The Migration Conference 2022

Abstracts Book

The Migration Conference Team

كلية العلوم القانونية و الاقتصادية
و الاجتماعية اكدال ـ الرباط
FACULTE DES SCIENCES JURIDIQUES,
ECONOMIQUES ET SOCIALES, AGDAL-RABAT

جامعة محمد الخامس بالرباط
Université Mohammed V de Rabat

AMERM

TRANSNATIONAL PRESS® LONDON

INTERNATIONAL BUSINESS SCHOOL

المملكة المغربية
ROYAUME DU MAROC

CCme
مجلس الجالية المغربية بالخارج
CONSEIL DE LA COMMUNAUTE MAROCAINE A L'ETRANGER

UNFPA

مؤسسة الحسن الثاني للمغاربة المقيمين بالخارج
Fondation Hassan II pour les Marocains Résidant à l'Etranger

المملكة المغربية
وزارة الداخلية
Royaume du Maroc
Ministère de l'Intérieur

The Migration Conference 2022
Abstracts Book

by

The Migration Conference Team

كلية العلوم القانونية و الاقتصادية
و الاجتماعية أكدال، الرباط
+₀ΘVΣ૫₀Ħ I +€ƉΘΙΣⵓΣΙ ΣⵌΘΧₒⵏΣ�I,
+Σⵍₒ⟅ΘₒⵏΣⵏ ⋀ +Σⵏₒ⟅ṠⵏΣⵏ-ₒⵅⵏₒⵏ
FACULTE DES SCIENCES JURIDIQUES,
ECONOMIQUES ET SOCIALES, AGDAL-RABAT

جامعة محمد الخامس بالرباط
Université Mohammed V de Rabat

A M E R M

TRANSNATIONAL PRESS® LONDON

INTERNATIONAL
BUSINESS
SCHOOL

TRANSNATIONAL PRESS LONDON

2022

The Migration Conference 2022 Abstracts Book

By The Migration Conference Team

Copyright © 2022 by Transnational Press London

First Published in 2020 by TRANSNATIONAL PRESS LONDON *in the United Kingdom, 13 Stamford Place, Sale, M33 3BT, UK.*

www.tplondon.com

Paperback

ISBN: 978-1-80135-160-7

Digital: 978-1-80135-161-4

Cover Design: Nihal Yazgan

www.tplondon.com

CONTENT AND TIMETABLE

President's Address

MOT DU CO-PRESIDENT DE LA "THE MIGRATION CONFERENCE 2022 RABAT"

Nous accueillons avec plaisir cette édition de « The Migration Conference 2000 Rabat » qui se tient au Maroc et qui est accueillie par l'Université Mohammed V de Rabat.

Ce rassemblement scientifique considéré comme le plus important traitant des questions migratoires réunit des académiciens, des chercheurs, des représentants de médias et de la société civile ainsi que des décideurs depuis dix ans et représente une occasion pour lancer une réflexion profonde autour de la thématique dans la mesure où les migrations sont érigées aujourd'hui en sujets prioritaires de débat sociétaux.

Dans ce contexte, des catégories de migrants apparaissent, les pays de départ se transforment en pays de transit ou d'accueil et réciproquement et la formulation d'un droit à la mobilité des personnes apparait. Sans oublier qu'aujourd'hui, la pandémie a accru la situation de précarité des migrants, les discriminations à leur égard et leur vulnérabilité.

Pour le Maroc, de par son positionnement géographique et sa position géostratégique particulière, la question migratoire est devenue depuis les années 60 un phénomène sociétal de grande envergure notamment pour une bonne partie de la jeunesse.

De même, et durant les dernières décennies, le Maroc est passé au début d'un espace de transit pour se convertir en pays d'établissement pour les migrants provenant de pays d'Afrique subsaharienne.

Cette réalité nous interpelle tous aujourd'hui puisque toutes les composantes de la société sont sollicitées et sont appelés à apporter des réponses adaptées à cette nouvelle réalité.

En effet, et étant donné le caractère pluriel et complexe des questions soulevées par la problématique de la migration, les politiques publiques dans leurs différentes dimensions : politique, économique, sociale et culturelle sont sollicitées ; tous les départements étatiques sont interpellés et tenus d'apporter des réponses adaptées à cette problématique à caractère transversal y compris la santé, l'emploi, l'éducation et la formation, la sécurité, etc.

De plus, ces mouvements migratoires modifient et affectent les relations internationales ce qui implique par conséquent une diplomatie nouvelle et repensée prenant en compte cette dimension migratoire.

Cette rencontre, par le biais de débats d'idées, pourra apporter des propositions innovantes qui permettraient d'aller de l'avant dans la compréhension de cette question qu'est la Migration et la proposition de résolutions aux situations complexes., tel est notre souhait.

Professeur Mohammed **Rhachi**

Mohammed V University of Rabat, Morocco

Chair's Welcome

Dear colleagues,

We are pleased to welcome you to The Migration Conference 2022 Rabat. The Migration Conference series attracted a few thousand colleagues over the last 10 years and surely became one of the largest ongoing events on migration and the largest scholarly gathering with a global scope.

The conference covers all areas of social sciences, humanities, economics, business and management. More popular areas so far included work, employment, integration, refugees and asylum, migration policy and law, spatial patterns, culture, arts and legal and political aspects which are key areas in the current migration debates and research.

Throughout the program of the Migration Conference, you will find key debates and scholarship discussed in 87 sessions accommodating about 350 presentations by over 400 contributors from all around the world, from Australia to Canada, China to Morocco, Brazil to Japan, and South Africa to Norway. We are proud to bring together experts from universities, independent research organisations, governments, NGOs and the media.

We are also proud to bring you opportunities to meet with some of the leading scholars in the field.

Although the main language of the conference is English, every year we host a good number of sessions in other languages. This year is not an exception as we will have sessions in English, Arabic, French, Spanish, and Turkish.

We thank all participants, reviewers, track chairs, session chairs, invited speakers and conference committees for their efforts and contribution. We also thank many colleagues who were interested in and submitted abstracts but could not make it this year. We are particularly grateful to colleagues who served as reviewers and helped us in the selection process.

We are grateful to the host organisations, Mohamed V University, Faculty of Social and Legal Studies in Agdal, AMERM, and International Business School as well as all other supporters and friends of the TMC.

Please do not hesitate to get in touch with us through the conference email (migrationscholar@gmail.com).

Ibrahim **Sirkeci** and Mohamed **Khachani**, Conference Chairs

On behalf of The Migration Conference Committee

TMC 2022 Rabat

"The Migration Conference" (TMC)

Cette conférence que le Maroc accueillera en septembre 2022 est la manifestation scientifique la plus importante au niveau international sur les questions migratoires.

C'est une série annuelle de forums rassemblements universitaires réunissant des académiciens, des chercheurs, des décideurs, des représentants des médias et de la société civile et des étudiants depuis 2012.

Chaque année, environ 500 participants d'environ 60 pays assistent et participent à plus de 80 sessions parallèles, tables rondes, ateliers et plénières.

Les initiateurs:

La Conférence sur la migration a été lancée par un comité exécutif composé du professeur Ibrahim Sirkeci de l'International Business School au Royaume-Un, le professeur Jeffrey H. Cohen, de l'Ohio State University et le Pr Philip L. Martin de l'Université de Californie, Davis aux États-Unis.

Les premières conférences sur la migration ont été lancées en 2012 au Centre d'études transnationales sur le campus Regent's Park de l'Université Regent de Londres. Les conférences suivantes ont été organisées respectivement à Londres (2014), Prague (2015), Vienne (2016), Athènes (2017), Lisbonne (2018), Bari (2019), Tetovo (2020) et Londres (2021). En raison de la crise du COVID-19, les deux dernières éditions de la conférence se sont tenues en ligne.

Comment l'idée est née pour organiser la TMC 2022 au Maroc

La première participation de l'Association Marocaine d'Etudes et de Recherches sur les Migrations (AMERM) à ces conférences date de 2019 à l'université de Bari (500 participants) organisée par la Prof Michela Pellicani (membre du Conseil scientifique de l'AMERM). Lors de l'édition de Londres de 2021, le conseil scientifique de la TMC a proposé à l'AMERM d'organiser une session en français sur la migration marocaine coordonnée par le Pr Mohamed Khachani à laquelle ont pris part 6 chercheurs marocains, alors que la langue officielle de la Conférence est l'anglais. C'est lors de cette conférence de Londres que la proposition d'organiser l'édition 2022 au Maroc a été faite au président de l'AMERM.

Compte tenu de l'importance de cet événement qui demeure la principale et la plus importante manifestation scientifique mondiale sur la question migratoire, ce projet a été accueilli favorablement par Mr le président de l'Université Mohammed V de Rabat désigné comme co-président de la TMC 2022 Rabat.

Création d'un comité d'organisation et d'un comité scientifique

Le comité d'organisation est présidé par Prof Ismail Kassou, vice président de l'Université Mohammed V de Rabat chargé de la Recherche et de la Coopération. Il est composé de:

- Prof Mohammed Dafir Echcherif El Kettani, Vice Président chargé de la Gouvernance et du Système d'information de l'Université Mohammed V de Rabat.

- Mr Abderrahmane Amkour, Secrétaire Général de l'Université Mohammed V de Rabat.

7

- Prof Ihsanne El Mansouri, conseillère du Président chargée du pôle de la vie étudiante.

- Prof Djamila Chekrouni, professeure à la Faculté des sciences juridiques, économiques et sociales Agdal- Université Mohammed V de Rabat, coordinatrice du master "Migrations et Sociétés".

- Mr Abdelouahab Figuigui, secrétaire général de la la Faculté des sciences juridiques, économiques et sociales Agdal- Université Mohammed V de Rabat.

Ce comité sera chargé de traiter toutes les questions relatives à la logistique et au séjour des participants : propositions d'hôtels à des tarifs préférentiels, restauration à proximité de l'université, transport, dossiers, etc.

Un comité scientifique National a été constitué , composé des enseignant-e-s chercheur-e-s du master "Migrations et Sociétés", des membres de l'AMERM et d'autres institutions. Il sera chargé d'instruire les propositions de communication. Il est composé des professeur-e-s:

- Djamila Chekrouni, Prof à la Faculté des sciences juridiques, économiques et sociales, coordinatrice du master "Migrations et Sociétés".

- Malika Benradi, Prof émérite à la Faculté des sciences juridiques, économiques et sociales, Agdal, membre de la Chaire Académique Lalla Meryem pour la Femme et l'Enfant et membre du CNDH.

- Michela Pellicani, Prof au Département des sciences politiques à l'Université de Bari en Italie

- Hind Ayoubi, Prof à la Faculté des sciences juridiques, économiques et sociales Soussi , membre de la Chaire Académique Lalla Meryem pour la Femme et l'Enfant et membre de la Commission des Nations Unies pour les Droits de l'enfant

- Boutaina Ismaeli Idrissi, Prof à la à la Faculté des sciences juridiques, économiques et sociales - Agdal

- Abdesslam El Ftouh, Ex directeur du Pôle économique à la Fondations Hassan II pour les Marocains Résidant à l'Etranger

- Ali Mhamdi, Diplomate ex responsable de la Direction des Affaires économiques et sociales, de la Direction juridique et Administrative et Financière au Ministère des Affaire Étrangères

- Ahmed Zekri, Prof à la à la Faculté des sciences juridiques, économiques et sociales - Agdal

- Le comité est coordonné par Mohamed Khachani, professeur à la Faculté des sciences juridiques, économiques et sociales Agdal, président de l'AMERM, partenaire scientifique de TMC 2022 Rabat et président du Comité National Marocain du Réseau Académique Nord-Africain sur la Migration (North African Migration Academic Network, NAMAN)

Date et lieu de la conférence

Il a été convenu avec la coprésidence anglaise que la Conférence débutera le mercredi 7 septembre à 14 heures avec une séance d'ouverture et une plénière et se terminera en début d'après-midi le samedi 10 septembre avec un panel de clôture. La plénière d'ouverture aura lieu dans les deux Amphi de la faculté des sciences juridiques, économiques et sociales Agdal, l'Amphi 1 (300 places) et l'Amphi 2 (250 places) qui sera relié par vidéo à l'Amphi 1. Les séances thématiques seront organisées dans 8 salles d'une capacité de plus de 40 places de 8h à 19h.

Financement

Les conférences sur la migration sont autonomes sur la base des frais d'inscription et des parrainages assurés par différentes institutions.

Au Maroc, les institutions suivantes seront sollicitées pour un éventuel partenariat à charge pour eux de contribuer à l'organisation de la conférence selon des modalités qui seront définies lors des réunions organisées à ce sujet:

- Les départements ministériels: Le Ministère des Affaires étrangères, de la Coopération Africaine et des Marocains Résidant à l'étranger, Le Ministère de l'Intérieur, Le Ministère de l'Emploi et le Ministère de la Justice.

- Les institutions Nationales: Le Conseil Consultatif des Marocains Résidant à l'Etranger, Le Conseil National des Droits de l'Homme, La Fondation Hassan II pour les Marocains Résidant à l'Etranger, Le Haut Commissariat au Plan, La région de Rabat Salé Zemmour Zaer, La Mairie de Rabat.

- Les agences des Nations unies concernées: le HCR, le FNUAP, UNIFEMME, l'UNICEF, l'OIM, le PNUD.

The Migration Conference 2022

The Migration Conference is a global venue for academics, policy makers, practitioners, students and everybody who is interested in intelligent debate and research informed discussions on human mobility and its impacts around the world. The Migration Conference 2022 is the 10th conference in the series. The Migration Conferences were launched at the Regent's Centre for Transnational Studies in 2012 when the first large scale well attended international peer-reviewed conference with a focus on Turkish migration in Europe in Regent's Park campus of Regent's College London. The migration conferences have been attended by thousands of participants coming from all around the world in London (2012), London (2014), Prague (2015), Vienna (2016), Athens (2017), Lisbon (2018), Bari (2019), Tetovo (2020), and London (2021).

The Migration Conference 2022 is hosted by Mohammed V University of Rabat and its Faculty of Economic and Social Legal Sciences in Agdal, Rabat, Morocco.

Supporters of The Migration Conferences included:

- Mohammed V University of Rabat, Morocco (TMC2022 Host)
- Faculty of Economic and Social Legal Sciences Agdal, Morocco (TMC2022 Host
- Association Marocaine d'Etudes & de Recherches sur les Migrations (AMERM), Morocco (TMC2022 Host)
- International Business School, Mobility Research Centre, United Kingdom
- The Ministry of Education, Morocco
- United Nations Population Fund (UNFPA)
- The National Human Rights Council (CNDH), Morocco
- National Office of Social and Cultural University Works, Morocco
- Hassan II Foundation for Moroccans Residing Abroad, Morocco
- The Council of the Moroccan Community Abroad, Morocco
- Ming-Ai (London) Institute, United Kingdom
- Centre for Development Evaluation and Social Science Research (CREDI), Sarajevo, Bosnia and Herzegovina
- Global Migration Research Centre, Social Sciences University of Ankara, Turkey
- Institut de Recherche, Formation et Action sur les Migrations, Belgium
- Migration Institute, Finland
- Migration Policies Research Centre, Istanbul Topkapi University, Turkey
- Research Centre in Economic and Organizational Sociology (SOCIUS), Universidade de Lisboa, Portugal
- Ruhr-Universität Bochum, Centre for Mediterranean Studies, Germany

- Sino-German Economic Development and Innovation Research Centre, Hefei University, P.R. China
- The Global Mobility Project, The Ohio State University, USA
- Unidad Académica en Estudios del Desarrollo, Mexico
- Universidad de Burgos, Spain
- Universidad Latina de México, Mexico
- Universidad Tecnica Particular de Loja, Ecuador
- Universität Hamburg, Germany
- University of California, Davis, Gifford Center for Population Studies, USA
- University of Nottingham, Faculty of Humanities and Social Sciences, China
- Urban Development and Social Research Association, Turkey
- Western Balkans Migration Network (WB-MIGNET), Bosnia and Herzegovina
- Yaşar University Jean Monnet Migration Chair, Turkey
- Migration and Diversity
- Remittances Review
- Migration Letters
- International Journal of Religion
- Göç Dergisi
- Journal of Gypsy Studies
- Border Crossing
- Journal of Posthumanism
- Journal of Ecohumanism
- AVAR journal
- Kurdish Studies
- Transnational Press London, UK
- Faculty of Contemporary Social Sciences, South East European University
- University of Bari Aldo Moro, Italy
- Dipartimento di Scienze Politiche, University of Bari, Italy
- Puglia Regional Administration, Italy
- Municipality of Bari, Italy
- Regent's University London Centre for Transnational Business and Management, UK
- ISTAT (Italian National Statistics Office), Italy
- Red Cross, Italy
- International Organisation for Migration, Italy
- Association Marocaine d'Etudes & de Recherches sur les Migrations, Morocco
- Ordine Assistenti Sociali Regione Puglia, Italy
- Tourism Office of Lisbon, Portugal
- ISEG and IGOT, University of Lisbon, Portugal

- Harokopio University, Athens, Greece
- Albrecht Mendelssohn Bartholdy Graduate School of Law, Germany
- Institut de Recherche, Formation et Action sur les Migrations, Belgium
- EKKE – The National Center of Social Research, Greece
- Hellenic Sociological Society, Greece
- Charles University Prague Faculty of Humanities, Czech Republic
- Regent's University Centre for Transnational Studies, UK
- Danube University Krems, Austria
- University of Vienna, Austria
- Ria Money Transfers
- J. Hornig Coffee, Austria
- Vienna Convention Bureau, Austria
- RGS Population Studies Group, United Kingdom
- IUSSP International Migration Expert Panel
- Austrian Air – Official Carrier for TMC 2016, Austria

migrationconference.net   @migrationevent

fb.me/MigrationConference

Email: migrationscholar@gmail.com

Host Institutions of The Migration Conferences

- Mohammed V University of Rabat, Morocco (TMC2022 Host)
- Faculty of Economic and Social Legal Sciences Agdal, Morocco (TMC2022 Host
- Association Marocaine d'Etudes & de Recherches sur les Migrations (AMERM), Morocco (TMC2022 Host)
- International Business School, United Kingdom (TMC2021 Host)
- Ming-Ai (London) Institute, United Kingdom (TMC2021 Host)
- Faculty of Contemporary Social Sciences, South East European University (TMC2020 Host)
- University of Bari Aldo Moro, Italy (TMC2019 Host)
- Dipartimento di Scienze Politiche, University of Bari, Italy (TMC2019 Host)
- ISEG and IGOT, University of Lisbon, Portugal (TMC2018 Host)
- Research Centre in Economic and Organizational Sociology (SOCIUS), Universidade de Lisboa, Portugal (TMC2018 Host)
- Harokopio University, Athens, Greece (TMC2017 Host)
- University of Vienna, Austria (TMC2016 Host)
- Charles University Prague Faculty of Humanities, Czech Republic (TMC2015 Host)
- Regent's University Centre for Transnational Studies, UK (TMC2014 Host)
- Regent's College London, UK (TMiE2012 Host)

People

The Migration Conference President

Prof Mohammed Rhachi, President, Mohammed V University, Rabat, Morocco

The Migration Conference Chairs

Prof Farid El Bacha, Dean of the Faculty, Mohammed V University, Rabat, Morocco (Co-Chair)

Prof Mohamed Khachani, AMERM & Mohammed V University of Rabat, Morocco (Co-Chair)

Prof Ibrahim Sirkeci, International Business School, UK (Chair)

The Migration Conference Executive Committee

Prof Jeffrey H. Cohen, Ohio State University, USA

Prof Philip L Martin, University of California Davis, USA

Prof Ibrahim Sirkeci, International Business School, UK

The Migration Conference National Organisation Committee

Ismail Kassou, Vice Président chargé de la recherche et de la coopération de l'Université Mohammed V de Rabat.

Mohammed Dafir Echcherif El Kettani, Vice Président chargé de la Gouvernance et du Système d'information de l'Université Mohammed V de Rabat.

Abderrahmane Amkour, Secrétaire Général de l'Université Mohammed V de Rabat.

Ihsanne El Mansouri, Conseillère du Président chargée du pôle de la vie étudiante Université Mohammed V de Rabat

Djamila Chekrouni, professeure à la Faculté des sciences juridiques, économiques et sociales Agdal- Université Mohammed V de Rabat, coordinatrice du master "Migrations et Sociétés"

Abdelaziz Laaroussi, Vice Dean de la Faculté des sciences juridiques, économiques et sociales Agadal- Université Mohammed V de Rabat

Abdelouahab Figuigui, secrétaire général de la Faculté des sciences juridiques, économiques et sociales Agdal- Université Mohammed V de Rabat

Transnational Advisory Committee

Prof Deborah Anker, Harvard University, United States

Prof Gudrun Biffl, Krems, Austria

Prof Lucinda Fonseca, University of Lisbon, Portugal

Prof Elli Heikkila, Migration Institute of Finland, Finland

Prof Beatrice Knerr, Kassell University, Germany and Hefei University, China

Prof Markus Kotzur, Universität Hamburg, Germany

Prof Jonathan Liu, International Business School, UK

Prof Apostolos G Papadopoulos, Harokopio University of Athens, Greece

Prof João Peixoto, University of Lisbon, Portugal

Prof Michela C. Pellicani, University of Bari "Aldo Moro", Italy

Prof Giuseppe Sciortino, University of Trento, Italy

Scientific Review Committee

Africa

Agnes Igoye, Ministry of Interior Affairs, Uganda

Prof Mohamed Khachani, AMERM & Mohammed V University of Rabat, Morocco

Dr Rania Rafik Khalil, The British University in Egypt, Egypt

Dr Sadhana Manik, University of KwaZulu-Natal, South Africa

Prof Claude Sumata, National Pedagogical University, DR Congo

Dr Ayman Zohry, Egyptian Society for Migration Studies, Egypt

Americas

Prof Jeffrey H. Cohen, Ohio State University, USA

Dr José Salvador Cueto-Calderón, Universidad Autónoma de Sinaloa, Mexico

Dr Ana Vila Freyer, Universidad Latina de México, Mexico

Dr Pascual Gerardo García-Macías, Universidad Técnica Particular de Loja, Ecuador

Dr Carlos Alberto González Zepeda, Universidad Autónoma Metropolitana-Cuajimalpa, Mexico

Dr Torunn Haaland, Gonzaga University, USA

Prof Liliana Jubilut, Universidade Católica de Santos, Brazil

14

Prof Philip L Martin, University of California Davis, USA

Dr Eric M. Trinka, James Madison University, USA

Karla Angélica Valenzuela-Moreno, Universidad Iberoamericana, Mexico

Dr Hassan Vatanparast, Saskatchewan University, Canada

Prof Rodolfo García Zamora, Autonomous University of Zacatecas, Mexico

Dr Monette Zard, Columbia University, USA

Asia-Pacific

Prof Ram Bhagat, International Institute for Population Sciences, India

Dr Amira Halperin, University of Nottingham Ningbo, P.R. China

Dr Sadaf Mahmood, Government College University, Pakistan

Dr Shweta Sinha Deshpande, Symbiosis School for Liberal Arts, India

Prof Nicholas Procter, University of South Australia, Australia

Dr Ruchi Singh, Prin.L.N.Welingkar Institute of Management Development & Research, India

Dr AKM Ahsan Ullah, University Brunei Darussalam, Brunei

Dr Zhongwei Xing, University of Technology Brunei, Brunei

Dr Xi Zhao, Hefei University, P.R. China

Eastern Europe

Dr Merita Zulfiu-Alili, South East European University, N. Macedonia

Dr Olga R. Gulina, RUSMPI- Institute on Migration Policy, Russian Federation

Dr Tuncay Bilecen, Kocaeli University, Turkey, UK

Prof Dilek Cindoglu, Kadir Has University, Turkey

Dr Yaprak Civelek, Anadolu University, Turkey

Dr Z. Banu Dalaman, Istanbul Ayvansaray University, Turkey

Prof Sevim Atilla Demir, Sakarya University, Turkey

Prof Vladimir Iontsev, Moscow State University, Russian Federation

Dr İnci Aksu Kargın, Uşak University, Turkey

Prof Sebnem Koser Akcapar, Ankara Social Sciences University, Turkey

Dr Murat Lehimler, Urban Development and Social Research Association, Turkey

Dr Armagan Teke Lloyd, Abdullah Gul University, Turkey

Dr Vildan Mahmutoğlu, Galatasaray University, Turkey

Dr Nermin Oruc, Centre for Development Evaluation and Social Science Research (CREDI), Sarajevo, Bosnia and Herzegovina

Dr Gökay Özerim, Yaşar University, Turkey

Prof Irina Savchenko, Linguistics University of Nizhny Novgorod, Russian Federation

Dr Onur Unutulmaz, Ankara Social Sciences University, Turkey

Dr Deniz Eroglu Utku, Trakya University, Turkey

Dr Pınar Yazgan, Sakarya University, Turkey

Dr Sinan Zeyneloglu, Kent University, Turkey

Western Europe

Dr Nirmala Devi Arunasalam, Global Banking School, United Kingdom

Dr Bahar Baser, Durham University, United Kingdom

Dr Gülseli Baysu, Queen's University Belfast, United Kingdom

Prof Petra Bendel, Friedrich-Alexander University of Erlangen-Nuremberg, Germany

Dr Gul Ince Beqo, University of Bari, Italy

Prof Aron Anselem Cohen, University of Granada, Spain

Dr Martina Cvajner, University of Trento, Italy

Dr Carla de Tona, Migration Letters, Italy

Dr Sureya Sonmez Efe, University of Lincoln, United Kingdom

Dr Deniz Cosan Eke, University of Vienna, Austria

Dr Alina Esteves, Universidade de Lisboa, Portugal

Dr Serena Hussain, Coventry University, United Kingdom

Prof Monica Ibáñez-Angulo, University of Burgos, Spain

Prof Markus Koller, Ruhr University Bochum, Germany

Dr Emre Eren Korkmaz, University of Oxford, United Kingdom

Dr Oksana Koshulko, The Technical University of Munich, Germany

Prof Jonathan Liu, International Business School, United Kingdom

Dr Lan Lo, University of Nottingham, United Kingdom

Dr Altay Manço, IRFAM, Belgium

Dr A. Erdi Öztürk, London Metropolitan University, United Kingdom

Isabella Piracci, Avvocatura Generale dello Stato, Rome, Italy

Dr Sahizer Samuk-Carignani, University of Pisa, Italy

Prof Giuseppe Sciortino, University of Trento, Italy

Dr Selma Akay Sert, University College London, UK

Dr Caner Tekin, Ruhr-Universität Bochum, Germany

Irene Tuzi, Sapienza University of Rome, Italy

Dr Emilia Lana de Freitas Castro, Berlin, Germany

Dr Ülkü Sezgi Sözen, University of Hamburg, Germany

Near East

Dr Rania M Rafik Khalil, The British University in Egypt, Egypt

Dr Yakhnich Liat, Beit Berl College, Israel

Dr Simeon Magliveras, King Fahd University of Petroleum and Minerals, Saudi Arabia

Dr Bradley Saunders, American University of Bahrain, Bahrain

Dr Paulette K. Schuster, Reichman University, AMILAT, Israel

Dr Omar Al Serhan, Higher Colleges of Technology, United Arab Emirates

Dr Md Mizanur Rahman, Qatar University, Qatar

The Migration Conference Technical Organisation Committee

Dr Aytac Yerden, Gedik University, Turkey (IT)

Ege Cakir, Middle East Technical University, Turkey (Admin)

Nihal Yazgan, Transnational Press London, UK (Admin)

Keynote Speakers

The Migration Conferences team are proud to have leading scholars in the field as keynote speakers whose details are listed below.

- Prof Markus **Koller**, Ruhr-Universität Bochum, Germany
- Prof Mustafa **Ozbilgin**, Brunel University London, UK
- Prof Jeffrey H. **Cohen**, Ohio State University, United States
- Prof Irudaya **Rajan**, IIMAD, Kerala, India
- Prof Parvati **Nair**, University of London, UK
- Sanjay **Awasthi**, IOM
- Dr V.J. **Varghese**, University of Hyderabad, India

In previous years, The Migration Conferences entertained distinguished scholars delivering keynote speeches including:

Theresa Alfaro-Velcamp, Emeritus Professor, Sonoma State University, USA, Dr Élise Féron, Tampere Peace Research Institute, Tampere University, Finland, Ruth Gomberg-Muñoz, Associate Professor, Department of Anthropology, Loyola University Chicago, USA, James F. Hollifield, Director of the Tower Center for Public Policy and International Affairs at Southern Methodist University, Dallas, USA, Camilla Orjuela, Professor, School of Global Studies, University of Gothenburg, Sweden, Pia M. Orrenius, Vice President and Senior Economist Federal Reserve Bank of Dallas, USA, Dr Rodolfo Cruz Piñeiro, Director, Departamento de Estudios de Población, El Colegio de la Frontera Norte, Mexico, Hna. Leticia Gutiérrez Valderrama, Scalabrinian Missionary, founder of SMR and Sergio Mendez Arceo National Human Rights Prize in Mexico; Diocesan Delegate for Migration – Diocese of Sigüenza-Guadalajara-Spain, Martina Cvajner, University of Trento, Italy, Jelena Dzankic, European University Institute, Italy, Nissa Finney, University of St Andrews, UK, Elli Heikkilä, Migration Institute of Finland, Finland, Agnes Igoye, Ministry of Internal Affairs, Uganda, Helén Nilsson, Nordic Council of Ministers Office in Lithuania, Giuseppe Brescia, MP, Parliamento Italiano, Italy, Markus Kotzur, Universität Hamburg, Germany, Karsten Paerregaard, Gothenburg University, Sweden, Martin Ruhs, European University Institute, Italy, Carlos Vargas Silva, University of Oxford, UK, Sasskia Sassen, Columbia University, USA, Oded Stark, U of Bonn, Germany, Giuseppe Sciortino, University of Trento, Italy, Joaquin Arango, Complutense University of Madrid, Spain, Ruba Salih, SOAS, University of London, UK, Fiona B. Adamson, SOAS, University of London, UK, Pedro Calado, The High Commissioner for Migration, Lisbon, Portugal, Ferruccio Pastore, FIERI – Forum of International and European Research on Immigration, Italy, Michelle Leighton, International Labour Organization, Genève, Switzerland, Yuksel Pazarkaya, Novelist, Turkey, Caroline Brettell, Southern Methodist University, USA, Barry Chiswick, George Washington University, USA, Karen Phalet, KU Leuven, Belgium, Douglas S. Massey, Princeton University, USA, Ibrahim Sirkeci, Regent's University London, UK, Jeffrey H. Cohen, Ohio State University, USA, Samim Akgonul, Strasbourg University, France, Kemal Kirisci, Bogazici University, Turkey, Nedim Gürsel, CNRS, CETOBaC & INALCO, France, Turkey, Philip L. Martin, University of California, Davis, USA, Tariq Modood, University of Bristol, United Kingdom.

Summary Programme

7 September 2022, Wednesday | DAY 1

12:00-16:00 – Registration

12:30-13:30 – Opening Session: Higher Education in a World of mobility restrictions

Panel Chair: Prof Farid El Bacha, Dean of the Faculty, Mohammed V University, Rabat, Morocco (Host Chair)

- The Minister of Higher Education, Scientific Research and Innovation
- Prof Mohammed Rhachi, President, Mohammed V University of Rabat, Morocco (President of the Conference)
- Driss El Yazami, CCME President
- Amina Bouayach, President of the CNDH
- Dr Laila Baker, Regional Director of UNFPA (Regional Office for Arab States)
- Prof Mohamed Khachani, President of AMERM & Mohamed V University of Rabat, Morocco (Co-Chair)
- Prof Ibrahim Sirkeci, International Business School, UK (Co-Chair)

13:30-15:15 – Plenary Session I
Moderator: Prof Philip L. Martin, University of California, Davis, USA
Keynote Speakers:

- Prof Jeffrey H. **Cohen**, Ohio State University, USA: **"Covid-19 and the direct and indirect challenges to mobility, settlement and security"**

- Prof Mustafa **Ozbilgin**, Brunel University London, UK: **Refugee Integrating Industry**

15:15-16:30 – Welcome Reception/Coctail

16:30-18:30 – Parallel Sessions I

8 September 2022, Thursday | DAY 2

09:00-10:30 – Parallel Sessions II

10:30-10:45 – Break

10:45-12:15 – Parallel Sessions III

12:15-13:15 – **Lunch Break**

13:15-14:15 – Plenary Session II
Moderator: Prof Jeffrey H. **Cohen**, Ohio State University, USA
Keynote Speaker:

- Prof Markus **Koller**, Ruhr-Universität Bochum, Germany: **The "Languages of Migration" and the Actor-Network Theory – Transregional Mobility of Artisans and Merchants from Ottoman Bosnia in the 18th and 19th Centuries**

14:15-14:30 – Break

14:30-16:00 – Parallel Sessions IV

16:00-16:15 – Break

16:15-17:45 – Parallel Sessions V

9 September 2022, Friday | DAY 3

09:00-10:30 – Parallel Sessions VI
10:30-10:45 – Break

10:45-12:15 – Parallel Sessions VII
12:15-13:00 – Lunch Break

13:15-14:45 – Plenary Session III: Modernity, Aspirations, and the Culture of Migration in India
Moderator: S. Irudaya **Rajan**, IIMAD, Kerala, India
Speakers:
- V.J. Varghese, University of Hyderabad, India
- Parvati Nair, University of London, UK
- Sanjay Awasthi, IOM

14:45-15:00 – Break
15:00-16:30 – Parallel Sessions VIII
16:30-16:45 – Break
15:00-16:30 – Parallel Sessions IX
19:15-21:30 – CONFERENCE DINNER

10 September 2022, Saturday| DAY 4

09:30-11:00 – Parallel Sessions X
11:00-11:15 – Break

11:15-12:45 – Parallel Sessions XI

12:45 END OF THE PROGRAMME

Please note this programme is subject to change without notice.

Day One 7 September 2022 Wednesday

Day One 7 September 2022 - 12:30-15:15

Opening Panel:

Panel Chair: Prof Farid El Bacha, Dean of the Faculty, Mohammed V University, Rabat, Morocco (Host Chair)

- The Minister of Higher Education, Scientific Research and Innovation
- Prof Mohammed Rhachi, President, Mohammed V University of Rabat, Morocco (President of the Conference)
- Driss El Yazami, CCME President
- Amina Bouayach, President of the CNDH
- Dr Laila Baker, Regional Director of UNFPA (Regional Office for Arab States)
- Prof Mohamed Khachani, President of AMERM & Mohamed V University of Rabat, Morocco (Co-Chair)
- Prof Ibrahim Sirkeci, International Business School, UK (Co-Chair)

Plenary Session I

Moderator: Prof Ibrahim **Sirkeci**, International Business School, UK
Keynote Speakers:

- Prof Jeffrey H. **Cohen**, Ohio State University, USA: **"Covid-19 and the direct and indirect challenges to mobility, settlement and security"**
- Prof Mustafa **Ozbilgin**, Brunel University London, UK: **"Refugee Integrating Industry"**

15:15-16:30 Opening Reception – Coctail

[Sponsored by the Dean of the Faculty of Economic and Legal Sciences, Mohammed V University, Agdal, Rabat, Morocco]

Day One 7 September 2022 Wednesday

Day One 7 September 2022 - 16:30-18:30

1A   Migration Issues in North Africa [AR] AMPHI 1

ـ الجلسة الأولى :قضايا الهجرة في شمال افريقيا

رئيس الجلسة :د .إبراهيم عوض ، مدير مركز الدراسات حول الهجرة و اللاجئين، الجامعة الأمريكية بالقاهرة

Chair: Dr. Ibrahim Awad, Director of the Center for Studies on Migration and Refugees, American University in Cairo

-      دة. سارة صادق: أستاذة مساعدة بمركز دراسات الهجرة واللاجئين: سياسات *الهجرة في مصر: تحليل لواقعية التحديات والفرص"*.
-      د. محمد علي أحمد وزارة التعليم والبحث العلمي – ليبيا : *الهجرة غير النظامية من أفريقيا جنوب الصحراء نحو بلدان المغرب العربي :دراسة حالة ليبيا* .

Dr. Hassan Boubakri, professeur de géographie et d'études migratoires. Université de Sousse, Tunisie: *Migration et asile en Afrique du Nord entre voisinages subsaharien et européen(Cas de la Tunisie et de la Libye)*

-      Dr Mohamed Musette: Centre de Recherche en Économie Appliquée pour le Développement: *La politique migratoire en Algérie*
-      Aziz Jilali Sghir Direction de la migration et de la surveillance des frontières (Ministère de l'intérieur): *La gouvernance de la migration au Maroc*

1B   PANEL: Statistics and Migrations AMPHI 2

Organised by The United Nations Population Fund (UNFPA)

Moderator: Mr. Luis Mora, UNFPA Representative in Morocco

Speakers:

-      An overview of the migration statistics status in Arab countries: measurement issues

Mr. Ismaïl Lubbad, UNFPA Regional Advisor (ASRO) in Population and Development;

-      Arab countries' experiences in international migration statistics measurement methods:

Morocco:

Mr. Mohamed Mghari, Regional Director at the High Commission for Planning;

Tunisia:

Mrs Yosra Massoudi, deputy director at National Institute of Statistics (INS);

Palestine:

Mr. Hatem Qrareya, Head of Division Demography of Palestinians Abroad;

Egypt:

Ms. Heba Said, Professor of Statistics at the Faculty of Economics and Political Science at Cairo University and a consultant for the Central Agency for Public Mobilization and Statistics (CAPMAS);

Golf Countries: (TBC)

1C   Education and High Skilled Migration   AMPHI 3

Chair   Marianne Garvik, NTNU, Norway

1275   Migration and Education: The Case of Integrating Sub-Saharan Immigrants' Children's into Moroccan Public Schools

Zineb Gormat, Ibn Toufail University, Kenitra, Morocco

990   International Students from the Global South to the Global North. Capabilities, Aspirations and Stepwise Migration Trajectories

Marianne Garvik, NTNU, Norway

1312   Children's educational experience following parental work migration. Between challenges and rewards

Georgiana Udrea, National University of Political Studies and Public Administration

Gabriela Gugu, National University of Political Studies and Public Administration

548   Maximizing Previously Acquired Competences of non-EU citizens at European Universities

Aleidis Devillé, Thomas Moore U., Belgium
Luc Wilms, Thomas Moore U., Belgium

Migration and Education: The Case of Integrating Sub-Saharan Immigrants' Children's into Moroccan Public Schools

(1275) Zineb Gormat, Ibn Toufail University, Kenitra, Morocco

Much has been written about the new shift in the migration movements in Morocco, from a country of emigration to that of immigration, receiving a diverse group of immigrants, asylum seekers, and refugees. Since mid-90s, there has also been an extensive debate over the international and national policies regarding the situation of the immigrants coming from Sub-Saharan Africa to Morocco in transit to Europe. Their number has drastically increased because of civil wars, political instability and economic crises in their own home countries (Cherti, & Grant, 2013). Their presence has confronted Morocco with various legal and social issues, most urgently, the uncertain future of the children born on the way to or in Morocco (de Hass, 2014). These children, who have no birth certificates or a nationality, also grow up in a state of irregularity, in other words, a lost generation deprived of its very basic rights (Cherti, & Grant, 2013). Therefore, the king's decision to regularize the undocumented immigrants in September 2013 meant setting the stage for their integration into Moroccan society, thereby, enjoying access to public services, including education (de Hass, 2014). The process of the children's school integration has been entrusted to civil society and NGOs in collaboration with the Ministry of Education. To better understand this process and gain an-in-depth insight into the migrant children's learning and cultural experiences in public schools, it is essential to thoroughly investigate the education programs available for them, and the challenges their integration has encountered thus far. To do so, a wide range of methods are being used. These include class observations at two public schools, semi-structured interviews at a local association, focus groups with the migrant parents and drawing workshops with their children. In this context, this paper, which is part of an ongoing research project currently being undertaken, first presents a brief overview of the process of integrating the migrant children into public schools, highlighting particularly the pivotal role of NGOs and civil society in the process. It then discusses the different challenges encountered up to now; which calls for the need of considering a new approach that can enable these children to participate effectively and appropriately in Moroccan society in the long run. The incorporation of Intercultural education based on embracing cultural diversity in the school curriculum should, hence, be the foundation for such integration. Unlike multicultural education which relies on learning about other cultures in order to create a culture of tolerance and acceptance of the other, 'intercultural education aims to go beyond passive coexistence, to achieve a developing and sustainable way of living together in multicultural societies through the creation of understanding of, respect for and dialogue between the different cultural groups' (UNESCO, 2006).

International Students from the Global South to the Global North. Capabilities, Aspirations and Stepwise Migration Trajectories

(990) Marianne Garvik, NTNU, Norway

Migrant workers and their migratory projects to improve lives have been significant objects of research interest. Anyhow, few studies have focused on international student migration as a strategy to create better life chances. Based on in-depth interviews, this article investigates Sub-Saharan African (SSA) international students' capabilities, aspirations and trajectories towards the Global North. The study will explore how students from the global south plan, implement and cope with their migratory paths building on the analytical framework of stepwise migration. We will also discuss the impact different actors have on their movements. Globalisation is increasingly expressed by migration and development through remittances, brain circulation and ideologies of a shared pool of labour and education. However, accessibility and opportunities are not evenly distributed between the global north and the global south. Strict visa requirements and lack of resources still create closed borders and inequality between the south and the north. Inequalities are constructed on hierarchies of class, race, ethnicity, gender, place in the global economy, and migration status structured by social, economic, and political forces. By intersecting various inequality indicators, such as socio-economic background, ethnicity, education, time (life-course), gender, knowledge and network, we will shed light on the intersectional identities that characterise international students. Through the intersectional identities, we will highlight the contradictory tensions the students encounter, which also frames their aspirations and coping strategies. Further, the intersectional perspective provides analyses of the students' expectations (aims and goals), as well as their negotiating of inclusion and exclusion through the theoretical lens of agency and structure.

24

Children's educational experience following parental work migration. Between challenges and rewards

(1312) Georgiana Udrea, National University of Political Studies and Public Administration

Gabriela Gugu, National University of Political Studies and Public Administration

This paper investigates the influence of parental labor migration on children's school performance and the coping mechanisms developed to accommodate their parents' absence. We focus on the dynamics of learning motivation following the departure of one or both parents to work abroad and children's perceived responsibility to improve their educational outcomes for a better future.

Given the opportunities offered by the enlarged European labor market after the 2007 and the 2014 phases (Beciu, Ciocea, Mădroane & Cârlan 2018; Bian 2018), a significant number of Romanian workers accepted the challenge of working abroad in search of better life prospects. Recently, the Statistical Office of the European Commission (2021) ranked Romania first in the EU in terms of migration, with more than 20% of total working population living in different EU countries. Globally, in the most recent World Migration Report (McAuliffe & Khadria, 2021), Romania ranked 14th in the Top 20 countries of origin of migrants, with the Romanian diaspora considered the fifth largest in the world (OECD, 2019).

Based on this dimension of the migration phenomenon, we argue for the importance of studying the consequences of migration flows on left-behind children in terms of their educational trajectories and how relationships with near and distant ones can affect them. Our research addresses a subject of secondary importance in the previous studies, which have mainly focused on economic, demographic and political effects of migration (Gherghina, Plopeanu, & Necula, 2020; Goschin, Roman, & Danciu, 2013; Sandu, 2016). This will help make the reality of these children better known in its depth and visible beyond statistics. Also, a deeper understanding of the different ways in which parents' migration can impact on children's educational behaviour provides important information that can be turned into solutions aimed at minimizing the negative effects of this process.

In order to achieve our objectives and obtain valuable insights on children's perceptions, we conducted in-depth semi-structured interviews with 15 adolescents from rural south-western Romania whose parents have been working abroad for at least 5 years. An important part of the discussion revolved around children's educational experience as they perceive it. Opinions and personal accounts were encouraged as we were interested to learn as much as possible about their peers and teachers, favourite subjects and best school achievements, challenges, future career plans and intentions to emigrate. Results show that most respondents understand the efforts parents make for the wellbeing of the family in general and their future in particular. Thus, they feel motivated and indebted to do well at school as a form of gratitude to their parents, but also as the only chance to overcome their condition. However, there are cases where, following parental migration, children's educational outcomes have deteriorated due to lack of motivation, lack of paternal authority, bad time management or changing priorities. We elaborate on these findings and provide evidence-based recommendations for policy makers.

References:

Beciu, C., Ciocea, M., Mădroane, I. D., & Cârlan, I. A. (2018). *Introduction: Intra-EU Labor Migration and Transnationalism in Media Dicourses: A Public Problem Approach.* In: C. Beciu, M. Ciocea, I. D. Mădroane, I. A. Cârlan (Eds.), *Debating migration as a Public Problem. National Publics and Transnational Fields* (pp. 1-37). New York: Peter Lang.

Bian, N. (2018, August). *Harta diasporei. Campioni în UE la migrația internă. Câți români trăiesc în afara țării* [Map of the diaspora. EU champions in internal migration. How many Romanians live abroad]. Retrieved on March 15, 2022 from: https://www.g4media.ro/harta-diasporei-campioni-in-ue-la-imigratia-interna-cati-romani-traiesc-in-afara-tarii.html.

Gherghina, S., Plopeanu, A. P., & Necula, C. V. (2020). *The Impact of Socio-Cultural Integration on Return Intentions: Evidence from a Survey on Romanian Migrants.* Journal of Immigrant & Refugee Studies, 18(4), 515–528.

Goschin, Z., Roman, M., & Danciu, A. R. (2013). *The brain drain phenomenon in Romania. Magnitude, characteristics, implications.* Economica, 65(5), 190–206.

McAuliffe, M., Triandafyllidou, A. (Eds.). (2021). *World Migration Report 2022.* Geneva: International Organization for Migration (IOM).

OECD. (2019). *Talent Abroad: A Review of Romanian Emigrants.* Paris: OECD iLibrary.

Sandu, D. (2016). *Remittances as Home Orientation Rooted in the Lifeworlds of Immigrants.* Central and Eastern European Migration Review, 5(2), 81–98.

Statistical Office of the European Commission. (2021). *Migration and migrant population statistics.* Retrieved on March 15th, 2022 from: https://ec.europa.eu/eurostat/statistics-explained/index.php?title=Migration_and_migrant_population_statistics#Acquisitions_of_citizenship:_EU_Member_States_granted_citizenship_to_706_thousand_persons_in_2019.

Maximizing Previously Acquired Competences of non-EU citizens at European Universities

(548) Aleidis Devillé, Thomas Moore U., Belgium

Luc Wilms, Thomas Moore U., Belgium

European Universities tend to attract students from all over the world. The procedure to recognize 'Elsewere Acquired Competences' is rather one-sidedly focused on Europe, the U.S. and Canada. The 'Lisbon Recognition Convention' (1997) nevertheless is a judicial basis that also allows non-EU citizens to follow a shortened study trajectory in Europe. 'Maximizing Previously Acquired Competences' - in short MaxiPAC - is a European project that promotes valorization of these competences of non-EU citizens in European higher education. Students who earned their degree or gained working experience outside of Europe can obtain a European diploma in a shortened process. Thomas More was the first University in Belgium to grant a bachelor's degree to a Palestinian refugee this way. Other Belgian and European universities are about to follow their example. The MaxiPAC procedure consists of 4 steps, which consist in essence of building a portfolio and providing an assessment of the foreign student. This is the basis to grant exemptions in order to achieve a shortened study route. At the end, a diploma is awarded by a specific

European university. We hope to contribute to an improved cross-border recognition of university degrees and competences.

1D   Conflicts, Insecurities, Migration   AMPHI 4

Chair: Ana Vila-Freyer, Universidad Latina de México, México

546   Self-Organization among Migrants and the (Re)Configuration of Urban Public Space in Morocco

Saad Alami Merrouni, Mohammed 1st University of Oujda, Morocco and Utah State University, USA

1151   The changing patterns of Ukrainian immigration in Hungary, Revisited

Zoltán Csányi, University of Barcelona, Spain

1124   Turkey as a "Safe" Third Country

Emrah Cengiz, Duisburg-Essen University, Germany

1259   Being a Palestinian refugee in Europe: effects of statelessness on fragmented identities and socio-political inequalities

Fanny Christou, Malmö University, Sweden & University of Poitiers & Institut Convergences Migrations, France

Self-Organization among Migrants and the (Re)Configuration of Urban Public Space in Morocco

(546) Saad Alami Merrouni, Mohammed 1st University of Oujda, Morocco and Utah State University, USA

Immigration to Morocco has gradually shifted from a transitory phase to a permanent form of settlement of migrants originating from multiple regions of the world. Most studies on immigration have focused on migrants' living conditions, basically from a human rights-based approach. These arguments, though insightful, reinforce the migrant's victimization and hinder their empowerment and agency. Similarly, the emphasis on migrants' experiences in Morocco varies according to several variables, especially concerning the status of residence. The regular/irregular dichotomy determines the ways migrants appropriate and use space. Besides, it influences the various strategies they adopt as they cope with social, cultural, and legal/structural obstacles that obstruct their access to it. Despite the abundance of migration scholarship in Morocco, the urban scale, as a unit of analysis, remained ignored. The implications of "methodological nationalism" (Wimmer and Glick Schiller, 2003) dominates both scholarly and political debates on migration and integration, in ways that fail to identify the richness of social and cultural interactions between migrants and the host society occurring in the urban realm.

Based on the results of an ongoing doctoral research, this paper seeks to highlight self-organization among migrants in Morocco as a novel strategy in seeking access and use of the urban public space (Lefebvre, 1991). Migrants' presence, as a "new" parameter, impacts the social and cultural fabric of Moroccan society and calls for a new conceptualization of issues like nationhood and citizenship. The fieldwork conducted in the cities of Oujda and Rabat, as two cities with different migration realities, is based on a case study methodology and focuses on self-organizations as a strategy coined by migrants as a strategy in coping with political dispossession and cultural discrimination. The results highlight the role of migrants' activism in altering the nationalistic configurations of the urban public sphere towards a realm of cultural and ethnic diversity.

References:

Lefebvre, H. (1991). The production of space. Oxford: Blackwell.

Wimmer, A., & Schiller, N. G. (2003). Methodological Nationalism, the Social Sciences, and the Study of Migration: An Essay in Historical Epistemology. The International Migration Review, 37(3), 576–610. http://www.jstor.org/stable/30037750

The changing patterns of Ukrainian immigration in Hungary, Revisited

(1151) Zoltán Csányi, University of Barcelona, Spain

While most Hungarian migration scholars agreed that the 2010s brought substantial changes in the patterns of international mobility from Ukraine to Hungary, it is clear that the new decade turned evolving migration trends upside down in multiple ways. After several years of vertiginous increases in the net migration balances of Ukrainians in Hungary - more than sixty-fold growth (!) for Ukrainian citizens between 2013 and 2019 -, the first shocks of COVID-19 resulted in a strongly negative net migration in 2020, being negative for the first time since yearly migration flows from this country are measured in Hungary. Although data is not yet available for 2021, it is expected that the lowering restrictions on border crossings in the second year of the pandemic brought about more equilibrated in- and outmigration flows between the two countries. Since the outbreak of the Ukrainian-Russian military conflict however, that took place only weeks before this abstract is being written, demographers are no longer in the position to develop expectations on the future developments of the Hungarian-Ukrainian migration system. While some sporadic data is already at hand on related topics as daily border crossings and applications for temporary protection in Hungary, reliable data will be a scarce resource for a longer period to be used for in-depths analyses of the socio-demographic and migratory impacts of the war. Instead, this presentation aims at nothing more than to review available data and knowledge to be accumulated in Hungary until TMC 2022, and to offer a longer term view on the changing patterns of Ukrainian immigration in Hungary.

Turkey as a "Safe" Third Country

(1124) Emrah Cengiz, Duisburg-Essen University, Germany

The goal of this research is to take a close look at Turkey in terms of safe third country as it was acknowledged so during the reputed 2015 EU migration crisis and as result of that acknowledgement, a readmission agreement was signed between the EU and Turkey. According to the mentioned agreement, Turkey had the obligation to prevent the migrants most of whom were fleeing from the conflicts in the middle eastern countries from crossing EU border. EU in return, pledged certain incentives such as providing financial support and visa liberalization. However the agreement caused criticisms from human right organizations, NGOs, migrants rights associations etc. because Turkey is a signatory of the Geneva Refugee Convention with geographical limitation and looking at Turkey's human rights violation records and current political situation, one might want to think twice before putting it in the safety third countries category. This research will question this critical point and reevaluate this designation based which the readmission agreement was established.The study will begin with a literature review of history of EU's readmission agreements as an implication of its externalisation policy in the migration issue. Following that, the study will critically examine the EU-Turkey Readmission Agreement focusing on Turkey's being designated as a safe third country by the EU and in which extend it deserves that title. And finally, the study will discuss what kind of improvement can be done to facilitate better conditions for refugees in Turkey.

Being a Palestinian refugee in Europe: effects of statelessness on fragmented identities and socio-political inequalities

(1259) Fanny Christou, Malmö University, Sweden & University of Poitiers & Institut Convergences Migrations, France

Thousands of migrants fleeing conflicts in the Middle East and North Africa attempt to cross the Mediterranean to reach Europe, often in unseaworthy vessels, and too many have died at sea. Over the last three years, Cyprus, an island with a complex history of conflict located in the most south-eastern region of the Mediterranean, has received the largest number recorded of asylum applications, Syria being the first country of origin and asylum seekers entering the south via the "Green Line" after having crossed Turkey. Germany and Sweden have recently been challenged by waves of migration and different political measures have been adopted since 2015, in the context of the so-called "migrants' crisis".Against this background, departing from testimonies and participant observations gathered through fieldwork with the Palestinian diaspora in Sweden between 2015-2017 (Malmö) and in Germany (Berlin) between 2018-2019, and based on an extensive literature review (state of the art and grey literature) dealing with the situation of the Palestinians in Cyprus, this paper aims to provide some preliminary reflexions regarding the plurality of the Palestinian refugees in different European countries.This paper thus aims to reinvigorate the current debate about immigration by exploring features of Palestinian living conditions in Europe. The Palestinian diaspora oscillates between experiences of inclusion and exclusion, citizenship rights and urban discrimination, belonging and non-belonging that contribute reframing the concept of integration. In this respect, one should explore the relevance of the so-called Palestinian stateless conflict-generated diaspora by identifying the various experiences of the Palestinian diaspora, drawing a space for identity where politics endorse a new dimension. In addition, stressing how a Palestinian identity is interrogated and negotiated in Europe will give the opportunity to probe the fragmented and plural elements of the Palestinian refugees.This paper will address Palestinian migrant experiences from a social, political, cultural and religious perspective while analysing the implications of their various situations in different European countries, thus contributing to a wider understanding of the impacts of statelessness and conflict-generated diasporas on the Palestinian fragmented identities and socio-political inequalities in Europe.Last but not least, this proposal aims to open for discussion and share knowledge. This presentation seeks to strengthen a current research project that seek to give a voice to those seeking refuge, and in doing so, help to challenge the media and political discourses associated with them. This presentation during the Migration Conference 2022 will thus give the opportunity to introduce some of the preliminary results but also to discuss challenges with the audience and develop partnerships to build a project that seeks to overall document and promote migrants' experiences, preserving and making accessible their complex interplays of narrative, to make societies more inclusive, resilient and sustainable.

1E   Gender and Migration AMPHI 5

Chair: Martina Cvajner, University of Trento, Italy

1196   From transnational to local governance: the reproductive care of immigrant women in the city of Sao Paulo, Brazil

Jaciane Milanezi, CEBRAP - Brazilian Center of Analysis and Planning, Switzerland

1273   Shaking Gender Roles: Syrian Refugee women's entrance to the Turkish labour force and its impact on empowerment and resilience

Julie Gamze Aydoğan and Funda Yıldırım, Turkey

525   Not Only A Man's World: Women Also Cross Borders

Maryam Liman, Bayero University, Kano, Nigeria

1306   Declining birthrate and seeking for living together with foreign workers in Japan: with reference to Taiwan

Yumiko Nakahara, Faculty of Economics, Kyushu Sangyo University

From transnational to local governance: the reproductive care of immigrant women in the city of Sao Paulo, Brazil

(1196) Jaciane Milanezi, CEBRAP - Brazilian Center of Analysis and Planning, Switzerland

A new international immigration profile has emerged in Brazil since the early 21st century, with immigrants originating from intra-American routes and the Global South. It is leading to a change in the racial profile of immigrants in the country, compared to the mostly European and white immigration of the last century. For instance, the universal health system has been classifying these new immigrants as Black, Brown, and Indigenous, according to the official racial categories of the Brazilian State. In the new context of international displacements in the country, the city of SÃ£o Paulo is still a central place to govern these flows. For example, municipal public policies for immigrant women have been under pressure to be adapted to this population and the reproductive care of the Family Health Strategy (FHS) falls under this category. The paper is based on postdoctoral research, which analyzes the racialization processes of international immigrant women in the city of SÃ£o Paulo within bureaucracies of primary health care, and, furthermore, how these racialization processes relate to the access and use of reproductive care. The paper will explore one preliminary finding, which is the changes in public policies in the city regarding the health of immigrant women between 2010 and 2020. Based on official health documents adopted by the city of SÃ£o Paulo in the last decade, it will show how the new public policy vocabulary intertwines with the racialization of immigrant women as Blacks and Indigenous in the Brazilian context. The paper contributes to the fields of international immigration, race relations, and Primary Healthcare through an analysis of the local governance of racial inequalities among immigrants.

Shaking Gender Roles: Syrian Refugee women's entrance to the Turkish labour force and its impact on empowerment and resilience

(1273) Julie Gamze Aydoğan and Funda Yıldırım, Turkey

Large influxes of migration from Syria has been witnessed since the start of the Syrian Civil War in 2011. Out of nearly 4 million Syrians under temporary protection, available statistics indicate that there are about 1.734.202 Syrian women residing in Turkey.[1] It is commonly known that Syrian refugee women are exposed to serious troubles such as gender-based violence, lack of education, early marriage, multiple pregnancies, and trauma due to losing family members,[2] and studies have shown that for many Syrian refugee women in Turkey, they had no or little experience from paid work prior to migrating, and those who have worked have done so within gendered work regimes.[3] Although there are lots of studies concerning the multidimensional challenges faced by Syrian refugee women, not a lot is known on the actual impact that entering labour in Turkey has had on their empowerment, which is well-known to have the potential to foster capacities that might translate into resilience.[4] Through the research questions of this study, we aim to address some of the mechanisms that may have been present during the women's processes of empowerment. At the same time, we also want to locate barriers to perceived empowerment, as well as considering the women's integration. As framework, we will use Feminist Standpoint Epistemology, which builds on (1) seeing and understanding the world through the eyes and experiences of oppressed women and (2) apply the vision and knowledge of oppressed women to social activism and social change.

The main objective in this study is to find out whether migration from Syria to Turkey has a transformative capacity to empower Syrian women, 1) through integration into labor force, 2) change in gender roles. We will adopt in-depth interview method in order to collect data on Syrian refugee women coming from different socio-economic statuses. We aim to use a life story approach, as it offers a unique way to step inside the personal world of the storyteller and discover larger worlds. Variables for examining migration and its impact on empowerment among Syrian women is inspired from OXFAMs framework, which evaluates women's empowerment through change in three levels: personal, relational and environmental.[5] We choose this framework as the indications represent the

[1] GIGM. https://en.goc.gov.tr/temporary-protection27 (Access: 31.03.2022)
[2] Mirici, I. (2018). Syrian refugee women's profile and their expectations in their host country: a case study in Turkey. *Quaity & Quantity, 52*, 1437-1443.
[3] Körükmez, L., Karakılıç, I., & Didem, D. (2020). *Exigency, Negotioation, Change: The Work Experiences of Refugee Women and Gendered Relations.* GAR Book Series No. 3.
[4] Leder, S. (2016). Linking women's empowerment and resilience. Literature Review. DOI: 10.13140/RG.2.1.3395.0809
[5] Lombardini, S., Bowman, K., & Garwood, R. (2017). A 'HOW TO' GUIDE TO MEASURING WOMEN'S EMPOWERMENT: Sharing experiences from Oxfams impact evaluation. Oxfam GB.

characteristics of an "empowered women" within a socio-economic context that is flexible to each unique setting. In this regard, we will attempt to answer the following questions:

- How does paid employment in Turkey facilitate processes of integration among Syrian women, and what are the implications involved in regard to gender ideologies?
- How does new distribution of gender roles after migration affect women's domestic life, and to what extent are their new role perceived as permanent (or temporary)?
- How do the women experience change in gendered spaces?

Not Only A Man's World: Women Also Cross Borders

(525) Maryam Liman, Bayero University, Kano, Nigeria

People move across borders for several reasons. The migrants from Niger Republic move into the neighboring Nigerian communities in numbers in search for greener pastures. Previously, research in the region has shown migration to be male dominated (Liman, 2021). However, a new wave of women participation was noticed hence the need for literature update. This study aims at understanding the reason behind this new wave.

The study was conducted at Daura Local Government Area, Katsina state in Nigeria. The study area shares with Niger Republic a manned border at Kongolom and unmanned borders throughout the expanse of its several remote villages making the influx of both human and animal resources uncontrolled. Women, just like men move freely into the study area yearly. In order to understand the reasons behind the decision by these women to cross the borders, four (4) Focus Group Discussions (FGDs, 8-10participants) were conducted with the 35 migrants using a checklist as a guide. Four (4) Key Informant Interviews (KIIs) also held with their hostesses. Qualitative data was therefore collected and reported in tables and descriptive narration. The results of the FGD show all respondents were female within the age range of 12-56years. Some were married, some widowed, a good number divorced and the rest were spinsters. None of them had formal education but some had basic Islamic knowledge. About 50% engaged in farming and post harvest activities that do not pay much. 39% partook in domestic chores such as cleaning, cooking and babysitting where the earnings range from N3,000-N6,000 monthly(aprox.$7-$14) and 11% engaged in street begging. Findings reveal that economic gains were the major reason for coming to Nigeria and money was raised for different activities. Further investigations about the use of the money revealed about a quarter are savings to finance daughters' weddings; younger ladies are saving towards their own weddings, around 5.7% are saving to contribute towards the hospital bill of a sick relative, some came to find means of family sustenance while others came just for the fun of it! While a few of the women have only just begun (11.4%), partaking for the first time, others have had the joy of returning yearly thereby making them circular migrants. These ladies and others practicing this migration type are commonly referred to as 'Yan Tabiradi.

Information gathered from the 3 of 4 of the hostesses, who were elderly women, all widowed and lived in 2-3 room houses explained that some migrants pay a token fee to stay (N150-N200 monthly-less than 50cents) for accomodation. The fourth hostess, relatively younger, entertained her relatives at no cost.

Finally, it can be concluded that, women from southern Niger Republic do partake actively in short distance, seasonal, circular migration in parts of northern Nigeria. They come due to availability of work, a good network of family and friends that secure the work and accommodate them and also the ease of crossing the border.

1306   Declining birthrate and seeking for living together with foreign workers in Japan: with reference to Taiwan

(1306) Yumiko Nakahara, Faculty of Economics, Kyushu Sangyo University

Japan's society has entered a labor shortage due to the rapidly declining birthrate and aging population. To make up for this shortage, the number of foreigners working in Japan has surged, reaching approximately 1.73 million in 2021 [1] , foreign workers account for 2.5% of Japan's total workforce [2]. The employment has spread to diverse fields, such as nursing and care facilities, restaurants, convenience stores, and delicatessen factories. Care workers from Southeast Asia are engaged in facilities for the elderly. In addition, foreign students take up part-time jobs at convenience stores to cover for their living expenses and tuitions, becoming an indispensable labor force in Japan which is already suffering from labor shortages. It is apparent that the policy regarding foreign workers has reached the stage of "how to accept" rather than "to accept or not." However, are Japanese people ready to accept an increasing number of foreign workers as neighbors? To accept foreign workers, it is important to create an environment, which has not yet been established in present day Japan. For example, religious considerations are needed if we want foreign workers to settle in Japan as an indispensable work force in the field of nursing and care work which suffers labor shortage. In addition, there is the issue of education for children of foreign workers

Contrarily, Japan's neighboring country Taiwan, has a relatively longer history of employing foreign workers than Japan; the percentage of total foreign workers to the total workforce is already 5.3% [3] , more than twice of Japan. The foreign workers have been a part of Taiwanese society. There are a many NGOs in Taiwan that support foreign workers, some of which are subsidized by local governments, or play the role of shelter for disappearance or arbitration institutions in the event of labor-management disputes. In other words, in Taiwan, since NGOs have greater powers, they are doing the work that public institutions should be doing. Thus, there are many lessons that Japan can learn from Taiwan.

In this research, we will look at the current situation of foreign workers in Japan in light of increasing labor shortages due to the declining birthrate and aging population, and the problems associated them, with reference to Taiwan, a pioneering example of absorbing foreign workers in the society.

[1] Ministry of Health, Labour and Welfare (Japan)
https://www.mhlw.go.jp/stf/newpage_23495.html

[2] Calculated from footnote 1 and
https://www.stat.go.jp/data/roudou/sokuhou/nen/ft/pdf/index1.pdf

[3] Calculated from Ministry of Labor (Taiwan)
https://statdb.mol.gov.tw/html/mon/c12020.htm and
https://eng.stat.gov.tw/ct.asp?xItem=48099&ctNode=2064&mp=5

1F   COVID-19 and Migration AMPHI 6

Chair   Lan Lo, University of Nottingham, UK

1040   Germans' awareness for social support needs of refugees. A matter of previous
       intercultural contact experiences?

*Saskia Judith Schubert, Berlin School of Economics and Law; Charité University
Berlin*

1053   Psychosocial Stressors and Resources of Women with a Migration Background -
       Final Results of a Labor Market Integration Program in Germany

*Sigrid James, University of Kassel, Germany
Franziska Seidel, University of Kassel, Germany
Julian Trostmann, University of Kassel, Germany*

524   Talking Trees: A virtual journey to the East in the time of the Covid-19 pandemic

*Lan Lo, University of Nottingham, UK
Michael Pinchbeck, Manchester Metropolitan University, UK*

1245   COVID-19 Emergency and Migrants' Health Protection in Southern Italy: A
       focus on the Apulia region

*Alda Kushi, Universita degli Studi di Bari, Italia
Michela Camilla Pellicani, Universita degli Studi di Bari, Italia
Gul Ince Beqo, Universita degli Studi di Bari, Italia*

**Germans' awareness for social support needs of refugees. A matter of previous
intercultural contact experiences?**

(1040) Saskia Judith Schubert, Berlin School of Economics and Law; Charité University
Berlin

Objectives Research in the past has shown that refugees' access to health care is
obstructed, partly due to negative attitudes of the receiving society (Penka et al., 2015;
Karpenstein & Nordheim, 2019) and a lack of knowledge on their support needs (Penka
et al., 2015; Sandhu et al., 2013). It is still largely unknown, which antecedents have a
positive effect on the perception of refugees' health care-related needs (Glen et al. 2019).
Prior research found empathy and positive attitudes towards another group (Glen et al.
2019; Vezzali et al., 2015) as well as intercultural contact to play an important role for the
readiness to help (van Assche, 2018, Hodson & Hewstone 2013). Using and expanding
the Empathy-Attitude-Action model (EAA; Batson et al., 2002), the current study
examined selected predictors of Germans' perception of support needs that refugees in
Germany may have as a precondition of Germans' readiness to help refugees. We
hypnotized Germans' greater awareness for refugees' need for emotional support to be
linked to a greater perception of refugees' perceived need for information regarding

health care services, directly and indirectly via more positive attitudes towards refugees' rights. Placing specific emphasis on the role of previous intercultural contact experiences as additional predictor, we expected it to serve as an antecedent for the remaining study variables. Method Data collection included a sample of 910 Germans (Mage = 48.40, SD = 14.79), matching the German census regarding central demographics. Participants completed a cross-sectional online survey with validated self-report measures. Assessments covered Germans' intercultural contact experiences, Germans' attitudes on refugees' rights, and Germans' perception of refugees' needs regarding emotional and informational support. After a multi-factor confirmatory factor analysis (CFA) was run to evaluate the measurement model and determine the latent correlations among the study variables, we computed three different structural equation models and increased the number of paths from quality of intercultural to the remaining study variables step-wise. Results Comparing the resulting models and choosing the least restrictive model as a result of significance testing, we found that previous positive intercultural contact experiences were related to greater perceptions of refugees' emotional support needs, as well as to more positive attitudes on their rights. Further, perceived emotional support needs were positively linked to perceived information needs, both directly and indirectly via attitudes on refugees' rights. The quality of intercultural contact had an indirect amplifying effect on perceived information needs via the other three variables but, surprisingly, had a negative direct effect. Conclusion Our results support the Empathy-Attitude-Action model, indicating that positive intercultural contact may help (1) to raise awareness for emotional support needs of refugees, (2) to improve Germans' attitudes on refugees' rights, and mediated through a rising awareness of emotional support needs of refugees and positive attitudes on refugees' rights (3) to sensitize the receiving community for information that needs to be made available in order for refugees to receive health care. A raised awareness for the perspective and support needs of refugees is a crucial step towards a healthier society, which acknowledges the needs of everyone living in it.

Psychosocial Stressors and Resources of Women with a Migration Background - Final Results of a Labor Market Integration Program in Germany

(1053) Sigrid James, University of Kassel, Germany

Franziska Seidel, University of Kassel, Germany

Julian Trostmann, University of Kassel, Germany

Women with migration background (WMB) are one of the most disadvantaged groups on the labor market. They face particular challenges, and psychosocial factors are believed to play an important role in affecting outcomes. Data on WMBs in labor market integration programs remains sparse however. - This analysis uses final evaluation data from a four-year labor market integration project for WMBs in Germany. The aim is to describe women's psychosocial stressors and resources (e.g., stress, resilience, social support) and examine their impact on outcome. Methods: The mixed-method evaluation collected data from multiple sources over three-and-a-half years. Basis for this analysis are data from 132 women who participated in baseline and follow-up surveys aimed at capturing data on their sociodemographic profiles, psychosocial stressors and barriers. The survey instrument included multiple standardized instruments. Descriptive, bivariate and logistic regression analysis was used to capture women's psychosocial profiles, examine changes over time and determine their predictive value for project outcome. Findings: Participants are highly heterogeneous regarding sociodemographic characteristics. They had medium levels of stress (M=38.5, SD=9.9) with 10% of women experiencing elevated stress. Sixty percent of women fall into the 'high,' 24.4% in the 'medium' and 15.6% in the 'low' resilience category. Social support is reported to be high on average. However, 10.8% experience social support rarely" or never." Bivariate analysis shows significant associations between lower stress and high resilience levels and early dropping out. The likelihood of staying in the project increases by 12% with every month in the project (Exp(B)=1.12; p<.001). Conclusion: Results suggest that being part of the project may contribute to higher stress and that women with higher resilience are more likely to drop out and seize other opportunities that present themselves. Results will be triangulated with findings from other data sources and implications for labor market integration efforts discussed.

Talking Trees: A virtual journey to the East in the time of the Covid-19 pandemic

(524) Lan Lo, University of Nottingham, UK

Michael Pinchbeck, Manchester Metropolitan University, UK

This paper presents a collaborative research project that provides students from the Universities of Nottingham (UoN) and Manchester Metropolitan (MMU) with the opportunity to 'Journey to the East' without actually travelling to the country. It is located within the literature on student migration and chimes with previous projects delivered either separately or in partnership by Lo and Pinchbeck around notions of migration and belonging.

It was devised in collaboration between Dr Lan Lo, Assistant Professor in Chinese Language and Society, from the UoN and Dr Michael Pinchbeck, Reader in Theatre, at MMU during the Covid-19 pandemic as an alternative to study placement for students taking Chinese on university degree programmes. It was part of a package of measures designed to address these students' language and cultural study needs in the context of lockdown and restrictions on international travel including to China.

The project, which is titled, Talking Trees/树说/述说 involves a living archive of stories listened to either from speakers in trees, imported from China or by downloading the audio via a QR code. The stories explore the notion of roots/routes and how trees have grown over time as a metaphor for migration and belonging.

One tree represents the idea of 'leaving home' while the other tree represents the idea of 'arriving home'. At each of the two trees students listen to verbatim interviews with Chinese speakers on a range of relevant themes. The voices were provided by international students from a range of backgrounds. A fictional narrative drawn from archival research and images explores the journey the trees might have taken from China to the UK, how they might be talking to each other and what they might say. This fictional narrative frames the interviews and forms an audio trail between the trees for visitors to follow.

COVID-19 Emergency and Migrants' Health Protection in Southern Italy: A focus on the Apulia region

(1245) Alda Kushi, Universita degli Studi di Bari, Italia

Michela Camilla Pellicani, Universita degli Studi di Bari, Italia

Gul Ince Beqo, Universita degli Studi di Bari, Italia

The aim of this article is to analyse the impact that the COVID-19 pandemic and the consequent health emergency have had on local governance, with particular focus on the protection of migrants' health in the Apulia Region (Southern Italy). The Apulian context represents an exception in the Italian national territory since, thanks to the legislative competence in the field of health provided for by the Constitution, the region has been able to detach itself from the political line of both the central government and the other regions, extending the basic medical care and health services provided to Italians and regular migrants also to irregular migrants. In this context, however, the health emergency, which has strongly destabilised the National Health System, has not only reinforced existing inequalities in terms of access to health care, particularly for vulnerable groups, such as irregular migrants, asylum seekers and seasonal workers established in informal settlements, but has also reorganised the State-Region relationship in the distribution of health services. The analysis conducted then examines a series of activities implemented by the regional administration (within the limits granted by the Government), and representatives of the third sector aimed at protecting the health of the most vulnerable groups with a focus on the governance of health services at various administrative levels.

1G   Economics of Migration   AMPHI 7

Chair   Elli Heikkilä, Migration Institute of Finland, Finland

1191   Female migrant sex workers in the UK, remittances, and entrepreneurship

Shirley Velasquez-Hoque, Oxford Brookes University, UK

1105   Remittances and Institutions - An Instrumental Variable Analysis

Zeeshan Hashim, Brunel University London, UK & Policy Research Institute of Market Economy (PRIME), Islamabad – Pakistan
Jan Fidrmuc, Université de Lille, France
Sugata Ghosh, Brunel University London, UK

1006   A Longitudinal Diary Study of Perceived Overqualification Between Brazilian and Venezuelan Immigrants Living in Portugal

Paulo Sousa Nascimento, University of Lisbon, Portugal

536   Seasonal migration and commuting in the tourism sector in Northern Finland

Elli Heikkilä, Migration Institute of Finland, Finland
Merja Paksuniemi, The University of Lapland, Finland

Female migrant sex workers in the UK, remittances, and entrepreneurship

(1191) Shirley Velasquez-Hoque, Oxford Brookes University, UK

The COVID-19 pandemic not only exposed pre-existing inequalities, but also deepened and exposed the gaps that further marginalise vulnerable people, including sex workers. Sex workers in this study are referred to as individuals who provide sexual services and companionship in exchange for monetary remuneration, organising their work in a largely independent manner (Analoui and Herath 2019). Despite the fact that sex workers have been adversely affected by the pandemic, they have been excluded from government relief and protection programmes, as well as health services (Lam 2020). Yet, sex workers, and more specifically migrant sex workers (particularly women), make significant direct and indirect contributions to local, national, and global economies, not only as a result of their labour, but as a result of their remittances sent back home (NSWP 2017). The ONS (2022) estimates that prostitution contributed £10.4 billion to the UK economy in 2021. Statistics on the remittances practices undertaken by sex workers are challenging to find and quantify, given that many are sent via informal channels. Nonetheless, it is well documented, that international economic remittances are a major source of external funding for developing countries, dwarfing foreign direct investment, foreign aid, and even public social welfare provisions. The World Bank (2021) for instance, forecasts that remittances sent by migrant workers to low and middle-income countries will reach $605 billion in 2022. As a result of the gaps in the literature and the opportunity and challenges that Covid-19 has presented migrant sex workers, this pilot qualitative study composed of semi-structured interviews and thematic analysis aims to explore the implications that economic remittances sent by female migrant sex workers in the UK have in their lives by studying how they use/invest this money back home. Preliminary findings from five interviews suggest four key findings. First, while the reasons for becoming sex workers vary, financial need and survival, particularly as a result of Covid prevail. Second, maintenance remittances predominate, although saving, investment, debt-repayment, emergency, and gift remittances are also regularly sent to close (largely female) family members. Third, these women have made investments back home in the form of land, property, and/or luxury good, which in some instances, are already offering them additional sources of income. Finally, all of the women interviewed plan to leave their current self-employment practices in the future by setting up different entrepreneurial ventures back home. The above findings are significant because although sex work is not encouraged in this research, as acknowledged by Analoui and Herath (2019), NSWP (2017), and Lam (2020) further research on this area is need, not the least due to the difficulties of tracking these remittances and their usages. Research into this topics will potentially contribute to further challenge the perceptions which lead to the stigmatisation of sex workers. Equally, this research can help explore in context, the value-added entrepreneurship activities these women engage in (Analoui and Herath 2019, Gaddefors and Anderson 2017), as well as the different forms of investments these women make/are planning to make back home. Thus shedding light on the implications of such entrepreneurial ventures on the current/future self-employment practices of these women, but potentially also on the lives of their families and their economies back home. References Analoui, B. D. and Herath, D. B. (2019) 'Independent female escorts: Stigmatized, value-adding entrepreneurs', The International Journal of Entrepreneurship and Innovation, 20(2), pp. 119-129. Gaddefors, J. and Anderson, A. (2017) 'Entrepreneursheep and context: when entrepreneurship is greater than entrepreneurs',

International journal of entrepreneurial behavior and research, 23 (2), pp. 267-278. Lam, E. (2020) 'Pandemic sex workers' resilience: COVID-19 crisis met with rapid responses by sex worker communities', International Social Work, 63(6), pp. 777-781. doi: 10.1177/0020872820962202. NSWP (2017) Migrant Sex Workers. Edinburgh, Scotland: nswp (Global Network of Sex Work Projects) Available at: https://www.nswp.org/sites/ nswp.org/files/briefing_paper_migrant_sex_workers_nswp_-_2017.pdf (Accessed: 31 March 2022). ONS (2022) Prostitution IDEF NSA. Available at: https://www.ons. gov.uk/economy/nationalaccounts/satelliteaccounts/timeseries/mnd4/ct (Accessed: 31 March 2022). World Bank (2021) 'Recovery: Covid-19 Crisis Through a Migration Lens, Migration and Development Brief 35': World Bank. Available at: https://www.knomad. org /publication/migration-and-development-brief-35 (Accessed: 30 March 2022).

Remittances and Institutions - An Instrumental Variable Analysis

(1105) Zeeshan Hashim, Brunel University London, UK & Policy Research Institute of Market Economy (PRIME), Islamabad – Pakistan

Jan Fidrmuc, Université de Lille, France

Sugata Ghosh, Brunel University London, UK

This paper explores how remittances influence political and economic liberalization in developing economies. We investigate four channels of remittances - income effect, social remittances, voice after exit, and modernization effect - through which remittances promote liberalization and one channel - stability effect - which discourages liberalization. Endogeneity is a potential problem since lack of freedom is a factor associated with peoples' incentive to emigrate and economies' dependence on remittances, and the analysis can be plagued by measurement error in official figures of remittances and omitted variable bias. The results using the instrumental variable approach show that remittances promote both political and economic liberalization. Some of the significant contributions of this research include demonstrating that remittances help recipient countries in solving their structural problems, and pave the way for political and economic convergence; introducing an instrumental variable, exposure to natural disasters, to resolve the endogeneity of remittances; and indicating how both political and economic outcomes are interconnected in developing economies.

A Longitudinal Diary Study of Perceived Overqualification Between Brazilian and Venezuelan Immigrants Living in Portugal

(1006) Paulo Sousa Nascimento, University of Lisbon, Portugal

Objectives: When a person perceives herself as overqualified, she considers having more qualifications and experience for her current occupation than the ones being used and required (Hsing-Ming et al., 2016). This element is particularly salient among migrants struggling with labour migration governance to validate and recognize their qualifications and competencies (Larsen et al., 2018). Those struggles put those migrants at risk of being overqualified and increase their chance of developing health issues, leading to higher stress levels and lower wellbeing (Crollard et al., 2012). The current study contributes to the literature gap by providing a diary study on the perceived overqualification of Brazilian and Venezuelan immigrants living in Portugal. Although lacking, a longitudinal perspective on the topic is required (Leschke & Weiss, 2020) because the migration experience is dynamic, full of diverse migration profiles and continuous changes (Altorjai, 2013). Methods: Every 3 months, a convenience sample of Brazilian (n = 17) and Venezuelan (n = 15) immigrants filled a questionnaire online. Each participant reported their perceived overqualification level at that moment in time (Perceived Overqualification Questionnaire, Fine & Nevo, 2008). Participants filled an open box question if substantial changes occurred during the 3 months, clarifying those issues if considered relevant. Sociodemographic variables were recorded to characterize the sample. Longitudinal diary data were analyzed using a random-intercept multilevel model for 456 individual-level observations nested within 32 level-2 immigrants. Results: An interaction effect between time and immigrant group was found, suggesting Venezuelan immigrants' perceived overqualification increased from baseline to 12-month follow-up compared to Brazilian immigrants (B = 0.30, SE = 0.12, p = .014). Spaghetti plots analyzed immigrant-specific trends over time, also suggesting different trajectories.Conclusions: Perceived overqualification appears to decrease over time, but changes may not occur similarly to all migrant groups and can also be extreme within each group. Future studies should explore the mechanisms of change of perceived overqualification. Particularly, studies should explore the contributions of migrants' length of time in the host country, their level of identification with the host country, and the overqualification nature (forced vs voluntary; Nascimento et al., 2022). In addition, social determinants of perceived overqualification (e.g., social capital) and wellbeing correlates (e.g., migrants' mental health, job satisfaction) should be explored to provide a better picture of this labour force characteristic more salient among immigrants, to design better services and care (Crollard et al., 2012; Wassermann & Hoppe, 2019).

Seasonal migration and commuting in the tourism sector in Northern Finland

(536) Elli Heikkilä, Migration Institute of Finland, Finland

Merja Paksuniemi, The University of Lapland, Finland

Problems with the functioning of the labor market are reflected in recruitment problems and labor supply problems. The growth of tourism in Lapland and Koillismaa in the Northern Finland is overshadowed by the shortage of skilled labor, which is particularly pronounced in seasonal sectors: it can be difficult to get enough people to work only during the high season. An additional challenge is the housing shortage.

This paper explores as a case study of tourism sector and the mobile, i.e. seasonally moving and commuting workforce in Lapland and Koillismaa in 2019. We analyse what are the consequences of the growing demand for labor in the tourism sector and the role of seasonal labour force which migrate and commute seasonally. Are there also consequences for the service system of the municipality subject to seasonal migration and commuting? In addition, we explore how the municipality could assist companies to increase a flexible workforce, i.e. seasonal migrants and commuters to tourism sector. The effects of the COVID-19 pandemic on the tourism sector in Lapland and Koillismaa are also highlighted.

The collected research material through a Webropol survey and interviews consists of 19 tourism entrepreneurs and three city and municipal leaders in the study area. In addition, publicly available and separately purchased statistical data of Statistics Finland, as well as Finnavia's air traffic statistics and traffic statistics were used as research data.

In twelve of the nineteen companies surveyed worked seasonal migrants in 2019. All companies with more than five employees had seasonal migrants. One of the companies employed 100 seasonal migrants, six companies each had 10–40 seasonal migrants, and five companies had less than ten seasonal migrants. The seasonal migrants worked mainly in so-called secondary labour market positions in 2019. Most of them worked in jobs in the catering industry or in customer service positions. The role of the seasonal migrants is thus essential in the labour force of tourism sector in the Northern Finland.

Seasonal workers were often from Finland but also from abroad. The main recruitment countries were Poland and Belgium, in addition to which other European countries were mentioned. Seasonal migrants were usually not the same people in different years. However, six respondents reported that seasonal migrants were mostly the same individuals as in previous years.

The number of commuters in the companies was clearly lower than the number of seasonal migrants. In most companies, there were one or two commuters, but no more than five people. The annual turnover of commuters was also not high, but they were the same people in different years.

The companies that responded to the survey felt that the importance of tourism activities and the services operating around them was great for municipalities, and that the importance was even expected to grow.

1H   Integration, Acculturation and Diasporas SALLES DES ACTES

Chair: Almudena Macías León, University of Malaga, Spain

949   The Importance of Skin Colour in Central Eastern Europe

David Andreas Bell, Norwegian University of Science and Technology, Norway

1084   Assimilation or Integration? Or should we develop a new approach to resettlement?

Nicole Dubus, San Jose State University, USA

521   Community sustainability of immigrants: a geographical overview from the Northern Region

Yeasmin Nafisa, University of Lapland, Finland

519   Community integration of foreigners residing in Spain: Risk and protection factors

Gianluigi Moscato, University of Malaga, Spain
Almudena Macías León, University of Malaga, Spain

The Importance of Skin Colour in Central Eastern Europe

(949) David Andreas Bell, Norwegian University of Science and Technology, Norway

The importance of skin colour is often neglected in empirical studies of negative attitudes towards minorities. In this study we use data from the 2014/2015 wave of the European Social Survey to analyse explicitly racist attitudes in Hungary, Poland and the Czech Republic. The study demonstrates how theoretical perspectives commonly used in explorations of negative attitudes based on ethnicity may be effectively used to analyse racist attitudes. The results show high levels of racist attitudes in both Hungary and the Czech Republic, despite there being very few non-white immigrants in these countries, while in Poland the racist attitudes are less widespread. Symbolic threats seem to be very important for understanding racist attitudes. Realistic threats, on the other hand, seem to be of less importance. There is also the surprising result that voters of more moderate political parties are not less racist than the voters of the more radical political parties in any of the three countries.

Assimilation or Integration? Or should we develop a new approach to resettlement?

(1084) Nicole Dubus, San Jose State University, USA

The resettlement process varies in every region, country, and town in small and large ways. But one element exists in each of them: how do new arrivals into a country thrive? Assimilation and Integration are often the stated goals of resettlement programs and have been operationalized via obtaining safe housing, employment, dominant language acquisition. Many times, assimilation and integration are used interchangeably. However, in the literature, assimilation connotes the new arrival adopting many of the host country's culture and values. Integration connotes a sharing of culture and values between the host country and the new arrival that preserves each party's distinct cultural attributes. Are assimilation and integration helpful with the continued disruptive and growing refugee crisis? Study This study explores the history of assimilation and integration in the United States and posits that both concepts assume a power dynamic where one country subsumes another, or tolerantly co-exist. This study suggests a new approach to the resettlement process, one that sees forced migration through a globalized lens. Through interviews with social service workers, program managers, educators, policymakers, and forced migrants, the study sought to understand the goals of those who work with forced migrants and the forced migrant's goals.

Methods

This is a qualitative study that examines the self-perceived experiences of professionals working with forced migrants and forced migrants receiving resettlement services. The data was collected in several countries, Iceland, Germany, Greece, Mexico, Sweden, Switzerland, and the United States, and represented migrants from SouthEast Asia, several African countries, Central, and South America, Syria, the Baltic region, Bhutan, Burma/Myanmar, Pakistan, and Afghanistan. Institutional board approval was obtained. Participants gave informed consent. Findings Participants described complex reactions that were dynamically influenced by personal expectations, past experiences, and were affected by the participant's experiences with racism and oppression. These findings are explored further and their implications for policymakers, providers, and migrants are discussed. In particular, the concepts of assimilation vs integration are examined in relation to forced migration. The data suggest that focusing on resilience might be a more effective approach than assimilation or integration.

Community sustainability of immigrants: a geographical overview from the Northern Region

(521) Yeasmin Nafisa, University of Lapland, Finland

Immigrants apply a planned behavior theory to preserve their culture and religious beliefs and maintain a regular relationship with transnational families and their own communities. Transnational families and communities of own become an unseparated part of their lives. These ties with one´s own have an impact on exercising different socio-legal systems and normative orderings (i.e. family laws) of their country of origins in the host society which become their everyday practices. This tendency has an impact on legally pluralist settings of the host country. Whether (or not) this tendency supports their integration into the host society is a concern of the moment in the Northern society. The study will explore how social exclusion and insecurity influence the motivation of immigrants to preserve their collectivist thought that leads to a diverse legal regime and influence a multi-level pluralistic conceptual framework in the host society. The objectives of this study are to broaden our knowledge of planned behavior theory and the role of motivation in any changing situation that can stimulate human desires to upkeep relationships with transnational families and own in-group networks.

Community integration of foreigners residing in Spain: Risk and protection factors

(519) Gianluigi Moscato, University of Malaga, Spain

Almudena Macías León, University of Malaga, Spain

The migrants' dream of finding a job and integrating into the host society is very often frustrated by various factors such as language difficulties, ethnicity, lack of social support, unemployment, etc. (Moscato, 2022). (Moscato, 2022). All these factors, in turn, can generate a feeling of perceived discrimination in the foreigner that hinders their integration (Tonsing, 2013). At the same time, the migration process itself can generate certain social, cultural and coexistence dynamics between immigrants and natives that feed negative perceptions of immigrants and hinder their adaptation process (Berry, 1997). In addition to the difficulties intrinsic to the migration process, Spain has experienced a growing anti-foreigner ideology that contributes to the implementation of stereotypes towards foreigners and their consequent discrimination. This makes their integration even more difficult (Moscato, 2022). The aim of this research is to determine the predictive capacity of certain psychosocial variables (perceived discrimination, social support, community participation, ingroup and outgroup identification) and sociodemographic variables (sex, employment status, years of residence, etc.) on the community integration of immigrants living in Spain. The snowball method was used for sampling and a questionnaire was used to collect the data, including scales validated with foreigners. Finally, 449 immigrants from different countries participated, although most of them (20.1%) came from Morocco. An analysis of variance was carried out to determine whether there were significant differences in relation to certain socio-demographic variables. A bilateral correlation analysis was carried out to determine the degree of relationship between integration and the independent variables. Finally, a linear regression analysis is carried out to determine the predictive capacity of each of the proposed psychosocial variables. With regard to the socio-demographic variables, and in line with other research, it was found that having a job, mastering the native language and having been resident for at least 5 years are protective factors for integration. In relation to psychosocial variables, perceived discrimination ($\beta=-.180$, $p<.01$) is a factor that hinders integration. Meanwhile, identification with Spanish culture ($\beta=206$, $p<.01$), community participation ($\beta=432$, $p<.01$) and formal ($\beta=132$, $p<.05$) and informal ($\beta=166$, $p<.01$) social support are protective factors. The model predicts 52.5% of the variance. Possible limitations of the study are discussed and new lines of research and intervention to improve the social and community integration of immigrants are suggested.

References:

Berry, J.W. (1997). Immigration, acculturation and adaptation. Applied Psychology: An Internatioal Review, 46(1), 5-68.

Moscato, G. (2022). ¿Qué factores psicosociales explican la integración comunitaria de los inmigrantes? Una experiencia entre lo digital y lo presencial. Comunitania. Revista Internacional De Trabajo Social Y Ciencias Sociales, (23), 53–71. https://doi.org/10.5944/comunitania.23.4

Tonsing, K. N. (2013). Predictors of psychological adaptation of south asian immigrants in Hong Kong. International Journal of Intercultural Relations, 37, 238-248.

Day Two 8 September 2022 Thursday

Day Two 8 September 2022 - 09:00-10:30

2A   Brain Drain in North Africa [AR-FR] _ AMPHI 1

الجلسة الثانية: هجرة الكفاءات في بلدان شمال أفريقيا

رئيس الجلسة :د. محمد العباسي ، رئيس شعبة الاقتصاد بكلية العلوم القانونية والاقتصادية و الاجتماعية. أكدال جامعة محمد الخامس

Chair: Dr. Idris Al Abbasi, Department Head - Department of Economics, Faculty of Legal, Economic and Social Sciences, Mohammed V University of Rabat, Morocco

556   Dr Mehdi Lahlou: Secrétaire Général du NAMAN: l'exode des compétences marocaines: à propos d'une enquête

511   Dr Boutaina Ismaili Idrissi & Hafsa Taya Sara Kawkaba: L'intention migratoire des professionnels de la Santé Publique au Maroc: Résultats d'une enquête

554   Dr Chekrouni Djamila & Benabdellah Zaynab: L'émigration des personnes qualifiées du Maroc

L'intention migratoire des professionnels de la Santé Publique au Maroc: Résultats d'une enquête

(511) Dr Boutaina Ismaili Idrissi & Hafsa Taya Sara Kawkaba

La crise sanitaire liée à la pandémie qui a touché le monde en 2020 a révélé, entre autres, l'état des hôpitaux (manque de matériel, de médicaments, de lits dans les services de réanimation) et a particulièrement mis en lumière la pénurie de personnel médical et soignant. Elle a aussi été l'occasion de rappeler une réalité méconnue au sujet de la présence de professionnels de santé à diplôme étranger notamment en Europe facilitée par une politique d'attraction et de migration choisie destinée à drainer davantage de médecins et autres professionnels de santé pour combler leurs besoins dans ce secteur.

Le nombre des médecins avec un diplôme européen ou extra-européen inscrit au tableau de l'ordre des médecins a quasiment été multiplié par deux (+ 90 %) entre 2007 et 2017 et devrait atteindre les 30 000 en 2020. En 2021, l'ordre des médecins comptait 22 568 médecins à diplôme étranger en activité régulière. Un peu moins de la moitié de ces effectifs sont constitués de praticiens à diplôme européen (45,5 %). Le reste est constitué de médecins immigré (e) s originaires de pays extra-européens. Ces dernièr(e)s sont majoritairement titulaires d'un diplôme obtenu au Maghreb et en Afrique sub-saharienne. Le choix des médecins étrangers notamment maghrébins d'exercer en France pays de prédilection en Europe est motivé essentiellement par leur trajectoire personnelle expliquée par certains facteurs récurrents, à la fois historiques et socio-économiques .

Selon une étude réalisée par le conseil national de l'ordre des médecins de France en 2018, le nombre de médecins marocains exerçant sur le territoire français avoisine les 7 000, dont 6510 médecins exerçant leur profession de façon continue et 430 médecins les exerçant de manière intermittente. Tandis que le nombre des médecins en France et supérieure à ceux au Maroc. La France fournit 6.475 médecins pour 1000 habitants, alors qu'au Maroc ce pourcentage ne dépasse passe pas 1 soit 0.7308 médecins pour 1000 habitants en 2017. Ceci dit le nombre de médecins marocains exerçant à l'étranger est estimé à 14000. Ce chiffre est appelé à évoluer compte tenu des conditions de travail des médecins au Maroc qui restent insuffisantes et peu propices pour leur évolution personnelle et professionnelle. Autant de facteurs push expliquant cet engouement pour exercer leur métier ailleurs notamment en Europe. Cette migration médicale marocaine coûte cher aux finances de l'économie marocaine et a un effet direct sur l'économie marocaine qui se manifeste par la dépréciation du capital humain et par conséquent des effets pervers sur la croissance économique alors que ce type de migration devient un gain pour les pays qui en bénéficient. Bhagwati et Hamada (1974) a montré que l'émigration des personnes les plus qualifiées génère une externalité fiscale associée à un biais du système fiscal optimal, et cela à deux niveaux. En outre, sachant que les agents les plus qualifiés sont les mieux rémunérés, le gouvernement perd en termes de revenu fiscal suite à la fuite de ces agents, ce qui affecte la taille potentielle de la redistribution des revenus. De même, l'investissement en termes d'éducation et de formation présente un large coût pour les pays en voie de développement qui ne peuvent recevoir les bénéfices en retour. De plus, d'après la théorie de la croissance endogène, la migration des compétences impose une externalité dont la source réside dans la réduction du stock de capital humain local disponible pour les générations présentes et futures. Cela implique un effet négatif sur le revenu des travailleurs non émigrés ou sur le taux de la croissance du pays de départ.

L'objet de cet article est d'examiner le phénomène de la fuite des compétences des professionnels de la santé dans le secteur public au Maroc. Il s'appuiera, entre autres, sur une enquête auprès des professionnels de la santé (Médecins, infirmiers et personnels paramédicaux (autres que les infirmiers) en exercice dans les principaux centres hospitaliers publics au Maroc notamment ceux des régions de Casablanca, Rabat et Fès afin d'apprécier le potentiel migratoire et les facteurs push et pull qui pourraient les inciter à quitter le pays.

L'émigration des personnes qualifiées du Maroc

(554) Dr Chekrouni Djamila & Benabdellah Zaynab

L'exode des compétences en Tunisie

(555) Dr Mohamed Kriaa (Université de Tunis)

2B   Migration Theory and Methods   AMPHI 2

Chair: Elli Heikkila, Migration Institute, Finland

1135   Building trust with refugee women - six guidelines for qualitative researchers

Khadijah Kainat, Abo Academy, Finland
Maria Hokkinen, Abo Academy, Finland
Elli Heikkila, Migration Institute, Finland

1173   A Radiation model for migration with directional preferences

Lucas Kluge, Potsdam Institute for Climate Impact Research, Germany

1010   From Aspiration to Action: Estimating Refugee's Capability to Migrate

Haodong Qi, Malmö University, Sweden
Tuba Bircan, Vrije Universiteit Brussel, Belgium

1215   New perspectives on migration patterns in Sudan in the context of climate change

Fanny Christou, Malmö University, Sweden & Migrinter & Institut Convergences Migrations, France

Building trust with refugee women - six guidelines for qualitative researchers

(1135) Khadijah Kainat, Abo Academy, Finland

Maria Hokkinen, Abo Academy, Finland

Elli Heikkila, Migration Institute, Finland

This paper explores the methodological challenges and the role of trust when conducting qualitative research with refugee women from the Middle East. It offers guidelines for researchers to ease access and gain rapport in an ethically sustainable way. Trust is a positive feeling about the intentions or behavior of another. It is an emotion and practice embedded in the relations between the 'trustor' and the 'trustee' (Lyytinen, 2016). Due to the events leading to refugeeness, such as conflicts and persecution, refugees are more susceptible to losing trust in the society (Hynes, 2017). When conducting research with minorities, the question of trust and access become central for collecting relevant research data (Miller, 2004). It is generally considered hard to develop relations of trust and access in refugee communities that are often closed to outsiders. Due to gender issues, national cultural and religious restrictions and family concerns, refugee women can be even more isolated from the mainstream communities than their male counterparts, making access even harder (Kainat et al., 2021). This paper is empirically based on two different ethnographic studies among refugee women in Sweden/Finland. Study 1, dealing with "integration issues of women refugees in Sweden" was conducted by participant observations and semi-structured in-depth interviews (n=20) with refugee women from Syria, Iraq and Palestine living in Sweden. Study 2, about consumer behavior of refugees, was conducted as small focus group interviews (n=23) in Finland, among refugees - both women and men - from Iraq, Turkey and Syria. In the former study, the participant observations and interviews were conducted in English, while the interviews of the latter study were supported by a translator. In both studies, we found that trust was closely associated with gender, cultural and religious aspects. In Study 1, the researcher was a so-called "insider", with cultural and religious similarities with the participants. In study 2, the researcher belonged to the mainstream population of Finland, thus making her an "outsider" in certain aspects and initially impeding the access, which later was solved by enlisting an interpreter. Study 2 also included male participants, which shed light on the specifics of interviewing men vs. women. Based on our analysis, we suggest six guidelines for researchers who wish to build trust while conducting qualitative research with Middle Eastern refugee women. Our suggestions, which we will elaborate on in our conference presentation and later full paper, include: 1) finding and involving participants in a culturally-appropriate way, 2) being mindful of the position of women in each context, 3) understanding the background of the participants, e.g. social, cultural, political, religious, economic and linguistic factors, 4) having common cultural competencies with the participants, 5) respecting the confidentiality and privacy of the participants, and 6) seeking ways to alleviate the imbalance of power in interviews. Building trust with a new informant is hard especially during COVID-19 pandemic without face-to-face meetings and time spent together. The pandemic has also provided opportunities to deepen and expand our understanding on how to adapt to new ways of doing fieldwork and data collection (Tiilikainen, Kaukko & Mubeen, 2021).

A Radiation model for migration with directional preferences

(1173) Lucas Kluge, Potsdam Institute for Climate Impact Research, Germany

The radiation model is a parameter-free model of human mobility that has been applied primarily for short-distance moves, such as commuting. When applied to migration, it underestimates the number of long-range moves, such as between different US states. Here, we show that it additionally suffers from a conceptual inconsistency that can have substantial numerical effects for long-distance moves. We propose a modification of the radiation model that introduces a dependence on the angle between any two alternative, potential destinations; accounting for the possibility that migrants have preferences about the approximate direction of their move. We demonstrate that this modification mitigates the conceptual inconsistency and improves the model fit to observational migration data, without introducing any fitting parameters.

From Aspiration to Action: Estimating Refugee's Capability to Migrate

(1010) Haodong Qi, Malmö University, Sweden

Tuba Bircan, Vrije Universiteit Brussel, Belgium

Migration is a selective process; not all desired migratory movements can be realized. However, there has been very limited empirical research on how migrants are (self-)selected along the migratory process. In this paper, we seek to examine refugees' capability to realize their desired migratory movements. Using Google search data and EUROSTAT statistics on asylum applications, we show that, for Syrians, the capability to migrate to the EU vary substantially across destinations. Most strikingly, for Syrians seeking asylum in Germany, the action tends to increase with the level of desire in a non-linear fashion. This suggests that there could be a tipping point at which the capability of migrating starts to grow and reinforces aspirations and actions simultaneously.

New perspectives on migration patterns in Sudan in the context of climate change

(1215) Fanny Christou, Malmö University, Sweden & Migrinter & Institut Convergences Migrations, France

Sudan is currently witnessing rapid urbanization as a result of decades of protracted conflict which has displaced millions of people inside the country who have migrated to urban centres like Khartoum. Indeed, Sudan has experienced conflict throughout the past decades with two civil wars (1955-1972 and 1983-2005) and the conflict that broke out after South Sudan's independence in 2011. This conflict has resulted in 1.1 million internally displaced people (IDPs), while the Darfur conflict of 2003 has resulted in 2 million displaced people and thousands of deaths. South Sudan's independence also meant the loss of a quarters of Sudan's oil production, a driving power of Sudan's economy. This shock has exacerbated the fragile structure of Sudan's economy, which, tied to the lack of infrastructure and reliance on subsistence agriculture, keeps almost half of the population below the poverty line. Moreover, the country is severely affected by upcoming climate change and challenged by various environment hazards such erratic rainfall, drought and extreme floods, dust storms, thunderstorms, and heat waves, also contributing to the displacement of people. The top three countries of origin for migrants in Sudan are South Sudan, Eritrea, Ethiopia, and Chad but we also need to consider displaced people inside the country due to historical change of borders. In parallel, conflicts and crisis in the neighbourhood countries have generated an influx of refugees. The most recent wave of migration to Sudan is the Syrian one, without any restriction entry for Syrians, due to various reasons regarding common features that exist between Sudan and Syria. Syrians in Sudan have access to education and healthcare as if they were nationals of the country, they have the right to work and run businesses in their names. There is no restriction on their movement because the Syrian community is not seen or granted to status of refugees and they tend to be called visitors or guests instead.Based on a current research project funded by the Swedish Research Council that deals with resilience in urban Sudan and its associated fieldwork, this article aims to review the current migratory patterns in Sudan, and more precisely in Khartoum. After a deep state of the art and an analysis of international organisations' reports, this article will 1/ introduce an historical background of the migration distribution in Sudan, 2/ focus on the migration patterns in Khartoum (migration waves induced by climate change and conflicts) and 3/ analyse strategies that are developed by migrants and local communities in two Sudanese neighbourhoods to face current challenges in Khartoum (urbanisation and environmental hazards). Finally, while migrants are often portrayed as victims in the context of climate change, empirical evidence also shows that in the face of environmental and climatic stress, migration is a common household strategy aimed at supporting basic needs and livelihoods. In this respect, this article aims to discuss and open perspectives on the role of migrants in Khartoum, questioning the sense of social cohesion that may occur to face environmental crisis.

2C   Youth Migration   AMPHI 3

Chair: Jeffrey Cohen, Ohio State Universtiy, USA

999   Religious affiliation as a risk and/or resource? A qualitative study of refugee youth and youth of immigrant descent in Germany

Julia Marie Christina Wenzing, Martin-Luther-University Halle-Wittenberg, Germany
Lina Alhaddad, Martin-Luther-University Halle-Wittenberg, Germany
Maja Katharina Schachner, Martin-Luther-University Halle-Wittenberg, Germany
Sophie Ingrid Elisabeth Hoelscher, Martin-Luther-University Halle-Wittenberg, Germany

1085   How unplanned turning points, social connections, and transnational linkages change the trajectories of sub-Saharan African migrants who live/lived in Morocco

Catherine Therrien, Al Akhawayn University, Morocco

1270   Is return easier than emigrating? A look at children of emigrants from Latvia and returnee children to Latvia and the factors that affect their psychosocial well-being.

Daina Grosa, University of Latvia, Latvia and University of Sussex, UK

951   Sense of belonging as being at home': Narratives of forced migrant youth in Southeast Asia

Rashin Lamouchi, University of Victoria, Canada

Religious affiliation as a risk and/or resource? A qualitative study of refugee youth and youth of immigrant descent in Germany

(999) Julia Marie Christina Wenzing, Martin-Luther-University Halle-Wittenberg, Germany

Lina Alhaddad, Martin-Luther-University Halle-Wittenberg, Germany

Maja Katharina Schachner, Martin-Luther-University Halle-Wittenberg, Germany Sophie Ingrid Elisabeth Hoelscher, Martin-Luther-University Halle-Wittenberg, Germany

Background: Worldwide crises and conflicts have resulted in rising numbers of forcibly displaced persons in recent years. Germany has received about almost 1.5 million refugees by 2020, half of them children and youth under the age of 18 (Federal Office for Migration and Refugees, 2020). In comparison to youth of immigrant descent, who have been in Germany for longer and are often born and raised in Germany, refugee youth commonly have to cope with traumatic experiences and additional acculturative challenges, such as learning a new language and adapting to different cultural values and norms. Religion has been shown to play a significant role for coping with acculturative hassles, considering its prevalence in immigrant communities and its positive relation to psychological well-being (Davis & Kiang, 2016). In view of the numerous stressors both refugee youth and youth of immigrant descent face, religious affiliation can be a source of personal and social support and act as a promotive and protective factor regarding their social-psychological adjustment in Germany (Suárez-Orozco et al., 2018). Especially for refugee youth religious affiliation could serve as an important resource, helping them to avoid an unstable environment after arriving newly in Germany and experiencing a sense of belonging in their religious community (Güngor et al., 2013). Nevertheless, especially for Muslim youth, which make up a large proportion in both groups and are often exposed to particularly high rates of discrimination, their religious affiliation can also present a risk factor as a source of exclusion and rejection by members of the cultural majority and other immigrant groups. However, especially in the light of discrimination, they may see their religious affiliation as a personal resource and source of strength (Abo-Zena & Barry, 2013).Aims: Previous research on refugee youth and youth of immigrant descent in Germany paid little attention to the role of religious affiliation in regard of their social-psychological adjustment, and there is little research comparing these groups. Our study therefore investigates religious affiliation as a risk and/or resource. Further, we explore potential similarities and differences between refugee youth and youth of immigrant descent regarding the role of religious affiliation as a risk and/or resource.Method: To address our research questions, explorative and semi-structured interviews (N = 11) were conducted with ethnically and religiously diverse immigrant-origin youth, aged 14 to 16 years (Mage = 15.45, SD = 0.69, 80% male). Six of the adolescents indicated having a refugee experience. Data will be coded by two coders to establish inter-rater reliability and analyzed using qualitative content analysis.Conclusion & Implications: The study adds to the current research on refugee youth' and youth of immigrant descents' resources and challenges while developing a better understanding of religious affiliation as a risk and/or resource. Furthermore, our study aims to provide potential implications for educational and social policies promoting the social-psychological adjustment of refugee youth and youth of immigrant descent. Our research emphasizes the importance of differentiating between minority groups, by focusing on refugee youth and youth of immigrant descent.

How unplanned turning points, social connections, and transnational linkages change the trajectories of sub-Saharan African migrants who live/lived in Morocco

(1085) Catherine Therrien, Al Akhawayn University, Morocco

My contribution to this conference will be based on the preliminary results of an ongoing research project on migration narratives funded by the European Commission [1]. This consortium includes 12 partners from origin, transit, and host countries. Morocco has initially been included in this project as a 'transit country'. However, adopting a decolonial approach (Gross-Wyrtzen & Gazzotti, 2021)[2] and a pro-South tone (Messari 2018[3]) challenges this Euro-centric view on Morocco and allows for a more complex description of the multifaceted realities of this context which bridges the Euro-African migratory system (Berriane and al., 2015)[4]. The analysis of diverse migration narratives (Bibler Coutin & Vogel, 2016) [5] will allow me to show how the migratory trajectories are impermanent and changing. To do so, I will first provide an ethnographic description of six different migration narratives. A young man migrant who spent a while in a protection house for minor migrants, underwent professional training and an internship in Morocco, reached Spain illegally and ended legally in France. A woman student who was recruited by a Moroccan school and decided to make Morocco her second home. A highly skilled man migrant who was locally recruited as an engineer, pursued a relationship with a Moroccan woman, but lost contact with her during the pandemic. An undocumented migrant, mother of six children (four left behind, one who traveled with her, and one born 'en route') who thought of Morocco as a transit space to Europe, lost hope when she discovered, the day after her wedding, that a migrant had stolen the money she had saved during the 4 years she had spent in Morocco, and fought to start again from scratch. An 'illegalized' man migrant who tried to reach Europe for some years, had the opportunity to get his paperwork during the second regularization campaign, worked as a mediator in a migrant association, and got multiple visas to legally travel in the Schengen area. And finally, an undocumented homosexual woman migrant who arrived in Morocco by crossing the borders illegally, and who, after many attempts to reach Europe by boat, sought refuge to the UNHCR and succeeded in being relocated in the USA where she recently got her American citizenship. I will then highlight the different turning points (political, biographical, economical, familial, etc.) that contributed to changing the trajectories of these sub-Saharan African migrants I met during the fieldwork and connect them to some elements that seem to be crucial in shifting the trajectories: the social connections and transnational links (Stock, 2016) these migrants built, broke, or maintained throughout their fragmented journey (Collyer, 2010). Ultimately, this analysis will allow me to highlight some common themes between the narratives: the concepts of hope, betrayal, home, God, and adventure. [1] ITHACA Interconnecting Histories and Archives for Migrant Agency: Entangled Narratives Across Europe and the Mediterranean Region (2021-2025). https://ithacahorizon.eu/ [2] Leslie Gross-Wyrtzen

& Lorena Gazzotti (2021) Telling histories of the present: postcolonial perspectives on Morocco's 'radically new' migration policy, The Journal of North African Studies, 26:5, 827-843. [3] Messari, N. 2018. Morocco's Africa Policy. MENARA Future Notes. 12: 1-6. [4] Berriane, Mohamed; de Haas, Hein; Natter, Katharina (2015) Introduction: revisiting Moroccan migrations, The Journal of North African Studies, 20:4, 503-521. [5] Bibler Colin, C., Vogel E. 2016. Migrant narratives and ethnographic tropes: navigating tragedy, creating possibilities. Journal of contemporary ethnography

Is return easier than emigrating? A look at children of emigrants from Latvia and returnee children to Latvia and the factors that affect their psychosocial well-being.

(1270) Daina Grosa, University of Latvia, Latvia and University of Sussex, UK

Latvian citizens who emigrate must stabilise their lives quickly in many different spheres of life after moving to their new country of residence. One area is the education and emotional well-being of children who move with their parents. Each country has its own system for enrolling newly arrived children in kindergarten and school. Some host countries have years of experience in integrating newcomer children, while others are less well prepared in terms of clear principles of inclusion in their education systems because of less historical experience with immigration issues. For children themselves, settling into a new environment socially, emotionally and psychologically is not without difficulties; it all depends on the individual and also on the environment, including the support of the family itself.

Regarding return migration – this may be much more challenging, particularly in this case in reference to government schools in Central Eastern European countries. Some of the challenges are: little or poor knowledge of Latvian (in the case of Latvia), a mismatch of age and knowledge levels, lack of preparedness and interest of Latvian educators to welcome children with different life experiences, a lack of information of returnee families about the Latvian educational system; the expectations that are set by families and how they differ from what was expected of the children in their host country.

This mixed methods study examines the different experiences of Latvian families emigrating and integrating into another country and also of returnee families integrating back into Latvia after several years of absence. The objectives of the study are to unpack the factors that influence the psychosocial well-being of children who migrate between countries. Quantitative data from a survey in Latvia, titled "Well-being and Integration in the Context of Migration" is used in this study, analysing the responses of emigrants living in the diaspora with children under 18 (n=1452), compared with the responses of returnees with children under 18 (n=351). Qualitative data from 67 interviews in total - 22 with Latvian nationals living outside Latvia and 17 returnee families who have migrated back to Latvia was also used in the study.

The findings indicate a lack of empathy towards newcomers and lack of knowledge in the school community about how to welcome and include them (both children and parents). Because of the school culture in government schools, returnee families have little interaction with teachers, administrators and other families and consequently live in an information "vacuum". Parents also do not always adequately prepare for the move beforehand. Among recommendations to schools is the need for intercultural education programmes in schools for teachers and school pupils, in order for them to be fully prepared for inclusion of newcomers into the school in a welcoming manner. Schools are encouraged to develop a handbook for newcomers, outlining the school rules and culture. Parents are recommended to prepare for the move beforehand, so that children have some information about what is in store for them in the new environment (including learning the language of the home country) and also be actively involved and informed about their child's progress - both academically and socially.

References

Berry, J. W. (1997) Immigration, acculturation and adaptation. *Applied Psychology, 46(1), 5–34.*

Bronfenbrenner, U. (1994). *Ecological models of human development. In: International Encyclopedia of Education, Vol. 3 (pp. 37–43). Oxford: Elsevier.*

Brooks, R., Goldstein. S. (2001). *Raising resilient children: Fostering strength, hope, and optimism in your child. New York: Contemporary Books.*

Cassarino, J.-P. (2004). *Theorising return migration: The conceptual approach to return migrants revisited. International Journal on Multicultural Societies, 6(2), 253–279.*

Grosa, D. (2022). *The return migration of children: (re) integration is not always plain sailing. In: King, R., Kutschminder, K. (eds.). Handbook of Return Migration. Cheltenham, UK; Northampton, MA, USA: Edward Elgar Publishing.*

Grzymała-Moszczyńska, H., Grzymała-Moszczyńska, J., Durlik, J., Szydłowska, P. (2015). *(Nie)łatwe powroty do domu? Funkcjonowanie dzieci i młodzieży powracających z emigracji [(Un)easy returns home? A study of the functioning of children and young people returning from emigration]. Warszawa: Fundacja Centrum im. prof. Bronisława Geremka.*

Sime, D., Fox, R. (2015). *Migrant children, social capital and access to services post-migration: transitions, negotiations and complex agencies. Children and Society, 29(6), 524–534.*

Vathi, Z., King, R. (2021). *Memory, place and agency: transnational mirroring of otherness among young Albanian "returnees". Children's Geographies, 19(2), 197–209.*

Sense of belonging as being at home': Narratives of forced migrant youth in Southeast Asia

(951) Rashin Lamouchi, University of Victoria, Canada

This paper is part of the Youth Migration Project (YMP), a research in progress that explores how young forced migrants continuously construct their identity and future aspirations while perched on the edge of mainstream society without access to normative entitlements or a voice in decision-making about their future. This study brings into view the developmental needs and aspirations of forced migrant youth who are currently residing in Kuala Lumpur, Malaysia. The project asks youth participants what is it like to grow up 'on the move' with a shattered sense of sense of home and belonging to a nation-state. Through purposive and snowball recruitment methods this participatory research gathers the migration and identity narratives of approximately forty forced migrant youth 13 to16 years-old mostly originated from countries in conflict in Asia and Africa, especially from Myanmar, Afghanistan, Syria, Pakistan, Iran and Somalia. The construction of belonging as an emotional feeling of 'being at home' in a place is the focus of this research. Belonging as feeling at home has not been frequently analyzed by scholars; rather, belonging has often been used as a synonym of collective identity or citizenship (Antonsich, 2010). Evocations of the concept of belonging, such as by Yuval-Davis (2006) and others, overlook the notion of place, "as if feelings, discourses, and practices of belonging exist in a geographical vacuum" (Antonsich, 2010, p. 647). Yet consideration of the geographical situation of the participants in this study is imperative if only because they had, as forced migrants, been rejected and/or ejected from their homes. As youth in transit, they are not fixed in their geographical locale, and yet many had been in prolonged displacement and may have found ways to reconstruct a sense of being at home at least temporarily. In exploring belonging as feeling at home, a reflexive thematic analysis was used to look for youths' accounts of their sense of 'being at home.' The results show this factor can contribute to generate feeling of belonging as being at home. Our study is unique in its focus on telling stories of forced migrant children and exploring migrant participants' perceptions of their own best interests in finding sustainable, equitable solutions to their displacement.

2D   Work, Employment, Society   AMPHI 4

Chair: Iliuta Cumpanasu, Border Police, Romania, Romania

547   Reporting from the Field- U.S. Immigration Policy and Citizen Driven initiatives to attend the root causes of the irregular migration from the Northern Triangle

Aileen Walborsky, Esq., Honorary Consul of Guatemala, USA

1157   The Concept of "Memory Effect" in Irregular Migration and Related Criminality

Iliuta Cumpanasu, Border Police, Romania, Romania
Veronica Oana Cumpanasu, Border Police, Romania

1220   Chinese Entrepreneurs in Casablanca: Experiencing and Narrating Contemporary Morocco

Jalil Jie Gao, The University of Arizona, USA

1303   Escaping irregularity through entrepreneurship: Irregular migrant's claims for recognition in Tunis

Hiba Sha'ath, York University, Canada

Reporting from the Field- U.S. Immigration Policy and Citizen Driven initiatives to attend the root causes of the irregular migration from the Northern Triangle

(547) Aileen Walborsky, Esq., Honorary Consul of Guatemala, USA

Migration is central to human history, yet how we deal with the sojourners among us says much about the soul of a nation. Freedom of movement is an inherent basic human right, yet the protection of a nation's borders and the decision of who and in what conditions people are admitted is also a right that belongs to nation states. It is in this tension that good immigration policy should be found, yet the U.S. Congress and many administrations have failed to enact such a policy for over two decades. Aileen Walborsky writes with authority and insight based on her 30 years of experience working as an immigration attorney in West Palm Beach, Florida. In her critical analysis of the current immigration policy of America, she suggests ways to revamp some aspects of U. S. immigration law and shares her involvement with citizen driven initiatives that attend the root causes of the irregular migration of teenagers from Guatemala.

The Concept of "Memory Effect" in Irregular Migration and Related Criminality

(1157) Iliuta Cumpanasu, Border Police, Romania, Romania

Veronica Oana Cumpanasu, Border Police, Romania

This paper focuses on studying the interrelations between the smuggling of migrants and the irregular migration along the Balkan Route, and their impact on the border management, bringing about a scientific advancement in the field, by identifying the patterns corresponding to the linkage of the two phenomena and scientifically developing for the first time a theoretical explanation with respect to their mutual influence and its effect on border security. The data from the past 6 years was collected by making use of semi-structured interviews with experts in the field of migration and desk research within some Organisations involved in border security, pursuing the gathering of genuine insights from the afore mentioned field which was constantly addressed the existing literature and subsequently subjected to the mixed methods of analysis, including the use of the Vector Auto- Regression estimates model. Thereafter, the analysis of the data followed the processes and outcomes in Grounded Theory and a new Substantive Theory emerged, explaining how the phenomena of smuggling of migrants and illegal migration are decisive impetus for each other, by using the proposed pattern. Related to the new arisen thesis, the findings of the study are also able to capture an area which has not yet benefitted from a comprehensive approach in the scientific community such as the prevalence of the concept of "Memory Effect" (concept of lazy battery/battery memory from Physics) in irregular migration, an interesting merge between science and a nowadays key international phenomenon, highlighting also how the recent 'Pandemic' interfered with border management. Therefore, the present paper gives a pro bono and unique opportunity to the policy makers, strategists and practitioners in the area of migration, to use the new born concepts as scientific tools and to apply the proposed model when drafting migration and criminality combating policies but also on the occasion of developing cooperation with third countries, be they of origin or transit, by concluding working arrangements, agreements, protocols, financial assistance programs or developing joint field operations, training, different country evaluations, etc, since the findings of this study bring both valuable, reliable and generalizable historical data and predictions. The scientific outcomes of this study were validated on June 30, 2021 when the author defended his dissertation for the European Joint Master's in Strategic Border Management, a two years prestigious program supported by European Commission and Frontex Agency and a Consortium of six European Universities.

Chinese Entrepreneurs in Casablanca: Experiencing and Narrating Contemporary Morocco

(1220) Jalil Jie Gao, The University of Arizona, USA

China has been increasingly engaging with Africa and the Middle East since the 2000s. Having been actively promoting its tourism and investment opportunities among Chinese audiences since the mid-2010s, Morocco has become one of China's most enthusiastic business partners in North Africa (Ghafar & Jacobs 2019). The ever-closer Sino-Moroccan economic relations have been well attested by the influx of tens of thousands of Chinese tourists, entrepreneurs, and investors to this faraway country in the past ten years (El Ouardighi 2019). Among these Chinese nationals in Morocco, Chinese entrepreneurs are often economic migrants who tend to stay in Morocco for an extended period of time. Although the formation of a highly visible Chinese business community in Morocco is a rather recent phenomenon, a small number of Chinese entrepreneurs are reported to have already arrived in Casablanca in the late 1990s and early 2000s (Lee 2018). This article is an histoire du temps présent of Chinese migrant entrepreneurs in Casablanca. It investigates two specific questions: How has the everyday life of these Chinese entrepreneurs been since their arrival in Morocco? And what have they experienced about Morocco's socio-economic changes in the past two decades? With the absence of official archives or extensive scholarship on a specific migrant community, constructing an oral history of the under-recorded or under-studied community with the help of a small number of the community members is an exceptionally efficient method of providing basic information on the historical development of this migrant community (Brettell 2003, Darian-Smith & Hamiltan 2019). This is precisely the case with the Chinese community in Morocco. Drawing on oral historical accounts from five Chinese entrepreneurs who have stayed in Casablanca for around two decades, this research has established a historical profile of the Chinese entrepreneurs' community in Casablanca since the 2000s and constructed a unique historical narrative of Morocco's socio-economic changes in the past twenty years through the perspective of Chinese migrant entrepreneurs in the country. On the one hand, this research found that Morocco's growing geo-economic importance in North Africa and the increasing domestic competition in China since the 2010s constitute the most important factors that led to the abrupt increase in the size of the Chinese entrepreneurs' community in Casablanca. On the other hand, these Chinese entrepreneurs' struggles with unexpected socio-economic tumult are similar to those of Morocco's urban middle class. This has been well reflected in their comparative narratives of their own experiences of and their observations of local Moroccans' susceptibility to critical historical events that have substantially impacted Morocco, such as the 2003 Casablanca bombings, the 2008 global financial crisis, the "Arab Spring," and the COVID-19 global pandemic.
References:Brettell, C. B. (2003). Anthropology and migration: essays on transnationalism, ethnicity, and identity. Altamira.Darian-smith, K., & Hoskins, A. (Eds.). (2019). Remembering Migration: Oral Histories and Heritage in Australia. Palgrave Macmillan.El Ouardighi, S. (2019, April 24). Tourisme: La dynamique des arrivées des Chinois s'essouffle. Medias24. https://www.medias24.com/2019/04/24/tourisme-la-dynamique-des-arrivees-des-chinois-sessouffle/Ghafar, A. A., & Jacobs, A. (2019). Beijing Calling: Assessing China's Growing Footprint in North Africa. Brookings Institute. https://www.brookings.edu/wp-content/uploads/2019/09/Beijing-Calling-Assessing-China%E2%80%99s-Growing-Footprint-in-North-Africa_English-1.pdfLee,

S. (2018). Friendly Outsiders? Exploring the dynamics between Chinese entrepreneurs and Moroccans in Derb Omar, Casablanca [MA Thesis].

Escaping irregularity through entrepreneurship: Irregular migrant's claims for recognition in Tunis

(1303) Hiba Sha'ath, York University, Canada

This paper explores the use of entrepreneurship as a strategy of "becoming less illegal" (Chauvin & Garcés-Mascareñas, 2014) for sub-Saharan migrants with precarious status living in Tunis, and the implications of this strategy on the irregular migrant population at large in Tunisia. In Tunisia, access to the formal labour market is highly restricted and official policy encourages entrepreneurship as a viable economic strategy for citizens and foreign investors; in this context, some migrants choose to position themselves as entrepreneurs as a means of formalizing their economic activities and as a strategy for obtaining residency papers.

While studies of migrant illegality (McNevin, 2006; Ustubici, 2018) explore various strategies migrants deploy for survival, safety, recognition, and incorporation, they do not sufficiently explore the recent and growing trend of migrant entrepreneurship in Global South contexts as a strategy for obtaining status and seeking legitimacy. On the other hand, studies of immigrant entrepreneurship tend to focus more on Global North contexts where the research subjects already possess legal status. By bringing these literatures into conversation, this paper contributes to this literature by examining *who* is able to benefit from the privileges this subjectivity confers and is recognized as such, and what implications this has for the subjectivities and politics of belonging for irregular migrants.

This paper draws on conceptualizations of migrant illegality as both a legally and a socially constructed process (De Genova, 2002), which can be experienced differentially by migrants based on various social characteristics (Ambrosini, 2016). In order to access pathways to regular status, migrants often assert their deservingness for regular status through various means: some rely on humanitarian and human rights grounds, others might emphasize cultural proximity and values. Finally, many will draw on frames of economic deservingness in order to assert their rights to legal status (Chauvin, S., & Garcés-Mascareñas, 2014).

In my analysis, I draw on doctoral fieldwork conducted in 2020 and 2021 consisting of 24 semi-structured interviews with migrants with precarious status living in Tunis, and 17 semi-structured interviews with activists and professionals working on migrant advocacy and assistance in Tunisia.

This paper contends that the ability to successfully present oneself as an entrepreneur and be recognized as such by key institutions in the host society is highly classed and gendered, with the benefits accruing mainly to wealthy male migrants. This means that inequalities within irregular migrant populations widen, as those who are already in a privileged economic and social position are better able to access rights, services, and claim recognition as foreigners deserving of status, while those who are already in more precarious social positions find their options for being recognized as legitimate economic actors and residents become more elusive. This paper opens the door for further research into the differentiated impacts and subjectivizing effects of policies encouraging migrant entrepreneurship on irregular migrants residing in Global South countries.

References:

Ambrosini, M. (2016). From "illegality" to Tolerance and Beyond: Irregular Immigration as a Selective and Dynamic Process. International Migration, 54(2), 144–159. https://doi.org/10.1111/imig.12214

Chauvin, S., & Garcés-Mascareñas, B. (2014). Becoming Less Illegal: Deservingness Frames and Undocumented Migrant Incorporation. Sociology Compass, 8(4), 422–432. https://doi.org/10.1111/soc4.12145

De Genova, N. P. (2002). Migrant "Illegality" and Deportability in Everyday Life. Annual Review of Anthropology, 31(1), 419–447. https://doi.org/10.1146/annurev.anthro.31.

040402.085432

McNevin, A. (2006). Political Belonging in a Neoliberal Era: The Struggle of the Sans-Papiers. Citizenship Studies, 10(2), 135–151. https://doi.org/10.1080/13621020600633051

Ustubici, A. (2018). The governance of international migration: Irregular migrants' access to right to stay in Turkey and Morocco. Amsterdam University Press.

2E   Gender and Migration   AMPHI 5

Chair: Martina Cvajner, University of Trento, Italy

515   The Hidden Side of Turkish Migration: Understanding sexuality as an aspiration to migrate to the UK

Dilvin D Usta, University of York, UK
Mustafa Özbilgin, Brunel University, UK

1261   Gender Climate Migration: Innovative European Union socio-legal avenues

Susana Borras Pentinat, Universita degli Studi di Macerata, Italy

1025   Social perception of Marriage Migration and Mixedness in Morocco from the early 20th-century to the Present: how Race, Gender and Social Class draw lines of difference

Catherine Therrien, Al Akhawayn University, Morocco
Catherine Phipps, University of Oxford, UK

997   Dealing with gender in the country of destination: A formative research among refugee people in Frankfurt am Main, Germany

Syed Imran Haider, Allama Iqbal Open University Islamabad, Pakistan
Muhammad Ali Awan, Jinah Sindh Medical University, Pakistan

The Hidden Side of Turkish Migration: Understanding sexuality as an aspiration to migrate to the UK

(515) Dilvin D Usta, University of York, UK

Mustafa Özbilgin, Brunel University, UK

Sexuality is an understated yet important motive for migration. Historically, Turkish migration studies reflect the factors explaining the conventional reasons, motivations, and flow of Turkish migrants, particularly in Western Europe. However, recent Turkish migration flow and migratory reasons are more complex and require empirical examination beyond the traditional economic and political factors. The way that the traditional socio-political boundaries between countries are transcended in contemporary migration practices is called transnationalism. Drawing on insight from 25 interviews, the article discusses migratory reasons of Turkish migrants should not solely be viewed from a polarised lens: the pursuit of economic security and access to human rights have been two traditional roots on which social policy is predicated; they also involve significant hidden interrelated factors, including sexuality. This article offers empirical insight by utilising transnationalism as methodological and theoretical tools to explore how sexuality shapes the contemporary migratory reasons of Turkish migrants in the UK.

Gender Climate Migration: Innovative European Union socio-legal avenues

(1261) Susana Borras Pentinat, Universita degli Studi di Macerata, Italy

This paper addresses the challenging socio-legal avenues for the European Union (EU) to respond the climate migration from a gender perspective. The main objective of this paper is to examine the climate change-induced migration in the EU from a gender perspective, offering a critical and social knowledge to respond to an urgent and complex social challenge in the EU. The specific objectives are first, analyse the possible regulatory improvements at EU; second, provide a comparative analysis on legal framework of the EU member states on migration, climate change and gender to identify good practices and regulatory improvements.

Social perception of Marriage Migration and Mixedness in Morocco from the early 20th-century to the Present: how Race, Gender and Social Class draw lines of difference

(1025) Catherine Therrien, Al Akhawayn University, Morocco

Catherine Phipps, University of Oxford, UK

This multidisciplinary contribution brings together both anthropology and history to explore Moroccan social perceptions of marriage migration. Mixed marriages were increasingly popular in Morocco during the early 20th-century, a rise that began with the establishment of the French protectorate and continued to grow markedly after independence.[1] There has been little previous historical study of marriage migration in Morocco during the colonial period, which caused the first major wave of modern migration to North Africa.[2] Furthermore, contemporary anthropological studies on mixedness have not had the opportunity to draw historical comparisons. Our contribution contextualizes and historicizes contemporary attitudes around mixedness in Morocco by comparing social perception of current mixed identities with attitudes that were also present in the early 20th-century to see how they shifted throughout the imperial moment, the post-independence period, and up to today's globalized world.The paper examines colonial records from the Archives Diplomatiques, sociological research from the 1930s, magazine articles on mixed marriage from the 1960s, reader's letters in response to these articles, and literary resources like memoires, novels and plays. We compare this data to contemporary ethnographic interviews recently conducted with mixed individuals who have been mainly socialized in Morocco and with some of their parents to understand the societal impact of marriage migration. The data was initially collected in two different research projects, one funded by the Moroccan government on the plural identities of mixed individuals in Morocco[3], and the other as part of a historical doctoral thesis on interracial relationships in French Morocco.[4] The European Commission-funded ITHACA project on migration brought these projects together to analyze marriage migration, mixedness, and the construction of racial categories the Moroccan context.[5]Immediately following Moroccan independence, mixed marriages provoked fears of cultural neo-imperialism.[6] Many considered it a threat to a Moroccan culture that had been tightly controlled for decades by France. In a globalized society, mixedness is now considered a positive phenomenon by many Moroccans, one that can offer social capital, cultural competences, and increased opportunities, but these historic concerns still impact attitudes around mixedness and draw lines of difference.[7] These persisting symbolic boundaries (race, language, gender, social class) have been shaped by historical factors, such as the perception that mixed marriages only take place within certain social classes, the belief that mixed children will not speak Moroccan Arabic and consequently will not be considered fully Moroccan, and the deep-rooted idea that marrying a nsrani(a) threatens the transmission of Islam. If experiences of discrimination have changed over the course of the 20th and 21st century, racial hierarchies are still prevalent and clearly delimitate lines of colour[8]in Morocco even though racial classifications were increasingly homogenized by the colonizer during post-colonial Morocco.[9] This paper historicizes these changes to understand social perceptions of marriage migration in contemporary Morocco.[1] Jean Dejeux, Image de l'étrange¨re: unions mixtes franco-maghrébines (Paris: La Boite e Documents, 1989).[2] Jocelyne Streiff-Fénart. "Le "Metissage" Franco-Algerien", Annuaire de l'Afrique du Nord, CNRS Editions, XXXIX, (1990), 343-351.[3] Catherine Therrien (2019 to present) 'Plural identity of mixed children in Morocco: transmission, agency and social constraints', Research Project funded by Ibn Khaldoun program (CNRST). It is a comparative project research with a Canadian team led by Josiane Le Gall.[4] Catherine Phipps (in process, 2019 to present), "Interracial Sexuality in French Morocco, (1912-1956)", doctoral thesis at History Faculty at the University of Oxford, funded by the Oxford-Anderson scholarship at University College, Oxford.[5] ITHACA Interconnecting Histories and Archives for Migrant Agency: Entangled Narratives Across Europe and the Mediterranean Region (2021-2025). https://ithacahorizon.eu/[6] Zakya Daoud, Les Ait Cheris (Casablanca: Sirocco, 2018).[7] Catherine Therrien (2020). "It's more complex than 'black' and 'white'. Social perception of mixed parentage children in Morocco", Hespéris-Tamuda 55(3): 275-307. www.hesperis-tamuda.com/fr/index.php/nouveaux-numeros/volume-lv-fascicule-3-2020/895-14.[8] Mahamed Timera, "La religion en partage, la "couleur" et l'origine comme frontie¨re. Les migrants sénégalais au Maroc,

"Cahiers d'études africaines 51, 201(2011): 148.[9] Gilliéron, Gwendolyne. (2020), Making the invisible visible: experiences of mixedness for binational people in Morocco. In Z. L. Rocha & P. J. Aspinall (Eds.), The Palgrave International Handbook of Mixed Racial and Ethnic Classification" (pp. 535-548). Cham: Palgrave Macmillan. doi.org/10.1007/978-3-030-22874-3

Dealing with gender in the country of destination: A formative research among refugee people in Frankfurt am Main, Germany

(997) Syed Imran Haider, Allama Iqbal Open University Islamabad, Pakistan

Muhammad Ali Awan, Jinah Sindh Medical University, Pakistan

This paper deals with the gender conflict which refugee people face in their country of destination which challenges their traditional gender roles acquired in the country of origin. Resulting, contestation, conflict and challenge in terms of gender and performance of acquired masculinities in the country of destination. Nevertheless, to cope and sustain in the social arena, the same traditional masculine identities remain in the process of negotiation, and construction in relation to their daily life interaction and during life span in host countries. It can be reflected through their own experiences and future prospective they have about their future children. Hence in relation to this, formative research was conducted to get the broader answer to the question "How gender encompasses the lives of the refugee people in the country of destination?"☐ . A total of 20 in-depth interviews were conducted by the refugees of the Pakistani, Syrian, Afghanistan, Irani nationalities in Frankfurt am Main, Germany between August to September 2019. Deriving from the country of origin among refugee people, the perceived value of masculinity was revolving around assertiveness, bread earner and protector of the family. While having very limited or no intimate relation with women in their country of origin. Mainly due to social pressure, limited access and normative practices where premarital sexual relation are taboos.Interestingly, respondents significantly negotiated these attributes of masculinity while staying in the country of destination to achieve their social and economic stability. However, it appears that this negotiation was situational and contextual which specifically restricted to the certain spaces and nature of interaction. Particularly, in terms of intimate relations with the opposite gender, keeping in mind their refugee status they were open to accept normative gender practices of the women who were from the mainstream culture. However, when it comes to long term relationships then they felt challenged and preferred the women of their country of origin or were expecting similar roles from their partner. Nevertheless, such expectations were varying among the respondents' education and duration of the stay and in the country of destination. Similarly, there was a significant perceived disparity about their opinion towards sons' and daughters' gender roles in the country of destination. In their perceived masculine gender roles, wife of their sons may not have a history of boyfriends, body may not be exposed in dress code, and should not drink alcohol, and should not be fond of parties. However, at same time they have shown acceptability for the sons if they choose their life partner as per their preferences. While, when it came to about their daughters, they were in favors of their education, jobs and were completely against their western dress code, alcohol and premarital sexual relation. Nevertheless, they understood the rights of the children and expressed helplessness if their children decide for themselves, either if it comes about the premarital sexual relation, dress pattern or another things which is not against the law, they can not control them. Hence, this research concludes that refugee masculinities remain in the process of negotiation which is situational and context based. In each of the situations, they position themselves and decide about the negotiation based on perceived outcome. They create justifications of their own negotiation of masculinity and make it acceptable in the configuration of 'self' where they themselves position. However, their self-positioning is somehow observable in the masculinities of their sons. Nevertheless, this newly constructed masculinities, its functionality and mechanism of justification is not applicable to their daughters. And for daughters, adaptation of normative feminine gender roles particularly in terms of intimate relationships can make them "other". It is imperative to educate gender in relation to sexuality to the refugee people who may equally accept or respect the differences of culture and give equal space to equal genders.

2F   Understanding Migration Experiences   AMPHI 6

Chair: Lejla Sunagic, Lund University, Sweden

1009   Situated rationality of risk-taking in boat migration: Dancing between despair and wisdom

Lejla Sunagic, Lund University, Sweden

1007   Highlighting the Role of Hijrah in Migration Studies

Talha Bhamji, University of Wales Trinity Saint David, UK

929   Impacts of the National Migration and Asylum Strategy on Sub-Saharan Immigrants' Livelihood in Morocco

Abdeslam Badre, Mohammed V University of Rabat, Morocco

1111   Racialising sub-Saharan African Presence and the Politics of Migration Securitisation in Tunisia

Yasmine Akrimi, Brussels International Center, Belgium

Situated rationality of risk-taking in boat migration: Dancing between despair and wisdom

(1009) Lejla Sunagic, Lund University, Sweden

Every day thousands of migrants originating in the Middle East (notably Syria and Iraq) are leaving the shores of the Mediterranean Sea in tiny inflatable boats heading for Europe. The policy makers initially assumed that migrants were not aware of the risk they faced in the course of journey, hence the awareness raising campaigns have been taking place in the countries of departure with a view of informing, persuading and changing the behaviour of potential migrants. The absence of the impact of the campaigns should not come as a surprise. Generally, policies and strategies to reduce people's risk taking are often less successful than expected. The reason is rarely ignorance. Even though people's risk taking is extreme complex, dynamic and contradictory process, people often have good understanding of risk they are about the take (Zinn, 2019).

The explanation of the continued boat migration despite the deterrence has been modified through an adjusted assumption that migrants are quite aware of the risk they take, but they take it anyway as they have noting to lose. Such assumption rules out any calculation of risk and benefit, as the elements of rational decision-making. Instead, their decision is believed to be motivated solely by the absence of choice.

As a reflection to the above contradicting assumptions, this presentation aims to bring a nuanced understating of how material needs, normative pressure and individual desire affect risk-taking by migrants. This presentation offers an interpretivist shift: rather than considering the risk as an evolutionary drive, a part of one's in-born personality, or a result of cognitive limits to calculate the risk, which has been dominant approach in behavioural-economic paradigm, this presentation will explore the risk-taking related to boat migration as a phenomenon rooted in social processes. In such approach the understanding of risk-taking requires examining of social experience and imagined future.

To surface this understanding, loosely structured interviews with Syrians and Iraqis living Sweden have been conducted, applying hermeneutic approach in order to grasp the migrants' motivation through analysis of the risk perception. The presentation shares the preliminary analysis that the risk-taking- although unanimously reported by migrants to be a result of the lack of reasonable alternative-is rooted in an analysis of the current social and life situations and supplemented with an analysis of future gains. Contrary to the risk-taking in situations with reasonable alternative where the response to loss is bigger than response to gain, in situations with no reasonable alternative action, response to gain overshadows the response to risk.

References:

Vandermause, R. K. and Fleming, S. E. (2011) 'Philosophical Hermeneutic Interviewing', International Journal of Qualitative Methods, 10(4), pp. 367–377. doi: 10.1177/160940691101000405.

Zinn, J. (2019) 'The meaning of risk-taking – key concepts and dimensions', Journal of Risk Research, 22(1), pp. 1–15. doi: 10.1080/13669877.2017.1351465.

Highlighting the Role of Hijrah in Migration Studies

(1007) Talha Bhamji, University of Wales Trinity Saint David, UK

Hijrah in the Islamic tradition refers to migration undertaken by Muhammad and his companions from Mecca to Medina in 622 C.E. So crucial is Hijrah that on numerous occasions the Qur'an and the Ahadith, reiterate the significance of this event. Historically, scholars from various discipline have sought to understand, interpret, and contextualize Hijrah. Muhammad Shafi (d. 767 A.H /820 C.E) was perhaps the first scholar to synthesise the Qur'anic injunction on Hijrah and the Hijrah ahadith. He maintained that a place where the level of temptation is unbearable, it becomes obligatory for a Muslim to relocate to another place (Shafi', 1999. Pp. 353-355). Similarly, Tabari (d.839 A.H/ 923 C.E) argued that any place that guarantees religious freedom is sacred (Tabari, 2003, pp. 379-381). Other scholars, in contrast, such as Ibn Taymiyyah (d. 1263 A.H/ 1328 C.E) shifted the sacredness of a place onto the individual by suggesting that the level of piety demonstrated by the individual determines the sacredness of the space (Taymiyyah cited in Michot, 2006. Pp. 74-85). More recently, however, Zafarul Islam Khan's holistic approach to Hijrah, in his book titled 'Hijrah in Islam', illuminates how Hijrah from the perspective of the Qur'an and the Sunnah (Muhammad's actions, words and behaviour condoned) influences the terms under which Muslims may reside in a place. He concludes that at best there is a consensus amongst scholars, based on the model of Hijrah, that Muslims may remain in a variety of locations providing they can preserve their religion and can actively participate in dawah (proselytising). In the case of any prohibition against the practice of religion or forced conversion the dictates of Hijrah come into play (Khan, pp. 216-217).MethodIn this paper, some examples are provided to illuminate the importance of Hijrah. Firstly, Hijrah is not understood as a single event in the history of Islam, rather it is regarded as a theological construct with doctrinal importance. Secondly, significant attention is given to the interconnectedness of Hijrah and the conception of space. In Islam there are numerous examples of how sacred space is contextualised ranging from sanctified buildings, such as the two haramains (two mosques in Mecca/Medina), to the religious ritual of tawaf around the Ka'bah. Similarly, there are also instances where the sacredness of a place is defined by a specific time, such as the Hajj pilgrimage. In light of this assessment, this presentation proposes to argue that Hijrah is a unique theological issue in Islam and that Muhammad's Hijrah stipulates the conditions of sacred spaces that transcends the event of Hijrah itself.Results and ConclusionHijrah is a theological issue that has been too little explored by academics and scholars who have given little attention to the various ways in which Hijrah impacts Muslims and influences the conception of space in Islam. This presentation is an attempt to propose new and original ways of representing and contextualising Hijrah in today's world. Reflecting on Hijrah through historical and textual analysis, enables us to reconsider new approaches to Islamic theology. Seeing Hijrah through theological perspective adds a further dimension in highlighting how Hijrah can help illuminate other themes in the academic study of Islam.

Impacts of the National Migration and Asylum Strategy on Sub-Saharan Immigrants' Livelihood in Morocco

(929) Abdeslam Badre, Mohammed V University of Rabat, Morocco

Since its implementation in late 2014, Morocco's National Migration and Asylum Strategy (NMAS) has enabled thousands of illegal sub-Saharan migrants and asylum seekers to obtain status regularization, enabling them equal access to basic social services (jobs, health services, housing, and child education) (HCP, 2018). To date, the country's official discourse speaks of a successful migration policy and integration strategy, which has turned the country into an immigration destination, after years of serving as a transit and emigrant exporting country (MFA, 2018). Whether or not these new-settlers have, or at least feel, integrated needs investigation, given the absence of a nation-wide systematic data and lack of institutional and human capital experience in matter of migration management. Additionally, the evaluation of the new strategy may not be comprehensive if it does not explicitly address the perspective of immigrants' perceptions about the host country and people as well as about themselves. This field-based research paper investigates the impacts of Morocco's National Migration and Asylum Strategy (NMAS) on the actual livelihood of these immigrants. Based on a bottom-up approach, It qualitatively (N=514 informants) and qualitatively (N=21 interviewees) analyzed the impacts MNAS' implementation has on livelihood of in country sub-Saharan migrants by looking at how they, sub-Saharan themselves, perceive their integration process within the various societal tissues of Morocco. The service provisions of 5 Moroccan sectors in public services were investigated, taking the gender dimension as a crosscutting edge. The finding revealed. The finding revealed fluctuating immigrants' attitudes toward various Morocco's public services across gender, migration status, and family status.[1]. This paper is a partial outcome of a post-doctorate fellowship project the author benefited from under the auspice of a joint-fellowship project offered by Princeton University; the University of Michigan; and Arab Barometer; under a project title: "Contributing to solutions for marginalized communities in the Arab region", 2019-2020, which was founded by Carnegie Cooperation.

Racialising sub-Saharan African Presence and the Politics of Migration Securitisation in Tunisia

(1111) Yasmine Akrimi, Brussels International Center, Belgium

Along its north-African neighbours, Tunisia has witnessed a transformation of its migratory status since the 1990s with the development of the European Union's border externalisation policies and the gradual establishment of individual visa requirements for certain categories of third-country nationals. The following multiplication of western-style militarised borders within Africa disrupted the traditional fluidity of migratory fluxes, along with border economies. Similarly to Morocco through the Gibraltar Strait, Tunisia has consequently been witnessing an increasing number of sub-Saharan migrants transiting from its soil to reach Italy's Lampedusa through risky boat trips, particularly following the escalation of the Libyan conflict which deviated the traditional Central Mediterranean route to neighbouring Tunisia. These new trends of South to South migration morphed the country's migratory status into a complex one, from a traditional emigration country to both a transit and receiving destination. In parallel, Tunisia developed a strict legal arsenal as to both limit the regular access of migrants to labour, and prevent mobility towards Europe both for nationals and non-nationals. However, countering the understanding of migration securitisation in the Maghreb as a mere translation of Western imperatives, this paper argues the internal process of racialised 'othering' of sub-Saharan African migrants (El Miri, 2018) serves to reinforce the internal cohesion of national identity as an 'imagined community' through the discursive perpetuation of a shared national past, present and future, a shared national culture, and a 'national body' (Helal, 2019). Adopting the theoretical framework of Giorgio Agamben's Homo Sacer (Agamben, 1995), we posit the 'state of exception' irregular sub-Saharan African migrants evolve in is not an anomaly to the functioning of the Tunisian nation state. By their categorisation as 'outcasts', irregular migrants contribute to strengthening the nation's political borders and ensuring national cohesion. In what De Genova calls 'the obscene of inclusion' (De Genova, 2013), irregular migrants, framed as a threat to internal cohesion, are included through exclusion as their perceived threat legitimises the securitisation of state practices (Rajaram and Grundy-Warr, 2004). Contrary to the classic perception of 'underdeveloped' countries as recipients of imposed migration policies, this rather posits a continuation in the spectrum of state interests between both shores of the Mediterranean. Using critical discourse analysis, precisely discourse-historical approach (Reisigl and Wodak, 2001), this paper will focus on key legal texts, state practices and state narratives from the 1990s to present day as to understand the processes of creation, perpetuation, transformation and destruction (Wodak, 2018) of Tunisia's migratory practices in terms of racialising and securitising sub-Saharan African migration, adapting to external European pressures while also reinforcing the legitimacy of internal repressive policies.

2G   Culture and Communication   AMPHI 7

Chair: Paulette K. Schuster, Reichman University, AMILAT, Israel

943   Crossing Borders: Nationalism in Maghrebian Literature and the Emergence of a New Reading Mode

Amal El Mansouri, Abdelmalek Essaadi University, Morocco

1222   Media, Politics, and the Lived Experience of Refugees in Italy

Wendy Stickle, University of Maryland, USA
Gabriella D'Avino, University of Birmingham, UK
Sandra Pertek, University of Birmingham, UK

1265   Self-Representation of Sub-Saharan Migrants in Morocco in Digital Media

Kenza Oumlil, Al Akhawayn University in Ifrane, Morocco

Crossing Borders: Nationalism in Maghrebian Literature and the Emergence of a New Reading Mode

(943) Amal El Mansouri, Abdelmalek Essaadi University, Morocco

The migration of people from the Maghreb countries crossing the Mediterranean and their settlement in various European countries including France has led to the emanation of a plethora of Maghrebian authors who play a major role in the emergence of Maghrebian literature of French expression. In fact, the main concern of this paper is to discuss the role of Maghrebian literature of French expression in the rise of nationalism. The first part of the paper focuses on the functional conception of literature as a witness of Maghrebian being. It explores how literature can lead to Maghrebinity and the construction of a specific Maghrebian mindset. The second part of this paper revolves around the reading mode of Maghrebian texts. The argument is that the creation of any literary work is the result of the fusion and interpretation of two modes of thought: that of the author, who creates the work, and that of the observer, who moves through space and time, giving the work its breath, adopting it, and understanding it. This arrangement of causality between author, work and public is obligatory for the accomplishment and the finality of the work.

Media, Politics, and the Lived Experience of Refugees in Italy

(1222) Wendy Stickle, University of Maryland, USA

Gabriella D'Avino, University of Birmingham, UK

Sandra Pertek, University of Birmingham, UK

Objective: This paper will explore the portrayal of migrants, particularly refugees, in the Italian media and how that portrayal aligns with the lived experiences of refugees. Specifically, this mixed methods research will explore the following research questions:

(1) How predominant are stories on immigration in mainstream Italian newspapers? (2) Is the presence of immigration stories related to political events (e.g., elections, legislation)? (3) What is the general tone of immigration stories? (4) How does the tone of mainstream newspapers compare to lived experience of refugees? Relevant literature: Not since World War II has there been such a large influx in displaced persons. This comes at a critical time when the strength of democracy hangs in the balance. As democratic values are in decline around the world, questionable actions on the part of powerful nations in their treatment of refugees and asylum seekers bring attention to a perennial human rights issue. Displaced persons experience extreme trauma, violence, and exploitation en route to and upon settling in the countries where they seek asylum (United Nations High Commissioner for Refugees, 2021). The general negative political sentiment to creating pathways for displaced persons to obtain a legal refugee status, particularly for those coming from non-European countries, increases their vulnerabilities when they, inevitably, must leave their home countries. Asylum-seekers, after enduring traumatic, life-threatening situations, only to arrive a new country with less than welcoming policies, politicians, and public perceptions (Blitz, 2017; Greussing & Boomgaarden, 2017; van der Brug & Harteveld, 2021). At the same time, research shows migrants rarely have a negative impact on the countries in which they resettle and, in fact, can offer many benefits (Zamfir, 2015). Methods: This research offers a mixed methods approach to understanding the perceived and lived experiences of asylum-seekers in Italy, a country that accepts a high rate of asylum-seekers thanks to its geographic location in the European Union. Despite a stable infrastructure in place to support refugees, Italian politicians and rightist media continue to portray refugees as burdensome and dangerous. This mixed-methods research will use Frame Analysis (Benford & Snow, 2000), to explore how Italian media frames immigration and related issues. Qualitative data stemming from semi-structured interviews with refugees and service providers who serve refugees, will seek to understand the true experience and impact of refugees settling in Italy. Conclusions: Using a mixed methodology this research will compare the media's portrayal of refugees and how closely it aligns with the experiences of refugees and those who work with them. Findings will highlight the importance of incorporating the lived experiences of refugees and the danger of media to impact the ability of refugees to successfully resettle in Italy and the European Union.

Self-Representation of Sub-Saharan Migrants in Morocco in Digital Media

(1265) Kenza Oumlil, Al Akhawayn University in Ifrane, Morocco

This paper explores digital self-representation of sub-Saharan migrants in Morocco, with particular attention to gendered representations. Previous research has examined the topic of migration in the Moroccan context from the vantage points of sociology, anthropology, geography (Alioua, 2014; Therrien, 2019; Gross-Wyrtzen, 2020), with some studies focusing on a gender studies perspective (Stock, 2012; Freedman, 2012; Tyszler, 2019). Communication and media studies about the topic of migration in Morocco are lacking. It is worth mentioning however Ennaji and Bignami's (2019) study of the use of smartphones and social media by refugees and undocumented migrants. This paper therefore aims to look at the topic of sub-Saharan migration from a gender and media perspective and is informed by alternative media scholarship.

Dominant representation of sub-Saharan migration is limited and tends to be negative (Alexander, 2019); migrant self-representation in the Moroccan digital sphere is hence an important question. Alternative media scholars indicate that it is imperative for under-represented and misrepresented communities to participate in the creation of their own images and influence the discourses that are inscribed on their bodies (Baltruschat, 2004; Ginsburg, 1995; Juhasz, 1995; Oumlil, 2016; Rodriguez, 2001; Salaita, 2006). Therefore, this study aims to bridge this gap in the literature.

In the Moroccan media landscape, due to the precarious situation of sub-Saharan migrants, there are few migrant voices that are expressing themselves on their socio-political conditions. In 2012, the number of sub-Saharan migrants in Morocco was estimated to be between 4'500 and 10'000 (Stock, 2012). In 2013, King Mohammed VI announced a new Moroccan migration policy, which led to two regularization campaigns in 2014 and 2016 (Natter, 2018). However, it seems that a regression of the status of migrants has taken place since these processes of "regularization" have taken a halt. Some of the most prominent voices that have emerged in the search for migrant voices include: (1) Association REFIME (Immigrant Women and Wives' Network – *Réseau des Femmes Immigrées et Épouses*), which has a Facebook page with 600 likes and subscribers; (2) Hassan Yemcheu's YouTube account with over 2000 subscribers, on which he uploads videos for the association Planet Migrant; and (3) Franck Nama's "Identité Africaine" blog with over 50 articles. Whereas "Identité Africaine" represents a male-dominated perspective, Association REFIME sheds light onto opportunities for support for migrant women and children. Similarly, Planet Migrant's YouTube platform includes a discussion of migrant women's entrepreneurship and domestic violence.

This paper investigates the construction of self-representation by sub-Saharan migrants in Morocco through textual analysis (Bainbridge, 2010) and netnographic analysis (Kozinets,2015) of qualitative Facebook posts, YouTube videos, and blog posts. Although these mediated interventions have a small reach, these migrants deploy digital storytelling tools in counter-public spheres. They present narratives that diverge from dominant discourse and take voice to bring about positive socio-political change for their communities.

2H   Migratory stratifications SALLES DES ACTES

Chair: Francesco Della Puppa, Ca' Foscari University of Venice, Italy

1048   "The relationship between the supervisor and the worker is never one of cordiality." Examining migrant stratifications between co-ethnic supervisors and South Asian male agrarian migrant workers in Greece

Reena Kukreja, Queen's University, Kingston, Canada

1112   Migratory stratifications and cultures of singledom: a case study on the Bangladeshi community in Rome

Andrea Priori, Fulda University, Germany

1052   Women migrancy and social change - the case of Slovenian domestic workers in Egypt

Mirjam Milharčič Hladnik, Slovenian Migration Institute, ZRC SAZU,
Ljubljana &; University of Nova Gorica, Nova Gorica, Slovenia

1089 "You can't get into Europe sitting like a woman". Refugee men in Athens tactically resisting the gendered migrant stratification

Árdís Kristín Ingvars, University of Iceland, Iceland

"The relationship between the supervisor and the worker is never one of cordiality." Examining migrant stratifications between co-ethnic supervisors and South Asian male agrarian migrant workers in Greece

(1048) Reena Kukreja, Queen's University, Kingston, Canada

Chasing the dream of a 'Europe filled with riches', a significant number of poor rural male migrants from the South Asian countries of Pakistan, Bangladesh, and India come to Greece in the hope of making an onward journey to preferred north European countries. With restrictive border regimes making this unrealisable, they end up living in Greece, marked by their migrant illegality and 'othering' on counts of their ethnic and religious identities. These undocumented male migrants have filled a vital labour gap in the rural agrarian economy with their cheap and flex labour. To give a context, Greek agriculture, from the 1990s onwards, has been transformed with the global migratory flows with over 90 percent of the labour in agriculture provided by migrants. This talk is based on my ongoing research in four agrarian communities of Thiva, Megara, Argos and Manolada where the South Asian men are engaged in seasonal and all year agricultural activity. It focusses on "masculine stratifications" within the South Asian migrant male population based on (un)equal relations of power embodied through migrant labour regimes. In particular, it discusses masculine encounters between co-ethnic supervisors and farmhands to showcase how border regimes and racial capitalism enable and benefit from reinforcing stratifications within the larger mass of homogenised male migrant others. In Greek agriculture, increasingly, labour management is one step removed from the farmers who do not interact directly with their farmhands for recruitment, daily supervision, allocation of tasks, keeping tab of work hours, or payment of wages. These tasks are overwhelmingly delegated to co-ethnic supervisors who share kin or village ties with the workers. Known as "Thekedar," "Commander," or "Mastura," these supervisors have the coveted regularised status, fluency in Greek, knowledge of local farming practices, trust of the farmers, and much higher earnings. Drawing on an intersectional approach of feminist political economy, Critical Studies in Men and Masculinities, and migration studies, the talk reveals the processes by which migrant stratifications are set up and/or reinforced by the supervisors in their bid to assert a successful "hegemonic" masculine hierarchical status among co-ethnic migrant men. Relational hierarchies of masculinities "dependent on immigrant status, age, and relations of power" which are enacted between different sets of men, such as co-ethnic supervisors and workers and between the workers themselves, emerge as critical in ensuring the docility of migrant male labourers. The workers seek to bridge this stratification by seeking to become supervisors themselves. The talk also reveals how stratifications emerge between national groups of migrant men as they internalise and replicate dominant discourses of othering in Greek society onto each other in a bid to maximise gains from the labour and bordering regimes and jockey themselves as the model minority male subjects.

Migratory stratifications and cultures of singledom: a case study on the Bangladeshi community in Rome

(1112) Andrea Priori, Fulda University, Germany

The so-called 'Bangladeshi community' in Rome (Italy) has developed through a series of migratory stratifications that have taken place since 1990. After an initial moment in which the protagonists of the migration were mainly men from middle-class urban households (Knights 1994), the social background of the migration expanded, together with the number of brokers in charge of the functioning of the migration chains. Subsequent waves, as well as including women, have been characterised by considerable diversification in geographical terms and greater variety in terms of social background, with large numbers of men from rural households who not only have less social and economic capital at their disposal than the urban middle classes, but also carry a different culture of emigration (Priori 2012).

Single, heterosexual and cis males play a fundamental role in Bangladeshi migration to Italy since most of the newcomers define themselves as 'bachelor' and see emigration as an important opportunity to accumulate economic and symbolic capital in view of an arranged marriage (Mapril 2014; Della Puppa 2014). In this way, the adventure in Europe often ends up being characterised by an ethos of singledom, which in the representations of many migrants takes on a normative form, establishing canons of respectability and behaviour that are considered "normal". The attitude of cis-male migrants towards this gendered ethos varies considerably according to the stratification of migrant generations, the socio-cultural characteristics of the different social groups involved, and the interaction between the evolving conditions of incorporation into Italian society and the changing conditions of life in the motherland.

This paper considers the diversification of a culture of singledom within the Bangladeshi diaspora based on ethnographic research in the city of Rome, analysing the interaction between different gendered ethos, that is the one of the motherland and the one that migrant men define as "European", and taking into account the different attitudes towards an idea of religious morality of the different social groups that constitute the backbone of the migrant generations that have succeeded in the last thirty years.

References:

Della Puppa, F., 2014, *Uomini in movimento. Il lavoro della maschilità tra Bangladesh e Italia*, Torino, Rosenberg & Sellier.

Knights, M, 1996, *Migration in the new world order: The case of Bangladeshi migration to Rome*, Sussex University Thesis.

Mapril, J., 2014, *The dreams of middle class: consumption, life-course and migration between Bangladesh and Portugal*, «Modern Asian Studies», XLVIII:3, pp. 693-719.

Priori, A., 2012, *Romer probashira. Reti sociali e itinerari transnazionali bangladesi a Roma*, Rome, Meti Edizioni.

Women migrancy and social change - the case of Slovenian domestic workers in Egypt

(1052) Mirjam Milharčič Hladnik, Slovenian Migration Institute, ZRC SAZU, Ljubljana &; University of Nova Gorica, Nova Gorica, Slovenia

The paper will present social, economic, cultural, political, religious and emotional universe of the Goriška region, which had been reshaped by the women's mobility between the cluster of villages in Slovenia and Egyptian cities (1870-1940). The women, called *aleksandrinke* (the women from Alexandria) worked as very well paid care workers for affluent Egyptian families in the different modes of migrancy. The phenomenon, called *aleksandrinstvo* brought with it rearrangements of the traditional roles within local economy, family and community and threatened the established system of community on many levels (Milharčič Hladnik, 2015). Even if the decisions to go to work in Egypt were the result of family deliberations under dire social, political and economic circumstances, the fact that women became breadwinners challenged the prescribed gender roles and the social representations of masculinity and femininity.

Aleksandrinstvo as a total social fact (Sayad, 2004) caused "the gender paradox" (Parreñas, 2005): the more changes of traditional family and community were necessary because of the absent women, the more persistent everyone involved was to preserve them. The fact that women were far from the tight social control of church, family and village prompted local priests and political opinion makers to condemn the practice as a threat to morality, ignoring the economic and political causes of migrancy as well as the economic benefit of the remittances regularly sent home. The reduction of women to the role of "mothers of the nation" was intense in all political and ideological varieties and it was institutionalized on the legislative, cultural, and ideological levels. For this very reason, the concrete experiences, achievements, contributions, and importance of female migrants had to be silenced, overlooked, forgotten, or wrapped into traumatic intimate memories (Hoerder, 2015). Moralistic accusations and condemnations of women migrants from Goriška to Egypt caused a collective trauma of families in the region that lasted for generations.

Migratory stratifications, transculturation processes and dynamics of social change will be analyzed through ego documents: family correspondences, testimonies, and life stories. With the use of the narrative methodological approach, the ego documents offer a glimpse of the subtle and complex emotional landscapes resulting from the rearrangement of gender roles and of the embedded sensibilities of femininity and masculinity caused by migration. The dominant discourse that constructed the landscape of collective memory where aleksandrinke did not have voice until recently will be challenged with the intimate level of exchange of love, loyalty, care and support of those who left and those who stayed that has been preserved and maintained through generations. The biographies of the agents of aleksandrinstvo expose the impact of the experience of mobility on people and community dynamic identity transformations visible still today in the remnants of food practices and material artefacts in the Goriška villages.

References:

Rhacel Salazar Parreñas, Children of Global Migration: Transnational Families and Gendered Woes, Stanford, CA: Stanford University Press, 2005.

Mirjam Milharčič Hladnik (ed.), *From Slovenia to Egypt: Aleksandrinke's Trans-Mediterranean Domestic Workers' Migration and National Imagination.* Göttingen, Ger.: V and R Unipress, 2015.

Dirk Hoerder, "Re-remembering Women Who Chose Caregiving Careers in a Global Perspective: Mothers of the Nation or Agents in Their Own Lives?" in Mirjam Milharčič Hladnik (ed.), *From Slovenia to Egypt*, 117–30.

Ingrid Jerve Ramsøy, *Expectations and Experiences of Exchange: Migrancy in the Global Market of Care Between Spain and Bolivia.* Malmö University, 2019.

Francesco Della Puppa, "A redeemed biography? Migration as an intrafamily redemption device", *Rassegna Italiana di Sociologia*, 2019.

Abdelmalek Sayad, *The Suffering of the Immigrant*, Cambridge, Polity Press, 2004.

"You can't get into Europe sitting like a woman". Refugee men in Athens tactically resisting the gendered migrant stratification

(1089) Árdís Kristín Ingvars, University of Iceland, Iceland

In December 2014, a group of Syrian refugees organized a sit-in at the Syntagma Square in front of the Greek parliament building. Greece, in midst of financial crisis at the time, offered them no means of aspiration to restore their social role as men and help their families. Thus, they demanded permission to travel further into Europe by implementing new tactics based on peaceful sit-ins, assemblies, and reciprocity towards the locals and other displaced Arabs. This paper is based on engaged ethnography conducted in Greece between 2012-2018, centred around masculinities among border activists from Middle Eastern and Sub-Saharan nation states. The Syrian organizers countered resistance from previously arrived Arab men, who persisted that sitting was feminine and that the way to resist bordering stratification of men, was to endure the precarious street life in Athens until the system could be outsmarted. This was framed within the militaristic discourse of serving time. However, as the Greek government accepted a "fast track" procedure for the "sitters" and required a list from the organizers of those deemed worthy enough, the Syrian's counted worthiness by who endured the process of sitting outside for five weeks. Afghan men, who had previously been stuck in the zone between extreme feminization and terrorist masculinities, at first resented the "fast-track" procedure offered to the Syrians, but by employing similar gendered tactics were able to follow the Syrian trajectories until the spring of 2016. In this way, the Syrians were temporarily able to reconstruct the migration performance and form new gendered pathways.

2J PANEL: Climate Change, Conflict and Displacement in India [ONLINE]

Moderator: Sana Vaidya

Speakers

Dr. Ritu Dewan, Indian Society of Labour Economics, India

Dr. Priyadarshini Karve, Symbiosis School for Liberal Arts, India

Ms. Roshni Shanker, Ara Trust, India

Day Two 8 September 2022 Thursday

Day Two 8 September 2022 - 10:45-12:15   AMPHI 1

3A   Media and Migration in North Africa [AR-FR]

الجلسة الثالثة: التناول الإعلامي لقضايا الهجرة

Chair: Dr. Abdul Majïd Fadhil, former Director of the Institute of Media and Communication Sciences, Morocco

557 ذ محمد القزاز جريدة الأهرام : الهجرة و الإعلام في مصر

Hicham Houdaifa, Secrétaire général du Réseau marocain des journalistes des migrations: Pour un traitement professionnel, juste et éthique de la migration: l'expérience du Réseau Marocain des Journalistes des Migrations.

556 - ذ حسن بنطالب : الهجرة و الإعلام في المغرب

559 Dr Hajar El Moukhi: Médias, jeunesse et immigrés au Maroc: La perception des jeunes vis-à-vis de l'image médiatisée de l'immigré-e au Maroc

560 Dr Khalid Mouna: Médias et migration au Maroc: entre clichés, populisme et discours d'accommodation

571 Dr Mohamed ElKazaz: الهجرة والإعلام في مصر

3B   Conflicts, Insecurities, Migration   AMPHI 2

Chair   Ülkü Güney, Karl-Franzens University Graz and Alpen-Adria University Klagenfurt, Austria

1246   Factors Influencing Immobility in Global South

> *Kristyna Kvasnickova, Charles University, Czech Republic*
> *Eliska Masna, Charles University, Czech Republic*
> *Aneta Seidlova, Charles University, Czech Republic*
> *Takuya Nakagawa, Charles University, Czech Republic*
> *Yeboah Mohammed, Charles University, Czech Republic*

1156   Ukrainian Arrivals in Austria (UkrAiA): A Rapid-Response Survey on Sociodemographic Characteristics, Needs and Resources

> *Isabella Buber-Ennser, Austrian Academy of Sciences, Austria*
> *Judith Kohlenberger, Vienna University of Economics and Business, Austria*
> *Bernhard Riederer, Austrian Academy of Sciences, Austria*
> *Ingrid Setz, Austrian Academy of Sciences, Austria*
> *Bernhard Rengs, Austrian Academy of Sciences, Austria*
> *Olena Tarasiuk, IIASA, Austria*

1254   Migration Policy Implementation and its Politics in South Africa

Toyin Cotties Adetiba, University of Zululand, South Africa

1013   Emigrants against will: A narrative Autoethnography Exploring Experiences between Migration and Exile

Ülkü Güney, Karl-Franzens University Graz and Alpen-Adria University Klagenfurt, Austria

Factors Influencing Immobility in Global South

(1246) Kristyna Kvasnickova, Charles University, Czech Republic

Eliska Masna, Charles University, Czech Republic

Aneta Seidlova, Charles University, Czech Republic

Takuya Nakagawa, Charles University, Czech Republic

Yeboah Mohammed, Charles University, Czech Republic

Past research has predominantly focused on how migration is driven by various economic, environmental, or political disturbances. In contrast, the understanding of how alternative livelihood strategies result in immobility has been relatively neglected despite its prevalence in most parts of the world (Schewel 2020). These skewed perceptions are made apparent by the large number of studies that focus on migration from the Global South to the Global North, forming a dominant discursive framework. We respond to these imbalances by examining the determinants of immobility through a unique comparison of our case studies conducted in 4 countries of the Global South: Ghana, Zambia, Lebanon, and India. The individual case studies have a common conceptual base that combines the livelihoods approach (De Haan 2012) and the distinction between necessity and opportunity-led livelihood strategies (Ellis 2000, Margolis 2014), aspiration-capability framework (Carling, Schewel 2018), and the theory of planned behaviour (Ajzen 1991).

We examine the drivers of immobility across diverse geographical settings and different thematic domains of links between migration/immobility and development. These thematic domains include livelihood interventions and their impact on immobility, environmentally induced immobility, immobility concerning rural livelihood diversification, livelihood strategies of refugees, and immobility of university graduates. Within the case studies, qualitative methods such as focus group discussions and semi-structured interviews are employed for data collection. Our findings highlight the importance of mediating factors including social norms, aspirations, and individual attitudes toward immobility, albeit influenced by specific contextual drivers. Considering a larger set of influencing factors identified in individual case studies, we propose a classification of immobility drivers combining the notions of necessity and opportunity-led immobility with the aspiration-capability framework and theory of planned behaviour.

References:

Ajzen, I. (1991). The theory of planned behavior. *Organizational behavior and human decision processes*, 50(2), 179-211.

Carling, J., & Schewel, K. (2018). Revisiting aspiration and ability in international migration. *Journal of Ethnic and Migration Studies*, 44(6), 945-963.

De Haan, L. J. (2012). The livelihood approach: A critical exploration. *Erdkunde*, 345-357.

Ellis, F. (2000). *Rural livelihoods and diversity in developing countries.* Oxford university press.

Margolis, D. N. (2014). By choice and by necessity: Entrepreneurship and self-employment in the developing world. *The European Journal of Development Research, 26*(4), 419-436.

Schewel, K. (2020). Understanding immobility: Moving beyond the mobility bias in migration studies. *International Migration Review, 54*(2), 328-355.

Ukrainian Arrivals in Austria (UkrAiA): A Rapid-Response Survey on Sociodemographic Characteristics, Needs and Resources

(1156) Isabella Buber-Ennser, Austrian Academy of Sciences, Austria

Judith Kohlenberger, Vienna University of Economics and Business, Austria

Bernhard Riederer, Austrian Academy of Sciences, Austria

Ingrid Setz, Austrian Academy of Sciences, Austria

Bernhard Rengs, Austrian Academy of Sciences, Austria

Olena Tarasiuk, IIASA, Austria

According to UNHCR (2022) estimates, due to the war in Ukraine roughly 4 million people have left the country by the end of March 2022, mainly women, children and elderly. While the neighbouring countries Poland, Moldova, Hungary and Slovakia are most affected, more and more people are also finding their way to Austria. Experts estimate that up to 200,000 Ukrainians might come to Austria in the near future (Brickner & Völker, 2022).

In April and May 2022, a survey in Ukrainian and Russian will be carried out among recent arrivals of Ukrainians in a registration center in Vienna. The questionnaire is based on a survey conducted in autumn 2015 among refugees (primarily from Syria and Afghanistan), which became one of the first quantitative surveys among refugees in Europe (Displaced Persons in Austria Survey - DiPAS). The findings on human capital, values and attitudes became an important reference in the academic and societal discussion on refugees in 2015 (Buber-Ennser et al., 2016; Ichou et al., 2017).

Data collection will be via paper questionnaires (PAPI) and online (CAWI). A sample of around 500 questionnaires is targeted. Since questions on the family context (marital status, children) are included in the survey, information on a larger number of individuals can be obtained. The focus is on the socio-demographic characteristics, human capital and values of people who have fled Ukraine to Vienna and want to find refuge in Austria.

At the Migration Conference 2022 in Rabat, first results of the survey will be presented. They will include marital status and (extended) family context in the host country and country of origin, thus also providing insight into family reunification potential. Furthermore, the human capital of the refugees is analysed, such as educational attainment, language skills, professional qualifications or work experience. Finally, first insights into refugees' values on gender equity and democracy based on the World Value Survey will be provided.

The planned paper aims to contribute to the academic and public discourse on newly arrived refugees from Ukraine. The aim is to assess the residential and integration needs of Ukrainian refugees. Through the data collected, resources for participation as well as potentials and challenges for integration and coexistence can be identified.

References:

Brickner, I., & Völker, M. (2022). Knapp 5.000 Ukraine-Flüchtlinge ließen sich in Österreich registrieren. Der Standard. Retrieved from https://www.derstandard.at/story/2000134168774/ knapp-5-000-fluechtlinge-liessen-sich-registrieren?ref=rec

Buber-Ennser, I., Kohlenberger, J., Rengs, B., et al. (2016) Human capital, values, and attitudes of persons seeking refuge in Austria in 2015. PLoS ONE, 11(9), e0163481. doi:10.1371/journal.pone.0163481

Ichou, M., Goujon, A., Buber-Ennser, I., et al. (2017) Immigrants' educational attainment: A mixed picture, but often higher than the average in their country of origin. Population and societies, 541(1), 1-4. Retrieved from https://www.ined.fr/en/publications/population-and-societies/Immigrants-educational-attainment/

UNHCR. (2022) Ukraine situation. Flash update #3. 15 March 2022. Genève: UNHCR.

Migration Policy Implementation and its Politics in South Africa

(1254) Toyin Cotties Adetiba, University of Zululand, South Africa

Globally, and among scholars, migration is to a certain degree an important and highly debated political topic because of its peculiarity to human movement and relationship between states. Migration is fundamental to liberal democracies and a function of the international system of states. The chronic structural problems associated with the developing countries particularly African states seems to have engendered mass displacement of people and has become a threat to the integrity of national borders and to the socio-economic and political stability of the state system. Following the demise of the apartheid system and the adoption of inclusive governance in South Africa in 1994, the country has continued to witness an influx of migrants. However, the call for the deportation and rejection of migrants amongst South Africans has continued to increase, with black foreign nationals at the receiving end of xenophobic attacks sometimes openly or clandestinely done by government officials. South Africa's preoccupation with restrictionism policies through the Department of the Home Affairs and driven by xenophobism and political interest, seems to have compromised inroads for immigrants that are very important to its economic growth. From the realist school of thought, the state plays the role of a guardian and the protector of the national interest [which are those things that are essential to the survival and well-being of a state as a whole] and security within the international community. Using a qualitative research method, this study is underpinned by the following questions (i) Is South Africa playing politics with its migration policies while surreptitiously legalizing xenophobism? (ii) Can a well-managed migration policies allay the fears of foreign nationals particularly the blacks in South Africa? (iii) What effects would anti-immigrants' laws and attitudes have on South Africa's relations with other [African] countries?

Emigrants against will: A narrative Autoethnography Exploring Experiences between Migration and Exile

(1013) Ülkü Güney, Karl-Franzens University Graz and Alpen-Adria University Klagenfurt, Austria

In my presentation, I examine my own experiences as an immigrant and an exiled scholar. Drawing on the autoethnographic method (Ellis 2004; Smith 2005; Hauber-Özer 2019) I contextualize and analyze the transformation in my lived practices of recurrent migration and my biography between "home" and "abroad". Approached as a reflexive positionality statement, I explore my shifting roles of a child of German-Turkish - working-class - migrants and an academic in exile and how these inform my personal and professional identity. The research presents a narrative autoethnographic reflection (Anderson 2006) on my past and present experiences navigating life between Turkey, Germany and Austria. This research builds on an inward-looking understanding of personal narrative while addressing migration more broadly.

3C   Migration Policy, Law, Politics   AMPHI 3

Chair: Giuseppe Sciortino, University of Trento, Italy

1030   A Wall of Words: Remaking Asylum in the United States

Alexandra Eléan Villarreal, University of Texas at Austin, US

1280   Seeking Asylum is for everyone? The distinct legal treatment given to Ukrainian, African and Middle Eastern asylum seekers in the EU

Tiago Scher Soares de Amorim, Germany

1238   A tale of failed policy convergence: exploring why is the achievement of an EU effective return policy so difficult?

Irene Landini, School of International Studies, University of Trento, Italy
Giuseppe Sciortino, University of Trento, Italy

537   AI applied to decision-making process in the field of international protection: current proposals in the EU and their impact on fundamental rights of asylum seekers

Andrea Romano, Universität Hamburg, Germany
Ülkü Sezgi Sözen, Universität Hamburg, Germany

A Wall of Words: Remaking Asylum in the United States

(1030) Alexandra Eléan Villarreal, University of Texas at Austin, US

Whom does the United States recognize as a legitimate asylum seeker? U.S. statute delineates refugees and asylees as anyone fleeing "persecution on account of race, religion, nationality, membership in a particular social group, or political opinion, "□ a definition that "" at least in theory "" renders U.S. asylum protections egalitarian and universally applicable. Yet for decades, an Anglo-American ideological project of exclusion has reinterpreted this seemingly agnostic language to destabilize any notion of impartiality, universality, or dependability within the asylum apparatus, relegating many displaced peoples of color to the dredges of what I call not-asylum. In this paper, I will consider the former Attorney General Jeff Sessions' 2018 precedential decision in the immigration court case, Matter of A-B-, and its wider implications for Central American asylum seekers fleeing domestic and gang-related violence. My analysis will demonstrate how racialized interpretations of U.S. asylum law have reified, deconstructed, and rebuilt the existing statute in a way that strategically narrows who qualifies for asylum. I will explore Sessions' opinion as not only an exposition of facts, but also a remaking of them, examining how he deploys speciously authoritative prose to enforce a radically reconceived definition of who asylum seekers are and are not. Then, I will consider how advocates, attorneys, judges, and experts have challenged Sessions' decision through court documents, letters, practice advisories, and other primary sources, where they excavate the ideological project of exclusion beneath his facially neutral language. Taken together, Sessions' opinion "" which has since been overruled "" and the pushback it engendered represent one of the clearest recent examples of how American definitions of asylum are actively unstable, multifarious, and controversial, shedding light on why inequity and confusion permeate the U.S. asylum system today.

Seeking Asylum is for everyone? The distinct legal treatment given to Ukrainian, African and Middle Eastern asylum seekers in the EU

(1280) Tiago Scher Soares de Amorim, Germany

The hypothesis presented here is that the European Union's (EU) legal treatment of asylum is unequal among different asylum seekers arriving in the bloc. The recent migratory flow due to the war in Ukraine demonstrates the EU's concern regarding the protection of human beings in accordance with international humanitarian law. It is a model of a "humane approach" (Michelle Bachelet) that should be the rule, nevertheless it contrasts with the strict migration policies developed by the EU in recent years for other asylum seekers. Since the beginning of the Ukraine migration crisis, millions of Ukrainians and non-Ukrainians have sought asylum in EU countries. Just before the war completed a week, the EU Council unanimously decided to adopt an unprecedented measure called Temporary Protective Directive, designed after the breakup of the former Yugoslavia, that guarantees temporary protection for persons fleeing the war in Ukraine. This emergency mechanism makes it possible for asylum seekers from Ukrainian territory to be granted immediate refugee status for at least one year, guaranteeing immediate access to the labor market, housing, health care and access to education for children (Council Implementing Decision EU 2022/ 382). In opposition to this measure, the EU has been intensifying its migration policies that hamper access to fundamental human rights for asylum seekers arriving from Africa and the Middle East via the Mediterranean Sea. According to article 19 of the European Charter of Fundamental Rights, collective expulsions are prohibited. However, only during the Pandemic, EU Member States have used illegal push back operations against at least 40,000 asylum seekers (Lorenzo Tondo, The Guardian). Border operations in EU countries are supported by FRONTEX - the European Border and Coast Guard Agency, which had a, 543 million budget in 2021 (more than 70% higher compared to 2019). Through FRONTEX's investments, there is an EU strategy to strongly monitor the Mediterranean Sea, expanding virtual borders to stop migrants before they get near a physical border. The EU tries to excuse itself from an obligation to save seafarers, culminating in the consequent processing of asylum applications when they are already on European soil (Lucas Laursen, IEEE Spectrum).

There are also reports on violations of fundamental human rights in camps installed in countries such as Greece, where the asylum seekers are forced to stay for long periods of time without the right to liberty, security, education, to a standard of living adequate for health and well being and the right to leisure and rest (Aegean Grassroots Report, 2020). The contradictions of both approaches need to be analyzed from the perspective of European and international humanitarian laws to implement fairer migration policies within the European bloc in the future.

A tale of failed policy convergence: exploring why is the achievement of an EU effective return policy so difficult?

(1238) Irene Landini, School of International Studies, University of Trento, Italy

Giuseppe Sciortino, University of Trento, Italy

Return policy is one of the most controversial components of the Common European Asylum System. EU readmission agreements with extra-EU sending countries have shown to be largely ineffective (Carrera 2016[1]; Lindberg and Khosravi 2021[2]). Moreover, policy harmonization and/or intergovernmental cooperation in return policies and practices among member states (MS) have always remained low. This is puzzling, as strong harmonization and coordination could be useful, for example, in exerting unified pressure on sending and transit countries. The topic of return has received little scholarly attention. Sociologists have focused on other related fields, especially border control, and visa policies (Baldwin-Edwards 2001[3]; Finotelli & Sciortino 2013[4]; Infantino 2020[5]). Legal scholars have highlighted the limitations of returns, especially in terms of human rights violations (Moraru, 2021[6]). Surprisingly enough, scholarly research has failed to adequately address the elephant in the room: why do the attempts to promote supranational policy harmonization, or operational cooperation, have systematically failed despite the advantages they may bring to states? This article addresses this unsolved question, from the angle of social research. First, we provide a general overview of the main international law instruments in the field of return and the major historical developments of return policies and practices in Europe. Secondly, we investigate the positions of six EU MSs about the return issue, i.e., Germany, France, Sweden, Italy, Spain, and Poland. Which of them push for increased cooperation and the establishment of a more effective EU return policy? Which are the positions of national political parties? Is there a domestic debate about why are national and EU returns policies and operations so ineffective and how to improve them? Finally, we dwell on the main attempts (by both EU institutions and, eventually, some MSs) to increase harmonization/cooperation over time. We examine the role played by different types of factors in hindering this process - i.e., problematic legal aspects, political obstacles, practical feasibility, ext. Based on this analysis, we inductively outline a number of potential driving factors behind failed harmonization and/or cooperation. Both legal and social research can benefit from incorporating these aspects into studies of immigration control policies to further explore the functioning and limits of return policies and practices.

AI applied to decision-making process in the field of international protection: current proposals in the EU and their impact on fundamental rights of asylum seekers

(537) Andrea Romano, Universität Hamburg, Germany

Ülkü Sezgi Sözen, Universität Hamburg, Germany

Digital innovation in the field of borders, migration and asylum has progressively become a crucial topic for migration law scholars, due to the increasing number of technological tools adopted in these field, such as biometric collection systems, facial recognition techniques or monitoring migrants' activity on social networks.

This paper aims at focusing on a new facet of this phenomenon, which is represented by the increasing application of artificial intelligence techniques to support decision-making processes in the area of international protection in the EU. This means that asylum officers are or will be assisted in their borders, visa and asylum procedures by automated decision-making systems that support or even replace human decision.

Between 2013 and 2019, the EU Commission funded the experimentation of the Intelligent Portable Control System (iBorderCtrl) an AI system directed at automatically detecting travelers that may pose a security risk on the basis of an interview conducted by an avatar that screened data, information and emotional behavior. Following such experiment, several projects applying automated recognition systems are ongoing in the EU (see for instance TRESPASS). Lastly, the EU Commission proposed in April 2021 an EU Regulation on Artificial Intelligence which covers, inter alia, how AI might be used in the areas of migration and asylum and contemplating the possibility that public authorities may use AI tools for the examination of applications for asylum and apply "polygraphs and similar tools or to detect the emotional state of a natural person".

These examples showcase that the use of AI is becoming salient in the area of migration and asylum and this poses a number of legal challenges for legal scholar such as the respect of principles of EU administrative action, e.g. transparency proportionality and non-discrimination, its impact on fundamental rights and particularly on vulnerable individuals, as well as the possibility to contemplate effective administrative and judicial remedies.

In particular, this paper will focus on how AI is currently used in the field of international protection, with the view of exploring how current EU proposals intend to include automated decision-making within the international protection procedure. In order to do that, we will first define automated decision-making and then use the comparative method to look into the initiatives carried out in non-EU (e.g. US, Canada and the UK) and EU Member States. Finally, we will use the hermeneutic method to analyze the current EU Commission proposal on the AI Regulation describing how it may affect international protection procedure and addressing how it may pose challenges to fundamental rights of asylum applicants.

Chairs: Karolina Sobczak-Szelc, Center for Advanced Studies of Population and Religion (CASPAR) CUE, Denmark and Marcin Stonawski, Institute Statistics Denmark

1251   Lived experience in rural and urban areas of origin countries and their role in shaping migration trajectories, temporalities and aspirations: A case study of Duhok and Zakho in the Iraqi Kurdistan

Lanciné Eric Diop, Aalborg University, Denmark
Basheer Saeed, University of Duhok, American University of Kurdistan, Iraq & University of Maryland, USA

1252   Complexities of internal and external mobilities from migrants' perspectives in Ukraine before the 2022 war

Dobroslawa Wiktor-Mach, Cracow University of Economics, Poland
Konrad Pędziwiatr, Cracow University of Economics, Poland

1256   Trajectories of Migration Aspirations within Senegal and beyond. Notes of preliminary analysis.

Stefano degli Uberti, National Research Council, the Institute for Research on Population and Social Policies (CNR-IRPPS), Italy
Lanciné Diop, Aalborg University, Denmark
Mohamadou Sall, Cheikh Anta Diop University, Senegal

1250   The role of city experiences in the migration decision-making process - the example of internal migrants in Sousse, Tunisia

Karolina Sobczak-Szelc, CASPAR, Cracow University of Economics, Poland
Konrad Pędziwiatr, CASPAR, Cracow University of Economics, Poland
Hassen Boubakri, University of Sousse, Tunisia

Lived experience in rural and urban areas of origin countries and their role in shaping migration trajectories, temporalities and aspirations: A case study of Duhok and Zakho in the Iraqi Kurdistan

(1251) Lanciné Eric Diop, Aalborg University, Denmark

Basheer Saeed, University of Duhok, American University of Kurdistan, Iraq & University of Maryland, USA

An urban laboratory to explore the migration decision making processTMC Conference Tracks: General paper / Area Focus and GeographiesAbstract Recent developments in migration research highlight the need to go beyond traditional theoretical frameworks to understand why people migrate at a particular time. This is especially true for approaches such as the push-and-pull approach, which, despite its relevance for understanding migration decisions and processes, is limited (Jónsson, 2010). Moreover, little attention is paid to the importance of the linkage between internal intra-regional and transnational migration decisions. Mobility is often consubstantial to everyday experiences and opportunities in countries of origin, particularly in rural areas and small villages, but also in the growing urban areas of countries of origin (Brachet, 2009; de Bruijn, Van Dijk & Foeken 2001: 1). These experiences in turn shape migrants' aspirations (Carling, 2014) and their inclination to either migrate internationally or stay. In this paper, we build on the analytical approach of the project FUME (Future Migration Scenarios in Europe), which calls for analyzing migration as a non-linear and fragmented process whereby cities can, on the one hand, serve as a stepping stone for further transnational migration or, on the other hand, become a destination for people who originally wanted to migrate internationally. Thus, grasping how the complexity of the interaction between different temporalities and trajectories and lived experiences in urban areas inform and help re-evaluate migration aspirations and projects is a prerequisite for understanding the current and future determinants of migration decisions (Carling & Collins , 2018). The data used draws on ethnographic research with experts and potential migrants in two cities in the Kurdistan Region of Iraq and advocates for an understanding of migration decisions that takes into account sociocultural as well as geographic and temporal perspectives. In other words, the changes reflect the lived experience of Iraqis, especially those belonging to religious or ethnic minorities (Paasche, 2020). Iraq's transition to a relatively stable economy has shifted the migration processes from a security-related phenomenon to an economic one. Regardless of when they arrived in the cities of Duhok and Zakho, informants, especially those who have stayed for more than 10 years, show a sense of belonging to a place, especially if their families manage to build a safe and peaceful life. However, the government has failed to improve job opportunities, so many informants dream of a possible move to Europe, which is perceived as an achievable dream rather than a concrete and realistic project.

Complexities of internal and external mobilities from migrants' perspectives in Ukraine before the 2022 war

(1252) Dobroslawa Wiktor-Mach, Cracow University of Economics, Poland

Konrad Pędziwiatr, Cracow University of Economics, Poland

Drawing upon a recent turn in migration studies which redirects the focus towards agency, aspirations, capabilities and decision-making (cf. Preibisch, Dodd, Su, 2016), the proposed paper presents the findings of a qualitative study on contemporary migration in Ukraine carried out within the Future Migration Scenarios for Europe project (FUME). Ukraine was selected as one of four origin countries (along with Tunisia, Senegal and Iraq) to provide a qualitative input into a multi-layered migration scenario for Europe. So far, the topic of interrelation between internal and international migration in Ukraine has been under researched, and the project intended to fill this gap. The fieldwork was carried out in Kyiv and in its suburbs from February to June 2021. During this period, in spite of the lockdown and anti-epidemic measures, the research team carried out focus groups with migration experts and then conducted 30 in-depth interviews (some face-to-face, some online) according to an interview scenario. Kyiv was chosen as the capital and the administrative and business center of Ukraine, which for years topped the Regional Human Development Index (Libanova, 2017), and attracted a large number of internal migrants. Our sample included people who moved from various regions of Ukraine, both remote and those bordering the Kyiv region and represented various sectors of economy, education levels and life trajectories. Research questions included inquiries into migration drivers and experience, assessment of current life in the capital city, aspirations for the future and capabilities to migrate abroad. The findings of the research indicate the fluidity of migration decision-making and the influence of interlinked factors, including economic, political, social and cultural upon mobility plans. The research also shows that the economic drivers have always been the key drivers of migration to the capital, in the last couple of years socio-cultural factors began to play a greater role especially among the younger generation, where aspirations for self-development are visible. Since 2014, political drivers also began to play a role and led to huge numbers of IDPs leaving their homes in Donbas and Luhansk regions as well as Crimea. With regards to the future migrations, four major types of intentions were discerned: 1) planning to return to the places of origin, 2) migration within the country or abroad , 3) staying in the city and the country, 4) "undecided," or "still searching," which is a category similar to the one identified by Eade et al. during their research on Poles in the UK and classified as "searchers" or by the category of "intentional unpredictability" (2007).

References:

Eade J., Drinkwater S., Garapich M. (2007). Class and Ethnicity: Polish Migrant Workers in London. End of Award Research Report, ESRC. Swindon: Economic and Social Research Council.

Libanova E.M. et al (2017) Zaklyuch zvit "Indeks-lyudskogo-rozvitku" [online]. Available at: https://www.minregion.gov.ua/wp-content/uploads/2017/01/Zaklyuch-zvit-Indeks-lyudskogo-rozvitku.pdf.

Preibisch, K., Dodd, W., & Su, Y. (2016). Pursuing the capabilities approach within the migration–development nexus. Journal of Ethnic and Migration Studies, 42(13), 2111-2127.

Trajectories of Migration Aspirations within Senegal and beyond. Notes of preliminary analysis.

(1256) Stefano degli Uberti, National Research Council, the Institute for Research on Population and Social Policies (CNR-IRPPS), Italy

Lanciné Diop, Aalborg University, Denmark

Mohamadou Sall, Cheikh Anta Diop University, Senegal

During the last decade, several specialists in migration studies have examined the processes of migration decision-making and how they inform the propensions of people to move, to stay or to return (Carlin and Schewel 2018; de Haas 2014). However, rather few studies attempted to addresses migrants' aspirations, (cap)abilities and behaviours taking into account the interrelationship between internal and international migration processes in the places of origin. In this perspective the theoretical perspective of the mobility studies (Sheller and Urry, 2006), by urging to conceptualize 'migration' as a 'way of life' (culture of migration) rather than an exception (De Bruijn, Van Dijk and Foeken 2001), provides a fertile ground for the understanding of the fluid nature of migration trajectories which are shaped by intersecting forms of mobilities (e.g. internal, intra-regional, transnational…) and immobilities.

Building on the analytical contributions of this approach, the aim of the paper is to discuss the evidences of the ethnographic research conducted in the framework of the Future Migration Scenarios for Europe project (FUME) which focuses on imagining possible futures scenarios of migration to Europe through the understanding of migration patterns and motivations at multiple geographical scales. The paper discussion draws from the information collected from January to April 2021 through a selection of in-depth interviews of "would-be migrants" and key-experts in the urban and peri-urban areas of the Dakar region. In fact, despite the recent changes Dakar still remains for the young generation of Senegalese migrants an important step in the migration routes, not only of internal migration; this urban area is a "stepping stone" to destinations abroad for many potential international migrants coming from villages and small towns (Sinatti 2008; Melly 2010).

The paper argues for an understanding of the "trajectory of aspirations" as a synthesis of different, interlinked motivations, attitudes and often, extemporaneous opportunities which shape the migration experiences more often as less planned, unsettled and fragmented. Social networks continue to play a key role in mediating migrant aspirations and the concrete organization of departures within and beyond the country (both regular and irregular) although an increasing rely on informal networks is documented. Both the temporality of migration and the socio-cultural and economic factors are at stake, shedding light on the complexity and fluid nature of migrant propensities to go abroad.

References:

de Bruijn, M., Van Dijk, R., Foeken, D. (2001). Mobile Africa. Changing Patterns of Movements in Africa and Beyond. Leiden: Brill.

de Haas, H. (2014). Migration Theory Quo Vadis? DEMIG project paper 24. IMI Working Papers Series. Oxford: IMI, University of Oxford. Available at: https://www.imi.ox.ac.uk/publications/wp-100-14/@@download/file

Carling, J. & Schewel, K. (2018). Revisiting aspiration and ability in international migration. Journal of Ethnic and Migration Studies, 44(6), 945-963. Doi: 10.1080/1369183X.2017.1384146

Melly C. (2010). Inside-Out Houses: Urban Belonging and Imagined Futures in Dakar, Senegal. Comparative Studies in Society and History, 52(1), 37-65. Available at: http://www.jstor.org/stable/40603071

Sheller, M., J. Urry (2006) "The New Mobilities Paradigm", in Environment and Planning, 38, pp. 207-226.

Sinatti, G. (2008) The making of urban translocalities: Senegalese migrants in Dakar and Zingonia. In M. P. Smith, and J. Eade (Eds.), Transnational Ties: Cities, Migrations, and Identities (pp. 61-76). Transaction Publishers.

The role of city experiences in the migration decision-making process - the example of internal migrants in Sousse, Tunisia

(1250) Karolina Sobczak-Szelc, CASPAR, Cracow University of Economics, Poland

Konrad Pędziwiatr, CASPAR, Cracow University of Economics, Poland

Hassen Boubakri, University of Sousse, Tunisia

An urban laboratory to explore the migration decision making processAbstract:Current research on migration indicates that different persons given the same factors make different migratory decisions. As long as the minority of them emigrates the majority will usually not consider moving. External immobility is also an important aspect of the processes of internal mobility. Therefore, the aim of this paper is to present the decision-making practices that drive potential migrants to leave the investigated city as well as to settle in it after the initial move out of their places of origin. We are going to look at motivations and propensities driving many people to stay in the city or to return to their region of origin. Within the framework, we compare and contrast the role of different environmental, socio-cultural, demographic, economic and political factors influencing migration decision making in a local context. The presentation will shed light on the main results of the research carried out between 2020-2021 within the H2020-funded Future Migration Scenarios for Europe project (FUME) in Sousse - the third-largest city in Tunisia. The research involved analysis of the existing data of qualitative and quantitative nature as well as in-depth interviews with experts and with prospective international migrants to Europe - those already living in Sousse, but who came to the city from rural areas of Tunisia up to 15 years ago.The results indicate that the migrants who came to the city over 10 years ago are quite firmly anchored in it and rarely think about external migration. International migration is much more often on the agenda of those recently arrived in the city and frequently younger people. They are looking for better life prospects and in case they cannot find them in Sousse, they are ready to go abroad with a first possibility as they have fewer anchors in their current place of residence.

3E   Integration, Acculturation and Diasporas   AMPHI 5

Chair: Almudena Macías León, University of Malaga, Spain

1297   Immigrants of Arab descent on the Hungarian-Serbian border

Meszár Tárik, Migration Research Institute, Hungary

1037   Socio-economic and adjustment challenges to Pakistani migrant workers in UAE

Syed Imran Haider, Department of Sociology Allama Iqbal Open University Islamabad, Pakistan
Ali Awan, Jinnah Sindh Medical University, Karachi, Pakistan
Asma Khalid, Allama Iqbal Open University Islamabad, Pakistan

1005   Bhutanese Refugees: New Diasporic Citizens of the United States or Still Dispossessed Refugees?

Retika Adhikari, University of Michigan, Ann Arbor, Michigan, USA

520   Covid 19 and the mobility of Roma population within Europe

Almudena Macías León, University of Malaga, Spain
Gianluigi Moscato, University of Malaga, Spain

Immigrants of Arab descent on the Hungarian-Serbian border

(1297) Meszár Tárik, Migration Research Institute, Hungary

Organized by the Migration Research Institute, in 2022 we visited the Serbian side of the Hungarian-Serbian border several times, where we conducted interviews with immigrants of Arab descent. During these conversations, information was revealed that was largely unknown to the Hungarian public. We were able to learn first-hand about the motivations of migrants in Serbia, as well as gain insight into their everyday lives and a close-up view of their temporary residences. A common feature of native Arabic-speaking immigrants in Serbia is that they intend to enter Western Europe illegally through Hungary, especially to Austria, France or Germany. The Hungarian border fence and strict controls make it significantly more difficult to achieve their goals, but their persistence is characterized by their ability to try to cross the border 8-10 times - or even more than 50 times in extreme cases. Immigrants and refugees in Serbia have been temporarily housed in dilapidated buildings, most of which are extremely neglected. Rain is falling on the buildings and the wind is blowing through them. Buildings that have become completely unsuitable for human habitation have presumably already served as temporary homes for many thousands of people. During the lecture, we will shed light on the difficulties faced by people wishing to cross the Hungarian border during their journey, and the reason for the increasing pressure on the Hungarian-Serbian border.

Socio-economic and adjustment challenges to Pakistani migrant workers in UAE

(1037) Syed Imran Haider, Department of Sociology Allama Iqbal Open University Islamabad, Pakistan

Ali Awan, Jinnah Sindh Medical University, Karachi, Pakistan

Asma Khalid, Allama Iqbal Open University Islamabad, Pakistan

The study aims to explore Pakistani diaspora living in the UAE. As per UAE government's residency policy, all non-citizens living and working in the UAE "85% of the UAE population" have a little chance to get citizenship (Ali, 2011), thus leaving people to be on the move. Pakistan has a patriarchal society where men migrate to other countries to earn a living and to support immediate and extended families. It is argued that people change their attitude and behaviour as per settings of the working and living environment, however, face many social, economic, religious, cultural, and political (to some extent) challenges. These can be derived from their socio-economic standing, religious affiliation, and most importantly performance of associated migrant identity in public and workspaces (Jasso, 2011). It becomes important to analyze how Pakistani men cop with the pressures and challenges to accommodate and adapt accordingly. In this research, 25 semi-structured interviews were conducted with Pakistani men who worked and lived in UAE for at least 6 years. Social scientific theory of migration is used as theoretical underpinning (Alba and Nee, 2003). The results reveal that there are continuous visa processing and confirmation issues (kafala system) which keep the migrants' minds occupied and cause them stress and depression due to insecure future where they are treated under contractual law rather than immigrant law (Ali, 2011). Economics always remained a continuous challenge to the migrants due to lack of technical and vocational skills including lack of understanding and fluency of English and Arabic language. Thus, their status remain low in the society and integration into the society seems difficult in the absence of permanent legal status, socio-cultural practices of the country of destination which restrict social interaction, leading to social exclusion. It is concluded that if permanent residence status is given by the UAE governments, technically skilled and English/ Arabic-speaking migrants move to UAE, they will have better opportunities and less uncertainties in their lives.

Bhutanese Refugees: New Diasporic Citizens of the United States or Still Dispossessed Refugees?

(1005) Retika Adhikari, University of Michigan, Ann Arbor, Michigan, USA

In 1989, the government of Bhutan implemented a Drukpa-Buddhist cultural policy, which sought to create a culturally and linguistically homogeneous Bhutan. One of the major consequences of this nationalist effort was a government-enforced assimilation of Bhutanese citizens from southern Bhutan, who had Nepali ancestry and were native Nepali speakers. Refusing to conform to the new changes, approximately 100,000 Bhutanese citizens with Nepali ancestry were expelled from Bhutan in the early 1990s and forced to live in refugee camps in Nepal. More than two decades later, approximately 100,000 Bhutanese refugees began being relocated to the United States as part of the US-funded and United Nations-managed refugee resettlement project.

Based on transnational ethnographic research between 2014-2019, this paper follows the movement of Bhutanese refugees, as they travel through the nodes of the resettlement trail—from refugee camps in Eastern Nepal, processing centers in Kathmandu, and international airports through the Gulf region and finally to the United States. By examining how newly arrived Bhutanese refugees strategically navigate their unfamiliar American neighborhood as well as resettlement bureaucracy, I demonstrate that refugees in their post-resettlement life continue to endure future uncertainties and economic precarity—just as they did while in refugee camps. My analysis of refugee arrival in the United States affords us new ways to imagine and engage the idea of refugee integration and American refuge.

Covid 19 and the mobility of Roma population within Europe

(520) Almudena Macías León, University of Malaga, Spain

Gianluigi Moscato, University of Malaga, Spain

This work focuses on the analysis of the incidence of Covid-19 in the Roma population mobility within Europe. For this purpose, a thematic/monographic review was carried out on recent studies of the consequences of the pandemic on the Roma ethnic minority. The Roma population has suffered a disproportionate impact of the pandemic in all the countries of Europe, mainly because of its high levels of exclusion and poor living conditions. The anti-Roma increase has also increased the risk for this group (FRA 2020). The mobility of this population seems to constitute an additional risk factor that conditions their precarious living conditions. The behaviour of this migratory flow responds to the interaction of global factors that respond to economic globalisation. Bauman (2000) states that although globalisation affects all members of society, it does not affect everyone in the same way. In this work, the Covid-19 pandemic has been considered a new global factor that makes up a new scenario, influencing pre-existing exclusion dynamics. These always seem to affect the same population sectors, the most vulnerable, which occupy a more marginal position in the social stratification that emerges from global dynamics. We will analyze the impact of the pandemic in the different areas: employment, health, housing, migration project,... We shall observe how the high levels of social exclusion of this ethnic group make it more likely to suffer a higher risk of morbidity, mortality, and the psychological, social, and economic effects of the pandemic.

The decline in the precarious living conditions of this population has reached alarming levels in most European countries during the pandemic, increasing levels of food insecurity and revealing new processes of discrimination and stigmatization towards this group (Warmisham, 2016).. Once again we witness human rights abuses against Roma in the EU context closely linked to the process of etnization of the pandemic (ERRC, 2020).

References:

Bauman, Zigmun. 2000. *Globalization: The Human Consequences.* Cambridge, Blackwell Publishers.

ERRC, 2020. *Roma Rights in the Time of Covid.*

EC, 2020. *Overview of the impact of the coronavirus measures on the marginalised roma communities in the EU.*

FRA (2020). *Implications of COVID-19 pandemic on Roma and Travellers communities.* University Institute of Studies on Migration y FRA. Junio 2020.

FRA, 2020. *Coronavirus pandemic in the UE- Impact on Roma and Travellers (Bulletin N°5).*

Warmisham J. (2016). *The situation of Roma and Travellers in the context of rising extremism, xenophobia and the refugee crisis in Europe.* Congress of local and regional authorities.

3F   Migration, Development and Remittances   AMPHI 6

Chair: *Boutania Ismaili Idrissi, Mohammed V University of Rabat, Morocco*

1136   The Impact of Economic Sanctions (on Russia) on Kyrgyz Labor Migrants and their Remittances.

Liudmila Konstants, American University of Central Asia, Kyrgyzstan

1181   Migrant Remittances and the Diffusion of Information and Communication Technology

Ubaid Ali, Université de Pau et des Pays de l'Adour, E2S UPPA, CNRS, TREE, Pau, France
Mazhar Mughal, ESC Pau Business School, Pau France
Muhammad Ayaz, Université de Pau et des Pays de l'Adour, E2S UPPA, CNRS, TREE, Pau, France
Junaid, Ahmad, Pakistan Institute of Development Economics, Islamabad, Pakistan

950   Migration and Development in Mexico: a revisit

Liliana Meza Gonzalez, Universidad Iberoamericana, Mexico

1023   The Impact of Remittances on Household Consumption in Morocco: A Micro Econometric Analysis

Boutaina Ismaili Idrissi, Mohammed V University of Rabat, Morocco
Sara Kawkaba, Mohammed V University of Rabat, Morocco

The Impact of Economic Sanctions (on Russia) on Kyrgyz Labor Migrants and their Remittances.

(1136) Liudmila Konstants, American University of Central Asia, Kyrgyzstan

The importance of the topic nowadays. Within the last several years Kyrgyzstan always occupies one of three first - places in the share of remittances in its GDP. Remittances comprise around one-third of the republic's GDP. Prevailed part of them - 85-95 percent goes from Russia. Due to this, Kyrgyzstan directly and significantly depends on the power of the Russian ruble, the banks' stability and convenience for money transactions, labor market conditions, and internal Russia's policy toward labor migrants. Due to all of these, and the sanctions that Russia experiences nowadays, its current and future prospective economic situations can't help but inspire concern for the future of Kyrgyz labor migrants, their remittances flow to the country, and the economic situation of Kyrgyzstan which depends on these remittances. The problem statement. On the one hand, it is expected that many Russian businesses will have to shut down or even exit markets. Moreover, the weakness and reduced purchasing power of the Russian ruble could make working there unprofitable for our migrants. On the other hand, most of our labor migrants work in industries that are not connected (significantly or at all) to any kind of Russia's imports from the West: construction, public catering, cleaning services, etc. Nevertheless, it's clear that decreasing the overall well-being within Russia will reduce demand in these industries as well, though some experts predict the development of "import substitution of businesses" and avoiding any demand decreases in those industries. Anyway, continuing working in Russia could be attractive for labor migrants just in case the Russian ruble won't plunge significantly and the conversion of rubles to other currencies and transfer of them won't be as expensive as meaningless. The primary objective of the planned study is to analyze the possible decrease of the employment level of labor migrants, the probability of their returns into Kyrgyzstan, and the effect of this on the remittances flow. The main method of the analysis. By August we will have the first data from the WB and ADB about remittances for the six months of this year. By September we plan to have the data of the National Bank of the Kyrgyz Republic for eight months. From the Russian statistics, we hope to get data about an approximate change in the level of employment of legally working labor migrants (as nobody knows the exact amount of illegal employees). Most of the information we plan to get from the periodical and (hopefully - professional) Russian and Kyrgyzstan sources of information and publications. Expected results. The data and information that we plan to collect within the four upcoming months (before the conference) could allow us to hope that we will be able to determine the trend. What kind of trend it could be - probably, nobody nowadays can predict exactly. Conclusion. Naturally, this preliminary analysis is/will be highly restricted with data and information. Anyway, the republic needs careful analysis of upcoming situation development.

Migrant Remittances and the Diffusion of Information and Communication Technology

(1181) Ubaid Ali, Université de Pau et des Pays de l'Adour, E2S UPPA, CNRS, TREE, Pau, France

Mazhar Mughal, ESC Pau Business School, Pau, France

Muhammad Ayaz, Université de Pau et des Pays de l'Adour, E2S UPPA, CNRS, TREE, Pau, France

Junaid, Ahmad, Pakistan Institute of Development Economics, Islamabad, Pakistan

The adoption of information and communication technology (ICT) and migration are two of the defining aspects of the 21st century. In this study, we examine whether migrant remittances are playing a significant role in the widespread adoption of ICT in developing countries? Does the behavior of households receiving remittances from the long-duration, long-distance international migration, and the short-duration, short-distance domestic migration differ significantly? And are different ICT technologies (mobile phones, internet, smartphones, and social media apps) impacted equally? We study these questions by first drawing a theoretical model and then testing the hypotheses empirically. We combine geocoded data on 160,624 households from the 2019-20 round of the Pakistan Social and Living Standards Measurement Survey (PSLM) and an instrumental-variable strategy to come up with significant effects of remittances on ICT adoption. Estimations show that recipient households have a 27% higher per capita mobile availability and a 12% higher probability of possessing internet facility compared to non-recipient households. This effect is visible more among international remittances recipient households than domestic remittances recipient households. ICT adoption also increases by the amount of remittances received by the recipient households. We find that remittances accelerate the adoption of smartphones and social media apps. Besides, while international remittances substantially increase the number of users of smartphones, internet, and social media apps at home, domestic remittance only leads to increasing in basic phone and smartphone usage whereas the adoption of other technologies among domestic remittances recipient households is lower compared to the non-recipient households.

Migration and Development in Mexico: a revisit

(950) Liliana Meza Gonzalez, Universidad Iberoamericana, Mexico

Using data at the municipal level for the period 2010-2015 for Mexico, this paper uses a two-stage least squares methodology to understand the relationship between migration, remittances and development, when development is measured through the Human Development Index of the United Nations Development Program. The question of whether migration and its consequent result of receiving remittances have a positive or negative effect on development has been approached from many perspectives (both theoretical and empirical), and the case of migration from Mexico to the United States has been of special interest. In this research, data from 5 different sources are used to understand whether migration/remittances and development are positively or negatively related, considering the endogeneity that exists in this relationship. The results show that migration and remittances promote development in the countries of origin, and that, at greater development, more migration is promoted at first and then reduced.

The Impact of Remittances on Household Consumption in Morocco: A Micro Econometric Analysis

(1023) Boutaina Ismaili Idrissi, Mohammed V University of Rabat, Morocco

Sara Kawkaba, Mohammed V University of Rabat, Morocco

Remittances have been growing rapidly in the past few years and now represents the largest source of foreign income for many developing economies and plays consequently an important role in the economic and social development of these countries. In addition to the investments that remittances may create, they contribute to increasing household income in the countries of origin and thus to raising the consumption of household. It is hard to estimate the exact size of remittance flows because many take place through unofficial channels. According to the World Bank, remittances to low and middle-income countries are projected to have grown a strong 7.3 percent to reach \$589 billion in 2021. Many authors have looked at the impact of remittances, and most show that remittances increase the final consumption of migrants' families in the country of origin. Remittance inflows can reduce poverty by increasing consumption and this importantly helps recipients of remittances to improve their living conditions (Ghosh, 2006; and Sorensen & Pedersen, 2002). However, Bouklia (2010) shows that remittances are mostly used in final consumption, they increase national income while Mouhoud (2013) has perceived remittances as an additional income that increases household income, which has implications for poverty reduction and increased consumption. Moreover, looking to the relationship between consumption and remittance, there has been an increasing interest from researchers, academics and policy makers around the world. Adams and Page (2005) found that remittances have a significant and positive impact on consumption. Similarly, Faini (2007) also found a positive relationship between remittances and saving, consumption and lifestyle of people. Gupta, Pattillo, and Wagh (2007) analyzed the impact of remittances across Africa using a panel of data from 76 developing countries including 24 African countries, the results of their empirical work confirm that remittances reduce poverty by improving the income of recipient households, increasing their consumption. Based upon a review of theoretical and empirical literature, this paper uses an econometric model to assess the impact of remittances on household consumption in Morocco. The National Survey on Household Consumption and Expenditure (ENCDM) of 2013-2014 carried out by the High Commissioner for Planning will be used as the main source. The matching method to apprehend the impact of these remittances on the population's living conditions will be used. The propensity score matching method (Rosenbaum and Rubin, 1983) consists in associating with each household that received remittances from a Moroccan resident abroad a household that did not receive remittances but that has similar demographic and socioeconomic characteristics. The result shows that there is a significate and positive relationship between remittances and consumption and also there is a relationship between domestic income and consumption which indicates that higher the level of domestic income, higher would be the consumption.Remittances, Household Consumption, Morocco, Economic development, Migrant.

Migratory stratifications and social ageing - Notes from a fieldwork within the Tunisian community in Modena

(1066) Andrea Calabretta, University of Padua, Italy

Vincenzo Romania, University of Padua, Italy

At the end of the '60s, with the arrival of a growing number of Tunisian migrants in Western Sicily, Italy entered in a new historical phase, becoming (also) a country of immigration (Colucci 2018). Since then, international immigration flows have multiplied, often intertwining with internal movements, and being called to adapt to economic cycles and policies changes. The paper employs the concept of migratory stratifications presenting the case of Tunisian migrants living in the town of Modena (Northern Italy). Issued from Southern Italy through a double passage (Daly 2001) or directly coming from Tunisia, characterised by different paths, migratory seniorities and generations, Tunisians in Modena seem to represent the prototype of a stratified migrant community. Focusing on this example, we ask how the migratory stratification characterising Modena and its Tunisian community influenced migrants' social ageing (Elias, Scotson 1963) determining (different) outcomes in terms of establishment in the local context and success of the migratory project. The paper answers this research question drawing on 30 qualitative interviews collected within the elder part of the Tunisian community in Modena and with Tunisians' descendants. The biographical dimension of the interviews allowed us to develop a diachronic perspective while addressing the research question. Once written out verbatim the interviews have been thematically analysed using Atlas.ti. The study presents the controverted and non-linear role of migratory sedimentations in influencing migrants' careers (Martiniello, Rea 2014) in the local area of Modena, where previous stratifications appear both as valuable resources and as sources of exclusion for new migrants. Therefore, while upholding the heuristic usefulness of the concept of migratory stratifications, the paper suggests its problematisation in the research use, considering the role of structural (economic, policies) changes for comprehending how migratory stratifications influence migrants' social ageing.

Migratory stratification, civic stratification and social stratifications in Japan. A persistent phenomena between labour market needs and cultural peculiarities

(1047) Nicola Costalunga, University of Macerata, Italy

Migration phenomena in Japan have been a controversial issue throughout the country's contemporary history. Japan's approach to migration has been of strong closure towards the outside and has affected not only those who were planning to move within the archipelago, but also those who were already living in the country. Indeed, migrants are embedded in a hierarchical pyramid constructed from the migration policies (Shipper 2008) and reinforced by an exclusivist ethno-nationalist rhetoric (Arudou 2015). The 'racial hierarchy' of foreigners is based on criteria related to employment and social, civil and political rights, determined by the level of personal belonging "or closeness" to the so called 'Japanese race': the closer a migrant is to the 'Japanese race', the higher is placed on the social and civic pyramid (Shipper 2008; Arudou 2015). This hierarchy in Japan is rigid and complex, and does not necessarily follow a diachronic perspective, according to the migratory stratification perspective: while the zainichi "the first to be present in the archipelago due to historical determinants" are also at the top of the pyramid, the position of other migrant categories does not strictly reflect the moment of arrival but are the result of other top-down dynamics and cultural (or phenotypic) contiguity. Nikkeijin, for example, who have arrived only in the 1990s (Brody 2002), are placed higher than other categories as direct descendants of the Japanese (Shipper 2008). There are also lateral positions, lacking any real vertical placement due to the protection of their country governments "e.g. foreign students", while others have climbed the pyramid instantaneously, such as highly skilled workers (Hamaguchi 2019). In fact, there is a correlation between labour market needs, migratory stratification, and social stratification, but it does not necessarily follow the chronological order of arrival. Thus, the relationship between migratory stratification and social stratifications is not always linear. What is surprising, instead, is the persistence of this social stratification despite the political-economic changes and the transformed needs of the labour market. This paper aims at analysing the extent to which migratory stratifications in Japan are determinants in the formation of social stratifications of migrants, and how these stratifications persist despite the potential transformative pushes dictated by the (variable) economic needs of the domestic and international labour markets.

Migratory stratifications in the labour market from a generational standpoint: a focus on the Italian context

(1209) Davide Girardi, Instituto Universitario Salesiano di Venezia, Italy

This paper aims to investigate the changes in labour market segments available to migrants in an economically leading Italian area, starting from the perspective of migratory stratifications.At the beginning of 2000s, Northern Italy showed an outstanding economic performance compared with the wider Italian context. The main trait of this process was a large participation to labour market driven by a spreading number of small and medium companies. Migrants' contribution was key to this dynamic. There was a clear segmentation between the migrants' workers - fundamental to fill labour shortages within industrial and services low-skilled jobs, often refused by natives - and native workers' jobs, with better skills assessment and symbolic recognition. The high low-skills job demand has favoured the transition from an economic migration to a family migration, characterised by the reunification of first-generation migrants (females and males) and the increasing role of second generations (reunified or born in Italy).Since the worldwide 2008-2009 financial crisis, however, these processes have slowed down. There has been a reduction of job demand caused by the growing difficulties of many small companies to compete within the international market and to boost product and process innovation. This dynamic has brought to a consequential reduction of immigrants' participation to labour market. Indeed, despite the enduring demand of care work in the second decade of the 2000s, the labour market structure in Northern Italy has substantially changed, resulting in a progressive segmentation between "insiders" - with well-paid skills inside companies and services based on the "Industry 4.0" paradigm - and outsiders, with devaluated skills inside less advanced companies. This polarization has also concerned the migrants' children in the phase of their transition to adulthood.These dynamics has been further exacerbated during the Covid-19 pandemic outbreak, that has affected immigrants in European countries from a health and more broadly social point of view. Immigrants too have experienced a so-called a "pan-syndemic".For these reasons, there is an urgent need for the identification of emerging patterns of immigrants' participation in the present context. What are the "tectonic shifts" of exclusion and inclusion of immigrants inside the labour market? More specifically, this paper aims to identify the economic "layers" concerning immigrants' jobs, national components and participation patterns. The migratory stratifications model seems appropriate also in order to focus on potential differences between generations, particularly in the phase of second generations' transition to adulthood.Based on a literature review and the elaboration of the most updated open data, the analysis of these stratifications will also be compared to the European "benchmarks" (France, Spain and Germany), in order to identify the potential turning points for Northern Italy.

Displaced memories in border area: layers of past that never past

(1049) Roberta Altin, University Trieste, Italy

This paper aims to analyze the different role and functions of migrants' memory through the comparison of different flows of refugees arrived in the border area of Trieste (Italy) in different stages: the Italian exodus after the WW2, the refugees from the former Jugoslavia in '90 and the asylum seekers arriving via Balkans from 2014 to the present.

Starting from the analysis of humanitarian reception and/ or rejection and considering the dynamics with local residents, stakeholders and other migrants, we want to understand how these factors influence the memory's maintenance or removal. The (eventually digital) connection with their origins or with a diasporic community, as well as the interferences played between the different stratifications of refugees and migrants in the same urban context in different times are just some of the many aspects to consider; others can be: trauma and removals, capability to rework and to think about the future (Horsti 2019). What happens when the rigid nationalist paradigm (inside/outside) takes over a more heterogeneous migration on a global scale with multiple reasons for displacement and a strong goal of transit rather than integration? Following an ethnographic approach, the main focus is to identify in which places, objects or other forms of identity expression the memories of refugees are deposited in different phases of displacement and, above all, how they stratify and intertwine with the others migratory transits in the same border area idealistically dividing western and eastern world.Horsti K. (ed) 2019. The Politics of Public Memories of Forced Migration and Bordering Europe, Basingstoke and New York, Palgrave Macmillan. Lorber M (ed) 2021. Beyond the Border, Exhibition catalogue, Trieste Civic Museums, Trieste. Glynn I., Kleist O.J (eds) 2012. History, memory and migration. Perceptions of the past and the politics of incorporation. Basingstoke and New York, Palgrave Macmillan.

Colonial, European and Qualified: The Stratification of Migration and Citizenship in the UK

(1110) Djordje Sredanovic, Université Libre de Bruxelles, Belgium

This presentation will explore the ways in which the history of migration and migration and nationality policies in the UK has created a complex stratification of statuses and rights. In the years between the end of World War II and the 1973 the UK diverged from the rest of North-Western Europe for a (post-)colonial policy that attributed different partial legal statuses to (former) colonial subjects, and in the fact that migration from the (former) colonies took the place of active recruitment of migrant workers. After progressively closing the borders to most former colonial subjects, the UK saw a significant migration from the European Union between the 1990s and the Brexit process, which saw the introduction of visa requirements in 2021. Currently the official migratory policy of the UK is strongly focused on 'qualified migration', with a points system determining which professional profiles can obtain a visa. Combining legislative analyses with the results of a qualitative research on the impact of Brexit on the experience of EU27 citizens in the UK, I will show how the effect of the sedimentation of different policies is the creation of several legal statuses with partial rights. Such statuses include Commonwealth citizens (with full voting rights but no specific mobility rights), holders of old colonial statuses, EU27 citizens who have obtained a settled status, as well as citizens of the Republic of Ireland, who have maintained a substantial bundle of rights during the whole period. I will discuss how such creation of 'legacy' legal statuses creates both a fragmentation of the rights of migrants, and the potential for problematic situation, such as the Windrush generation scandals, in which former colonial subjects who entered the UK with a legitimate status have been classified as irregular and in some cases deported because of lack of paper trails.

3H PANEL: Money, Merit and the Making of a Migrant in India [ONLINE]

Moderator: Dr. Sulakshana Sen, SSLA, India

Speakers

Ashley William Gois, Migrant Forum Asia, India

Dr. Shivkumar Jolad, Flame University, India

Dr. Mehrunnisa Ahmad Ali, Ryerson University, India

Day Two 8 September 2022 - 13:15-14:15

Plenary Session II [ONLINE]

Moderator: Prof Jeffrey H. **Cohen**, Ohio State University, USA
Keynote Speaker:

- Prof Markus **Koller**, Ruhr-Universität Bochum, Germany: **The "Languages of Migration" and the Actor-Network Theory – Transregional Mobility of Artisans and Merchants from Ottoman Bosnia in the 18th and 19th Centuries**

Day Two 8 September 2022 - 14:30-16:00   AMPHI 1

4A   Refugees and asylum seekers in North Africa [AR-FR]

الجلسة الرابعة: اللاجئين و طالبي اللجوء في شمال إفريقيا

رئيس الجلسة : د محمد عمارتي ، كلية العلوم القانونية و الاقتصادية و الاجتماعية جامعة محمد الأول بوجدة . عضو المجلس الوطني لحقوق الأنسان

Chair: Dr. Mohamed Amarti Professeur à l'université Mohammed Ier -Oujda , membre du CNDH

561 *Dr Ibrahim Awad Director of the Center for Studies on Migration and Refugees, American University in Cairo:* "Refugees and Asylum Seekers in Egypt: Protection and Livelihoods"

563ـ دـ ليبيا: د. البشير الكوت أستاذ العلوم السياسية بجامعة طرابلس : قضايا اللاجئين في ليبيا

Ali Mhamdi (Ex ambassadeur à Lahay, Beyrouth et Vienne): Les flux migratoires et la protection des réfugiés au Maroc

564 Haut-Commissariat aux Réfugiés - Maroc

562ـ دـ علي المحمدي : إشكالية اللجوء في المغرب

4B   Understanding Migration Experiences   AMPHI 2

Chair: Paulette K. Schuster, Reichman University, AMILAT, Israel

540   Afghan Migrant Women of Zeytinburnu: From Invisibility to Visibility

Zeynep Banu Dalaman, Istanbul Topkapi University, Turkey

1241 Qualified migration in the Olomouc region and its transnational dimension

Nikola Medova, Palacky University Olomouc, Czech Republic

1088 Life in transit areas: Sub-Saharan children in Rabat, Morocco, negotiating and shaping family transformations

Chiara Massaroni, University of Innsbruck, Austria

1015 Shrab, Jamam, Jazz and Chupah: Courtship and Weddings Rituals among Syrian Jewish women in Mexico City

Paulette K. Schuster, Reichman University, AMILAT, Israel

Afghan Migrant Women of Zeytinburnu: From Invisibility to Visibility

(540) Zeynep Banu Dalaman, Istanbul Topkapi University, Turkey

Turkey is home to nearly 4 million refugees, among which, Afghan constitute the second largest group after Iraq. In Istanbul, one of the biggest refugee receiving zones is Zeytinburnu, in which a significant number of Afghan population is noticed while crossing road, specially the "Yeşiltepe neighbourhood ‟ where it is known as the little city of Afghans, since Afghans made increased movements in it and started to develop businesses and working condition and obtained better integration within this society. Of course half of the Afghan population is comprised by women, but even yet, no research is conducted to address Afghan immigrant women‟s living conditions and experiences in Istanbul. Since there are no appropriate supporting systems relevant to the Afghan women's social integration at the local and state level. The feminist point of view implies that vulnerable women need the most secure social and labor environments. The challenge here is that receiving countries do not establish a well-being plan and policies for migrant women who want to stay permanently. This study emphasizes both the importance of uttering the social and economic conditions and social conditions and adjustment issues of Afghan women based in Zeytinburnu, İstanbul. Afghan Women's Social, Cultural and Solidarity Association is known as the first association established under the name of women. In this study, within the framework of the activities of this association in Zeytinburnu, the social problems experienced by Afghan women and the problems they face during the integration process will be examined. This research is based on face-to-face interviews from women who belong to the different provinces of Afghanistan and come from different backgrounds and different legal statuses.

Qualified migration in the Olomouc region and its transnational dimension

(1241) Nikola Medova, Palacky University Olomouc, Czech Republic

The aim of the research is to map qualified migration in the Olomouc region and its forms. The concept of qualified migration includes people who have completed tertiary education. These people can work in specific positions, and it is difficult to replace them with someone else. Research of qualified migration is generally carried out to a lesser extent than in the case of unskilled labor migration, worldwide and within the Czech Republic. Research in the Czech Republic focuses primarily on individual ethnic groups of migrants and their integration or, examines the impact of migration policies. Therefore, this work aims to fill this gap and examine skilled migration in a case study of the Olomouc Region. We will examine the migration trajectories of international migrants at different stages of migration.

Life in transit areas: Sub-Saharan children in Rabat, Morocco, negotiating and shaping family transformations

(1088) Chiara Massaroni, University of Innsbruck, Austria

This paper explores the ways in which young Sub-Saharan migrant children living in transnational households in Rabat, Morocco make sense and shape the social transformations affecting their families, the (re)negotiation of family roles and the ways in which families are fragmented, reunited, and reconstructed through migration.

While most migrants living in and around Rabat, Morocco, tend to reside in the country for years, if not for their entire life, most perceive their stay as temporary, hoping to reach Europe or North America at some point (Berriane et al., 2015). Living in a transit area shapes family life in unique ways: the liminal position of the migrants creates new relations, which, while perceived as temporary, might end up constructing *de-facto* new household relations. Households' members learn to negotiate new roles and are confronted with the ways in which the local community understands and embodies family life, while still longing for a new family life elsewhere.

While migration scholars have focused on the ways in which migration impacts family life and on how transitional ties contribute to create novel forms of family practices enacted across national borders (Bryceson & Vuorela, 2020; Mfoafo-M'Carthy & Akesson, 2019; Parreñas, 2002), very little is known about the ways in which family is renegotiated in transit areas, and how children make sense of such transformations.

To address this gap, this paper uses a qualitative, child-centred, multi-method approach, which brings forward the ways in young Sub-Saharan children living in Rabat make sense, experience, and contribute to shaping family transformations in transit. The paper will provide an understanding of the ways in which children cope with presences and absences of family members, how their fragmented and ambiguous narratives can signal the pain and loss that often accompany family migration, but also the construction of new forms of responsibilities and agency within the family. The paper contributes to shed new light on the active role that migrant children have in shaping family transformations through migration and more broadly it emphasis the relational nature of family life.

Bibliography

Berriane, M., de Haas, H., & Natter, K. (2015). Introduction: revisiting Moroccan migrations. The Journal of North African Studies, 20(4), 503–521. https://doi.org/10.1080/13629387.2015.1065036

Bryceson, D. F., & Vuorela, U. (2020). Transnational families in the 21st century. In D. F. Bryceson & U. Vuorela (Eds.), The Transnational family: New European frontiers and Global networks (pp. 3–30). Routledge.

Mfoafo-M'Carthy, M., & Akesson, B. (2019). "Family is everyone who comes through the doors of our home": West African concepts of family bridging the North-South divide in the diaspora. In T.-

D. A. Imoh, M. Bourdillon, & S. Meichsner (Eds.), *Global childhoods beyond the North-South divide (pp. 99–120). Palgrave Macmillan.*

Parreñas, R. S. (2002). *The care crisis in the Philippines: children and transnational families in the new global economy. In B. Ehrenreich & A. R. Hochschild (Eds.), Global woman: Nannies, maids and sex workers in the New Economy (pp. 39–54). Granta.*

Shrab, Jamam, Jazz and Chupah: Courtship and Weddings Rituals among Syrian Jewish women in Mexico City

(1015) Paulette K. Schuster, Reichman University, AMILAT, Israel

Syrian Jews first arrived in Mexico in the late 19th century. However, immigration began in earnest following the collapse of the Ottoman Empire. The characteristics of migration have evolved in the last decades to include new modes of analysis. I am interested in employing the spectrum of transnationalism as a point of departure. Jews from Syria came primarily from Aleppo (known as Halebis) and Damascus (known as Shamis). Syrian Jews brought many rituals with them. In this paper, I will describe those associated with pre-marriage courtship and wedding rituals across four generations of Syrian Jewish women in Mexico City. For example, attending a Jamam, drinking Shrab, receiving the Jazz and employing the Chupah (Wedding canopy). As Syrian Jews settled in Mexico, did their rituals converge with other Jewish and/or Mexican traditions? Through qualitative analysis, literature review and personal accounts, I will try to understand how they develop their sense of belonging and how they construct their identity through the use of rituals. Do they form their identity along ethno-religious lines (as Jews, as Jewish Arabs or Sepharadim)? or along national ones (as Mexicans)? Can these migrants be treated as transnational? This will be an interesting case study where gender, migration and religion are the main variables. Research is based on intergenerational interviews and Participant Observation conducted in Mexico City.

4C   Culture, Migration, Integration   AMPHI 3

Chair: Ece Cihan Ertem, University of Vienna, Austria

505   Diyanet's Religion Education for Turkish diaspora: Quran Courses for Turkish Migrant Children in Austrian Mosques

Ece Cihan Ertem, University of Vienna, Austria

1102   Trends in the European Union regarding Islamic culture and its heritage

Răzvan Dacian Cârciumaru, University of Oradea, Romania

1224   Chinese migrants in Africa: an exploration of cross-cultural place-making and geopolitical symbiosis

Erica Hu, Ohio State University, USA

Diyanet's Religion Education for Turkish diaspora: Quran Courses for Turkish Migrant Children in Austrian Mosques

505 Ece Cihan Ertem, University of Vienna, Austria

The Muslim community and their rights have been officially recognized by the Austrian state earlier than in many other European countries (Kolb, 2020) and in public secular primary schools of Austria, Islamic religious education has been provided since 1982 (Tuna, 2020; Aslan &Windisch, 2012). Despite being generally appreciated, there have been many theoretical discussions about Islamic religious education in Austria concerning the teaching methods, professionalization of teachers, teacher education, curricula and the context of secular schools. (Kramer, 2021, pp.255-257; Kolb, 2021, p.5; Aslan, & Hermansen, 2021) The Turkish community is one of the biggest migrant groups in Austria and more than half of the Turkish migrants define themselves as Sunni Muslims (Yağmur&Vijver, 2022; Sezgin, 2019). The Turkish community is largely engaged in the activities of religious education for their children however there have not been many studies either based on the impressions of Turkish parents or analysis of the discourse of Turkish educational policies for the Turkish diaspora. Hence, this paper focuses on the Quran courses that Turkish migrant children in Austria attend and it aims to research elaborating the thoughts and impressions of Turkish Sunni Muslim parents about Quran courses supplied by the Turkish government in Austria. Quran reciting education is mostly served by religious officers/Imams sent directly by the Turkish government with the approval of the Head of Religious Affairs (Diyanet) hence with this research, the religion education policy of contemporary Turkey for the Turkish diaspora will be analyzed with a comparison to Quran courses taught in Turkey. In order to scrutinize the subject, qualitative methods will be followed. In addition to document analysis, 20 semi-structured parent interviews are planned to be conducted. This paper presentation will include the literature review of the topic including the new educational policies of Turkish Diyanet, an analysis of the contemporary documents regarding Quran education of Turkish migrant children in Austria, and the preliminary results of parent interviews.

References:

Aslan, Ednan, and Marcia Hermansen, eds. Religious Diversity at School: Educating for New Pluralistic Contexts. Springer Nature, 2021.

Aslan, Ednan, and Zsófia Windisch. The Training of Imams and Teachers for Islamic Education in Europe. Wiener Islamstudien. Volume 1. Peter Lang GmbH, Internationaler Verlag der Wissenschaften. Germany, 2012.

Kramer, Michael. "Islamic Religious Education in Austria and Its Challenges for the Social Integration of Muslim Pupils." Religious Diversity at School. Springer VS, Wiesbaden, 2021. 253-273.

Kolb, Jonas. "Constituted Islam and Muslim Everyday Practices in Austria: The Diversity of the Ties to Religious Organizational Structures and Religious Authorities in the Process of Change." Journal of Muslim Minority Affairs 40.3 (2020): 371-394.

Kolb, Jonas. "Muslim diversity, religious formation and Islamic religious education. Everyday practical insights into Muslim parents' concepts of religious education in Austria." British Journal of Religious Education (2021): 1-14.

Sezgin, Zeynep. "Islam and Muslim minorities in Austria: Historical context and current challenges of integration." *Journal of International Migration and Integration* 20.3 (2019): 869-886.

Tuna, Mehmet H. "Islamic religious education in contemporary Austrian society: Muslim teachers dealing with controversial contemporary topics." *Religions* 11.8 (2020): 392.

Yagmur, Kutlay, and Fons JR van de Vijver. "Socio-cultural, Demographic, Educational and Linguistic Characteristics of Turkish Abroad." *Multidisciplinary Perspectives on Acculturation in Turkish Immigrants. Springer, Cham*, 2022. 13-38.

Trends in the European Union regarding Islamic culture and its heritage

1102 Răzvan Dacian Cârciumaru, University of Oradea, Romania

Muslims are the largest religious minority in Europe, and Islam is the fastest growing religion. The Muslim population of Europe is ethnically and linguistically diverse, and Muslim immigrants from Europe come from a variety of countries in the Middle East, Africa, and Asia, as well as Turkey. In recent years, European countries have intensified their efforts to better integrate their growing Muslim population. The study focuses on presenting the main current trends in the European Union countries and their attitude towards the Muslim community. As stated by Josep Borrell in 2019, it is first necessary to clarify the following anecdote: "Is the Arab-Muslim world an integral part of the European historical experience or can it be considered a foreign and imposed element?" The answer to this question is the key to coexistence between Muslims and European society in the European Union. The central question is how to avoid stereotypical generalizations, how to reduce fear and how to promote cohesion in our different European societies, while combating marginalization and discrimination based on race, ethnicity, religion or belief. To do this, we need to understand and, where appropriate, integrate this Islamic component, to an appropriate extent, into our history and, therefore, into European history as a whole. We cannot answer affirmative to the question of the Arab component of European culture unless we accept its presence in our European culture. Officially, this recognition has already been made within the Recommendation number 1162, on "The Contribution of Islamic Civilization to European Culture", issued by the Parliamentary Assembly of the Council of Europe on September 19, 1991. This research examined the different stages of migration flows, from temporary labor migration to permanent settlements, and showed the gradual construction of the Muslim problem in Europe and the emergence of extreme right-wing anti-Muslim parties. The paper dealt, in a non-exhaustive way, with some aspects related to the problem of extremism, and also discusses the policies of de-radicalization in European countries. The message the newspaper tried to convey is simple: the vast majority of immigrants, many of them Muslims, intend to settle in the European Union, and their numbers will increase in the coming years. Given this reality, European countries must do their best to continue their integration, and Muslims must contribute by demonstrating their attachment and loyalty to their new home countries. For all these reasons, and because we sometimes face narrow and xenophobic views of society, we must support a society that is open to ideas, influences, knowledge, and the transfer of technology, goods, services, and people through secure, regulated, and legal channels, in line with The Global Compact for Migration (Marrakech, Morocco). The imprint of Andalusia as part of the core of Europe provides us with a great opportunity to implement not only important cultural diplomacy initiatives, but also to strengthen our political dialogue with the Mediterranean region and the Arab and Muslim world, a dialogue that we must do our best to promote.

Chinese migrants in Africa: an exploration of cross-cultural place-making and geopolitical symbiosis

1224 Erica Hu, Ohio State University, USA

In 2013, China launched the Belt and Road Initiative (BRI), a global infrastructure development strategy with the goal of enhancing regional connectivity and economic development. As of 2020, countries in Africa own the largest Chinese debt compared to other BRI partners, signaling momentous cooperation and entanglement between the two. Similar to other diplomatic ambitions that facilitate the exchange of infrastructure, trade, and soft power at a transcontinental scale, BRI induces dichotomies of suspicion and trust, assimilation and isolation. Its complexity motivates me to question how China's rise to power affects the developmental trajectory in other regions. My research attempts to make sense of the significance of such ethnographic change from two angles. The first part of my research investigates how different types of Chinese migrants acclimate to local communities and how they shape local economic and cultural development. The second part gauges ways Africans respond to such demographic shifts through analyzing public opinion data in peer-reviewed articles and relevant cases of conflict and mutual support. Regarding migrants as agents of change and active nurturers of cultures and societies, I strive to elucidate the consequences of key socioeconomic policies through a human-centric approach that joins both qualitative and quantitative patterns to help us understand how we can better respond to communities' needs and improve their members' quality of life. As Chinese investment projects continue to proliferate in Africa, more multiethnic communities will emerge, bringing with them new challenges requiring cross-cultural adaptation and economic resilience.In my thesis, I discuss and draw connections between relevant historical context, economic development data (such as FDI, knowledge transfer, local employment rate, etc.), the presence and absence of cross-cultural organizations, popular opinion studies, and existing ethnography research that documents the lives of Afro-Chinese communities in various African countries (I use Kenya, Nigeria, and Namibia as my case studies). The mainstream narrative tends to reduce Chinese engagement in Africa to mere neocolonialism and theories such as "debt-trap diplomacy." However, through my analysis, I found that the tension and challenges present in African and Chinese migrant communities are largely a result of the lack of policy support and socioeconomic programs. These include unstandardized practices that fail to hold investors accountable for unassessed social impacts, the absence of dispute-mediation mechanisms, a series of implementation issues involving non-state actors beyond governmental control, and neglected needs of cultural integration on the ground.

4D   Work, Employment, Society   AMPHI 4

Chair: Martina Cvajner, University of Trento, Italy

542   An Agency without Agents - The Informality of Care Work Brokering in Italy

Martina Cvajner, University of Trento, Italy

An Agency without Agents - The Informality of Care Work Brokering in Italy

(542) Martina Cvajner, University of Trento, Italy

Transnational care chains are the engine of today's female migration to Southern Europe, Italy in particular. With its fast-growing elderly population, it's cultural attitude towards ageing and death paired with inadequate migration policies, Italy has become in the recent past one of the biggest markets for home elderly care. Using two data sets of in-depth interviews carried out with eastern European care workers interviewed in 2005 and in 2015 (N. 250), along with ethnographic data systematically collected over more than a decade, I shall discuss how access to care work has changed over a significant period of time (2000 – 2020) and how the stabilization of female flows has changed the brokering of elderly care in Italy. Back at the turn of the millennium, when I started the ethnographic part of my research much of the job brokering was carried out in informal venues -- like parking lots or bus stations -- and thru word of mouth. Some of it was a friendly exchange, some requested a monetary contribution. Much of it was carried out thanks to a shared linguistic past (i. e. ex-soviet migrants). Twenty years after, what has changed? How are can care workers access the job market? How can local families select a care worker? This contribution will offer a hypothetical explanation on why the brokering of elderly care in Italy has remained informal without transiting to a more formal, ad hoc agency model.

Work integration programs for refugees in Italy: a factory of invisible yet essential workers

(1190) Noemi Martorano, FISPPA- University of Padoua IDHE.S - Université Paris Nanterre, France

This paper aims to analyse the connection between the Italian reception system and humanitarian policies (Fassin 2010; Tazzioli 2015), integration policies (activation policies and workfare policies (Krinsky & Simonet 2012; Borghi 2005), and social reproduction (Bhattacharya 2017), through the study of labour integration programs addressed to refugees in reception projects in northern Italy. The programs studied in the paper are designed as work orientation and accompaniment services meant to encourage refugees that have obtained papers and are concluding their reception process to undertake job orientation, professional training, and internship, with the purpose to achieve progressive autonomy and "integration" into the labour market. The analysis is based on qualitative research that took place in different contexts in northern Italy, where participant observations of labour integration pathways in the reception context and interviews with program beneficiaries (45), reception workers (36), job centers and employment agencies (5), and enterprises (7) were carried out. The paper intends to analyse the work integration device through the lens of social reproduction theory (Bhattacharya 2017; Simonet 2018), which makes it possible to analyse, on the one hand the increasingly widespread use of internships, as a form of free, devalued and denied work; on the other, social reproduction theory intersecting the study of exploitation and social oppressions, allows us to understand how institutional actors in the labour integration process reformulate and reproduce religious, cultural, racial, and gender relations, which concretely orientate the job trajectories of the beneficiaries towards specific labour market sectors and segregate them within the broad spectrum of social reproduction jobs (from logistic to care work), that are essentials to the social reproduction of the society.

Foreign-born caregivers and the Southern European model of elder care: a reflection on the latest employment estimates

(1213) Hector Goldar Perrote, NTNU - Norwegian University of Science and Technology

Foreign-born caregivers have become essential to ensure the provision of elder care in Southern European countries. Indeed, some researchers, such as Da Roit and colleagues, speak of a 'Southern European migrant-based care model' (2013). In the case of Spain, for instance, Romero (2012) argues that said reliance has progressively led to the 'externalization' and 'denationalization' of elder care. While there is no question that these foreign workers play a fundamental role in this regard, estimating their numbers is a challenging task since a substantial proportion of them are irregularly employed. My objective in this working paper is to provide an estimate on the number of employed foreign born caregivers for both Italy and Spain. Depending on the granularity of the data, I may be able to focus on the situation in rural areas too, which is a particular interest of mine. To accomplish these goals, I will analyse Labour Force Survey data (Spanish Statistical Office/Italian National Institute of Statistics/Eurostat), which should allow me to account for irregular employment as well. My methodology section will draw from Gorfinkiel's and Martínez-Buján's example in their 2018 paper. References Da Roit, B., Gonzalez Ferrer, A., & Moreno-Fuentes, F. J. (2013). The Southern European migrant-based care model: long-term care and employment trajectories in Italy and Spain. European Societies, 15(4), 577-596. Gorfinkiel, D., & Magdalena, Y. R. M. B. (2018). Mujeres migrantes y trabajos de cuidados: transformaciones del sector doméstico en España. Panorama Social, (27), 23-36. Romero, B. A. (2012). Towards a model of externalisation and denationalisation of care? The role of female migrant care workers for dependent older people in Spain. European Journal of Social Work, 15(1), 45-61.

104

Mums@work - With migrant mothers and local decision-makers for better childcare. An innovative approach to improving day care in the Offenbach district".

(1081) Amira Bieber, European Project Management, Pro Arbeit Kreis Offenbach (AöR) Dreieich, Germany

The role of mothers in day care and reducing the lack of childcare - How to solve the lack of childcare with innovative approaches and joint effort at local level. The lack of childcare places is a structural problem in all European countries and affects both big cities and rural areas. The children of working mothers in the first years of life do not have the same framework conditions to grow up and be cared for in all European countries. Not every mother can return to work and not every child gets a place in a day care centre. For children of unemployed or single mothers, the situation is even more difficult. But what role do the mothers themselves play in this? What have mothers in Europe been demanding for decades? What are they entitled to, and what examples of successful care and reconciliation of work and family life can Europe show? This is one of the topics of european AMIF project "mums@work".

4E   Migration in the Turkish Context   AMPHI 5

Chair: Ergün Özgür, Freie Universitat Berlin & Leibniz- Zentrum Moderner Orient Berlin, Germany

1117   Homemaking in Istanbul after the fourth displacement of Syrian Circassians: The facilitating role of the Circassian diaspora networks

Ergün Özgür, Freie Universitat Berlin & Leibniz- Zentrum Moderner Orient Berlin, Germany

1285   Imagining Ἴμβρος: Conceptions of a Lost Homeland

Laura Brody, Charles University/Paul-Valery University

530   Perceptions of 1864 Circassian Migration in the Contemporary Ethnic Group Memory living in Turkey

Melike Batgiray, Max-Planck-Institut für Rechtsgeschichte und Rechtstheorie, Germany

1221   The Ones Who Walk Away': An Ethnography of Exiled Egyptian Artists in Istanbul

Mariam Diaa Agha, İbn Haldun University Istanbul, Turkey

Homemaking in Istanbul after the fourth displacement of Syrian Circassians: The facilitating role of the Circassian diaspora networks

(1117) Ergün Özgür, Freie Universitat Berlin & Leibniz- Zentrum Moderner Orient Berlin, Germany

Since the war started in Syria, many Syrian citizens, including Circassians, searched for a refugee in neighbouring countries such as Egypt, Jordan, Lebanon and Turkey. Some Syrian Circassians repatriated to their historical homelands in the Caucasus, such as

Adygea, Kabardino-Balkaria or Karachevo- Cherkessia; and Abkhazia; and others fled to the European countries. This research, based on 48 structured interviews with the representatives of NGOs, international organizations and public officials, analysis the facilitating role of the Circassian diaspora networks during the homemaking process of the Syrian Circassians in Turkey after 2011. Moreover, based on the interviews with the Syrian Circassians in Istanbul, the research discusses their perceptions about their new life, working conditions, contact with host citizens, the Circassian diaspora networks in Turkey, and their plans for the future. The ancestors of Syrian Circassians were deported from the Caucasus after 1864 (Russian - Caucasian War). Around two million people were sent to Anatolia, the Balkans, and the Middle East under the rule of the Ottoman Empire. Those Circassians in the Balkans were displaced after 1878 (Russian-Ottoman War) and resettled in the Middle East. In 1967 the Six-Day War of Israel against Syria led to their third displacement from the Golan Heights. Some resettled within Syria, and others were accepted by the USA as migrants when they gave up their land rights. In the last war that started in 2011, Syrian Circassians did not want to participate and were under the crossfire of oppositional forces and the Syrian army and displaced for the fourth time. Results show that the Circassian diaspora networks in Turkey were actively involved in the Syrian Circassians' homemaking and resettlement process. The first Circassian diaspora network having many associations in Turkey, provided humanitarian and financial materials, free accommodation, and tickets for their transfer to the cities, towns, and villages where Circassians live. They supported them to find a school for their children, tried to teach them Turkish and arranged employment opportunities. This network coordinated the repatriation of Syrian Circassians to the Caucasus, which did not reach the expected numbers. The second Circassian diaspora network arranged flights to bring Syrian Circassians to the Nizip II container camp in Gaziantep city in collaboration with the government. Their support for those Syrian Circassians outside the camp was limited compared to the first network. They gave a list of the Syrian Circassians who appealed to repatriate to the Caucasus to the Russian embassy. Both Circassian networks supported the citizenship application of the Syrian Circassians in Turkey, which is not possible for many still. In Istanbul, interviews with Syrian Circassians confirm their contacts with the Circassian diaspora networks, which became limited after the Covid-19 pandemic in 2020. Some Syrian Circassians established their work and found their association in Istanbul, and others lost their job and became more precarious after 2020. Thus, making a home in Turkey was not easy, while returning to Syria or their homelands in the Caucasus might not be an alternative for some Syrian Circassians.

Imagining Ἴμβρος: Conceptions of a Lost Homeland

(1285)   Laura Brody, Charles University/Paul-Valery University

This study turns towards the long-term impact of the 1923 Treaty of Lausanne on the island of Imvros (Gökçeada), one of the few formerly Greek Aegean islands ceded to Turkey in the aftermath of WWI. Its contents derive from 37 ethnographic interviews conducted with members of the first, second and third generations of the Imvriot diaspora who resided on Imvros, in Greece or part-time in both locations between August 2021 and March 2022. Although Imvros' native Greek-speaking population was exempt from taking part in the Greco-Turkish population exchange, the 1923 Treaty of Lausanne rendered it a minority within a new Turkish Republic, and due to Turkish nation-building strategies since 1923, most were ultimately displaced between the 1960s and 1980s. The Imvriot diaspora is unique insofar as many of its members – including those of the second and third generations – have returned to the island in recent decades for seasonal or permanent habitation, or to attend the reviving Panagia (Virgin Mary) Festival each year in August (e.g. Ercan 2020; Tsimouris 2014). Unlike many second and third generation members of other migrant diasporas who have never visited the diaspora homeland, many of those within the Imvriot diaspora thus possess not only tangible – but also frequent - memories of Imvros. As such, the Imvriot diaspora constitutes a unique case study through which to explore generational differences in migrant diasporas' relationships to their homeland, especially in cases in which tangible interactions with that homeland have increased. The objective of this paper is thus to explore patterns regarding both memories and imaginations of Imvros across differing generations of the diaspora, zoning in specifically in on two contrasting conceptions: Imvros as a place of sorrow, and Imvros as a place of joy. Due to the use of childhood memory as a reference point across generations, the patterns that have emerged from this study also relate to contrasting conceptions of Imvros' transformation over time in either a negative or positive manner. In this study, the philosopher Henri Lefebvre's (1991) notions of spatial practice (perceived space), representations of space (conceived space) and representational space (lived space) have served as a guiding lens. While much of the existing literature on Imvros focuses on issues related to the marginalisation and forced displacement of the Imvriot diaspora, as well as on transgenerational trauma evident in both memories and postmemories of these experiences (e.g. Babül 2006; Halstead 2019), this paper instead contributes new empirical data by demonstrating how different generations of the Imvriot diaspora independently negotiate their relationships to – and imaginations of - the island. In a more general sense, it also contributes on the centennial anniversary of the 1923 Treaty of Lausanne to our understanding of its continuously reverberating impact on Greek-speaking minority communities in Turkey.

References:

Babül, Elif. 2006. "No Home or Away? On the Connotations of Homeland Imaginaries in Imbros." In Diaspora and Memory: Figures of Displacement in Contemporary Literature, Arts and Politics, 43–54. Amsterdam: Rodopi.

Ercan, Sevcan. 2020. "Finding the Island of Imbros: A Spatial History of Displacement and Emplacement." UCL: Bartlett School of Architecture.

Halstead, Huw. 2019. Greeks Without Greece: Homelands, Belonging and Memory Amongst the Expatriated Greeks of Turkey. London: Routledge.

Lefebvre, Henri. 1991. The Production of Space (1974). Translated by Donald Nicholson-Smith. Oxford: Blackwell Publishing.

Tsimouris, Giorghos. 2014. "Pilgrimages to Gökçeada (Imvros), a Greco-Turkish Contested Place." In Pilgrimage, Politics and Place-Making in Eastern Europe Crossing the Borders, edited by John Eade and Mario Katić, 37–55. London: Routledge.

Perceptions of 1864 Circassian Migration in the Contemporary Ethnic Group Memory living in Turkey

(530) Melike Batgiray, Max-Planck-Institut für Rechtsgeschichte und Rechtstheorie, Germany

Circassian Migration transformed into the mass movement in the second half of the nineteenth century after the Tsarist Russia's oppressions in the area. Although it was investigated deeply, public opinion about the Circassian migration fell on stony ground. The article aims to understand how the process of migration was perceived by immigrants and how it was passed on to generations, how it was reproduced by third and the fourth generations and tries to understand their perceptions and feelings about migration. The purpose of this study was to show the perception of migration in the public's memory in the light of my experiences during the field researches I conducted in different cities of Turkey where the migrants were settled by the Ottoman Empire, not to reveal historicity. The method of the study was oral history. The study tries to explain how the immigrants' grandchildren perceives and explains the "1864". My research findings indicate that, although the Ottoman Empire's archive was relatively fertile to understand the settlements of the Circassians, there were great numbers of cases which did not reflect the Ottoman archival documents such as "lost villages". During the study, the term "lost village" was used for the abandoned or vanished villages which were given to the Circassians to settle by the Ottoman Empire. Although the first settlement history of the villages could be seen in the archival documents, it is impossible to understand the reason of being "lost" of these villages without field research and oral history. Thanks to the oral history, immigrants' unregistered stories during the road to Ottoman land filled some important gaps in migration studies thanks to the memories which were passed down by word of mouth. The another purpose of the research was to understand the ordinary immigrant who could not find a place himself in the archival documents, and the ordinary immigrant who we need to know in point of fact. It should not be forgotten that, migration was formed by individual concerns. At that point, historian needs to 153 know people's own concerns to understand the process in addition to written documents. As a result, this study has two purposes: the first is to understand the current migration perception of the descendants of the immigrants that started in 1856, and the second, more methodologically, is to reveal how useful oral history will be to historians in migration studies.

The Ones Who Walk Away': An Ethnography of Exiled Egyptian Artists in Istanbul

(1221) Mariam Diaa Agha, İbn Haldun University Istanbul, Turkey

This ethnographic fieldwork study delves into Egypt's post-2013 politically motivated migration wave. After the military takeover of the country in the summer of 2013, a considerable numbers of Islamists and members of the Muslim Brotherhood started fleeing the country in fear of the state crackdown. In the following years, they were gradually followed by a number of secular activists and intellectuals who also became targeted by the state due to their earlier affiliations and political involvement in the 2011 revolution. Exiled Egyptians found refuge in variant destinations; however, thousands of Islamists found in Turkey a sympathizing and supportive atmosphere due to the ideological ties between Turkish Islamist state officials and some Egyptian Islamic figures. Almost eight years have passed since the beginning of this migration wave, yet too little anthropological studies were carried out on this phenomenon. In this ethnography, I dig into the nuances of what it is like to be an Egyptian political migrant living in Istanbul with a particular focus on the community of exiled artists among them. Looking at the potentialities between the 'not yet' and the 'no longer' and the spaces between hope and despair, I attempt to fathom how these exiled artists interact with the political situation in Egypt given that their physical presence became elsewhere. This study was carried out between the years 2021 and 2022, combining several qualitative methodologies. I carried out 25 semi-structured in-depth interviews with variant members of that community. I also merged my interviews with a participant observation method which required me to attend social gatherings, a live concert and drama shooting days in which these artists were actively present. I also included a digital ethnography method which allowed me to explore how my interlocutors express their emotions over the digital space which is the only space that ties them to their homeland. This study also involves a discourse analysis of the Egyptian media representations of this community. Lastly, I integrated a content analysis method to highlight the recurrent themes in the drama works those artists produce. Using Victor's theory of liminality and Derrida's concept of hauntology, I argue that these artists are constantly haunted by the memory of their homeland and the spectre of the unfulfilled yearnings of the Arab Spring. In the artistic sphere, some of them find themselves reliving the pain of forcibly fleeing the country while they also find a way to escape their realities and create new meanings to transnational activism that ties them to their motherland. This ethnography adds to the quite scarce literature on the recent migration wave in Egypt and to the larger literature on political migration and exiles.

4F   Migraciones, Globalización and Transnacionalismo [ES] AMPH

Chair: Pascual Garcia, Universidad Técnica Particular de Loja, Ecuador

952   México 2021: Crisis Migratoria, de Fronteras e Institucional

> *Rodolfo García Zamora, University of Zacatecas, México*
> *Selene Gaspar Olvera, University of Zacatecas, México*
> *Francisco Javier Contreras Díaz, University of Zacatecas, México*

541   Palabras clave: Crisis Climática, Migración, Ecología, Justicia Ecológica

> *Zeynep Özlem Üskül Engin, Galatasaray University, Turkey*

1154   Migración internacional y transnacionalismo de jubilados en las costas del noroeste mexicano.

> *Pascual Garcia, Universidad Técnica Particular de Loja, Ecuador*

1228   Practicas de cuidados y acceso a la salud de las familias transnacionales que residen en Cosalá y Phoenix Arizona durante la pandemia del Sars-Cov 2

> *María José Enríquez Cabral, Universidad Autónoma de Sinaloa, Mexico*
> *Ismael García Castro, Universidad Autónoma de Sinaloa, Mexico*

México 2021: Crisis Migratoria, de Fronteras e Institucional

(952) Rodolfo García Zamora, University of Zacatecas, México

Selene Gaspar Olvera, University of Zacatecas, México

Francisco Javier Contreras Díaz, University of Zacatecas, México

Las caravanas migratorias de Centroamérica y los flujos migratorios de Haitianos de Brasil y Chile a México en 2021 coinciden con los problemas añejos de movilidad interna y hacia Estados Unidos generando una situación de crisis acumulada por décadas de ausencia de una política migratoria integral del gobierno ante las ocho dimensiones que asume la movilidad humana en el país, que provoca problemascrecientes en la Frontera Sur y Norte y en particular con Estados Unidos. Resulta evidente la crisis institucional del Estado mexicano ante la nueva realidad migratoria frente a la cual se profundiza la política de militarización contra los migrantes y de las fronteras con una mayor subordinación a las políticas migratorias, de control de fronteras y seguridad regional de Estados Unidos. México 2021: Migration Crisis, Border and Institutional Crisis The migratory caravans from Central America and the migratory flows of Haitians from Brazil and Chile in 2021 coincide with the long standing problems of internal mobility and to the United States, generating a situation of accumulated crisis due to the absence of a comprehensive migration policy by the Mexican government in the face of the eight dimensions that human mobility currently presents in the country and that causes growing problems in the Southern Border, Norther Border and in particular with the United States. Thus, it is evident the institucional crisis of Mexican State in the face of new migratory reallity, in the face of which the policy of militarization against migrants and a greater subordination to the migratory policy, border control and regional security of the United States is deeping.

Palabras clave: Crisis Climática, Migración, Ecología, Justicia Ecológica

(541) Zeynep Özlem Üskül Engin, Galatasaray University, Turkey

Durante los siglos en que el seres humano se dejó en manos de la naturaleza, no se hablaba de crisis climática. Durante siglos el hombre ha sido parte de la naturaleza, aunque ha tratado de transformarla y mejorarla, su poder no ha sido suficiente para trastornar el equilibrio del mundo. Este equilibrio se ha ido deteriorando gradualmente durante los últimos 150 años, y el punto al que hemos llegado es alentador.

El hombre moderno se siente cada vez más alejado de la naturaleza. Por un lado, da a las personas la sensación de que son modernas, que utilizan la tecnología y que están "ganando" en su lucha con la naturaleza. Se ve empujado a un entorno cada vez más artificial, cortando sus lazos con la naturaleza. Vivimos en una época en la que se considera un lujo destruir la vegetación y hacer crecer árboles en los balcones de nuestras casas inteligentes. Nuestra actitud está haciendo un gran daño al mundo y alterando el equilibrio del mundo.

Aunque se afirma que el calentamiento global afectará a varias partes del mundo, no es posible predecir cuánto se verá afectado un país a partir de hoy y si algunos lugares permanecerán intactos. Los científicos tampoco pueden predecir cómo y cuándo cambiará el clima. Queda por responder si el hemisferio norte o el hemisferio sur se calentarán.

El aire caliente hace que los glaciares se derritan, y el derretimiento de los glaciares eleva los niveles de los océanos y los mares. Esta situación amenaza por ahora a algunas islas del Océano Pacífico, y existe el peligro de que las islas queden sumergidas en un futuro próximo. El derretimiento de los glaciares también amenaza la vida de los esquimales que viven en Groenlandia. Si hay un movimiento migratorio global por sequías e inundaciones que pueden ocurrir por la crisis climática, no hay bases para solucionar el problema. Ningún país está dispuesto o preparado para recibir refugiados climáticos. Si no son los países occidentales los que no se verán obligados a migrar, es posible predecir que el mundo se enfrentará a una nueva injusticia.

Migración internacional y transnacionalismo de jubilados en las costas del noroeste mexicano.

(1154) Pascual Garcia, Universidad Técnica Particular de Loja, Ecuador

En los últimos treinta años, en el contexto de la globalización económica las migraciones han adquirido mayor importancia a nivel mundial, no sólo los flujos dirección del Sur al Norte, sino también entre regiones del Sur al Sur y en los últimos años, ha tomado un auge del Norte a Sur con determinados flujos migratorios como los de los pensionados (provenientes del norte económico) que buscan un mayor nivel de calidad de vida al final de su vida. Los cambios radicales en los medios de transporte y en las tecnologías de la información, así como el envejecimiento de la población de los países ricos, los impactos negativos de las políticas económicas de ajuste estructural en el norte y el deterioro de la calidad de vida de los jubilados, conlleva el plantearse migrar a sitios donde su bienestar no se vea mermado.

Practicas de cuidados y acceso a la salud de las familias transnacionales que residen en Cosalá y Phoenix Arizona durante la pandemia del Sars-Cov 2

(1228) María José Enríquez Cabral, Universidad Autónoma de Sinaloa, Mexico

Ismael García Castro, Universidad Autónoma de Sinaloa, Mexico

El objetivo de la presente investigación es analizar los retos y consecuencias que enfrenta la familia transnacional de estatus migratorio mixto en el acceso al derecho a la salud durante la pandemia del covid-19, y el papel del espacio social transnacional en la conformación de estrategias para enfrentar dicha problemática. En análisis que aquí se presenta es parte de un proyecto mucho más amplio que aún se encuentra en proceso. El trabajo empírico se divide en tres fases. Durante la primera fase, aplicaremos el instrumento (entrevistas a profundidad semiestructuradas) para obtener sus impresiones acerca de la problemática planteada anteriormente y las prácticas sociales que estructuran el espacio social trasnacional. Estudiar este espacio supone, entre otras cosas, la identificación y discernimiento de las prácticas sociales en la vida cotidiana que implican: comunicación transnacional, buscar y compartir informaciones, intercambiar experiencias, compartir recursos, etc. Asimismo, en este primer acercamiento indagaremos con los miembros de las FETMM que residen en Cosalá sobre contactos y distribución espacial de los familiares que residen en Phoenix. Nuestro criterio de selección en esta primera fase contempla dos exigencias: 1) miembros de familias (nuclear o extensa) que tengan familiares viviendo en Phoenix y 2) que los que están en Cosalá sean migrantes de retorno o bien, residentes del municipio por discontinuidad de la unidad familiar por migración. En el caso de que sea miembros de familia transmigrantes de retorno se considerará como parte de la muestra tanto a los retornados de manera voluntaria como por crisis económica o por causa de la pandemia. Para lograr lo anterior contamos con un portero al interior de Cosalá que nos introducirá a la comunidad y servirá de hilo conductor con familias que presenten las características mencionadas. Aplicaremos un muestreo intencionado y de referencia en cadena, este último esencial para recabar una muestra de, al menos, veinte familias transnacionales de estatus migratorio mixto. Entre las primeras afirmaciones que subyacen de esta investigación es que la esencia transnacional de las familias de estatus migratorio con lazos entre Phoenix y Cosalá, representa un recurso que les permite trazar redes de apoyo en ambos lados de la frontera y que facilitan estrategias de cuidado y acceso a la salud para sobrellevar la enfermedad producida por el virus del sars-cov 2. El apoyo no solo consiste en ayuda material, sino también en soporte emocional transnacional que coadyuva a la minimización del miedo que representa contraer dicho padecimiento. Algunos miembros que residen en Phoenix y no logran mantener sus redes sociales y sus prácticas transnacionales, tanto materiales como afectivas desarrollan, eventualmente, un retorno a Cosalá.

4G   Managing Migration   AMPHI 7

Chair: Sherry-Ann Singh, University of West Indies, Trinidad and Tobago

1295   Turkish Migrants in Russia: Problems and Prospects

Irina Alexandrovna Savchenko, Moscow City University and Linguistics University of Nizhny Novgorod and Nizhny Novgorod Academy of the Ministry of Internal Affairs of Russia
Ali Ihsan Genç, Linguistics University of Nizhny Novgorod, Russia

602   From India to the Caribbean: A Story of Indian Migration, Adaptation and Community (Re)constitution

Sherry-Ann Singh, University of West Indies, Trinidad and Tobago

1120   Between migration policy and migration management: The EU case

Marita Brcic Kuljis, University of Split, Croatia

1313   Birthplace Security: The Missing Link to Preventing Forced Migration and Displacement

Elizabeth Pearl Morgan, American University, USA

Turkish Migrants in Russia: Problems and Prospects

(1295) Irina Alexandrovna Savchenko, Moscow City University and Linguistics University of Nizhny Novgorod and Nizhny Novgorod Academy of the Ministry of Internal Affairs of Russia

Ali Ihsan Genç, Linguistics University of Nizhny Novgorod, Russia

Migrants from Turkey who come to Russia to work or study face certain problems and expectations [Içduygu A, Karaçay AB. 2012]. We will talk about the main difficulties, as well as the prospects for Turkish citizens in Russia. Our study is based on the data of a sociological survey (December 2021 - January 2022) held among Turkish citizens living in Russia (n=174).

The Turks' rejection of the gastronomic habits of Russians is not specific. Turks (as well as many other migrants (with the exception of people from East Slavic countries) are especially shocked by "raw foods" (meat or fish). Here is a typical Turkish opinion about Russian cuisine: "There is a herring (salted raw fish) that Russians eat even on holidays, but this is not at all suitable for Turks, we do not understand how it is possible to eat fish that is not cooked on fire."

Such a retreat is actually very representative and testifies to the difference in the worldviews of Russians and Turks. And such a difference is difficult to overcome. Russians are sure that fish or meat that has been salted abundantly ceases to be raw and suitable for food after a few days. Turks consider it inedible. Meanwhile, for Russians staying in Turkey, it is wild that it is impossible to find salted herring in a supermarket.

If we talk about the expectations of people who come to Russia from Turkey, then perhaps the most important of them is the hope that obtaining a visa and residence permit will be simplified. Currently, the simplified visa system is available only for truck drivers and so-called "white collar workers". Many people hope that the Russian government and the Turkish one will sign an agreement that will eliminate the problems and meet the expectation.

Of the surveyed migrants, 33.5% want to obtain Russian citizenship, and 20% dream of becoming a citizen of the United States. For 26.8%, the most pressing problem is money. Practically all migrants are concerned about the current political situation, rising airfare and changes that have swept the world's payment systems. In general, today we can talk about a "new" mutual influence of migration and remittances [Sirkeci et al 2012].

Despite all the difficulties that Turkish citizens face when coming to Russia, it still remains attractive for migration, and the number of Turkish citizens coming here is growing.

References:

Içduygu A., Karaçay A.B. 2012 'The international migration system between turkey and Russia: project-tied migrant workers in Moscow', International Migration'. V 50, no 1, pp. 55-74.

Sirkeci I, Cohen JH, Ratha D. 2012 'Migration and Remittances during the Global Financial Crisis and Beyond'. L. World Bank, 2012. 480 p.

From India to the Caribbean: A Story of Indian Migration, Adaptation and Community (Re)constitution

(602) Sherry-Ann Singh, University of West Indies, Trinidad and Tobago

Between 1838 and 1920, more than half a million Indians migrated to the Caribbean under the system of Indian indenture; about 85% of whom opted to make the Caribbean their permanent home. Though in essence an exploitative, apathetic and rapacious system, Indian indenture changed the lives of these Indians immigrants, and the face of the Caribbean. Today, Indians are ingrained into the very fabric of the Caribbean community; comprising the ethnic majorities in British Guiana, Trinidad and Tobago and Surinam. Moving arduously through the processes of rupture, dispersal, displacement, relocation, reconsolidation, assimilation and integration, the Indian communities throughout the Caribbean have made significant contributions to all facets of Caribbean life; both at the level of colony/country and at the regional level. Whether in agriculture, the professions, or the industrial, commercial, petroleum and energy sectors, Indians have become an integral part of the social and economic triumphs and travails of the Caribbean, and the region's social, cultural and religious life has been indelibly coloured by the Indian presence. Like all diaspora communities, however, they have engaged endlessly with the diasporic dilemma of straddling two worlds - the ancestral homeland and their Caribbean reality - a checkered journey fraught with sweat, tears and nostalgia, but also charged with new opportunities and challenges that held often indiscernible promises of fulfilment; personally and as a people. This paper seeks to examine the aforementioned issues within the framework of the Caribbean as essentially a diaspora-based region. It charts the journey via which Indians have emerged as communities ready to embark on the many new journeys and experiences necessary to take them from whole yet varyingly marginalized communities at the end of the system of Indian indenture, to the fully integrated yet distinct entities that they are today as both Caribbean people and Indo-Caribbean communities.

Between migration policy and migration management: The EU case

(1120) Marita Brcic Kuljis, University of Split, Croatia

In the first pages of the New Pact on Migration and Asylum 2020, the European Commission states that it strives to " build a system that manages and normalises migration for the long term and which is fully grounded in European values and international law". The process of agreeing on migration policies in the European Union is extremely complex. The reasons are multiple, but the key ones are those that refer to the relationship between the sovereignty of the national community and the goals of the supranational community. In addition, major problems for the implementation of an acceptable model of migration management and the ever-present anti-immigrant attitudes among the citizens of the European Union.

In this paper, we will present the model of migration management in the European Union in the context of the relationship between the man (human rights)- the nation-state (sovergenity)- the supranational community (?).

All this will be analyzed in the context of liberal democracy as the ruling political paradigm of the European Union. Special emphasis will be placed on the analysis of the relationship between migration policy, which is more national policy, and migration management, which is more supranational policy.

Birthplace Security: The Missing Link to Preventing Forced Migration and Displacement

(1313) Elizabeth Pearl Morgan, American University, USA

By the time the Drafting Committee for the 1948 Universal Declaration of Human Rights gathered to write the protocol, the nations involved had long forgotten their cultural memory and implication of forced uprooting. In fact, some of the members had not experienced being forced from their homeland. Rather, most of the Committee members—Charles Dukes (United Kingdom of Great Britain and Northern Ireland), John Peters Humphrey (Canada) Alexander E. Bogomolov (Soviet Union), René Cassin (France), Hernán Santa Cruz (Chile), William Hodgson (Australia), and Peng-chun Chang (China)—represented imperial legacies that enjoyed the opposite dimension of forced human movement. Beknown to them was a profound appreciation for the freedom of movement and its symbolism of free will. Yet their lack of experience with not having had to make the choice as nations to flee in order to survive has left a gap in the international community's understanding of what humanity is entitled to by natural right. Missing from the Declaration is the perspective of forced migrants, who, were it their choice to enjoy staying, would not risk a dangerous journey from their birthplace and homeland in search of survival, let alone to lead a dignified life.

The inevitable and unfortunate consequence of failing to protect the freedom of establishment—the freedom to stay where one was born and established their livelihood—is the international community's disregard for the long-term impact of causing forced uprooting. In our globalized world, international security depends on the sustainability of agricultural and resource rich nations and the capacity to self-determination of native populations. This research paper will demonstrate birthplace security—the freedom not to move—as the missing link in the post-imperial conceptualization of universal human rights. It employs quantitative research using the datasets from the Armed Conflict Location & Event Data Project, the Migration Governance Indicators (MGI), and The Economist Intelligence Unit to argue that improving the self-determination potential of native populations to stay (as well as to return home) within underdeveloped countries has a greater benefit for the national security of developed countries than imposing restrictive measures such as migration protocols and border detention and housing.

Key Preliminary Datasets and Sources

The Migration Data Portal. https://www.migrationdataportal.org/international-data?i=stock_abs_&t=2020. Last updated 20 January 2021.

The Universal Declaration of Human Rights. https://www.un.org/en/about-us/universal-declaration-of-human-rights.

The Economist Intelligence Unit. Democracy Index. https://www.eiu.com/n/campaigns/democracy-index-2020/.

Forced Migration Review. Return: voluntary, safe, dignified and durable? FMR 62, October 2019. https://www.fmreview.org/return.

Raleigh, Clionadh, Andrew Linke, Håvard Hegre, and Joakim Karlsen. (2010). "Introducing ACLED-Armed Conflict Location and Event Data." *Journal of Peace Research 47(5) 651- 660.* www.acleddata.com.

4H   Migratory Stratifications ONLINE

Chair: Giulia Storato, University of Turin, Italy

1076   Overwriting the (multicultural) city. The Arcella neighborhood in Padua (Italy) as an urban palimpsest

Adriano Cancellieri, Universite Iuav di Venezia, Italy

1050   Overlapping frontiers: Monfalcone and the stratification of labor migrations

Giuseppe Grimaldi, University of Trieste, Italy

1071   Purgatory of Transition: A Case Study among Migrant Weavers in the Perspective of Migratory Stratification in the City of Sambalpur, India

Bandana Meher, Sambalpur University, India
Kumar Acharya, Sambalpur University, India

1051   Agribusiness and migration: the analysis of the ages of Paraguayan rural emigration from the perspective of migratory stratifications

Juliana Carpinetti, Universidad Nacional de Rafaela (UNRaf) - Argentina Consejo Nacional de Investigaciones Científicas y Técnicas (CONICET), Argentina

1090   Victoria Square, Athens: crossroads of trajectories, space in transformation. Migratory movements and social stratifications in the centre of the Greek capital

Chiara Martini, Independent researcher, Greece

Overwriting the (multicultural) city. The Arcella neighborhood in Padua (Italy) as an urban palimpsest

(1076) Adriano Cancellieri, Universite Iuav di Venezia, Italy

The aim of the proposal is to analyze a portion of the multicultural neighborhood of Arcella in Padua (Italy) as an urban palimpsest in which urban traces and layers of different migratory cycles can be identified. The Arcella neighborhood is an area that has long been invested by a series of migratory stratifications, driven by changing global and local scenarios (e.g. Eastern enlargement of European Union and African refugee crisis). The case study sub-area is in *Via Bernina 18*, a small complex of former warehouses that, in the last fifteen years, have become the place of gathering for an Islamic cultural center, an evangelical Chinese church, a Moldovan Orthodox church, a Hindu Temple, eight different Pentecostal Nigerian communities and two African cultural centers.

A territorial and diachronic perspective will be adopted. This spatio-temporal perspective is quite rare in migration and even urban studies, but there are some notable exceptions. See in particular Maffi's (1995) urban history work on New York's Lower East Side and Quayson's (2014) work on Accra's Oxford Street and a range of longitudinal work in anthropology, geography and sociology (see for example Small, 2004; Çağlar and Glick Schiller, 2018; Flint Ashery and Stadler, 2021).

The paper will focus in particular: a) on the urban traces that the different migration cycles have left in urban spaces; b) on the entanglement between these different urban sediments that work as constraints and opportunities and the everyday *overwriting of the city*.

References:

Çağlar, A. and Glick Schiller, N. (2018). *Migrants and City-Making. Dispossession, Displacement, and Urban Regeneration*, Durham and London: Duke University Press.

Flint Ashery, S. and Stadler, N. (2021). *Palimpsests and urban pasts: The janus-faced nature of Whitechapel.* PLoS ONE, 16 (9).

Maffi, M. (1995). *Gateway to the Promised Land: Ethnicity and Culture in New York's Lower East Side.* New York: New York University Press.

Quayson, A. (2014). *Oxford Street, Accra.* Durham NC: Duke University Press.

Small, M. (2004). *Villa Victoria. The Transformation of Social Capital in a Boston Barrio.* Chicago: The Chicago University Press.

Overlapping frontiers: Monfalcone and the stratification of labor migrations

(1050) Giuseppe Grimaldi, University of Trieste, Italy

The paper explores the different meaning associated with frontier spaces in Europe and their effects in the stratification of its migrant labor force. It focuses on Monfalcone, in the Italian North East, a maritime town at the border with Slovenia that hosts the most important state-driven ship construction hub in Italy, Fincantieri. In the second part of the XX century Monfalcone represented part of the frontier between western and eastern world; for this reason, it was the recipient of massive industrial public investments with state driven hiring politics as part of the economic, political, military measures aimed at controlling the border. The cantiere, in this respect, represented a frontier space aimed at fixing the land and its people (Turner, 1921). With the fall of the iron curtain, however, public investments dramatically decreased: the "cantiere" survived thanks to private cooperatives that hired laborers for lower salaries and worse conditions. The new configuration attracted a very high flow of migrants from the Balkan regions, from southern Italy and especially from Bangladesh. The processes of reconfiguration of the labor force in Monfalcone suggests to consider different meanings associated to the concept of frontier in Europe: besides the Eastern-Western dichotomy, in fact, Europe, have always reproduced its identity along the frontier opposing "modernity" to "primitiveness". (Moe, 2004). This frontier materializes in the relation with the so-called Global South.Nowadays the highly productive economic contexts of the European peripheries (such as Monfalcone) that are connoted by huge economic flows and, at the same time, severe marginality of the labor force materialize this frontier (Raeymaekers, 2021). The ethnographic analysis of the way the frontiers between Europeanness and otherness modify and overlap represents a vantage point to consider the processes of stratification of the labor force in Europe.

Purgatory of Transition: A Case Study among Migrant Weavers in the Perspective of Migratory Stratification in the City of Sambalpur, India

(1071) Bandana Meher, Sambalpur University, India

Kumar Acharya, Sambalpur University, India

In the diachronic perspective of migration in urban spaces, there is the movement of human resources in each generation. It slowly shapes the new community developed in the shadow of change in occupation. The change in occupation result of migration to the new community impact the social representation of the group. In the above context, there was the occurrence of movement among weavers of Sambalpuri textile to the non-weaving profession. The change from skilled labour in rural to unskilled labour gave rise to migratory stratification. In search of a better future from a renowned caste-based occupation in the rural areas, they migrated to become working class in the urban space. The present study tries to explore the reason for their migration to urban areas through an inter-generational perspective. This study also did a situational analysis of their identity in the context of migratory stratification and how it affected their social status in the migrated community from their native one. The study was conducted among the weavers of Sambalpuri textile popularly known as Bhulia caste, found in the western part of Odisha, India. They are experts in weaving Sambalpuri textile with intricate designs in handloom, through tie and dye technique.

Agribusiness and migration: the analysis of the ages of Paraguayan rural emigration from the perspective of migratory stratifications

(1051) Juliana Carpinetti, Universidad Nacional de Rafaela (UNRaf) - Argentina Consejo Nacional de Investigaciones Científicas y Técnicas (CONICET), Argentina

The objective of this presentation is to analyze the relationship between: a) the transformations that the advance of the agribusiness model prints in the Paraguayan rural universe; b) the configuration of its inhabitants as potential emigrants; and c) the way in which the latter go through, redefine and signify their entire migratory process; through the perspective of migratory stratifications. To achieve its, utilizes the theoretical concept of "emigration ages" developed by A. Sayad. This category allows us to reflect on the relationship between the different stages in the transformations of the peasant social order, on the one hand, and the types of emigration and emigrants that they produce, on the other; assuming that the different ages of emigration correspond to different phases of the process of internal transformation of the rural communities that produce emigrants. The methodological strategy developed consists in a diachronic analysis, based on the confrontation of two large corpus of data: 1) the surveys carried out by T. Palau et al to residents of different rural communities of Paraguay during an investigation published in 2007; 2) the interviews conducted during my doctoral research with Paraguayan immigrants from rural areas and actually residing in the city of Rosario, Argentina, presented in 2020. The results obtained allow us to infer that, in the decade passed between the collection of both corpus of data, the transformations generated in the emigration society as a result of the expansion of the agribusiness model, finds its correlate in the sedimentation of various migratory ages that range from a first phase in which migration is completely at the service of the reproduction of the original peasant society, to a third in which it has become almost completely autonomous from it.

Victoria Square, Athens: crossroads of trajectories, space in transformation. Migratory movements and social stratifications in the centre of the Greek capital

(1090) Chiara Martini, Independent researcher, Greece

Greece is one of the European countries most frequently crossed by incoming and outgoing migratory movements. For decades it has been one of the main entry points into Europe. In different periods and to different extents, the people who have passed through or settled in Greece have brought about profound changes, transforming its places, dynamics and the whole social fabric. By using the concept of "migratory stratification", this paper will try to analyse the reality of a specific urban space, located in the Greek capital, namely Victoria Square, which has become over the years a symbol of the migratory phenomena that have invested and is still investing the city and the whole country. The transformations and stratifications affecting this square, and the entire surrounding neighbourhood, began when numerous immigrants from the Philippines in the late 1980s, from Albania in 1991 and from Eastern Europe after the fall of the Berlin Wall, settled in, profoundly changing its social fabric and dynamics. These processes continue today: over the last few years, Victoria Square has become a sort of hub for refugees, immigrants and asylum seekers, for their shops, their informal networks, their interactions and exchanges; it is a place of departure, arrival, meeting and conflict, a space where one can seek and give visibility to the dramatic conditions in which migrants are forced to live in Greece. Starting from an empirical research on the field and in the light of the migratory phenomena and social transformations occurred, in this paper we will therefore try to analyse this particular context, by highlighting the interactions, interweaving and relationships that are triggered in such plural, layered and heterogeneous situations.

4J   PANEL: Feminization of Migration in India [ONLINE]

Moderator: Dr Ruchi Singh, Prin.L.N.Welingkar Institute of Management Development & Research, India

Speakers

Dr. Marie Percot, IIMAD, India

Dr. Amba Pande, Jawaharlal Nehru University, New Delhi, India

Dr. Archana K Roy, International Institute for Population Sciences, India

Day Two 8 September 2022 Thursday

Day Two 8 September 2022 - 16:15-17:45   AMPHI 1

5A   Workshop: Immigration and Civil Society [AR – FR]

الجلسة الخامسة: المجتمع المدني و قضايا الهجرة

Chair: D. Malika Ibn Radi, Honorary Professor, Mohammed V University of Rabat, Morocco

منسقة الورشة: دة. مليكة ابن الراضي إستاذة فخرية جامعة محمد الخامس بالرباط، المغرب

565 Fondation Orient Occident: les femmes migrantes au Maroc

567 Caritas: les mineurs non accompagnés

GADEM: « Le cadre juridique relatif au droit des étrangers au Maroc ».

568 Jacques OULD AOUDIA, vice-président de l'ONG Migrations et Développement: le migrant comme acteur de développement dans sa région d'origine

565 Dr Ahmed Zekri: L'Association Marocaine d'Etudes et de Recherches sur les Migrations: La société civile actrice de la recherche sur les questions migratoires

5B   New Challenges in Migration Studies   AMPHI 2

Chair: Ülkü Sezgi Sözen, Universität Hamburg, Germany

1178   The Serbian Paradox: Negative Attitudes and Migration Aspirations Towards the West

Mirjana Stanojević, Faculty of Science, Masaryk University, Czech Republic

533   Who says what? Racial ratification of in-groups and social desirability

Caroline Adolfsson, Malmö University, Sweden

1199   Analysing migrants' perception of Europe - Security and Human Rights Implications

Aitana Radu, University of Malta, Malta
Joseph Cannataci, University of Groningen, Netherlands

1121   Pathologies of Living together: Integration of Immigrants, Recognition and Possibilities of Solidarity

Gulay Ugur Goksel, Istanbul Bilgi University, Turkey

The Serbian Paradox: Negative Attitudes and Migration Aspirations Towards the West

(1178) Mirjana Stanojević, Faculty of Science, Masaryk University, Czech Republic

Serbia and especially peripheral, rural regions bypassed by big industrialisation projects in SFR Yugoslavia, such is the Pomoravlje region, have been a significant source of economic migrants (the Gastarbeiter) since the '60. What was initially planned as a temporary stay gained more permanent characteristics when the Gastarbeiter were joined by their families. The Serbian diaspora's importance and power significantly grew in the 90s, when FR Yugoslavia became isolated due to wars and sanctions. Households with migratory experience became distinctive with their economic and material wealth and possession of western brands that were out of reach for those without family members abroad. Due to growing negative attitudes toward the West and growing mistrust in political elites and media, the diaspora's first-hand experience became the primary source of information about the West. However, many diaspora members did not integrate into host societies, and their perception of the West often encouraged existing occidentalist images of cold, soulless, money-driven Westerners. (Volčić, 2005) Antonijević (2013) also argues that the Gastarbeiter did not have characteristics of transmigrants due to their non-integration. Nonetheless, the West has been a popular destination for aspiring migrants because it is perceived as a contrast to Serbia in terms of employment, meritocracy, and wealth.

The migrant aspirations and attitudes toward the imagined West were examined amongst the youth in the Serbian region of Pomoravlje during the year 2021 via semi-structured interviews, focus groups and autoethnographic research. The youth incorporate persons who grew up in Serbia during the "era of entrapment", first due to wars and sanctions and subsequently due to strict visa regimes and poverty. (Jansen, 2009) As an international student residing in the EU and originating from this region, I was given a unique position of both an insider and outsider, and my presence has, without exception, provoked a debate about "here" and "there".

I argue that negative attitudes towards the West and strong national ethos, both reproduced through the diaspora's experience, push potential migrants into temporality even before they have experienced precarious jobs, strict immigration policies and segregation abroad. Since the West is perceived solely as a source of economic power and Serbia as a source of all the other values, many of my interlocutors plan to emigrate temporarily for the amount of time necessary to fulfil their career and financial goals. Since they do not plan their stay as permanent, they often mobilise only the minimal resources necessary for leaving. Many do not plan to join the Western societies but the Serbian diaspora in the West, so they do not consider integration. (Gardner, 1993) Anđić (2020) wrote about Serbian "blocked future "and futurelessness". I argue that Pomoravlje youth's future is not necessarily blocked but rather delayed. The delayed future relates to reproduced temporality – many interlocutors plan their future in Pomoravlje, but after returning from abroad. This mechanism enables the reproduction of negative sentiments toward the West together with migratory aspirations toward the West.

References:

Anđić, T. (2020). Futurelessness, migration, or a lucky break: narrative tropes of the 'blocked future'among Serbian high school students. Journal of Youth Studies, pp. 430-446.

Antonijević, D. (2013). Stranac ovde, stranac tamo. Srpski genealoški centar.

Gardner, K. (1993). Desh-Bidesh: Sylheti images of home and away. Man, pp. 1-15.

Jansen, S. (2009). After the Red Passport: Towards an Anthropology of the Everyday Geopolitics of Entrapment in the EU's 'Immediate Outside. The Journal of the Royal Anthropological Institute, pp. 815-832.

Volčić, Z. (2005). The notion of 'the West'in the Serbian national imaginary. pp. 155-175.

Who says what? Racial ratification of in-groups and social desirability

(533) Caroline Adolfsson, Malmö University, Sweden

Despite pushes towards colorblind and post racial ideology, Sweden remains entangled in its own ratification of whiteness as a mechanism for in-group inclusion. In this experiment, white natives and non-white natives/migrants descendants were asked to rate multiracial faces to estimate perceived Swedishness and then, afterwards in de-briefing interviews, reflected on their choices. Results show that the white faces were more predominately indicated as Swedish. Additionally, those with a foreign background were more likely to ratify ethnic Swedish racial stereotyping than Swedes. Most white respondents showed high social desirability effects, rejecting that they endorsed racial stereotyping around the ethnized perception of Swedishness, despite rating non-white faces as less Swedish. Previous research has shown that the stronger the social norm, the greater likelihood of social desirability bias is to occur (Fisher, 1993). Two conflicting social norms present themselves here: (1) that of Swedish post-racialism and colorblindness where discussions of racial and racialization are uncomfortable and preferably not discussed and (2) white hegemony within Sweden. Despite the Swedish participants guilt and claims of focusing on national over ethnic categorizations, survey data shows that Swedish participants were more likely to rate the white faces as more Swedish than the non-white faces. This article contributes to the growing body of racial and ethnic studies research in Sweden.

Analysing migrants' perception of Europe - Security and Human Rights Implications

(1199) Joseph Cannataci, University of Groningen, Netherlands

The perception of Europe and of individual European countries as a desired target for migration has a high impact on the decision-making process of individuals from outside Europe considering coming to Europe, both in terms of 'big' decisions, such as selection of final destination and transit route and of 'smaller' decisions such as interaction with border guards or willingness to undergo medical checks on arrival. Perception may well differ from reality due to incomplete information, wrongly understood information or intentional dissemination of fake information, among other factors. A good understanding of migrants' perceptions is therefore essential to ensure that both their well-being and security is preserved through culturally-sensitive treatment on arrival and the national security of Member States is protected by preventing the proliferation of potentially-dangerous or disruptive behaviour. This study will introduce a Perception Model for studying migrant's perceptions of Europe, based on the Theory of Planned Behaviour (Ajzen, 1991), which focuses on a set of undesirable behaviours (e.g. lying about one's identity, refusing to provide biometrics data, concealing the identity of human smugglers), which can, in certain circumstances, materialize into, on the one hand threats to the migrant's wellbeing, and/or chance to be granted asylum, and on the other threats to public order or national security. For each such behaviour the model identifies a number of behavioural, normative and control beliefs that can be employed to predict the probability of a certain behaviour being displayed and to better understand the reasons why an individual or community displays a certain behaviour. Furthermore, the study will then examine the policy implications of integrating such a model in the threat analysis models employed at European and national levels. The focus is to better understand what are the limitations of the existing risk analysis methodologies employed by Frontex (e.g. CIRAM) and national Member States and what could be the added value for policy-making in introducing an additional migrant-centric analytical component. In addition to the operational value, the study will also discuss the human rights perspective of employing such a model in border security. The focus here will not only be on the rights of privacy, data protection and association but the paper will explore broader implications such as discrimination, inequality, bias and lack of due process. In its analysis the paper will base itself on the results of two research projects (H2020 MIRROR and H2020 CRITERIA), which were the frameworks in which the Perception model was designed and tested within a broad base of stakeholders.

References:

Icek Ajzen, The theory of planned behavior, Organizational Behavior and Human Decision Processes, Volume 50, Issue 2, 1991, Pages 179-211, ISSN 0749-5978, https://doi.org/10.1016/07 49- 978(91)90020-T.

Migration-Related Risks caused by misconceptions of Opportunities and Requirement (MIRROR), https://h2020mirror.eu/ Comprehensive data-driven Risk and Threat Assessment Methods for the Early and Reliable Identification, Validation and Analysis of migration-related risks (CRITERIA), https://www.project-criteria.eu/

Pathologies of Living together: Integration of Immigrants, Recognition and Possibilities of Solidarity

(1121) Gulay Ugur Goksel, Istanbul Bilgi University, Turkey

"Integration" is a treacherous concept. It has been ideologically employed by many politicians and academics to perpetuate colonial inequalities, discrimination and exclusion. Today, many western scholars (Schinkel 2019) argue that immigrant integration studies are an imposition and warn us that by focusing on the integration studies, we reproduce historical epistemological categories that cause injustice in the first place. Many claims that the concept is normatively ideological and harmful. While I agree with these criticisms, I do not agree with the suggestion that we should discard the concept altogether. I contend that if we orient our focus away from unfounded ideals such as social cohesion and reinterpret the concept from a Recognition theoretical perspective, the obsession with nationalism, borders and security can be disfigured. Recognition theory can breathe life into the concept of "integration" and help us to better understand what it means to live together with diversity. In this chapter, through an analysis and an application of Parekh, Tully and Honneth's theories of recognition, I will lay out a new account of "just integration" based on normative values of inclusion and individualization. In addition, I will focus on possibilities of solidarity in society within the framework of theory of recognition. I will focus on immigrant groups'(invented) recognition orders to understand how the reconfigurations of host society by immigrant groups effect possibilities of solidarity and reduce some pathologies that emanate from living together.

5C   Impact of COVID-19 on Migration   AMPHI 3

Chair   Roberta Ricucci, University of Turin, Italy

1167   Health risks for international migrants during COVID-19 pandemic in Russia

Olga Borodkina, St Petersburg University, Russia
Maria Ivanova, St Petersburg University, Russia

Health risks for international migrants during COVID-19 pandemic in Russia

(1167) Olga Borodkina, St Petersburg University, Russia

Maria Ivanova, St Petersburg University, Russia

The COVID-19 epidemic has led to serious social and economic, but also significant health problems among international migrants. For many years, Russia is a host country for significant number of migrants, primarily from the countries of the former Soviet Union. **The research methods** were the analysis of statistical data and data from studies conducted among labor migrants in Russia, expert interviews and in-depth with migrants. **Research results** demonstrated Health risks of migrants, which have always been highly valued, have increased significantly in the context of the COVID-19 pandemic. In addition to tuberculosis and HIV, Covid-19 has taken a leading position among infectious diseases. This fact is largely due to the unfavorable living conditions of migrants, which excluded the possibility of ensuring social distancing, that increases the risk of the spread of COVID-19. International migrants remain one of the most stigmatized and discriminated groups; many of the infected migrants tend to hide diseases in order to avoid its greater stigmatization. In addition, as studies show the fear of being unemployed prevails over the fear of contracting coronaviruses. Online surveys conducted in Russia indicate a widespread covid dissidence among migrants (almost 25%), that is, a conscious refusal to vaccinate (V. Mukomel et al.). The unfavorable socioeconomic conditions, limited prevention resources, shortage of medicines, poor awareness about prevention measures, lead to high risks of COVID-19 and other diseases. In Russia, a foreign citizen is currently eligible for free COVID-19 treatment because this infection is included in the list of socially dangerous diseases, but subject to the availability of a compulsory medical insurance. However, only a very small part of migrants who are citizens of member countries of The Eurasian Economic Union (Armenia, Belarus, Kazakhstan, Kyrgyzstan) working under an employment contract, as well as having residence has this form of insurance have this kind of insurance.

Other migrants staying in the Russia on the basis of employment under patents cannot apply for this document. They are required to have a voluntary medical insurance, while most international migrants try to purchase the cheapest medical insurance program, that does not provide treatment for infectious diseases including COVID-19. As a result, a significant part of the international migrants remains out of obtaining the necessary medical care during a pandemic, which negatively affects not only the health of migrants, but also the epidemiological situation in general. In **conclusion**, it should be noted that reducing the health risks of international migrants requires, first of all, the adoption of state programs for the free COVID-19 vaccination of migrants and access of migrants to medical treatment for infectious diseases. Secondly, the state should support NGOs which play key role of disseminating information about infectious diseases and their prevention among international migrants, including in foreign languages.

Acknowledgment. The research was carried out in St. Petersburg University with the financial support of the RSF, the project № 22-18-00261.

Social vulnerability of international migrants in the context of the COVID-19 epidemic

(1207) Mariia Ivanova, St Petersburg University, Russia

Olga Borodkina, St Petersburg University, Russia

The COVID-19 epidemic has exacerbated the existing discrimination and social vulnerability of international migrants. Migrants now constitute a significant proportion of the labor force in many countries. Migrant workers and their families made a considerable contribution to economic development in their countries of origin, as well as to their countries of destination. The crisis made quite clear systemic inequalities between the native population and migrants. The Covid-19 pandemic has increased the vulnerability of international migrants. The research task related to the analysis of the main determinants of migrant vulnerability in current conditions is identified. As a theoretical framework for the study were the theory of social vulnerability" the pressure and release (PAR) model and the determinants of migrant vulnerability (DoMV) model. Research methods: the first stage of the study analysed background information based on data collected from available governmental and non-governmental sources (legislative acts, official statistics on international migration). The second stage of the study included the qualitative methods. In order to assess the general conditions of the COVID-19 pandemic crisis and the extent of its impact on the migration community, semi-structured expert interviews were conducted with heads of non-profit NGOs dealing with migration issues and in-depth interviews with international migrants in St. Petersburg, Russia.The findings of the study: The legal status of international migrants. The lack of official legal status of a migrant is a key determinant of vulnerability to the consequences of the COVID-19 pandemic; Access of international migrants to health services. Many migrants do not receive medical care during the pandemic, which negatively affects not only the health of migrants, but also the epidemiological situation in general; Professional risks of international migrants. Significant difficulties in the labor market are associated with informal relations with employers. In addition, the pandemic mainly affected employment in the service sectors, where migrants are mostly represented; The housing conditions of migrants. The housing conditions of migrants is characterized by a higher population density, which makes it difficult to provide of social distancing, thereby migrants are more vulnerable to COVID-19 infection and at the same time pose an epidemic threat to others; The public attitudes towards international migrants. Respondents among migrants claim that during the pandemic they have faced an increase in xenophobia; The education of migrant' children. Many children often do not have technical opportunities for online education, in addition, the low level of education and poor Russian language skills of their parents make difficult the home education since online classes require the support of adult family members; Social support for international migrants. Social support for migrants is fragmented, there is no systematic approach to reducing the social vulnerability of the migration community during the pandemic.The social vulnerability of migrants affects not only the social situation of migrants themselves but also the host society; that is especially important to take into account in the situation of the COVID-19 epidemic.

Acknowledgment. The research was carried out in St. Petersburg University with the financial support of the RSF, the project – 19-18-00246

Expect the Unexpected: The Impact of the Global Pandemic on Mobility Strategies. A Case Study with Italian Highly-Skilled Movers in and Beyond Europe

(1243) Tanja Schroot, University of Turin, Italy

Roberta Ricucci, University of Turin, Italy

Recent studies (World Bank 2021) confirm the massive consequences of the pandemic on human capital development and the urgent need for research in order to direct international human capital investment and recruitment.The fast-pacing formulations for needed skill sets in the near future and thus evolving lacunas for qualified labour, hamper the significance to investigate on drivers that cause, alter and amplify mobility decisions of knowledgeable movers (Lulle et 40 al. 2021). A vast body of research supports this perspective and point to the linked significance of family (King and Lulle 2016) and subjective indicators for a positively perceived life-quality that move beyond economic benefits (Schroot, Marroccoli 2021), which becomes even more central in the context of the worldwide pandemic and presumed altered decisional dynamics for onward or return migration. This is where the current study ties in, that investigated with data from a total of 25 qualitative interviews from highly-qualified Italians living abroad in and beyond the European space how the pandemic has impacted their thoughts on future mobility strategies in the context of the paradigmatic life course framework. Findings suggest a strong correlation between conditions caused by the global COVID crisis and the sense of belonging on the one hand, and the (re)definition of expected living standards in the host context on the other hand.

Impact of COVID19 on the Educational Experiences, Grassroots Research and Community Organizing of Latinx Immigrant Communities in Philadelphia, PA (USA).

(1100) Alicia Rusoja, University of California, Davis, USA

This multimodal presentation will focus on a subset of data from an ongoing and longitudinal participatory action research study, designed and led by Latinx immigrants themselves, that addresses the following questions: (1) What are the short-term and longer-term intergenerational impacts of COVID19 on the lives, the education, and political mobilization of Latinx immigrants who have been organizing together in Philadelphia (USA) for their own and fellow marginalized BIPOC (Black, Indigenous, Peoples of Color) communities' human rights?; (2) How do these Latinx immigrants make sense of and respond to the impact of COVID19 on their lives?; and (3) What needs, interests, questions, lenses and relationships (including with fellow marginalized Black Indigenous Peoples of Color) shape their individual and communal responses to the pandemic's short and long-term impact?Methods included in-depth interviews with 15 Latinx immigrants as well as fieldnotes and photography. Analysis was done iteratively through the use of analytical memos (Saldaña, 2015), thematic coding (Strauss & Corbin, 1998) and member checks (Delgado Bernal, 1998).A central finding is that COVID-19 has greatly impacted the political mobilization of Latinx immigrants in Philadelphia, including by leading them to utilize grassroots research to document silenced and ignored realities of Latinx immigrant children, youth and adults within schools, and to utilize their findings take action to advocate for themselves through what the author terms "communal research justice." ReferencesFalicov, C., Niño, A., & D'Urso, S. (2020). Expanding Possibilities: Flexibility and Solidarity with Under resourced Immigrant Families During the COVID_9 Pandemic. Family process, 59(3), 865-882.Jolivétte, A. (Ed.). (2015). Research justice: Methodologies for Social Change. Policy Press.

5D   Migration Theory and Methods   AMPHI 4

Chair: Justyna Salamonska, Kozminski University, Poland

1144   Re-conceptualising free movement: Empirical study on intra-European movers and their migration and motivation trajectories

Justyna Salamonska, Kozminski University, Poland

1140   Re-thinking in an employment contract and medical screening at recruitment phase of potential foreign workers in Malaysia: A mixed-method study

Sheikh Mohammad Maniruzzaman Al Masud, Universiti Malaysia Pahang, Malaysia
Rohana Binti Hamzah, Universiti Malaysia Pahang, Malaysia
Hasan Ahmad, Universiti Malaysia Pahang, Malaysia

517   Collectivity in waiting: families' reunification experiences in Sweden

Hilda Gustafsson, Malmö University, Sweden

1106   Democracies, Polities in Transition, and Refugees: The Struggle to be Generous

Min Ji Kim, University of California San Diego, US

Re-conceptualising free movement: Empirical study on intra-European movers and their migration and motivation trajectories

(1144) Justyna Salamonska, Kozminski University, Poland

In this presentation I utilise the European Internal Movers Social Survey (EIMSS) dataset to paint a quantitative picture of intra-European migrations, focusing on five EU member states: France, Germany, Great Britain, Italy and Spain, in each studying movers from the remaining four countries. First, I distinguish between one-off, repeat (to the same destination) and multiple migration (to different destinations) trajectories of the EU movers. Second, I focus on motivations of intra-European movers, analysing how they change over time. Third, I examine to what extent migration trajectories so far (one-off, repeat, multiple) are useful to predict aspirations for further international mobility. In relation to multiple migration trajectories, I find that majority of multiple migrants lived in at least two EU countries which I argue, makes them true free movers in the EU, hopping between the different destinations (they account for about 20 per cent of the whole sample). Combinations of destinations in the EU seem to be non-random, as clearly some combinations of destinations are more popular than others (the former include Italy and France; Great Britain and France; Germany and France; Great Britain and Germany, and Great Britain and Italy). As regards migration motivations, the free movement gives right to resettle within the EU for various reasons and here also EIMSS data points not only to great variety of reasons for current move, but perhaps more interestingly, how the motivations to hit the road changed over time. Unsurprisingly, repeat migrants seem to be more consistent in the repeated choice of the same motivation (labour migrants often remain labour migrants etc.), with an exception of educational motivations which seem to be a springboard to other, predominantly work and family related moves. Indeed, literature on student migration suggests such changing motivations for migration in case of educational migrants upon training completion. For multiple migrants there is more heterogeneity in transitions of migration motives over time, meaning that past motivations are less useful to predict the same motivations for the following move. However, past migration trajectory is a good predictor of future mobility on the whole. Multiple migrants have wider geographical horizons when drawing their future and their life course spatially, compared to one off migrants. Multiple movers are more willing to move outside of the EU if they could significantly improve their work or living conditions and more likely do declare to live in a place different than origin and current destination in five years time. In case of repeat migrants, one unexpected finding is that their imagined life course - in the long term - seems to be set in the destination, as they are more likely to declare to stay than to move, be it origin or elsewhere. Importantly, motivations for migration matter: moving for quality of life (a factor overlooked in predominantly labour focused analyses of migration intentions) is a single motivation that serves as a good predictor of staying in the current destination.

Re-thinking in an employment contract and medical screening at recruitment phase of potential foreign workers in Malaysia: A mixed-method study

(1140) Sheikh Mohammad Maniruzzaman Al Masud, Universiti Malaysia Pahang, Malaysia

Rohana Binti Hamzah, Universiti Malaysia Pahang, Malaysia

Hasan Ahmad, Universiti Malaysia Pahang, Malaysia

There has been an influx of foreign workers (FWs) into Malaysia since independence in 1957, mainly due to its rapidly expanding economy. However, since the introduction of Malaysian labour migration policies, it has remained a short-term solution to fill instant labour shortages (Fernandez, 2008). Simultaneously, the present systems were based on public safety and security rather than on labour administration and continuing sustainable development (ILO, 2016, p-3). Consequently, foreign workers suffer abuses and restrictions from employers and recruitment agents (Devadason & Meng, 2014). Whereas, in the SDGs (Sustainable Development Goals), migration was for the first time considered a vital contributor to sustainable development in the mainstream global development landscape (IOM, 2017). Therefore, there is an urgent need to redesign the migrant workers' key recruitment factors as this is the first step in FWs' management. Concentrating on recruitment factors, this study identified two important issues, such as employment contract (EC) and first medical screening (MS) that would require reconsideration for potential FWs at this phase (MEF, 2016). Besides, this study focused on SDG 08 due to the connection between FWs above recruitment factors and sustainability via decent work. This was a sequential exploratory mixed-method study. Data were collected using qualitative (in-depth interviews) and quantitative (face-to-face surveys) methods. This study used a mixed methodology mainly to obtain enriched information from both experts (in-depth interviews) and general workers (face-to-face surveys). The study found that the following issues should be reassessed, such as writing ECs in the foreign worker's native language as well as providing and explaining ECs before the placement of foreign workers in the destination country. Writing EC in FWs' native language is an international requirement (ILO, 2019). An explanation of the EC would help potential workers to understand it meticulously—service rules, regulations, working conditions and wages, etc. An EC is the first and foremost legal document for every foreign worker abroad. Furthermore, the study also explored that an initial medical examination should be done by FOMEMA (Foreign Workers' Medical Examination Monitoring Agency of Malaysia) for probable foreign workers. It would be helpful to prevent fraudulent selection of foreign workers in their country of origin. In addition, the first MS by FOMEMA in lieu of source country clinics or doctors might be lessened the repatriation risk of prospective foreign workers just after arrival in the destination country, Malaysia. The outcomes will aid the redesign of foreign worker recruitment policies. The results will also guide sustainable enhancement of workforce contributions to society and the Malaysian economy. Moreover, SDG 08 will be achieved if the proposals are implemented.

References:

Devadason, E. S., & Meng, C. W. (2014). Policies and laws regulating migrant workers in Malaysia: A critical appraisal. Journal of Contemporary Asia, 44(1), 19-35. https://www.tandfonline.com/doi/full/10.1080/00472336.2013.826420?casa_token=qNztTk1l-fYAAAAA%3A3v9eJ tjveLfwfYcPaGgfjD7-zqZPY9AYl8td0wGizu0zhCgskj9HH12-ah1CGRrBAgTTtOrITJL7 yLE

Fernandez, I. (2008). Recruitment and placement of migrant workers in Malaysia: Inconsistent, unclear and deregulated without a human rights approach. National Conference on Developing a Comprehensive Policy Framework for Migrant Labour, Malaysian Bar Council, Petaling Jaya, 18-19 February.

ILO. (2016, p-3). Review of labour migration policy in Malaysia. ILO Regional Office for Asia and the Pacific. https://www.ilo.org/wcmsp5/groups/public/---asia/---ro-bangkok/documents/publication/wcms_447687.pdf

ILO. (2019). General principles and operational guidelines for fair recruitment and Definition of recruitment fees and related costs https://www.ilo.org/global/topics/fair-recruitment/WCMS_536755/lang--en/index.htm

IOM. (2017). *World MIgration Report 2018* https://publications.iom.int/system/files/pdf/wmr_2018_en.pdf

MEF. (2016). *MEF Survey On Management Of Foreign Workers.* M. E. Federation. http://www.mef.org.my/publications/publication_info.aspx?ID=34

Collectivity in waiting: families' reunification experiences in Sweden

(517) Hilda Gustafsson, Malmö University, Sweden

The fundamental role of waiting in migration processes and migrants' everyday life is widely acknowledged in migration literature. Yet despite a notable body of knowledge, little attention has been drawn to waiting beyond the individual experience. This study highlights how families who reunify in Sweden experience waiting together. With a qualitative method including semi-structured interviews, the experiences of persons who undertook family reunification in Sweden reveal waiting as a collective experience. Together, the (to date 14) interviews display waiting for family reunification within refugee migration, student migration, among work permit holders, for Swedish citizens and their respective partners. The results show that waiting for family reunification includes shared goals based on mutual commitment, the delegation of care and communication flows across nation states, expectations, emotions and conflict. The study further shows how Sweden's recently adopted family reunification policy has consequences on the waiting experiences of families, including both close and distant family members who may or may not be included in the bureaucratic process of family reunification itself. These consequences are embodied through forced activity including work and finding housing in Sweden, as well as passivity and/or flexibility abroad as family members are expected to stay prepared to abandon their lives if granted permission to go to Sweden.

Democracies, Polities in Transition, and Refugees: The Struggle to be Generous

(1106) Min Ji Kim, University of California San Diego, US

Thanks to the discourse of human rights, which has historically been connected to political and economic liberalism, there is a widespread belief that democratic states - in particular Western liberal democracies such as the USA, the UK, and Australia - are more generous to refugees and asylum-seekers than their autocratic counterparts and would therefore host more refugees. As the world underwent a wave of democratisation in the 1990s after the fall of the Soviet Union (Huntington 1991; Diamond 2003), Gary Freeman (1995) observed that the institutional architecture of democratic states compels them to enact an expansive immigration policy. Joppke (1998) further observed that constitutional principles and the rule of law in democracies constrained governments from easily expelling foreigners on their territories. Anti-discrimination laws, as well as formal and informal anti-racism norms, have made it impossible for democracies to overtly select or exclude migrants and asylum seekers based on ethnicity (Joppke 2005; see also Gest and Boucher 2021). However, relatively recent research covering certain regions and historical periods suggest that democracies were among the first to adopt racist immigration laws - also negatively impacting de facto refugees - and the slowest in dismantling them, allowing autocratic states to perform better in this regards (FitzGerald and Cook-Martin 2010, 2014; FitzGerald 2019). Other studies suggest that democratic transition is accompanied by increasing restrictions and hostility toward refugees, implying that democracy and an unwelcoming humanitarian migration policy are correlated (Milner 2009; see also Ruhs 2008, 2013). In this paper, I investigate which of these hypotheses has more empirical support. Are politically liberal states really more generous than their autocratic counterparts toward refugees and asylum seekers? Does their hosting of refugees ultimately align with their much-landed democratic values? I analyse an original merged panel dataset covering 162 countries over a period of 1951 to 2018 built from data from the UNHCR and Polity 5, deriving refugees per capita and political regime type (democracy, anocracy, autocracy). I find that democracies - including democracies of the Global South - on average hosted fewer refugees relative to their populations than autocracies and posted lower asylum approval rates. Countries that underwent a transition to democracy in almost all cases hosted fewer refugees as democracies than they did as autocracies and/or anocracies. Including anocracies in the analysis complicated the picture, as anocracies have now overtaken autocracies in hosting the majority of the world's refugees on a per capita basis. Even so, democratic nations continued to post the lowest percentages, providing support to the notion that, contrary to the discourse of liberalist values and human rights, democracies struggle to be generous to humanitarian migrants.

5E   Gestión de crisis y nuevas reconfiguraciones de la movilidad humana ante la COVID-19 [ES]   AMPHI 5

Chair: José Salvador Cueto Calderón, Universidad Autónoma de Sinaloa, Mexico

1188   El efecto de la pandemia en el proyecto migratorio de los españoles emigrados en Reino Unido y Francia

Alberto Capote Lama, University of Granada, Spain
Iria Vazquez Silva, University of Vigo, Spain
Belen Fernandez Suarez, University of A Corunna, Spain

1281   Condiciones del desplazamiento de la migración de tránsito de origen centroamericano y el papel de la sociedad civil en su paso por México

José Salvador Cueto Calderón, Universidad Autónoma de Sinaloa, Mexico
Nayeli Burgueño Angulo, Universidad Autónoma de Sinaloa, Mexico
Stephanie Cortés Aguilar, Universidad Autónoma de Sinaloa, Mexico

1231   Dinámicas de exclusión de los nacionalismos modernos: necropolítica antiinmigrante

Laura Natalia Rodríguez Ariano, Universidad Autónoma Metropolitana, Mexico

518   Migración, gestión de crisis y el papel de los gobiernos subnacionales ante la COVID-19 en México

Carlos Alberto González Zepeda, Universidad Autónoma Metropolitana Unidad Cuajimalpa (UAM-C), Mexico

El efecto de la pandemia en el proyecto migratorio de los españoles emigrados en Reino Unido y Francia

(1188) Alberto Capote Lama, University of Granada, Spain

Iria Vazquez Silva, University of Vigo, Spain

Belen Fernandez Suarez, University of A Corunna, Spain

La irrupción de la pandemia de covid19 hizo que en el marco de los estudios migratorios se pasara de hablar de la movilidad a la inmovilidad. De hecho, en marzo de 2020 la UE cierra las fronteras a ciudadanos de terceros países. En el caso de las migraciones intraeuropeas se produjo el cierre transitorio y desordenado de las fronteras también a partir de marzo de 2020.Esta comunicación analiza el impacto que está teniendo la crisis del COVID-19 en el proyecto migratorio de los emigrantes españoles residentes en Francia y Reino Unido. Estudiaremos las consecuencias de la pandemia y su gestión en relación con la movilidad, el cambio residencial y los cambios a nivel laboral.La investigación que se presenta se basa en la realización en total de 50 entrevistas semiestructuradas; realizadas en Reino Unido y en Francia que se marcharon después de la crisis de 2008. Las entrevistas han sido llevadas a cabo entre los meses de septiembre 2021 a marzo de 2022. Estos datos forman parte de la investigación "Integración y retorno de la «nueva emigración española»: un análisis comparado de las comunidades de españoles en el Reino Unido y Francia (PID2019-105041RA-I00)".En el análisis del impacto de la pandemia sobre los proyectos y estrategias de movilidad de los emigrados españoles, cabe distinguir entre varias fases de la pandemia: a) el primer año, particularmente los primeros meses a partir de marzo de 2020, y b) una fase posterior basada en menos restricciones en 2021 y 2022. La incertidumbre del inicio de la pandemia se propagó también a los emigrantes españoles: las dudas iniciales se sitúan en qué decisión tomar: permanecer en Reino Unido o Francia, o regresar a España. En este sentido la coyuntura difiere sustancialmente en función de las condiciones del empleo que revelan un impacto social de la pandemia muy desigual. Cabe distinguir tres situaciones distintas: a) personas con empleos estables y con la posibilidad de teletrabajar, con libertad por tanto para regresar a España; b) emigrantes con empleos precarios y que implicaban presencialidad (antes de la pandemia) con imposibilidad de teletrabajar, cuyo empleo fue interrumpido por la covid 19 o incluso lo perdieron; c) personas con empleos considerados esenciales en los países de destino, por ejemplo, en el ámbito sanitario o de cuidados, que continuaron trabajando presencialmente a pesar del confinamiento. La crisis sanitaria demostró, desde un primer momento, un impacto diferencial marcado por la desigualdad social presente en nuestras sociedades: la covid19 ha supuesto para unos el desempleo y para otros el derecho al teletrabajo, impactando también en la renta de los hogares y en la (im)posibilidad de movilidad entre ciudades y países. Este impacto marcado por la desigualdad se ha reflejado claramente en los emigrantes españoles, en función principalmente de sus condiciones laborales.

Condiciones del desplazamiento de la migración de tránsito de origen centroamericano y el papel de la sociedad civil en su paso por México

(1281) José Salvador Cueto Calderón, Universidad Autónoma de Sinaloa, Mexico

Nayeli Burgueño Angulo, Universidad Autónoma de Sinaloa, Mexico

Stephanie Cortés Aguilar, Universidad Autónoma de Sinaloa, Mexico

El presente trabajo analiza el fenómeno de la migración de tránsito de origen centroamericano en su cruce por México, como un fenómeno emergente, que se presenta como resultado del desplazamiento y expulsión de miles de personas de sus países de origen. El incremento en los flujos de migrantes principalmente provenientes de países con altos niveles de pobreza, desempleo y por consiguiente de una violencia estructural, no solo ha generado uno de los principales retos en la agenda política de los gobiernos económicamente desarrollados, a los cuales se dirige la población migrante, sino también en aquellos países por donde el migrante transita como parte de sus trayectorias hacia el país destino. Tal es el caso de México que, aunque no deja de ser un país tradicionalmente expulsor de migrantes pasa a convertirse en un país de tránsito y destino, con la presencia de miles de migrantes principalmente de origen centroamericano que cruzan por el territorio nacional con el objetivo de llegar a los Estados Unidos de América. En este sentido, el trabajo tiene como objetivo enfatizar sobre las condiciones del desplazamiento de la migración de tránsito de origen centroamericano en su cruce por la ciudad de Culiacán, Sinaloa, como parte de la llamada Ruta del Pacífico y comprender desde la perspectiva del propio sujeto migrante sobre sus trayectorias, condiciones y retos presentes en su tránsito. El estudio parte de reconocer la complejidad que representa el "transitar" en donde el migrante entra en contacto, en diversos contextos y espacios sociales, como sitios de disputa y desplazamientos, caracterizados por contextos de inequidad, marginalización y violencia, así como el papel que juega la sociedad civil como un elemento que condiciona su tránsito a través de acciones de apoyo y solidaridad que inciden como recursos que permiten la continuidad y temporalidad de sus trayectorias. El trabajo analiza estos contextos de interacción del migrante con el espacio social y las reconfiguraciones que el propio migrante presenta en su condición transitoria, en su paso por la ciudad. Se analizan las condiciones, contextos, así como también el diseño de estrategias del sujeto migrante, que confluyen en la decisión sobre futuras trayectorias.

Dinámicas de exclusión de los nacionalismos modernos: necropolítica antiinmigrante

(1231) Laura Natalia Rodríguez Ariano, Universidad Autónoma Metropolitana, Mexico

El escenario denominado crisis migratoria que se vive en la actualidad en los países receptores de inmigrantes de occidente, principalmente de carácter nacionalista, es uno de los principales desafíos y desafíos para los principios de solidaridad y dignidad humana, estos principios fundamentan los pilares de la democracia liberal moderno. Los mecanismos políticos, sociales, económicos y jurídicos actuales propician un estado permanente de incertidumbre e inseguridad hacia la inmigración irregular, quienes parecen no estar a salvo durante todo el ciclo migratorio. El endurecimiento de las políticas migratorias cuya finalidad es detener los flujos de inmigrantes no deseados, propician el incremento de decesos de estos seres humanos. Los muros, son dispositivos de contención fronterizos y la representación física del poderío de un Estado Nación y de su soberanía frente a las demás naciones. Por otra parte, los discursos de odio fortalecen el rechazo del extranjero acorde con los ideales anti inmigratorios, los cuales no tienen nada que ofrecer solo engrandecer los costos que producen a la nación receptora y minimizar los beneficios que aseguran al lugar de destino; lo anterior se relaciona con los discursos de supremacía racial que datan de varios siglos atrás y permean en las democracias del siglo XXI. En consecuencia, fortalece la idea de la otredad, donde surge la política separatista de nosotros y la exclusión de ellos; de esta forma los derechos humanos pasan a ser garantía solo del primer grupo y las zonas fronterizas son espacios del Estado de excepción. Conceptualizar el fenómeno migratorio a través de la biopolítica y necropolítica nos permite evaluar políticas y acciones punitivas de carácter racistas y mercantilistas que permean en la sociedad mundial actual. El factor económico que domina el panorama global actual se rige bajo la lógica de exclusión y rechazo al inmigrante pobre, en la medida que su vida y goce de derechos se debe a su capacidad de reciprocidad y las políticas migratorias modernas lo reduce a una vida desechada, sin valor y sin derechos por su situación migratoria. La reducción del individuo, a una mercancía, a un medio de producción y consumo con facilidad de reemplazo ha implicado una concepción de los inmigrantes irregulares como consumidores fallidos, es decir, como una vida sin valor, de acuerdo con los criterios del mercado globalizado. De este modo se afirma que la necropolítica es la forma en la que opera el capitalismo neoliberal, donde aquellas vidas que no producen ni consumen nada, de acuerdo a esta lógica globalizada, son equivalentes a Vidas sin valor e importancia, arrojadas a la muerte.

Migración, gestión de crisis y el papel de los gobiernos subnacionales ante la COVID-19 en México

(518) Carlos Alberto González Zepeda, Universidad Autónoma Metropolitana Unidad Cuajimalpa (UAM-C), Mexico

El propósito del artículo es analizar las políticas dirigidas a reducir el impacto de la crisis originada por el brote de COVID-19 en los gobiernos subnacionales en México. Con base en la literatura sobre gestión de crisis y mediante el análisis comparativo se muestran las acciones, los programas y políticas implementadas por los gobiernos subnacionales específicamente dirigidas a la población migrante durante la pandemia. La ponencia contribuye a la discusión sobre gestión de crisis y migración en el contexto del brote de COVID-19. La premisa es que el tipo de crisis, las características político-administrativas, así como las trayectorias históricas y la coordinación con la estrategia federal influyen en la implementación de las acciones destinadas a disminuir el impacto de la crisis en un contexto de migración.

5F   Workshop and Book Launch: Youth Migration: Multiple borders to the
North   AMPHI 6

Chair: Liliana Meza Gonzalez, Universidad Iberoamericana, México

966   Immigrant's access to medical services in Mexico: the case of Central Americans.

Liliana Meza Gonzalez, Universidad Iberoamericana, México

972   Would you please tell me, which way I ought to go? Central Americans crossing by or settling in Guanajuato

Ana Vila-Freyer, Universidad Latina de México, México

1123   The use of leisure time by migrant and non-migrant teenagers

Paula Alonso, University of A Coruña, Spain

975   Suspended lives of Central American Youth in Mexico: Between Inclusion and Survival

Martha Luz Rojas-Wiesner, El Colegio de la Frontera Sur, México
Susan Hjorth Boisen, Centro de Investigaciones y Estudios Superiores en
Antropología Social (CIESAS), México

Immigrant's access to medical services in Mexico: the case of Central Americans.

(966) Liliana Meza Gonzalez, Universidad Iberoamericana, México

This chapter of the TPL book "Multiple borders to the North" analizes the access to public medical services of Central American migrants in Mexico, before and after the enactment of the 2011 Migration Law. Using a quantitative approach, we find that access to medical services decreases from 2010 to 2015, despite the welcoming discourses in the country.

Would you please tell me, which way I ought to go? Central Americans crossing by or settling in Guanajuato

(972) Ana Vila-Freyer, Universidad Latina de México, México

Young Central Americans migrants seek to go as far north as possible away from their communities of origin, changing the North American migratory system. Countries such as the United States, México and Guatemala, have reacted implementing policies centered on a national security perspective, criminalizing the migratory phenomenon. In clear contrast, and supporting their action on a human security perspective, civil society organizations supported on the Episcopate of human mobility of the catholic church the creation of a network of migrant sanctuary houses which set up protocols for the protection of persons leaving their communities. In parallel, and fleeing for safety, migrants have been changing the routes and becoming visible in states, as in Guanajuato, where they follow the train tracks to reach the north. We identified the sociodemographic characteristics, and the tangible and intangible resources they count on their Northway based on a survey answered by 387 persons in a Sanctuary house in Celaya. Based on this information, we explore the possibilities of piecing together a Sanctuary City in Celaya, Guanajuato, a strategic point in the new routes used to reach the North, which could ease their inclusion in the region.

The use of leisure time by migrant and non-migrant teenagers

(1123) Paula Alonso, University of A Coruña, Spain

This article analyzes the differential use of leisure time in migrant and non-migrant adolescents in their daily lives. At present, the research of the use of time has not been fully addressed in the field of migration, creating a framework not explored enough between both fields of sociology. The mail goal is to analyze the use of leisure time between the native and migrant population and to detect if, in global terms, based on their perceptions and narratives, there are asymmetries between them that cause a situation of disadvantage for the migrants. METHOD. The methodology used is quantitative, based on two surveys applied to 3,080 native and migrant teenagers. We used statistical data trough of contingency tables. We made a descriptive analysis of the practices, habits, desires and hobbies based on use of time to know how they carried out. RESULTS. The results certify a differential use that the students make of that time according to their origin and that they stage particular stories of their experience during their growth and socialization process. DISCUSSION. Knowledge about the leisure experiences of teenagers can be approached from the point of view of the use of time, so that it contributes to the diagnosis of the different realities that the school population poses and unmasks situations of differential use and disadvantage of one group compared to another.

Suspended lives of Central American Youth in Mexico: Between Inclusion and Survival

(975) Martha Luz Rojas-Wiesner, El Colegio de la Frontera Sur, México

Susan Hjorth Boisen, Centro de Investigaciones y Estudios Superiores en Antropología Social (CIESAS), México

In the countries of Northern Central America (NCA) (El Salvador, Guatemala, and Honduras), since the 1980s, there have been flows of refugees and migrants who have left for other countries to escape the violence and poverty that afflicts the region. At present, the growing precariousness and social inequality, lack of access to rights, weakening of democratic institutions, environmental deterioration, as well as increasing violence by gangs have worsened poverty, marginalization, and insecurity in the countries of origin, which has driven increasing processes of internal and international displacement of people who flee in search of alternatives for survival and to escape violence. Many migrants and displaced people arrive at Mexico's southern border in search of safety and better living conditions in Mexico or in the United States. Some of the people fleeing violence may qualify for international protection, although, for different reasons, not all of them want or succeed in carrying out a refugee claim. Others do not qualify for international protection, although insecurity or living conditions do not allow them to remain in their communities or countries of origin. People who do manage to apply for asylum in Mexico are forced to carry out the process at the southern border. Others, who lack the opportunity to apply for asylum, or who do not have the necessary legal status or the resources to move forward, are also "trapped" or "immobilized" in the border area in southern Mexico, in "areas of precarious transit" (Hess, 2012, p. 428), where they face difficult economic conditions, social marginalization and a precarious legal status (Basok and Rojas, 2017). Access to rights depends on the legal status of the migrants and displaced people in these areas of transit. Some obtain refugee status or complementary protection, while others are rejected or remain in an irregular status and may be subject to deportation. Despite the formal rights granted by the law, there are various formal and informal mechanisms that limit effective access to rights and services in this area of "involuntary immobility" (Carling, 2002, p. 5), which accentuates the vulnerability of this population. These spaces of forced immobility of migrants, displaced persons, and asylum seekers on the southern border of Mexico trap them in various situations of social and economic marginalization, which force them to develop daily strategies to survive, in conditions of unemployment, poverty and deprived of access to rights and services. This process produces a differential inclusion (Mezzadra, 2012, p. 171) in the lower strata of the receiving communities. This analysis is based on two different research projects carried out by the authors on the southern border of Mexico between 2017 and 2019. The two investigations were qualitative and based on in-depth interviews. We were able to select interviews in which forms of differential inclusion were evident. We have taken up three short stories by young adults, whose personal narratives give an account of different forms of entrapment, accumulated disadvantages, inequalities and experiences of daily survival, resistance, and resilience of youth in the border area. These personal stories reflect some of the multiple processes, as well as the formal and informal mechanisms, through which this precarious and differential inclusion occurs, which accentuates the vulnerability and forced immobility of these young people.

5G   Education and High Skilled Migration

Chair   Farid Makhlouf, ESC Pau Business School, France

924   The Spirit of The University of Al-Qarawiyyin: The Contribution of Qualified Migration on Higher Education in Morocco

Farid Makhlouf, ESC Pau Business School, France
Youssef Errami, ESC Pau Business School, France

1274   Accommodating Cosmopolitan Renegotiations: Re-examining traditional norms of mobility in transnational migration

Aena Asif, Symbiosis International University, India
Isha Banerjee, Symbiosis International University, India
Kuhelika Bisht, Symbiosis International University, India
Nayanika Shome, Symbiosis International University, India

1257   Brain Drain in Social Sciences in Turkey in the Context of Maslow Hierarchy

F Gamze Bozkurt, Ankara Social Science University, Turkey

The Spirit of The University of Al-Qarawiyyin: The Contribution of Qualified Migration on Higher Education in Morocco

(924) Farid Makhlouf, ESC Pau Business School, France

Youssef Errami, ESC Pau Business School, France

The phenomenon of migrant remittances has attracted keen interest among policymakers, scholars and researchers.In this communication we are interested in the effects of skilled migration on the education. In fact, the higher education and research sector has undergone profound changes since the beginning of the 21st century, as a consequence of the installation of hyper-competition. Morocco has not been an exception in this globalized history. In this paper we explore the possible impact of skilled migrants on education in Morocco.The Higher Education and Research sector has been undergoing profound changes since the beginning of the 21st century. The confirmed importance of this sector in the development of nations has been confronted with the saturation of supply in developed countries, leading them to engage in a frantic competition to attract students who pay tuition fees. Indeed, the number of seats offered by higher education and research institutions at the end of the 20th century was sufficient to cover the entire student demand and to push the actors in two directions. The first, internal, was to engage in a reputation war by reinforcing the perceived quality and notoriety of the brand, expressed in particular by national and international rankings (Shanghai Ranking Consultancy, Times Higher Education, QS World University Rankings, etc.). This was achieved through colossal investments in infrastructure, academic processes and scientific research, and by obtaining leading international accreditations (AACSB, EQUIS, AMBA), thus establishing the North American educational model.

Accommodating Cosmopolitan Renegotiations: Re-examining traditional norms of mobility in transnational migration

(1274) Aena Asif, Symbiosis International University, India

Isha Banerjee, Symbiosis International University, India

Kuhelika Bisht, Symbiosis International University, India

Nayanika Shome, Symbiosis International University, India

People's movement between and across places has concerned the social sciences and humanities over time. To understand this movement, it is crucial that we recognize the contemporary devaluation of the physical idea of 'place' that has come about with the accelerated development and dominance of information technologies. The processes of globalisation have furthered the drive to move across the world and allow cross-cultural spaces and identities to exist; this also reconstructed the idea of a community and gave rise to the concept of cultures without geographies. Toward this end, the chief dichotomy between 'origin' and 'destination' is destabilised, thereby warranting the need to re-examine traditional meanings, contributions and consequences surrounding mobility and migration. However, although new information technologies inform and influence societies and therefore regions and cities, "their effects vary according to their interaction with the economic, social, political and cultural processes that shape the production and use of the new technological medium" (Castells, 1989: 2). The study of the culture of migration, therefore, emphasises both structure and agency, and the three levels of macro (global influences), meso (enculturation by community) and micro (individual choices) in the study of migration. This paper analyses two pairs of voluntary migrants who left their home country in search for a "better life". This study analyses their reasons for the migration and their specific experiences once they did migrate. The paper does so by carrying out 5 in depth interviews with each pair in order to identify wider patterns in their decisions and experiences surrounding migration. The paper highlights the role of social capital, gendered expectations and the validity of traditional migration theories in order to examine the nuances that exist in migration of these subjects. The results of these case studies allowed us to gain insight into the shifting trends in migration of an affluent and highly-skilled class of migrants. The overarching trends that emerged in both the case studies were explored by understanding firstly, the push and pull factors behind their migration, which was not financially motivated but driven by 'lifestyle migration' (Li et al., 1995). To understand the ecosystem that allowed this form of migration, we explored the culture of migration in their domestic spaces. This theme was studied with an emphasis on the shift in the traditional trend of male-led migration as we observed that the individual experience of women was not overshadowed by others, allowing them personal freedom and choice in choosing to migrate (Piper, 2008). Secondly, their social capital and negotiations with their identity were observed through their navigation of urban, organisational and national spaces. The results demonstrated a rise in increased individualism as a sub-product of transnational migration in highly skilled personnel (Kõu et al., 2017, p. 2791). The study contributes to further migration theory building and aiding countries in policy formation.

References:

Benson, M., & O'Reilly, K. (2009). *Migration and the Search for a Better Way of Life: A Critical Exploration of Lifestyle Migration. The Sociological Review, 57(4),* 608–625. https://doi.org/10.1111/j.1467-954X.2009.01864.x

Castels, M. 1989. *The Informational City. Oxford: Blackwell.*

Kõu, A., Mulder, C. H., & Bailey, A. (2017). *'For the sake of the family and future': the linked lives of highly skilled Indian migrants. Journal of Ethnic and Migration Studies, 43(16),* 2788–2805. https://doi.org/10.1080/1369183x.2017.1314608

Li, F., Jowett, A., Findlay, A., & Skeldon, R. (1995). *Discourse on Migration and Ethnic Identity: Interviews with Professionals in Hong Kong. Transactions of the Institute of British Geographers, 20(3),* 342-356. doi:10.2307/622655

Piper, N. (2008). *Feminisation of Migration and the Social Dimensions of Development: the Asian case. Third World Quarterly, 29(7),* 1287–1303. https://doi.org/10.1080/01436590802386427

Brain Drain in Social Sciences in Turkey in the Context of Maslow Hierarchy

(1257) F Gamze Bozkurt, Ankara Social Science University, Turkey

The aim of the study is to compare in the center/context of students who have the thought of immigrating abroad due to the reasons while they continue their education in Turkey and Turkish citizens prefer abroad for undergraduate, graduate, post-doctoral, post-doctoral students studying abroad. This study is conducted students who is studying in the field of Social Sciences. The population of this study is determined specific departments in the social science field which have the highest ranking score in the university enter exam.The problem of external migration has an important place in Turkey's agenda, especially in the last 20 years. Considering the immigration data to and from Turkey, it is observed that there is a rapid increase in the number of outgoings. When these migration data are examined, it is the qualified-brain drain that is the most sensitive and should be the first to be resolved. The majority of the masses who migrated from Turkey put forward reasons such as getting more qualified education, having a more secure job, and getting rid of social and political pressure. Considering the increasing number of universities in Turkey on this situation; It is also possible to determine that many variables such as legal, political, economic, socio-psychological and self-actualization have different effects. The questions to be asked at this point are as follows: What are the effects of the individual's desire for self-actualization and the legal reforms, government policies and universities in the countries they live in, in the context of immigrants from Turkey -qualified migration, brain drain? However; According to undergraduate, graduate, doctoral and post-doctoral students, how is the research and free thought environment of universities? Are the legal and bureaucratic processes as effective as the desires and needs regarding the material in the brain drain? Is brain drain a remedy or a goal, and if so, how well does it serve this goal? What impact do the mentioned factors have on migration?In line with the analysis to be made; The aspects of universities in Turkey that cause migration, the effects of think tanks/career centers to direct students abroad, and the effects of structural/legal reforms in Turkey on migration will be examined. Within the scope of the study, answers will be sought within the framework of a questionnaire prepared on the basis of the Maslow hierarchy scale, to the desire of people to realize themselves. It is aimed to diagnose the problem by analyzing different types of factors both within themselves and comparatively. From this point of view, by creating solution proposals, by revealing the perceptions of qualified immigrants and the academy components, whose immigration status we measure, about what opportunities they can obtain abroad; policy recommendations can be developed in this regard.This research is primarily descriptive and causal-comparative research and has a correlational research design. It is both a quantitative and qualitative research. The quantitative part includes socio-demographic questions and a scale on Maslow's Hierarchy. The qualitative part includes in-depth interviews to prepare these questions. In the research, besides these primary data, TÜİK, YÖK, EU etc. secondary source data obtained from various institutions (national and international) will also be analyzed. The study sample of the research includes undergraduate, graduate, doctoral and post-doctoral students of Turkish origin, who have resided in Turkey or have migrated abroad, studying in the departments of business administration, international relations, psychology, sociology, economics and law.In this study, answers will be sought to our problematic, which will be created in the context of the research question, within the framework of Maslow hierarchy scale and a prepared questionnaire. While doing this, qualified manpower (students) who have stayed and migrated in Turkey will be determined and both groups will be subjected to a survey. When different types of factors are analyzed both internally and comparatively, the problem will be identified and solution proposals will be created, revealing the perceptions of immigrants about what they think they can achieve abroad, and policy recommendations can be developed on the basis of student centers regarding this.

5H   Work, Employment, Society

Chair: Afzalur Rahman, University of Chittagong, Thailand

1266   Political Economy of Drug Smuggling: The effect of Yaba drug on Bangladesh Economy

Afzalur Rahman, University of Chittagong, Thailand

1287   Between Ingratitude and Misunderstanding - Power Games and Counterpower in the Integration of Refugees in Portugal

Marta Lemos, CRIA/ISCTE-IUL, Portugal

1018   Out-migration of people from the Garhwal Himalaya: a Case Study

Saurav Kumar, Mizoram University, India

1073   The Integration System in Greece: Challenges and Problems

Dimitrios Georgiadis, University of Nicosia, Cyprus

Political Economy of Drug Smuggling: The effect of Yaba drug on Bangladesh Economy

(1266) Afzalur Rahman, University of Chittagong, Thailand

The purpose of this paper is to explore the political economy of drug smuggling known as Yaba from Myanmar to Bangladesh. However, this study will further estimate the economic loss suffered by Bangladesh due to this smuggling. Bangladesh is situated in the crucial point between the 'golden triangle' (Myanmar, Thailand and Laos) and the 'golden crescent' (Pakistan, Afghanistan and Iran) in terms of geographical location. Also, it is surrounded by the major drug producing countries of Asia, many of which are strengthening their narcotics legislation and stepping up enforcement measures (Azizul and Md., 2017). Bangladesh with its easy land, sea and air access is becoming a major transit point for drug trafficking (Haq, 2000). The mixed research methods followed in this study with analyzing the relevant documents and interviewed with the involving stakeholders to know the process comprehensively. The main questions framed for the research: What is the economic impact of yaba trade in Bangladesh? How is yaba money distributed Bangladesh and beyond? What is the socio-economic loss due to the trafficking of this drug? Several researches on illicit commerce may seem at first to be an odd case to investigate but the geography of illicit networks is a field that has been covered sporadically in the literature (Dell, 2015; Hastings, 2015; Vellinga et al., 1999; Weisheit and Wells, 2010). In the case of Myanmar, Patrick Meehan explored the relationship between state-building processes and the illicit opium/heroin economy in Shan State since 1988 and the study revealed how the opium/heroin trade has been co-opted by the Myanmar state to fortify its control in the region over the past twenty-five years (Meehan, 2015). M.Emdad-Ul Haque had explored the drug scenario of Bangladesh since the colonial opium trade of the nineteenth century and in his book the cross-border trafficking routes was also analyzed (Haq, 2000). The addiction rate is ever increasing in Bangladesh. Dr. Rifat Naoreen Islam alleged that even the teachers and physicians who are supposed to guide the society are more or less getting addicted and law enforcing agencies are in most cases either refraining from their job or are associated with the drug business (Islam et al., 2013). Nonetheless, after the outbreak of COVID-19, the trafficking of yaba during lockdown has been increased drastically. In a nutshell, this research will definitely make a breakthrough in the discourse of drug smuggling.

Between Ingratitude and Misunderstanding - Power Games and Counterpower in the Integration of Refugees in Portugal

(1287) Marta Lemos, CRIA/ISCTE-IUL, Portugal

In the Portuguese refugee reception and integration system, refugees are under the responsibility of public and private entities accountable for the "success" of their "autonomy". During this period, "taking care" of refugees serves as a form of control and in the relationship between entities and refugees, disagreements arise and compromise their integration.

The reception and integration of refugees in Portugal depends essentially on the mobilization of private reception entities or municipal consortia. Often the responsibility for the "success or failure" in the "autonomy" of refugees, within the deadlines stipulated by Statal financial support, falls on the staff of these institutions. These men and women, mostly social workers, are people who daily deal with the "responsibility of taking care" of refugees and to promote their "autonomy". This task is not the only one they must deal with. Every day these social workers accumulate this task to others previously assigned. Within a year and a half, refugee adults are expected to be employed, to speak and understand Portuguese language and to be able to rent a house without any financial support; children should be enrolled at school and perfectly adapted to school's environment. Faced with this situation plus a *lack of know-how, availability and resources*, social workers create an "autonomy plan" for refugees and reflect expectations during that year and a half. Most of the times this plan faces many complications as time goes by and mostly, it is not aligned with refugees' own life expectations. In this "autonomy plan" the act of "taking care" of refugees reveals as a way to discipline the body (Silva et al. 2018) in order to succeed the task assigned and to remain intact entity's public image. The relationship of those who care and those who are cared for generates disagreements, misunderstandings, and frustrations where social workers percept ingratitude for their work in refugees' actions and refugees percept that they despise their wills and/or their culture.

Bibliography:

Almeida da Silva, Eunice; Belletti Mutt Urasaki, Maristela; Rebeca Silva Flores, Quézia "Concepções de cuidado e relações de poder na saúde da mulher", Revista Família, Ciclos de Vida e Saúde no Contexto Social, vol. 6, núm. 1, 2018, Universidade Federal do Triângulo Mineiro, Brasil. Available on: https://www.redalyc.org/articulo.oa?id=497955422009

Out-migration of people from the Garhwal Himalaya: a Case Study

(1018) Saurav Kumar, Mizoram University, India

Since history, out-migration has significantly impacted the Garhwal Himalaya. This is a common phenomenon, and people have used it to diversify their risk and livelihood options. This paper evaluates the extent of out-migration in the Garhwal Himalaya and examines the different types, patterns, reasons, and implications of out-migration. It identifies the importance of age, gender, education, caste, and altitude in influencing out-migration. This study was conducted by gathering data from the 12 villages of the Garhwal Himalaya. A total of 560 households were surveyed from the villages, covering 100% sample from each village. The authors constructed a structured questionnaire and asked the heads of each surveyed household about the types of migration they practice, the locations of migration, the reasons for migration, and the consequences of such migration. In addition, the authors asked about migrants' age, sex, caste, education, income, and occupation. The study reveals that out-migration in the Garhwal Himalaya has become a major problem since it has led to many socio-economic problems in the region. And if it is not addressed at its earliest, a large number of villages will become depopulated. Additionally, this study suggests some policy measures to curb out-migration from the Garhwal Himalaya.

The Integration System in Greece: Challenges and Problems

(1073) Dimitrios Georgiadis, University of Nicosia, Cyprus

For most of its contemporary history, Greece was a migrant sending country. The geopolitical changes of 1989, quickly converted the country into a host of mainly undocumented immigrants from Southeast Europe, Central-Eastern Europe, the former Soviet Union, and later from South Asia, the Middle East and Sub-Saharan Africa. During the last decade and particularly since 2010-2015 Greece has faced important immigration pressures from irregular migrants and asylum seekers from Asia and Africa, reaching Greece via Turkey. Greece is the first country of arrival in Europe for irregular migrants and asylum seekers that are often heading west and north. During the last 3-4 years, the relevant irregular migration and asylum seeking routes through Morocco and Spain, and through Libya and Italy have been reduced to a trickle. Thus, the Greek Turkish corridor has absorbed the brunt of these pressures. At the same time, the Greek asylum system had been non-functioning, leaving thousands of people trapped in Greece, without documents, without assistance and without the means to make a living. Even though the European legislation on asylum and notably the Dublin II regulation foresees that asylum applications should be processed in the first safe country of arrival, in this case Greece. These two factors, the non-governance of asylum and irregular migration and the economic crisis, provoked a true humanitarian crisis in central Athens. Aim of this presentation is to analyze the Greek Integration System and to discuss about the problems that Refugees face through a quantitative research in Athens Greece.

5J   Gender and Migration

Chair: Pinar Yazgan, Mobility Research Centre, International Business School, UK

938   The racialised and gendered construction of the culture of disbelief in asylum. Analysis of the legal responses to asylum claims based on gender persecutions in Spain

         Diana Garcés-Amaya, Independent Researcher, Spain
1021   Migrants, the Informal Sector, and Prostitution in Trinidad and Tobago

         Andel Edwin Michael Andrew, Independent
         Lueanda Francis-Blackman, The University of the West Indies, St Augustine
948   A Gender Biased Approach to the Experiences of Women who Migrated to Turkey Through Marriages

         Senem Gürkan, Ondokuz Mayis University, Turkey
         Erkan Persembe, Ondokuz Mayis University, Turkey
939   Women Migrant Workers in the Gulf: The Gender Dimension of Impact of COVID19

         Anu Abraham, NMIMS University, Mumbai, India
         Ginu Zacharia Oommen, Kerala Public Service Commission, India

The racialised and gendered construction of the culture of disbelief in asylum. Analysis of the legal responses to asylum claims based on gender persecutions in Spain

(938) Diana Garcés-Amaya, Independent Researcher, Spain

This paper aims to contribute to the study of how gender and race are embedded in the admission/expulsion procedures of asylum systems in the multicultural societies of the Global North. Drawing on the concepts of the 'politics of suspicion' and the 'culture of disbelief' that Hass and Shuman (2019) and Jubany (2017) have identified as central features of asylum procedures, emphasising the existence of an ethos that systematically and structurally accompanies the 'global war on terrorism' and has since come to define asylum regimes. The same politics of suspicion have influenced shifting narratives about asylum seekers, which, while contextual and contingent, crucially affect the lives of those seeking protection. The latter are undoubtedly responsible for the production of subalternity and places of non-belonging for those excluded from the increasingly narrow category of "refugee". In this sense, I am interested in how legal discourses and resources intervene to produce subjects, categorise them and place them in certain social positions, i.e. the role of law and the authorities that decide on asylum in the processes of subalternisation and racialisation of those who are considered non-members of the political community. To this end, my central corpus of analysis consists of the judgments issued by the National Court and the Supreme Court between 2009 and 2019 in response to asylum claims on gender grounds in the Spanish state. The coding and analytical process relied on the tools of Critical Discourse Analysis. This made it possible to gain insight into these bureaucratic-legal contexts in which the production and reproduction of meanings, representations and ideologies take place (Wodak and Meyer 2003). This made it possible to recognize how racialised representations of gender, stereotypes and orientalist frames are mobilised to argue for negative decisions and how they play a role in the deployment of the politics of suspicion (Hass and Shuman, 2019). In the judgments I examined, I was able to identify at least three distinct patterns: 1. criminalisation of women asylum seekers based on their places of origin, the routes they travelled and the nature of their accounts, 2. discrediting of life experiences and the credibility of their claims in relation to pregnant women; 3. 'pathological visibility' (Phoenix, 1) of women who deviate from stereotypical victim portrayal. Finally, I argue that asylum seekers are portrayed as suspicious subjects by the same authorities with whom they seek protection. This becomes evident when discursive strategies of naming and categorising focus on the supposed 'intention' of 'taking advantage' and the mobilisation of contradictory representation by the authorities, where applicants are portrayed as both victims and suspects and criminals. This particularly affects women from Maghreb countries and West Africa. It is striking that in this assessment process, women applicants are no longer seen as passive victims and voiceless, but are hypervisibilised and categorised as doubly suspicious, using gender-based violence to generate empathy.

Migrants, the Informal Sector, and Prostitution in Trinidad and Tobago

(1021) Andel Edwin Michael Andrew, Independent

Lueanda Francis-Blackman, The University of the West Indies, St Augustine

This paper explores Venezuelan migrants and the informal sector in Trinidad and Tobago. Specifically, the chapter explores prostitution by female Venezuelan migrants in

Trinidad and Tobago. The Venezuelan migrant crisis has afforded an opportunity to examine the short term and long-term impact of the Venezuelan migrant population in Latin America and the Caribbean as the region has witnessed an unprecedented number of Venezuelans fleeing their native land. Trinidad and Tobago has been one of the recipient countries of these migrants. One of the outcomes of this has been the expansion of the unique informal sector that has developed to include services such as the preparation and sale of perishable food, retailing of clothes, jewellery, newspapers and other items. One aspect of the informal sector that has not been explored is that of prostitution. The growing sex industry in Trinidad and Tobago calls for an exploration of dark side of migration and the impact of prostitution on the society. There is the need to examine the exploitation of the female migrant and factors which led to resorting to prostitution and the consequences. The research adopts a qualitative methodology using semi-structured interviews to answer the main research questions: What factors have led to prostitution among female Venezuelan migrants in Trinidad and Tobago and what has been the social impact of prostitution in Trinidad and Tobago?

A Gender Biased Approach to the Experiences of Women who Migrated to Turkey Through Marriages

(948) Senem Gürkan, Ondokuz Mayis University, Turkey

Erkan Persembe, Ondokuz Mayis University, Turkey

As a result of globalization, the relations of individuals from different nations and the increase in the migration phenomenon have followed a directly proportional course. These migrations, which were carried out for various reasons, have caused immigrants to be affected in different ways. When the relevant literature is examined, it can be seen that women are affected by the phenomenon of migration more than men. Moreover, marriage migration, one of the types of migration that is described as specific to women, has become widespread. This study aims to examine the experiences of women of foreign origin, who migrated to Turkey through marriage and married to a Turkish man, in terms of gender. In this context, the daily life experiences and social integration processes of immigrant women at the end of marriage will be evaluated with a gender equality approach. The participants of this qualitative study consist of 13 women who immigrated to Turkey by marriage after marrying to a Turkish man. Data will be collected by in-depth interview method by creating a semi-structured interview form consisting of open-ended and demographic questions compiled from former studies in the existing literature. The questions in the semi-structured interview form are composed of socio-demographic information, information about daily life experiences, and information about marriage migration and integration process. Due to the risk of transmission of the viruses during the pandemic, some of the interviews will be conducted online. The findings and results of the study will be included in the conference presentation.

Women Migrant Workers in the Gulf: The Gender Dimension of Impact of COVID19

(939) Anu Abraham, NMIMS University, Mumbai, India

Ginu Zacharia Oommen, Kerala Public Service Commission, India

The ILO defines a migrant worker as "a person who migrates or who has migrated from one country to another with a view to being employed other than on his own account" (ILO, 2019). The GCC region hosts 23 million migrant workers, accounting for about three-quarters of the entire workforce of the region who contribute to 50 per cent of the regions GDP. The migrant workforce that dominates the workspace of GCC region, who are mostly on temporary contracts and engaged in low-wage occupations, predominantly hail from South and South-East Asian countries. India alone accounts for about 25 million labourers in GCC (ILO, 2018). Women account for 39 per cent of migrant workers in the GCC (ILO, 2019) and the number comes as no surprise taking into account the feminization of workers in multiple sectors. Among the South and South East Asian countries from where outmigration data is available, Sri Lanka reported women migrants' represented 65% of total migration, while Indonesia and the Philippines also reported 66% and 70% respectively. While we don't have the exact percentage of women among the migrant workers from India, they are still a large number and mainly originate from Kerala Andhra Pradesh and Tamil Nadu.Women migrants, who are in the skilled category are mainly nurses in the health sector and those in the semi- skilled or unskilled category are domestic workers, care workers, cleaning crew, manufacturing workers, salon staff and salespersons. These workers are vulnerable to numerous exploitations, for instance, domestic workers, who are mostly women are highly vulnerable to owing to the very nature of their workspace. As Gamburd (2015) writes about the women domestic workers from Srilanka, there is no laws to safeguard the labour rights, abuse and isolation of maids working in the households. Their vulnerability is magnified by the fact that these women come from lower socio-economic background and in many cases are not literate and thus having limited scope to access external help. Even so, the complaints that has been registered with the Indian Ministry of External Affairs complaint cell has been predominantly from women facing abuse and living and working in precarious conditions.Though there has been a lot of attention on the Indian migrants in the Gulf during the current COVID19 pandemic, the story was predominantly that of the 'male migrant worker'. While this in itself may not be an issue, it is crucial to note that gender is a dimension, which differentiates an individual's experiences. One of the major reasons for the lack of work on women migrant workers is due to the lack of access to these workers, especially those in the more vulnerable groups such as domestic workers, care workers whose work space is restricted to the domestic space of the employers. This is also visible in the fact that there is very scant representation of women from these occupational backgrounds in cultural or civil society organisations.The onset of COVID pandemic has exacerbated the issues faced by women migrant workers. For the purpose of understanding the impact of the pandemic on the migrant women workers, we interviewed about a dozen women in the six GCC countries working in different sectors to understand their experience. The two groups had widely different experiences to share and while it was easy to find respondents willing to be interviewed in the first group, it was much more difficult to contact respondents from the second group. For example, while many of the semi-skilled and unskilled workers lost their jobs, wages and their accommodation too, for the health-workers it was more about the deterioration of their working conditions than the problem of losing their jobs. This paper explores in detail the systemic nature of the vulnerabilities faced by women migrants in the GCC that was exacerbated during the pandemic.

Day Three 9 September 2022 Friday

Day Three 9 September 2022 - 09:00-10:30

6A   Immigration and Integration [AR FR]   AMPHI 1

الجلسة السادسة: الهجرة و إشكالية الاندماج

رئيس الجلسة: أحمد الودغيري أستاذ بشعبة القانون العام كلية العلوم القانونية و الاقتصادية و الاجتماعية أكدال جامعة محمد الخامس بالرباط

Chair: *Dr Ahmed Al-Wadagiri Professor, Public Law Division, Faculty of Legal, Economic and Social Sciences, Mohammed V University of Rabat, Morocco*

565 Michela Pellicani: Les défis de l'intégration des Marocains en Italie

566 Dr. Mohammed Dahiri, Université Complutense de Madrid (UCM): La migración en España y la problemática de la integración de la comunidad marroqui.

-       محمد عسيلة : « واقع الهجرة في ألمانيا و إشكالية اندماج مهاجري المغرب

Mamadou Bhoye Diallo Coordinateur du Collectif des communautés subsahariennes au Maroc: Accès des migrants aux services sociaux de base : réalisations et défis

567 Damnati Faycal: Gouvernance de la question migratoire au Maroc

6B   New Challenges in Migration Studies   AMPHI 2

Chair: *Ana Vila-Freyer, Universidad Latina de México, México*

962   Pope Pius XII, Nuncio Roncalli, and Rescue of Jews in the Holocaust

Yitzchak Kerem, The Hebrew University of Jerusalem, Israel

1233   Providing A Simple and Easily Accessible Diagnostic Tool Does Not Always Match Success in STD Screening Campaigns for Migrant Population

Laura Elena Pacifici Noja, Unicamillus University, Rome, Italy

928   Are social cohesion and transnationalism complementary? Migrant communities in Guanajuato, Mexico

Ana Vila-Freyer, Universidad Latina de México, México

523   Return migration with reference to relative insecurities

Sinan Zeyneloglu, Istanbul Kent University, Turkey
Ibrahim Sirkeci, International Business School, UK

Pope Pius XII, Nuncio Roncalli, and Rescue of Jews in the Holocaust

(962) Yitzchak Kerem, The Hebrew University of Jerusalem, Israel

While according to ongoing research Pope Pius Xii had a low key to negative image in the historiography on rescue of Jews, appeared removed and very conservative, a focus on Vatican delegate Roncalli, highlights much more rescue, although somewhat exaggerated and often did not materialize, but does note that after approached Roncalli toiled for rescue and succeeded in many cases. The Vatican did harbor at least 300 Jews in the Holocaust, and did initiate financing rescue and for Jewish converts endangered, but never issued strong statements promoting Jewish rescue and condemning Nazism. Eretz-Israel Chief Rabbis Herzog and Ouziel toiled for such messages, but they were never issued by Pius XII. Roncalli in Istanbul did assist illegal immigration to Palestine in the instances of the Tari boat, Jewish refugees passing through Turkey, and in larger and significant episodes like rescuing some 12,000 Jews in Hungary partially with baptismal papers, releasing a few hundred Jews from the Jasenovac death camp in Croatia, and assist supplying wheat to Greece in 1941-1942 when famine killed as many as 60 Jews a day in Salonika. He wrote to King Boris to rescue Bulgarian Jewry, but this has never been a serious factor in analyzing the non-implementation of the deportation orders or the sending of 20,000 Jews from Sofia for forced labor. Furthermore Boris signed for 20,000 Jews to be deported and in the end 12,000 Jews from the new territories of Yugoslavian Macedonian and Greek Thrace were deported by the Bulgarians and annihilated in Treblinka. The protests of the Bulgarian Orthodox Church, labor unions, and two mass public demonstrations are considered factors. When Boris died of a heart attack sometime in late August-early September 1943, German policy and practical action changed. Roncalli also intervened on behalf of rescue in Italy and Slovakia. After Jewish Agency emissary Haim Barlas showed Roncalli proof of mass execution in Auschwitz, Roncalli was devoted to rescue. He tried to divert annihilation of Jews in Transnistria, but only rescued a group of several hundred Jews. Rumors assessed that Roncalli had qualms toward Pious XII over passivity on rescue of Jews in the Holocaust, but this has never been shown. Roncalli claimed that he acted on behalf of the Pope and with great religious conviction. Roncalli's rescue activities made him closer to the Jewish people, prompted him to rethink Vatican attitudes on the Jews and Judaism, and this was instrumental when he became Pope John XXIII, and initiated Vatican II until his death in that same year of 1962.

Providing A Simple and Easily Accessible Diagnostic Tool Does Not Always Match Success in STD Screening Campaigns for Migrant Population

(1233) Laura Elena Pacifici Noja, Unicamillus University, Rome, Italy

From 20 to 27 November 2020, the extraordinary reception center (ERC) "Mondo Migliore" joined the notable continental event "European Testing Week", aimed at promoting screening campaigns for the diagnosis of HIV and viral hepatitis. The ERC, which overall hosted over 400 migrants largely from North Africa, the Gulf of Guinea, the Horn of Africa, Syria, Pakistan, and Bangladesh, is located in the hinterland of Rome and managed by the Italian Red Cross (CRI). In the medical clinic operating in the ERC worked a team of physicians accredited in internal medicine and infectious diseases and nurses and was open daily. As part of the initiative, a laboratory tool for molecular diagnostics (GeneXpert®) of sexually transmitted diseases (STD), provided free of charge by the manufacturer Cepheid, was made available at the ERC medical clinic. Free tests for the rapid diagnosis of HCV and HCV, carried out on a mini digital capillary blood sample, were offered free to guests during the "European Testing Week". The initiative was publicized in the ERC through the dissemination of cultural mediators. Also in the dedicated week, STD counseling was offered to all patients who for whatever reason had access to the ERC medical clinic. Out of 402 guests present during the "European Testing Week", only 8 (2%) people spontaneously requested to carry out the tests. in the same period of time, among the 63 guests who spontaneously had access to the clinic for different health reasons and received counseling dedicated to STDs, 35 joined the initiative and were tested while the other 28 did not accept to carry out the screening. In total, therefore, only 43 guests (10.7%) joined the initiative despite being offered free of charge and being easy to access. However, it should be noted that the counseling made it possible to recruit a significant number of people, not spontaneously motivated to carry out the screening. Regarding the results, all the people tested were negative for HCV and HIV. Limiting the analysis to the guests who were tested after STD counseling, it is observed that the acceptance of the test was higher in the population with a higher level of education, with a longer time away from the mother land, while gender and nationality do not seem to affect this aspect. Confusing factors can be the low number of the sample, the young age of migrants (average age 32 years), the shortness of the intervention (one week), the possible ineffectiveness of the transmission of information through mediation. On the basis of the available data, it can be concluded that free access to the test does not imply acceptance of the screening. Awareness of STDs through targeted health promotion interventions is a key factor for the success of screening campaigns. In the absence of these interventions, the easy accessibility of the test for STDs does not guarantee a success of the screening campaign.

Are social cohesion and transnationalism complementary? Migrant communities in Guanajuato, Mexico

928 Ana Vila-Freyer, Universidad Latina de México, México

How do migrant groups affect social cohesion, community values and the development of their communities of origin? To answer these questions, an exploratory survey was applied to 658 people, 21% of whom were returned migrants and/or their families. The goal was to identify the resources mobilized by migrants during their migratory trajectory based on the five dimensions that, according to Jane Jenson, compose social cohesion. This work had two findings: migrant groups have sustained their community values and commitments in a structure of social linkages supported by family and friendship relationships, as well as a low recognition of national and subnational political institutions. Evidence also suggests that some elements of community participation that constitute this linkage structure are present simultaneously in multiple geographic spaces. This would reinforce a sense of multiple belongings and create a notion of transnational social cohesion in expelling communities in Mexico.

Return migration with reference to relative insecurities

523 Sinan Zeyneloglu, Istanbul Kent University, Turkey

Ibrahim Sirkeci, International Business School, UK

This paper discusses the suitability of the concepts of independence and safety in understanding today's international human mobility patterns and mechanisms. It refers and contextualises the discussion within the framework of the Conflict Model of Migration and relates these to the concept of (in)security. The discussion is directed towards return migration and retirement migration as these particular types of migrations are more appropriate to the theoretical discussion intended here. The concepts of independence and safety were introduced in the 1930s by August Losch, a German economist. These concepts have the potential to explain the non-economic motives in relation to the economic motives in contemporary human mobility.

6C   Migration and representation   AMPHI 3

Chair: Zoltán Csányi, Hungarian Central Statistical Office, Hungary

1244   Human zoos around 1900 - reconstructing unheard voices of colonial and migration history

> *Johanna Franziska Katharina Tönsing, University of Paderborn, Germany*

1095   The figure of the refugee as a prisoner and macabre surrealism of oppression in No Friends but The Mountains by Behrouz Boochani

> *Ewelina Barbara Kaczmarczyk, Jagiellonian University, Cracow, Poland*

1234   The Birth of a New Global Health Journal. Who Feels the Need?

> *Laura Elena Pacifici Noja, Unicamillus University, Rome, Italy*

1072   Steps towards a historical analysis of the globalization-migration nexus [Pasos hacia un análisis histórico del nexo globalización-migración]

> *Zoltán Csányi, Hungarian Central Statistical Office, Hungary*

Human zoos around 1900 - reconstructing unheard voices of colonial and migration history

(1244) Johanna Franziska Katharina Tönsing, University of Paderborn, Germany

During the long 19th century, the zoo gradually replaced the menagerie. Certain epistemological transformations have been accompanied by architectural changes concerning the exhibition of animals.[6] Unlike the menagerie – where sovereignty showed its power – the zoo is a civilian institution, and therefore, dependent on economic return. It was Carl Hagenbeck who first had the idea of exhibiting "exotic" humans, who just like animals, had been brought back from German and other colonies. Thus, the zoo is a colonial space *en miniature*. As the leisure attraction of the 19th century, the zoo played a significant role in hammering in a racist outlook for the masses – for it literally constructed a racist perspective that appeared to be natural. Around 35,000 humans were

---

[6] Cf. Jacques, Derrida: The beast and the sovereign I. Chicago 2000.

exhibited in human zoos, and Hagenbeck had around 100,000 visitors on a daily basis since there was no competition with cinematographic visualizations yet.[7] A certain racist epistemology was first materialized in and through the human zoo. In the zoos, the visitors could experience colonialism without having to travel, and therefore, reinforced *en passant* their hierarchic concept of humankind. Most of those stereotype images remain yet today – such as the impression of the oversexualized black body.[8] Initiated by Carl Hagenbeck, the human exhibits were consciously staged in order to provoke unconscious feelings on the part of the visitor. The general populace could be more easily influenced by witnessing the "uncivilized other," in order to normalize perceptions of them.[9] Therefore, the zoo is an institution against the „Verwilderungstendenzen"[10] (wildness) of the zoo visitor.[11]

It is not surprising that the zoo plays a role in many scientific and fictional narratives and reports. Those that are written from a eurocentric perspective have been broadly viewed by many scholars. Narratives from the perspective of the exhibited humans, though, have been widely ignored. The search for them has just begun.[12] Since I understand the zoo with Homi Bhabha as a *third space*[13], I try to understand in-depth, the life stories, and in particular, to analyze the resistant practices against the patriarchal eurocentric ascriptions. Thus, my lecture will introduce you to the diary of Abraham Ulrikab[14] – an Inuk who was exhibited with his family in 1880/81. His story shows daily experiences and consequences of forced migration processes. Besides the physical abuse by Hagenbeck's employees, the embarrassing nakedness and the constant freezing in winterly Europe, his family's ordeal can also be read as evidence of a specific female body experience. For economic reasons, Hagenbeck played with the lust and sensationalism of the male visitors. And the diary shows how the female bodies were used for gynecological examinations by Ernst Haeckel. The diary, therefore, is of major interest, concerning the global history of exhibiting "exotic" humans.

The figure of the refugee as a prisoner and macabre surrealism of oppression in No Friends but The Mountains by Behrouz Boochani

---

[7] Cf. Nessel, Sabine: Medialität der Tiere. Zur Produktion von Präsenz am Beispiel von Zoo und Kino. In: Markus Rautzenberg und Andreas Wolfsteiner (Hrsg.): Hide and Seek. Das Spiel von Transparenz und Opazität. München 2010, S. 198-310.

[8] Cf. Gabriele Dietze: Sexueller Exzeptionalismus. Überlegenheitsnarrative in Migrationsabwehr und Rechtspopulismus. Bielefeld 2019.

[9] Cf. Philipp Sarasin: Zweierlei Rassismus? Die Selektion des Fremden als Problem in Michel Foucaults Verbindung von Biopolitik und Rassismus. In: Martin Stingelin (Hrsg.): Biopolitik und Rassismus. Frankfurt am Main 2003, S. 55-79.

[10] Peter Sloterdijk: Regeln für den Menschenpark. Ein Antwortschreiben zum Brief über den Humanismus. Frankfurt am Main 1999, S. 10.

[11] Geulen, Christian: „Center Parcs". Zur bürgerlichen Einrichtung natürlicher Räume. In: Manfred Hettling und Stefan-Ludwig Hoffmann (Hrsg.): Der bürgerliche Wertehimmel. Innenansichten des 19. Jahrhunderts. Göttingen 2000, S. 257-282.

[12] Projects such as „Vergessene Autobiographien" (https://www.vergessene-biografien.de/. 6.10.2020.) just started their reserach.)

[13] Cf. Bhabha, Homi: The location of culture. With a new preface by the author. London 2006.

[14] Hartmut Lutz und Kathrin Grollmuß (Hrsg.): Abraham Ulrikab im Zoo. Tagebuch eines Inuk 1880/1881. [Kapitel Vorwort und Einführung]. Rödermark 2007, S. 9-21 und S. 22-45.

(1095) Ewelina Barbara Kaczmarczyk, Jagiellonian University, Cracow, Poland

The reportage, the daybook, the prose called by the translator â€žmacabre surrealism" No Friends But The Mountains by Behrouz Boochani is a shocking autobiographical account of a prisoner of the Manus center. The story sent by WhatsApp application begins from the refugee crossing and ends by rebellion in prison coordinated by the Australian government. The book shows how in the twenty-first century comes to practices of objectifying people. Boochani's language is very earthy, poetic at times and affective. Its compositional dominant is constituted by comparisons of prisoners to animals, and of himself to meat. The brutalization of reality shows that the refugee is reduced to body and corporeality, a meaningless number, superfluous existence. He is like homo sacer. This figure is a symbol of politicization of human life because holy man" means the person who can be killed by anybody without comitting a crime. Boochani inspired by the thought of Michele Foucalt calls his meticulously analyzed prison system a kyriarchal system in which evil is banal and responsibility rests with others, giving prison staff a sense of impunity and distance from participating in the iniquities. In Boochani's work refugees are brought only to Agamben's bios, and all systemic actions are intended to confirm this belief. In my speech I would like to make a literary analysis and interpretation of the work, based on the concept of Giorgio Agamben's Homo sacer.

The Birth of a New Global Health Journal. Who Feels the Need?

(1234) Laura Elena Pacifici Noja, Unicamillus University, Rome, Italy

The birth of a new journal devoted to the study of Global Health seems trivial today; in fact, the topic is now sounded out from every angle and full of high-level contributions. However, as the SARSCoV2 pandemic has taught, global health, in its broadest sense, still reserves ample space for medical and above all methodological research. in fact, translational research is the new frontier of the study of health at a global level: much is expected from the application of expertise provided by apparently unrelated disciplines such as geology, zoology, geography, botany, meteorology, hydrology, cultural and religious anthropology. The ability to merge these skills in a syncretism can implement the academic vision of global health. What is currently needed is not only the systematic collection of data on the state of health, diseases, and modes of transmission of diseases. Above all, the ability to read events in anticipation is needed to be able to predict potentially significant events that can affect global health. The Copernican revolution will be in giving more and more space to innovative methodologies capable of interpreting the signs of modification of the state of health of populations and the planet at an early stage. In this sense, these disciplines hitherto neglected in the study of global health can represent a fruitful resource. With this in mind, the UniCamillus Global Health Journal (UGHJ) was very recently founded within the UniCamillus University of Rome (Italy). Its purpose is to give voice to methodological research, even in parallel disciplines that can contribute to the growth of understanding of the natural phenomena that govern health. the goal is to grow new generations of multidisciplinary teams dedicated to the study of global health and its determinants.

152

Steps towards a historical analysis of the globalization-migration nexus [Pasos hacia un análisis histórico del nexo globalización-migración]

(1072) Zoltán Csányi, Hungarian Central Statistical Office, Hungary

Nuestro análisis examina cómo la globalización afectó los niveles de emigración en los países del mundo. Se realizaron regresiones log-lineales en una muestra global de 77 países de tamaño grande y mediano para sacar conclusiones sobre cómo el cambio socioeconómico entre 1990 y 1995 afectó las tasas de emigración en los períodos posteriores. Los modelos utilizados en el estudio se basan en las teorías de la causalidad acumulativa, de la modernización y del sistema-mundo, contextualizadas en el cambio histórico. Por un lado, planteamos la hipótesis de que los efectos migratorios aparecerían más tarde en el tiempo y, por otro lado, en lugar de sus valores absolutos, tomamos en cuenta los cambios ocurridos en cada una de las variables. Los resultados sugieren que una combinación sorprendente de los factores de las tres teorías es la que mejor explica los cambios migratorios. Si bien los efectos de los determinantes cambian con el tiempo, es el análisis de sistemas-mundo, modificado hasta cierto punto, el que brinda el marco más apropiado para integrarlos.

6D   Workshop: Mexico as a Destination Country SALLES DES ACTES

Chair: Liliana Meza León, University of Malaga, Spain

969   Public policy recommendations for the socio-economic integration of migrants in Mexico

> *Karla Valenzuela, Universidad Iberoamericana Mexico City, Mexico*
> *Isaac García-Puertos, Universidad Iberoamericana Mexico City, Mexico*

970   Return Migration in Mexico: social and labor insertion

> *Liliana Meza Gonzalez, Universidad Iberoamericana, México*

971   A study of the labour market integration of immigrants in Mexico

> *Abigail Tun Mendicuti, Max Planck Institute of Demographic Research, Germany*

984   México país de origen, tránsito y detino de los flujos migratorios contemporáneos

> *Cristina Gomez Johnson, Universidad Iberoamericana, Mexico*

974   Central American migrants in Mexico

> *Carla Pederzini, Universidad Iberoamericana, A.C., Mexico*

977   US-born migrants in Mexico: Socioeconomic characteristics and labor market performance

> *Pedro Paulo Orraca Romano, El Colegio de la Frontera Norte, Mexico*

Public policy recommendations for the socio-economic integration of migrants in Mexico

(969) Karla Valenzuela, Universidad Iberoamericana Mexico City, Mexico

Isaac García-Puertos, Universidad Iberoamericana Mexico City, Mexico

In Mexico there are 1.2 million people born in other countries, which constitutes 0.96% of the population nationwide (INEGI, 2021). The patterns of international migration have undergone a rapid shift; several changes in the migration flows worldwide, the diversification of the migrants´ profiles and the border externalization policies have turned transit countries into a destination for mobile populations, and Mexico is no exception. For this country, return migration also constitutes a challenge for the returnees themselves, as well as for the communities that receive them. Given this scenario, the country is now confronted with a new reality, in which integration policies for both, foreigners and returnees, become of the outmost importance. The aim of this presentation is to suggest public policy recommendations in order to improve the federal government´s efforts to incoroporate returnees and foreign populations with differentiated profiles.

Return Migration in Mexico: social and labor insertion

(970) Liliana Meza Gonzalez, Universidad Iberoamericana, México

This paper uses census data to understand how returned migrants are reintegrating into the Mexican labor market. Returned migrants are stratified based on their destination: the US and other countries. I find a favorable treatment from the employers to the returned migrants, but while returnees from other countries are prefered in Mexico due to their observable characteristics, returnees from the US are preferred because of their unobservable characteristics.

A study of the labour market integration of immigrants in Mexico

(971) Abigail Tun Mendicuti, Max Planck Institute of Demographic Research, Germany

Immigrants from 4 different regions:Spain, Rest of Europe and Canada, Southamerica and the Caribbean, and Asia, Africa and Oceania. Using data from 2000,2010 and 2020 census and 2015 intercensal survey of Mexico.

México país de origen, tránsito y detino de los flujos migratorios contemporáneos

(984) Cristina Gomez Johnson, Universidad Iberoamericana, Mexico

Esta investigación busca resaltar los cambios y modificaciones en las fases del proceso migratorio en y a través de México. Evidentemente, la situación de violencia generalizada en gran parte del territorio marca estas transformaciones, así como la desmejora de la situación de los migrantes en tránsito. Estas transformaciones en todas las fases del proceso migratorio están articuladas a circunstancias de violencia, pero ¿cuáles son las violencias viejas y nuevas que afectan a los migrantes?, ¿qué las diferencia? Es posible que las violencias, tanto en el lugar de salida como en tránsito, tengan relación con el aumento en las solicitudes de refugio, por ello, ¿cómo se articulan las violencias con las solicitudes de refugio? A partir de una búsqueda bibliográfica, hemerográfica y una revisión de bases de datos oficiales se analiza la transformación de las migraciones conteporáneas en México a partir de tres aspectos: 1) la evolución de la política migratoria México- Estados Unidos; 2) el impacto de las violencias en la población migrante -propias de los contextos de origen, tránsito y destino-; 3) el incremento de las solicitudes de refugio que convierten a México en un país de destino y ya no solo de tránsito -con todas las implicaciones, observaciones y retos que implica esta transformación-. El trabajo de campo se realizó en tres ciudades de México —Tijuana, Tapachula y Ciudad de México—, definidas por su ubicación en el marco de las rutas migratorias: Tapachula, en el estado fronterizo de Chiapas, como principal zona de entrada de migrantes en la frontera sur; Tijuana, por representar la ciudad donde se concentra la mayor cantidad de migrantes y solicitantes de refugio en la frontera norte; y la Ciudad de México por representar un cambio en la ruta migratoria, ya que anteriormente no era una ciudad de amplia presencia de población migrante en tránsito. Actualmente, muchos migrantes llegan a este último destino porque allí se concentra gran parte de la institucionalidad y las oficinas a las que buscan acceder para regular su situación migratoria. Los flujos actuales han modificado el proceso migratorio en conjunto: rutas, estrategias de paso —muchos no cuentan con apoyos desde Estados Unidos—, se topan con mayores obstáculos —crimen organizado, tratantes, contrabando, mayor control migratorio, seguridad pública— y las razones para salir tienen mayor relación con una huida por cuestiones de seguridad que con factores únicamente económicos, son víctimas de una vulnerabilidad estructural que repercute en su día a día. Esta situación entorpece la planeación y, por tanto, el proceso migratorio puede tener un grado mayor de vulnerabilidad que ha modificado la meta: muchos deciden quedarse en México. Este es un giro que no solamente impacta a los propios migrantes y sus familias, sino también a México, que hasta ahora no había sido destino mayoritario de migración.

Central American migrants in Mexico

(974) Carla Pederzini, Universidad Iberoamericana, A.C., Mexico

Using data from the 2000, 2010 and 2020 censuses, as well as from the 2015 Intercensal Survey, this chapter analyzes the main characteristics as well as the labor insertion of migrants from Guatemala, El Salvador, Honduras and Nicaragua in Mexico.It first addresses the context in which Central American migration to Mexico occurs and the main conditions that have led to emigration from each of these countries, as well as their settlement conditions in Mexico.Then descriptive statistics are shown on the main characteristics of migrants from these four countries in the four points in time analyzed. The information is presented separately for men and women. The data shows a rapid growth of the Central American population residing in Mexico.Guatemalans are the most important group in terms, while Hondurans show the greatest dynamism during the period.Important differences are found in the levels of schooling according to nationality.Guatemalan migrants have a higher concentration in low levels of schooling while Nicaraguans are concentrated in the highest.In terms of geographical concentration, Guatemalans concentrate in the southeast, although throughout the period there is a diversification and a tendency to the greatest concentration of the Central American population in the north of the country.Regarding labor integration, only Guatemalans are concentrated in the primary sector, but it is observed that in general the

Central American population shows a high participation in the service and government sector. The econometric results show that the wage differentials of Central American migrants are favorable to them, after controlling for a series of variables such as their education, their age, their employment position, their place of residence or their marital status. However, this favorable situation decreases over the period analyzed. Observable characteristics of migrants from these countries largely explain favorable income differentials. The loss of income advantage may be explained by the reduction in the level of schooling of migrants who come from these three countries over the period analyzed.

US-born migrants in Mexico: Socioeconomic characteristics and labor market performance

(977) Pedro Paulo Orraca Romano, El Colegio de la Frontera Norte, Mexico

The migration of the US-born to Mexico has been scarcely examined. Some studies analyze the characteristics of migratory flows from the US to Mexico and the impacts that these generate in the receiving localities, others investigate the employment of young Americans in Mexico, some focus on the US-born who arrive in the country to retire, and others investigate the school insertion of children and adolescents born in the US who arrived in Mexico as a result of the return of their Mexican parents and their decisions to re-emigrate to the US. This study contributes to the literature that studies the US-born population in Mexico and analyzes the socio-economic and labor market characteristics of migrants born in the US who have chosen Mexico as their country of destination, paying particular attention to the evolution of wage differences between US and Mexican workers. Unlike much of the existing literature that focuses on cases of migration from developed countries to developed countries (south-north migration), this study examines a case of migration from a developed country to a developing country (north-south migration). The importance of analyzing the US-born in Mexico lies in part in the fact that they represent by far the largest and most important immigrant group in the country. It is estimated that, in 2020, the foreign-born population in Mexico amounted to approximately 1 million 200 thousand people. Among this population, the contingent made up of Americans amounted to a little more than 797 thousand, representing 65.8 percent of the immigrant population. The study shows that the number of US-born migrants in Mexico has increased substantially in recent years. It is observed that, in general, it is a young population made up mostly of people under 25 years of age. In addition, the US-born have higher levels of education and earn higher wages than Mexicans; however, the wage gap between the two groups has narrowed considerably in recent decades. Wage decompositions suggest that the US-born receive higher wages than Mexicans in part because they receive preferential treatment in Mexico's labor market.

6E   Integration, Acculturation and Diasporas

Chair: Valentyna Pliushch, Institute of Sociology, National Academy of Sciences, Ukraine

1094   Socio-cultural adaptation of migrants: concepts, stages, and dynamics

   Valentyna Pliushch, Institute of Sociology, National Academy of Sciences, Ukraine
1225   Intercultural Aspect of Refugee Integration: The Lithuanian Case

Socio-cultural adaptation of migrants: concepts, stages, and dynamics

1094 Valentyna Pliushch, Institute of Sociology, National Academy of Sciences, Ukraine

The subject of adaptation dynamics of migrants' stages of adjustment and adaptation to the new culture is studied for more than a century. During this time a number of practical concepts is proposed.

One of the earliest theoretical concepts of socio-cultural adaptation dynamics was proposed by Norwegian sociologist S. Lysgaard, suggesting three stages U-curve of adaptation, proportional in time to the migrant's contact with a new culture:

1. Positive primary adaptation;

2. Adaptation crisis;

3. Restoration of positive adaptation [Lysgaard, 1955, p. 51].

In 2010 J.&J. Gullahorns proposed the concept of the W-curve of adaptation, in which they conceptualized two interconnected U-curves, consisting five stages of adaptation:

1. Honeymoon;

2. Culture shock;

3. Initial adjustment;

4. Mental isolation;

5. Acceptance and integration.

The reseachers conclude that the problems of alienation and rejection may recur with different intensity when the migrant returns from time to time to his native culture which creats the W-curve of adaptation dynamics [Gullahorns, 2010, p. 45-46].

In 1975 the American sociologist P. Adler offers a three-level analysis regarding socio-cultural adaptation dynamics of migrants (at the levels of perception, emotional state and social behavior), and derives five stages of adjustment to the new culture:

1. Contact;

2. Disintegration;

3. Reintegration;

4. Autonomy;

5. Independence.

Mr. Adler argues that the migrant successfully adapts to the extent that he or she is able to experience new emotional, behavioral and social states [Adler, 1975, p. 20-23].

In 1986, T. Lewis and R. Jungman proposed six stages of adaptation, including the pre-adaptation stage and the post-adaptation stage in case of a migrant's return home.

1. Preliminary stage;

2. Spactator stage;

3. Increasing participation stage;

4. Stage of culture shock;

5. Stage of adaptation;

6. Stage of reentry into home culture.

Scientists are convinced that adaptation dynamics for each migrant may differ in stages and intensity. However, despite the differences in some cases, the pattern is usually true for most of migrants [Lewis, 1986, p. 45–51].

American researcher R. Kohls in 1996 offers a modern concept of the U-curve of the dynamics of adaptation of migrants, consisting of four stages

1. Initial euphoria;

2. Irritability and hostility;

3. Gradual adjustment;

4. Adaptation or biculturalism.

R. Kohls notes that "the dynamics of the process of adaptation depends not only on the duration of the migrant's stay in a non-cultural environment, but to some extent on the personal intentions and characteristics of the migrant" [Kohls, 2001, p. 96-100].

To conclude, it is noted that there are a significant number of concepts on the dynamics of the process of socio-cultural adaptation, however, they all agreed that socio-cultural adaptation is a complex multi-stage process that has a wave-like dynamics of the rise and fall of the migrant's social well-being and occurs over a long period of time.

References:

Adler P. The transitional experience: An alternative view of culture shock. Journal of Humanistic Psychology, 15, 13-23, 1975.

Gullahorn J., Gullahorn J. An Extension of the U-Curve Hypothesis. Journal of Social Issues, 19, 33-47, 2010.

Kohls L.R. Survival Kit for Overseas Living: For Americans Planning to Live and Work Abroad. 2001.

Lewis, T., Jugman, R. On Being Foreign: Culture Shock in Short Fiction, an International Anthology. Yarmouth. Intercultural Press. 1986.

Lysgaard S. *Adjustment in a foreign society: Norwegian Fulbright grantees visiting the United States.* International Social Sciences Bulletin. 7, 45-51, 1955.

Intercultural Aspect of Refugee Integration: The Lithuanian Case

(1225) Vaiva Chockeviciute, Vilnius University of Applied Sciences, Lithuania

Changing irregular immigration tendencies in Lithuania shows the fast-rising need to improve refugee integration processes in the country. The immigration statistics shows, Lithuanian institutions received at least 11 times more asylum request on 2021 comparing with 2020 (EMN, 2020). The Official Lithuanian 2018-2030 Strategy for demography, migration and integration declares aims to promote decent working and living conditions, inclusive local communities, trust in state institutions as well as tolerant receiving society. However, it still does not provide an action plan for integration of newly arrived foreigners (European Website on Integration, 2018). Therefore, integration issues challenges most vulnerable social groups such as refugees and refugee/asylum status seekers.

Adequate housing, jog opportunities, access to education and healthcare are fundamental needs, as well as the main challenges during integration process. Non the less, language barrier, the lack of community support, knowledge of institutional and systemic norms and practices can be equally challenging (Majka, Majka, 2015). The host country, like the migrants themselves, faces certain psychological and socio-cultural difficulties and must adapt in the face of a different culture (Ward, Kennedy, 2001). 2021 Public Opinion Poll conducted by the Social Research Centre revealed most Lithuanians form their opinion about non-EU immigrants from the media. Almost half of the recent Public Opinion Poll participants claimed they would not like to live in the same neighborhood with refugee or Muslim people. The negative attitudes visibly grew in a period of last year (LSTC, 2021). The raising numbers can be related to the unexpected Belarus-European Union border crisis, which started back in July 2021. Negative society attitudes can be considered as an additional obstacle for refugee integration.

The study presents the results of qualitative in-depth interviews with refugees and asylum/refugee status seekers as well as social workers/NGO representatives who provide refugees with services to support their integration process into the host country. The data of 7 interviews was collected in Vilnius, early 2022. The attention was broad to the assumption successful integration should include adaptation to the local cultural skills, norms and values while preserving native cultural identity (Neuliep, 2018). The findings of the research revealed systemic limitations of refugee integration, including mutual language barrier, the lack of intercultural knowledge of service providers, the lack of systemic practices and cultural knowledge of refugees as well as negative society attitudes experienced by the refugees after receiving their legal status and leaving refugee centre.

The interview data raised a question of effective cultural integration and invites to discuss the benefits of deeper intercultural knowledge provided to the immigrants in order to improve their integration opportunities as well as raising awareness in the society so mutual respect could be reached.

The Collateral Immigrant - A Closer Look at the new shape of Identities of Partners, Spouses, and Children of skilled Indian migrant workers who move with their families.

References:

European Migration Network Lithuania (2020). Migration in Numbers. Available at: https://123.emn.lt/en/#chart-14-desc .

European Web Site on Integration, Migrant integration information and good practices (2018). Strategy for demography, migration, and integration 2018-2030. Available at: https://ec.europa.eu/migrant-integration/librarydoc/strategy-for-demography-migration-and-integration-2018-2030 .

Institute for etnic studies of LSRC, (2021). Institute for etnic studies of the Lithuanian Center for Social Research orderd research results of the 2021 Public oppinion poll. Available at: Visuomenės-nuostatų-apklausos-rezultatai-2021.pdf (ces.lt) .

Majka T., Majka L. (2015) Refugee Integration: Issues and Challenges. In: Bean F., Brown S. (eds) Encyclopedia of Migration, (p. 2). Springer, Dordrecht. Available at: https://doi.org/10.1007/978-94-007-6179-7_106-1 .

Neuliep J., W. (2018). Intercultural Communication. A Contextual Approach, (658 p.). SAGE Publications, Inc.

Ward C., Kennedy A. (2001). Coping with Cross-Cultural Transition. Journal of Cross-Cultural Psychology. 32(5):636-642. doi:10.1177/0022022101032005007

The Collateral Immigrant - A Closer Look at the new shape of Identities of Partners, Spouses, and Children of skilled Indian migrant workers who move with their families

(1128) Paramita Roy, Women's College Calcutta, India

This paper analyses the breaking down and rebuilding of identities of Second Space immigrants who have moved away from India as companions to someone else. It's also about those among the Diaspora who, being born in the Third Space of Immigration, find themselves in a niche of "otherness" both at home as well as in the public sphere of the place their parents have immigrated to.

It derives the definition of First, Second, and Third Space from the postcolonial sociolinguistic theory of identity and community, which is attributed to Homi K Bhabha. It also takes a closer look at a few literary and cinematic narratives which draw conclusions on whether these changing identities have been instrumental in evolving a more accepting family or do these stories remain mere testaments to the pain incurred by being secondary to someone else's story, a by-product of someone else's plans of a better life. It includes a close look at Gauri and Bela's experience of identity from Jhumpa Lahiri's *The Lowland*. It talks about the experience of the secondary characters- mother and daughter Gauri and Bela as they traverse the newness of dislocation. Gauri being widowed, married off to her brother-in-law and shipped off to another country to avoid political ramifications, and Bela having to accept his traditional mother's sudden decision to abandon her and her father to understand herself. It also talk about Gurinder Chadha's 1993 film *Bhaji on the Beach* which highlights tensions of the generation gap between the traditional and modern perspectives within three generations of Indian immigrants.

The paper looks at *A Good Indian Wife* by Anne Cherian. The idea of collateral immigrant identity is the main theme of her book. Her novel exhibits empathy for her protagonist Leila Krishnan's cultural and emotional dilemma and efforts of adjustment in a far-away adoptive land. Cherian takes the deceptively common use of the institution of marriage to show how it is undergoing rapid transformation to accommodate the newness of globalization and economic prosperity. Cherian touches on the idea of social mobility and adaptive love that leads to a positive ending. This paper argue the positives and negatives of Cherian's novel. It compares her story both with Lahiri's and also with Revathi's 2002 film *Mitr, My Friend*, which deals with is a more disruptive story about cultural clashes between two different immigrant generations but eventually ends in reconciliation. While Cherian is able is encapsulate how things work out just fine with a greater degree of personal adaptability, it doesn't provide much insight into the equitable personal growth of the characters in question like Lahiri's or Revathi's works. The lesson is not in the creating of Identity, the moral of the story is that if you are adaptable you will survive.

The results and conclusion drawn from the literature and film review adds to the pre-existing scholarship on the modern Indian diaspora immigration literature. It provides more dimension to the secondary party in the narration of the skilled, global immigrant.

References:

Cherian, Anne. *A Good Indian Wife: A Novel.* W.W. Norton & Company, 2009.

Lahiri, Jhumpa. *Lowland.* Headline Publishing Group, 2014.

The Location of Culture, by Homi K. Bhabha, Routledge, 1994, p. 38.

Priya.V, and Sudha Kongara. *Mitr, My Friend.* Telephoto Entertainments Limited, 2002.

Syal, Meera. *Bhaji on the Beach.* Channel Four Films, 2007.

The Adultification of African Children: An Intersectional Analysis of the Spanish Refugee Response

(532) Mouna Massaoudi, Ruhr University Bochum, Germany

On March 4th, 2022, in response to the Russian invasion of Ukraine, the European Commission unanimously agreed to activate the EU Temporary Protection Directive, a previously dormant mandate that aims for EU member states to process a large influx of refugees while preventing adverse effects on domestic asylum systems. This rush to solidarity, although understandable, paralleled and even fueled the less generous measures provided for refugees fleeing other conflicts and sparked a discussion in many media outlets on the double standards by which EU states respond to those fleeing armed conflict or other disasters. These accusations of racial discrimination are not baseless; EU states have consistently displayed xenophobia and hostility towards immigrants, with right-leaning political discourse and austere policies. This directive has been inert since 2001, through various conflicts and refugee influxes from outside of Europe and was only activated following the war in Ukraine. Spain, in particular, expanded the scope of the directive and announced it will grant residence permits to Ukrainians who were present in Spain irregularly prior to the Russian aggression. This sharply contrasts with its treatment of migrants of African origin who attempt to cross the kingdom's borders every day. Although Spanish and EU legislation guarantee certain rights and protections to migrants, there is extensive documentation of instances of the Spanish asylum system bending the rules and violating these rights. Moreover, through its individual complaints' mechanism, the Committee on the Rights of the Child has found that Spain's methods of age-assessment of unaccompanied migrant children violated many of their rights under the Convention of the Rights of the Child, of which Spain is a signatory. Most importantly to this paper, the faulty age assessment procedure, on at least 14 instances, repeatedly misclassified unaccompanied minors as adults, consequently depriving them of protections they are entitled to. Through the analytic lens of Institutional Racism, and using the treatment of African Unaccompanied Minors by the Spanish Asylum system as a case study, this paper argues that the Adultification of Black Children, a term coined to describe the treatment of African American children by the U.S. Justice System as older than they factually are, leading to longer, more severe sentences than their white peers — can be extended to the treatment of African refugee children by the European Union Asylum system.

6F   Türkiye'nin Göç Deneyimi [TR]

Chair: Betül Dilara Şeker, Van Yüzüncü Yil University, Turkey

538   Yabancı Uyruklu Göçün Gayrimenkul Sektörü Üzerindeki Etkisi: İstanbul İli Fatih İlçesi Örneği

Gökçe Küçük, Bursa Technical University, Turkey
Sedanur Gezer, Bursa Technical University, Turkey
Ömer Bilen, Bursa Technical University, Turkey

1184   Avrupa Birliği İnsani Yardımlarında Nakit Transferi Yaklaşımı: Türkiye'de Yabancılara Yönelik Uygulanan Nakit Transferlerinin AB İnsani Yardım ilkeleri Açısından Değerlendirilmesi

Pınar Çağlayan, Usak University, Turkey
Rıdvan Kurtipek, Columbia University, Turkey

1174   Suriyeli Annelerin Kültürleşme Sürecinde Eğitim alan Çocuklarını Değerlendirmesi

Betül Dilara Şeker, Van Yüzüncü Yil University, Turkey

Yabancı Uyruklu Göçün Gayrimenkul Sektörü Üzerindeki Etkisi: İstanbul İli Fatih İlçesi Örneği

(538) Gökçe Küçük, Bursa Technical University, Turkey

Sedanur Gezer, Bursa Technical University, Turkey

Ömer Bilen, Bursa Technical University, Turkey

Avrupa Birliği İnsani Yardımlarında Nakit Transferi Yaklaşımı: Türkiye'de Yabancılara Yönelik Uygulanan Nakit Transferlerinin AB İnsani Yardım ilkeleri Açısından Değerlendirilmesi

(1184) Pınar Çağlayan, Usak University, Turkey

Rıdvan Kurtipek, Columbia University, Turkey

Avrupa Birliği kurumları ve üye devletlerin sağladığı finansman dünyadaki en büyük insani yardım tutarlarından birini oluşturmaktadır. AB, afet ya da acil insani yardımın gerektiği durumlarda farklı kıtalardaki 70'den fazla ülke için destek sağlamaktadır. Avrupa Birliğinin insani yardımlardan sorumlu kuruluşu İnsani Yardım ve Sivil Koruma Genel Müdürlüğü (DG ECHO)'nün bütçesi kurulduğu 1992 yılından bu yana yıllık 1 milyar Avro'nun üzerinde olup 2022 yılı için insani yardım bütçesi 1,5 milyar Avro civarındadır. Avrupa Birliği, insani yardım programlarının "en savunmasız olanların hedeflenmesi, yeterli, hakkaniyetli ve uygun zamanda olması, verimli ve etkili olması, hesap verebilir ve ölçülebilir olması" ilkeleri çerçevesinde yürütülmesini amaçlamaktadır. AB'nin insani yardım kapsamındaki en büyük operasyonlardan biride 2016 yılında imzalanan AB - Türkiye mutabakatı ile başlatılan ve 3 Milyar Avro bütçeye sahip olan Türkiye'deki Mülteciler için Mali İmkan (FRIT) "EU Facility for Refugees in Turkey" programıdır. Program bünyesinde özellikle Suriye'deki çatışmalar nedeniyle Türkiye'ye gelen yabancılar için AB finansmanlı projeler uygulanmaya başlamıştır. Bu projelerin finansman ve hedef kitle açısından en büyük ve kapsamlı olanı ise bir nakit transferi programı olan Sosyal Uyum Yardım Programı (SUY) (Emergency Social Safety Net-ESSN)" dır. 2016 yılında uygulanmaya başlayan SUY, Aile ve Sosyal Hizmetler Bakanlığı (ASHB) Sosyal Yardımlar Genel Müdürlüğü, Türk Kızılay ve Dünya Gıda Programı (WFP) ortaklığında uygulanmaya başlamış, daha sonra WFP'nin yerine Uluslararası Kızılhaç ve Kızılay Federasyonu (IFRC) geçmiştir. FRIT kapsamında uygulanan diğer iki büyük insani yardım programından biri SUY programının tamamlayıcısı olarak planlanan Tamamlayıcı Sosyal Uyum Yardımı (T-SUY), diğeri ise Yabancılara Yönelik Şartlı Eğitim Yardım Programı (YŞEY)'dir. Bu çalışmada öncelikle AB'nin insani yardım amacıyla desteklediği nakit transferi programlarının belirtilen ilkeleri üzerinde durulacak, daha sonra ise Türkiye'de FRIT aracılığıyla desteklenmiş olan SUY, T-SUY ve YŞEY programlarının bu ilkeler ile uyumlu bir şekilde uygulanıp uygulanmadığı tartışılacaktır. Araştırmanın temel kaynaklarını belirtilen programların izleme ve değerlendirilmesi kapsamında hazırlanmış olan raporlar ve bu programları değerlendirmek üzere yapılmış akademik çalışmalar oluşturacaktır.

Suriyeli Annelerin Kültürleşme Sürecinde Eğitim alan Çocuklarını Değerlendirmesi

(1174)   Betül Dilara Şeker, Van Yüzüncü Yil University, Turkey

Göç, günümüzde farklı yerlerde devam eden çatışma ve karmaşalar nedeniyle devam etmektedir. Göç hem yeniden yerleşim ve kaynaklara erişim fırsatlar sunarken hem de bu konularında belirsizlikler taşımaktadır. Mülteciler/geçici sığınmacılar planlanmadan ve zorunluluklar nedeniyle göç sürecini deneyimlerler. Mülteciler menşe ülkede, göç sürecinde ve yeni yerleşilen ülkede travmatik olaylara maruz kalarak çoklu kayıplar yaşarlar. Yeniden yerleşim, kültürleşme ve uyum süreci bu grup için daha zorlu geçmektedir. Genellikle komşu ülkelere yerleşen mülteciler için coğrafik yakınlık nedeniyle kültürel farklılıklar fazla olmasa da sosyal ve kültürel açıdan farklı bir yere yerleşmek, fiziksel, psikolojik ve sosyal bir takım zorluklar bireylere ek yük getirebilir. Bu süreçte özellikle çocuklar eğitim, çalışma gibi farklı nedenlerle baskın grupla daha fazla etkileşime girmektedir. Yaşanan etkileşim sosyal kimlik, ilişkiler, toplumsal cinsiyet, önyargılar, çatışma, ayrımcılık, uyum gibi kavramlara odaklanmamıza neden olmaktadır. Eğitim süreci yaşanan etkileşim özellikle kültürleşme sürecinde önemli olduğu için çalışmada ele alınarak değerlendirilmiştir. Çalışmanın amacı İzmir'de yaşayan Suriye'den gelmiş kadınların çocuklarının eğitim sürecinde yaşadıkları deneyimlerin ele alınarak, yeni yerleşim yeri çocuklar için yeni fırsatlar ve belirsizlikler temelinde incelenmesidir. Genel olarak Suriyeli kadınların yaşadıkları fiziksel, psikolojik, sosyal durumları üzerine çalışmalar yapılmıştır. Çalışmanın amacı genelden farklı olarak Suriyeli mülteci kadınların çocuklarının eğitim sürecinde yaşadıkları deneyimleri, sorunları nasıl değerlendirdiklerini ortaya koymaktır. Çalışmaya İzmir'de yaşayan çocuğu okula devam eden 19 kadın katılmıştır. Katılımcılarla yarı yapılandırılmış görüşmeler yapılmıştır. Çalışmada geçerli veriler elde edebilmek için gerekli durumlarda görüşmelerde tercüman yardımı da alınmıştır. Araştırmada veriler temel özellikleri özetleyebilen, esnek ve zengin betimlemeler yapılmasına olanak veren tematik analiz ile değerlendirilmiştir. Çalışma sonucunda kadınların özellikle kız çocuklarının eğitimine önem verdiği gözlenmiştir. Katılımcılar çocuklarının eğitim sürecinde bulunmalarını desteklediklerini ancak zaman zaman çocuklarının öğretmenleri ve akranları ile yaşadıkları sorunların çözümünde yetersiz kaldıklarını ifade etmişlerdir. Çocuklarının sınıfta farklılıkları nedeniyle dışlandıklarını belirtmişlerdir. Katılımcılar kendi dil yetersizliklerinin, farklı kültüre sahip olmalarının, maddi yetersizliklerin ve ağır şartlar altında çalışmalarının da çocuklarının eğitim ile ilgilenmelerini etkilediğini ifade etmişlerdir. Çalışma aile içinde annenin eğitim sürecine dahil olan mülteci çocukları ile birlikte yaşanan deneyimlerini ele almaktadır. Bu nedenle eğitim konusunun çocukla birlikte sürece eklenen paydaşlarla (anne) değerlendirilmesi; özellikle aile boyutunun sürece dahil edilmesini sağlamaktadır. Ayrıca kültürleşme süreci ve bu süreçte karşılaşılan sorunlara karşı geliştirilen mekanizmaların öğrenilmesinin uzun vadede uyum politikalarının belirlenmesinde alana katkı sağlayacağı düşünülmektedir.

6G   Identities and Migration

Chair: Ayşenur Talat Zrilli, Eastern Mediterranean University, North Cyprus

1126   Parental Negotiations in Naming Children among Mixed-Married Migrants

Mehmet Davut Çoştu, University of Lancaster, UK

1235   Migration, Memory, Motivation: The Quest for 'Meaningful' Education among Tibetan Nationals in Exile in India

Tsering Lhamo, Indian Institute of Technology, Delhi, India

1147   Vulnerable Borders or Vulnerable Migrants? EU External Migration Policies and Gendered Vulnerability

Kathrin Marie Walter, King's College London, UK and Sciences Po Paris, France

1291   Gender and identity formation: The case of second generation Turkish immigrants in North Cyprus

Parental Negotiations in Naming Children among Mixed-Married Migrants

(1126) Mehmet Davut Çoştu, University of Lancaster, UK

This study explores parental negotiations in naming practices of Turkish-speaking (TS) Muslim male migrants married to (non-) Muslim wives. It examines their decision-making processes in terms of the maintenance and transmission of heritage, and the smooth adjustments of their children to life in Britain. The naming practices provide a rich insight into how mixed families negotiate to balance different dynamics, such as Turkish/British ethnic or Muslim/non-Muslim sounding names. More specifically, I aim to examine how for Islam/Muslims the process of naming the child is inextricably linked to religious, social, cultural, ethnic, and political considerations within the minority status context. Furthermore, I examine how different considerations (such as the cultural-linguistic question of name pronunciation and spelling, ethnic or national belonging, and identification) operate when naming the child in mixed-married families and how the names became a contextual and relational constitution of identity through parents' name choices. Naming practices among TS migrants in the UK have not been studied yet, let alone the naming practices of mixed-married TS migrants. Little is known in the existing naming practices studies about the experiences; therefore, naming practices need more attention. To fill the gap in the literature, this study aims to explore how mixed-married TS Muslim male migrants name their children and what considerations inform their choices. The aim is to assesses the impact of mixed marriage over naming practices, the challenges TS male parents face, and the negotiations they experienced in naming processes. My argument is that interpretations of Islam are embedded in different aspects of their lives which are not explicitly religious. Through naming practices, I aim to show the engagement of Islam with these aspects and to bring to life the complex decision making involved in the naming process. The relationships between individuals (through the name) and others within their social contexts is discussed in terms of how the 'name' reflects the religion, kinship, ethnicity, values, culture, and gender to outsiders. As naming practices are closely associated with religious and cultural values, a 'name' plays a vital role in many aspects of our everyday life. For example, religious and ethnic identity can dwell in a name and can be displayed through it. How some TS migrants mark or hide their religious beliefs through the naming of their children is the focus of my analysis in this study.

Migration, Memory, Motivation: The Quest for 'Meaningful' Education among Tibetan Nationals in Exile in India

(1235) Tsering Lhamo, Indian Institute of Technology, Delhi, India

My paper examines the migration of children of Tibetan nationality to India. The Tibetan nationals in exile have been residing in India for several decades following the Chinese occupation of Tibet. Since 1959, there was a mass exodus of Tibetans seeking refuge in India. In this context, the paper investigates the intersections of "refugee" and "migrant" with regard to children of Tibetan nationality when they come to India. The primary reason why the children migrate to India is to attain "meaningful" education which they believe does not exist owing to the assimilationist educational policy in contemporary Tibet under Chinese state (Mishra, 2014). The paper gives an insight into their lived experience in the process of gaining education at Tibetan schools in India (for example, Tibetan Children's Village). It is a retrospective study wherein the respondents are Tibetan students who are currently pursuing their higher education studies in India and have completed their school education in India. In-depth interviews are used as a tool to interact with the respondents to elicit their lived experience. The respondents constitute both male and female students. They are of different generations, first or second or third generation in India, and further they come from different regions of Tibet, that is, *Amdo*, *U-Tsang* and *Kham*. Different social categories lead to diverse experience in their school educational journey.

The paper also underlines their experience of the journey undertaken to migrate from their homeland to India. The journey entails hazardous trails and involves the risk of being apprehended by the state who are vigil to deter this transgressive act. The paper dwells on the emotional and psychological impact on the respondents while staying away from family since a young age to pursue their education without administrative mechanism to return to visit home. On the one hand, there is a unanimous agreement that they are receiving "good" education in Tibetan schools in India wherein they possess knowledge of Tibet before its annexation by the Chinese state. This memory of Tibet is kept alive through the educational policy designed by the Tibetan Government-in-Exile (established in Dharamsala, India) to sustain their unique identity in exile which stands juxtaposed against the "other" Tibet as projected by the Chinese state. The memory of Tibet which the children learn at school is of Tibet before Chinese rule, before they were born therefore, hence it is not their individual memory rather a collective memory constructed of Tibet. It could be argued that the memory is not lived by them but manufactured to perpetuate Tibetan national identity in exile (Anand, 2000). However, on the other hand, they feel pangs of separation and yearn for home in their aspiration for good education which keeps them away from home (Frilund, 2018; Thapan, 2016). Therefore, this quest for meaningful education motivates them to continue with their education in exile.

The paper will discuss the contemporary scenario of migration by Tibetan nationals from Tibet to India especially post-2008, Olympics event in Beijing. The global event marked a remarkable point for both Chinese state and Tibetan nationals. While it was a national embarrassment to the former amidst increasing protest and self-immolation in Tibet, there was a stronger and more brutal crackdown to suppress for the latter and as a result, increasing restrictions to prevent migrating to India. The respondents voice that since 2008 event, there has been a decrease in the number of children migrating from Tibet to India.

References:

Anand, D. (2000). (Re)imagining Nationalism: Identity and Representation in the Tibetan Diaspora of South Asia. Contemporary South Asia, 9(3), 271-287.

Frilund, R. (2020). Exploring (Transit) Migration through a Postcolonial Lens: Tibetans Migrating to India and Beyond. Journal of Ethnic and Migration Studies, 46(7), 1425-1441.

Mishra, M. (2014). Tibetan Refugees in India: Education, Culture and Growing up in Exile. Orient Blackswan.

Thapan, M. (2016). 'Single' and Alone: Tibetan Youth in Exile in India. Society and Culture in South Asia, 2(2), 161-181.

Vulnerable Borders or Vulnerable Migrants? EU External Migration Policies and Gendered Vulnerability

(1147) Kathrin Marie Walter, King's College London, UK and Sciences Po Paris, France

My paper examines the migration of children of Tibetan nationality to India. The Tibetan nationals in exile have been residing in India for several decades following the Chinese occupation of Tibet. Since 1959, there was a mass exodus of Tibetans seeking refuge in India. In this context, the paper investigates the intersections of "refugee" and "migrant" with regard to children of Tibetan nationality when they come to India. The primary reason why the children migrate to India is to attain "meaningful" education which they believe does not exist owing to the assimilationist educational policy in contemporary Tibet under Chinese state (Mishra, 2014). The paper gives an insight into their lived experience in the process of gaining education at Tibetan schools in India (for example, Tibetan Children's Village). It is a retrospective study wherein the respondents are Tibetan students who are currently pursuing their higher education studies in India and have completed their school education in India. In-depth interviews are used as a tool to interact with the respondents to elicit their lived experience. The respondents constitute both male and female students. They are of different generations, first or second or third generation in India, and further they come from different regions of Tibet, that is, *Amdo*, *U-Tsang* and *Kham*. Different social categories lead to diverse experience in their school educational journey.

The paper also underlines their experience of the journey undertaken to migrate from their homeland to India. The journey entails hazardous trails and involves the risk of being apprehended by the state who are vigil to deter this transgressive act. The paper dwells on the emotional and psychological impact on the respondents while staying away from family since a young age to pursue their education without administrative mechanism to return to visit home. On the one hand, there is a unanimous agreement that they are receiving "good" education in Tibetan schools in India wherein they possess knowledge of Tibet before its annexation by the Chinese state. This memory of Tibet is kept alive through the educational policy designed by the Tibetan Government-in-Exile (established in Dharamsala, India) to sustain their unique identity in exile which stands juxtaposed against the "other" Tibet as projected by the Chinese state. The memory of Tibet which the children learn at school is of Tibet before Chinese rule, before they were born therefore, hence it is not their individual memory rather a collective memory constructed of Tibet. It could be argued that the memory is not lived by them but manufactured to perpetuate Tibetan national identity in exile (Anand, 2000). However, on the other hand, they feel pangs of separation and yearn for home in their aspiration for good education which keeps them away from home (Frilund, 2018; Thapan, 2016). Therefore, this quest for meaningful education motivates them to continue with their education in exile.

The paper will discuss the contemporary scenario of migration by Tibetan nationals from Tibet to India especially post-2008, Olympics event in Beijing. The global event marked a remarkable point for both Chinese state and Tibetan nationals. While it was a national embarrassment to the former amidst increasing protest and self-immolation in Tibet, there was a stronger and more brutal crackdown to suppress for the latter and as a result, increasing restrictions to prevent migrating to India. The respondents voice that since 2008 event, there has been a decrease in the number of children migrating from Tibet to India.

References:

Anand, D. (2000). (Re)imagining Nationalism: Identity and Representation in the Tibetan Diaspora of South Asia. Contemporary South Asia, 9(3), 271-287.

Frilund, R. (2020). Exploring (Transit) Migration through a Postcolonial Lens: Tibetans Migrating to India and Beyond. Journal of Ethnic and Migration Studies, 46(7), 1425-1441.

Mishra, M. (2014). Tibetan Refugees in India: Education, Culture and Growing up in Exile. Orient Blackswan.

Thapan, M. (2016). 'Single' and Alone: Tibetan Youth in Exile in India. Society and Culture in South Asia, 2(2), 161-181.

Gender and identity formation: The case of second generation Turkish immigrants in North Cyprus

(1291) Ayşenur Talat Zrilli, Eastern Mediterranean University, North Cyprus

Şerif Türkkal Yenigüç, Eastern Mediterranean University, North Cyprus

Migration has played an important role in the building of North Cyprus as a political as well as a cultural entity. As a result, despite not being an internationally recognized nation-state, Turkish Republic of Northern Cyprus has become a de-facto state for people from diverse cultural backgrounds. One of the main groups of population who consider this state their homeland in addition to native Turkish Cypriots, are populations which were transferred from Turkey after the partition of Cyprus in 1974. Today there live in the northern part of Cyprus at least three generations of immigrants and their offspring. Due to historical, cultural and political ties between Turkish Cypriots and Turkey, North Cyprus still remains one of the main destination countries for potential Turkish migrants. Yet, these close ties have, for many decades, obscured and complicated the way immigrants from Turkey were viewed both politically and socially. Turkish nationalist discourses among the Turkish Cypriot community denied this population immigrant identities and constructed them as kin. Yet, 'how do the immigrants see their own selves'? has been a question rarely asked.   In line with a social interactionist and constructivist perspective we argue that identities are constructed actively by individuals who interact in everyday life in different settings. We resort to Berzonsky's (1989;1992; 2004) theory, which argues that people have different styles of constructing their identities. Berzonsky differentiates between 'informational', 'normative' and 'diffuse avoidant styles' (Berzonsky, 1989; 1992; 2004) which depend on individual problem-solving strategies. We also argue that 'gender' as a social institution also play an important role in the determination of the strategy adopted.   Within this conceptual framework, our aim is to focus on second generation immigrants from Turkey and their experiences of self-identification. Our data comes from 20 semi-structured in-depth interviews with university students who have at least one immigrant parent from Turkey. We endeavour to answer questions relating to how they describe their ethnic and cultural identities, whether, to what degree and in which situations they identify with their country of origin and which strategies they follow in the process. At the same time, we try to understand how gender affects these processes, not only by creating differences in the strategies adopted by men and women, but also functioning as an intrinsic part of these identities.

6H   Establishing a Decent Labour Policy for Migrant Workers in Taiwan's Distant Water Fisheries

Chair: Lichuan Liuhuang, National Chung Cheng University, Taiwan

1177   Is Debt Bondage a Sufficient Indicator of Forced Labour for Migrant Workers?

Ming-Te Peng, National Chung Cheng University, Taiwan

1179   Assessing the Working Conditions for Migrant Workers in Distant Water Fisheries

Pao-Ann Hsiung, National Chung Cheng University, Taiwan
Hsiu-Chun Hsu, National Chung Cheng University, Taiwan

1263   Establish a Decent Labour Policy for Migrant Workers in Taiwan's Distant Walter Fisheries

Lichuan Liuhuang, National Chung Cheng University, Taiwan
Mingte Peng, National Chung Cheng University, Taiwan
Ruoyen Lee, National Chung Cheng University, Taiwan

1264   Development Blockchain as a Service of Offshore Application

Pao-Ta Yu, National Chung Cheng University, Taiwan

Is Debt Bondage a Sufficient Indicator of Forced Labour for Migrant Workers?

(1177) Ming-Te Peng, National Chung Cheng University, Taiwan

Introduction: Taiwan's distant water fisheries (DWF) plays a leading role in global seafood supply chains. Due to a harsh nature of DWF, its recruitment used to rely on laborers from rural areas, islands and native communities. Nowadays, its crew mainly consist of migrant workers from Indonesia, Vietnam and Philippine. In past decades, Taiwan's DWF has criticised for poor working conditions, forced labour or even trafficking in human beings. For instance, the Taiwanese vessel Fuh Sheng No.11 is the first case to be detained by South Africa due to violation against International Labour Office's (ILO) C188 Work in Fishing Convention. Hence, operational indicators of force labour, established by ILO, is adopted by NGOs and inspectors to measure migrants in Taiwan's DWF. Objectives: The main objective of this empirical study aims to investigate to which extent the phenomenon of debt bondage, one of the operational indicators, is strong enough to accurately identify trafficking and force labour. Second, this research explores the context where this debt takes place. Methods: This study employs two methods to collect empirical data. The first method is semi-structured interview. 22 migrant fishmen in Taiwan were interviewed in 2021 to delineate recruitment procedures and working conditions in DWF. To have a deep look at extreme conditions, this study turns to controversial cases by analysing 31 appeal cases. These 31 appeal cases were processed by the Fisheries Agency during 2021. Results: According to interviews with migrant crew, to have debts is a common pattern. Because departure fees, including passports, VISA, transport, crew certificate, insurance, training and health check, are costly, it is unlikely for migrants from rural areas to afford recruitment procedures without borrowing grants from local agencies. Migrants may require advanced payment for family before departure. This suggests the debt could be seen as an investment for migrant workers to have better life rather than mere bondage. Because having debts is such common among migrant workers, the indicator of debt bondage may not be enough to identify trafficking and force labour. Continuity between debt and debt bondage can not be reduced to one indicator. On the other hand, the controversy analysis show that deposits and its varieties generate considerable impacts on decreasing migrants' mobility. The deposit disables migrants from meeting their debts. Furthermore, the existence of deposits makes exit more difficult and costlier while migrant workers encounter deteriorated working conditions. Conclusion: ILO's C188 Convention suggests that no fishman should pay recruitment fees. Because international inequality and uneven development render migrant workers vulnerable to harsh contracts, this zero-cost policy alleviates disadvantages caused by structural poverty. Nevertheless, there is a vague zone whether some costs are included as part of recruitment fees. Despite this vulnerable situation, migrants still display their agency, considering working abroad as a temporary strategy for higher salary and future career. This complicated nature of working in DWF indicates that either continuity between debt and debt bondage or spectrum between exploitation, forced labour and trafficking should not be overly simplified.

Assessing the Working Conditions for Migrant Workers in Distant Water Fisheries

(1179) Pao-Ann Hsiung, National Chung Cheng University, Taiwan

Hsiu-Chun Hsu, National Chung Cheng University, Taiwan

Assessing the working conditions of fishermen onboard fishing vessel is always a challenging task due to the limited resources available such as completely no networking or very small bandwidth satellite communications with a very high cost, limited visual capturing through some CCTV cameras onboard, limited computing power for any real-time analysis. This work highlights the issues in this area of research and proposes a feasible solution for some of the issues. Mainly, we propose a 3-fold technique where firstly, fishermen labour (working hour) records are maintained electronically by a Pad-based APP, secondly, CCTV video cameras record automatically the working conditions on a vessel, and thirdly, we try to compare the afore-mentioned working records to make sure that the electronically maintained labour records have the same distribution as the automatically captured records. Here, deep learning techniques such as human detection, human tracking, pose estimation are used. Statistical techniques are used for distribution comparisons. The same method will also be used later to check for illegal long working hours in the future.

Establish a Decent Labour Policy for Migrant Workers in Taiwan's Distant Walter Fisheries

(1263) Lichuan Liuhuang, National Chung Cheng University, Taiwan

Mingte Peng, National Chung Cheng University, Taiwan

Ruoyen Lee, National Chung Cheng University, Taiwan

Taiwan's distant water fisheries (DWF) vessels have been long criticized by the civil society and environmental NGOs for the alleged cases of forced labour and human trafficking. In 2020, the fishery products have been even labelled as product of forced labour by the Ministry of Labour of the USA. The challenges ahead of policy reform and enforcement are various. Internally, the management of distant water fisheries involves with several government authorities while find hard to collaborate. In addition, the industries and the supply chain are composed with states of markets, coasts, ports and of labour sourcing, etc. In particular, the labour force of distant water fisheries relies on migrant fishers originated from Indonesia, the Philippines and Vietnam. Thus how to enforce ILO core Conventions and national legislations would need to find way to integrate main stakeholders between the sourcing countries and Taiwan. The aim of our research is to advocate for a fair working environment for the industry through the approach of creating a sustainable human centered ecosystem for migrant fishers on board of DWF. The current cross-national recruitment and employment institutions for migrant fishers have been criticized for its asymmetric information gap caused vulnerability and abuse of labour rights. The migrant fishers who are desperate to get on board of DWF might ignore the high risks of working environment and the process of labour and be entrapped in a vulnerable situation. The 3 years term project assumes that to remedy the vulnerability of migrant fishers on board of DWF would need to take a holistic approach to empower the recruitment and management system with stakeholders' engagement and continuous dialogue and collaboration.

The research team conducts desk review and accumulated research findings mapping out the problems and developing the benchmark standards and guideline. With the consent of fisheries association and voluntary engagement of 9 vessel companies, we would be able to apply the digital technology to identify working and rest time on board. By taking the action oriented methodological approach, we invite core stakeholders (vessel owners and staff, migrant fishers' organisation, training centers and recruitment agencies) to fulfil the benchmark standards via research seminars and dialogues in the field. The action research approach would be useful to provide evidence-based advice for policy implementation to the government and to provide a trustful platform for continuing dialogues to benefit all parties and stakeholders.

This research is now at the end of first year. 3 of 9 experimental vessels were equipped with CCTV for the analysis of working time and identification of wrong or dangerous behaviour on board. The blockchain technology has been developing to assure the transparency of data contributed by various stakeholders in the recruitment and management system. The ongoing engagement with various field practioners and stakeholders via solution-oriented dialogues provide precious lessons in the realisation of social peace at sea.

Development Blockchain as a Service of Offshore Application

(1264) Pao-Ta Yu, National Chung Cheng University, Taiwan

Blockchain technology has been in the news in recent years with the hype of virtual currencies and has been on the public's radar. What the public is aware of is based on the variants of virtual currencies related to fintech, rather than the benefits and technological changes that blockchain technology can bring. When it comes to implementing blockchain technology for different projects, it is not based on existing blockchains or a specific blockchain that can be the solution. The International Organization for Standardization TC307 Committee is still working on the standardization of blockchain classification, terminology, and related standards. Problems related to the state of offshore fishing labor include lack of transparency in administrative operations at sea, inaccurate documentation, low credibility in filling in work hours and fishing records...etc. The "trust" element based on blockchain technology can help to solve these long-standing problems. The purpose of choosing to implement blockchain technology is to make the process of exchanging data between parties faster, cheaper, more transparent, trustworthy, and accountable, so that the application can be recognized by the regulatory authorities and meet the evolving needs. In this study, we propose the framework core foundation of blockchain and the application services based on blockchain technology. The framework core foundation of blockchain includes a high-security digital signature, communication privacy, data fast verification algorithm, data retrieval algorithm, fault tolerance mechanism, etc., which are applied to decentralized database storage applications.

Day Three 9 September 2022 Friday

Day Three 9 September 2022 - 10:45-12:15   AMPHI 1

7A   North-South Migration: Moroccan Model [AR-FR]

الجلسة السابعة: هجرة شمال جنوب : نموذج المغرب

رئيس الجلسة : ذ. توفيق اليحياوي ، منسق ماستر الاقتصاد الترابي كلية العلوم القانونية و الاقتصادية و الاجتماعية أكدال جامعة محمد الخامس بالرباط

Chair: Y. Tawfiq Al-Yahyawi, Coordinator of The Master of Turabi Economics, Faculty of Legal, Economic and Social Sciences, Mohammed University of Rabat, Morocco

576 Djamila Chekrouni & Mohamed Khachani (Université Mohamed V de Rabat): Dimension historique et quantitative de la migration Nord/Sud au Maroc

Abdesslam El Ftouh (ex directeur du Pôle Economique à la Fondation Hassan II pour les Marocains Résidant à l'Etranger): L'intégration des Européens au Maroc

578 Ounir Abdellah: Cadre institutionnel et juridique de la question migratoire au Maroc

579 Boutaina Ismaili Idrissi: Quel apport de la migration du Nord à l'économie marocaine

7B   Migraciones, Globalización and Transnacionalismo [ES]

Chair: Encarnación La Spina, University of Deusto, Spain

1203   Control migratorio en el Mediterráneo: la deslocalización de las fronteras europeas

María Isolda Perelló Carrascosa, InMIDE, University of Valencia, Spain

1153   ¿Hacia una obsolescencia programada en la clasificación y categorización de los flujos migratorios en el siglo XXI?: nuevos y viejos retos

Encarnación La Spina, University of Deusto, Spain

1127   Diaspora del Austro Ecuatoriano: Practicas Transnacionales y Ayudas

Pablo Israel Canar Tenenpaguay, Investigador autónomo, Spain

Control migratorio en el Mediterráneo: la deslocalización de las fronteras europeas

(1203) María Isolda Perelló Carrascosa, InMIDE, University of Valencia, Spain

A través de esta comunicación, se pretende mostrar algunos resultados de la investigación llevada a cabo en 2020 dentro del marco de un informe sobre las migraciones y la movilidad en el Mediterráneo. Su finalidad es exponer cómo las políticas europeas de control migratorio han pretendido desalentar la entrada irregular de personas migrantes y refugiadas procedentes del Magreb, el África Subsahariana y Oriente Próximo, alineando las acciones diplomáticas de política exterior con las de defensa, y deslocalizando las fronteras mediante la vía de la cooperación al desarrollo.

Desde que en 2005 se adoptara el Enfoque Global de la Migración y la Movilidad (GAMM) como marco general de la política exterior de la UE en materia de migración y asilo, el fomento del desarrollo en los países de origen fue considerado esencial para garantizar una migración ordenada, legal y segura. Este proceso iniciado con la Conferencia de Rabat de 2006 continuaría en 2014 con la Cumbre de la Valeta sobre Migración y la Iniciativa sobre la Ruta Migratoria UE-Cuerno de África (o ruta migratoria oriental) conocida como Proceso de Jartum, monitoreando iniciativas y acciones para luchar contra la trata de seres humanos y el tráfico ilícito de migrantes (Comisión Europea, 2015). Posteriormente, se crearía el Fondo Fiduciario de Emergencia de la UE para África (EUTF) abordando las causas profundas de los desplazamientos forzosos y de la migración irregular. Asimismo, con el fin de atender las vulnerabilidades de los refugiados y las comunidades de acogida en los países de la franja mediterránea afectados por la crisis de Siria, se activó el Fondo Fiduciario Regional de la UE (Fondo MADAD) (European Comission, s. f.-a, s. f. -b). Pero también se han adoptado estrategias de contención, como el establecimiento de los "hotspots" griegos e italianos para la reubicación temporal de los solicitantes de asilo (Campesi 2020), o se han desplegado misiones civiles y militares en Libia, el Mediterráneo central y el Sahel dentro del mecanismo de concertación de política exterior (PESC) y la Política Común de Seguridad y Defensa (PCSD).

Para el levantamiento de información se ha recurrido a fuentes históricas (Mora, 2013), entre ellas documentos oficiales y memorias de organismos comunitarios e internacionales. Asimismo, para tener un conocimiento cuantitativo del tema investigado se han confeccionado datos procedentes de fuentes secundarias, en su mayor parte aportadas por la Agencia FRONTEX y la Comisión Europea.

Como se verá, un alto porcentaje de las cantidades presupuestarias asignadas a los Programas y proyectos EUTF en el Norte de África está destinado al fortalecimiento de la vigilancia fronteriza. Además, pese a la intervención europea en zonas como El Sahel y Libia, no se está garantizando la protección de migrantes y refugiados, que siguen quedando a merced de los grupos terroristas y las milicias armadas, o de las organizaciones de trata de personas. Igualmente, el bloqueo de las rutas mediterráneas ha provocado la reactivación de otras más mortíferas, como la ruta atlántica hacia las Islas Canarias.

Bibliografía:

Comisión Europea (2015). ¿Cómo coopera la UE con África en materia de migración? Recuperado de https://n9.cl/3x7q

Campesi, G. (2020). Normalising the Hotspot Approach? En Carrera S., Curtin D. Geddes A. (Eds.), 20 Year Anniversary of the Tampere Programme: Europeanisation Dynamics of the EU area of Freedom, Security and Justice, EUI, Fiesole, pp. 93-104.

European Comission (s. f. -a). EU Emergency Trust Fund for Africa. Recuperado de https://cutt.ly/sDPQRAk

European Comission (s. f. -b). EU Regional Trust Fund in Response to the Syrian crisis. Recuperado de https://ec.europa.eu/trustfund-syria-region/where-we-work_en

Mora, D. (2013). Metodología para la investigación de las migraciones. Integra Educativa, 6(1), 13-42. Recuperado de http://www.scielo.org.bo/pdf/rieiii/v6n1/v6n1a02.pdf

¿Hacia una obsolescencia programada en la clasificación y categorización de los flujos migratorios en el siglo XXI?: nuevos y viejos retos

(1153) Encarnación La Spina, University of Deusto, Spain

La clasificación entre migraciones forzadas y migraciones voluntarias o, migraciones (dictada por razones) económicas- así come aquella entre "verdaderas/os" y "falsas/os" solicitantes de protección internacional (y entre "verdaderas/os" y "falsas/os" refugiadas/os) no es nítida y en ocasiones resulta intencionadamente muy difuminada.. Básicamente porque el "nexo diferencial entre migración y asilo" se fundamenta en la multiplicidad y en la coincidencia de razones para la movilidad frente a la robustez/rigidez de las categorías o etiquetas que se intentan imponer (Castles, 2003, p. 16, De Genova, Mezzadra 2015, Crawley and Skleparis, 2018). Los antecedentes del debate académico sobre el nexo migración-desplazamiento-asilo (Naranjo Giraldo, 2015), mantienen a la investigación dividida según clasificaciones normativas o políticas y por ende traducen de forma acrítica categorías políticas y etiquetas en categorías científicas (Zetter 2007, Robertson 2018, Collyer y De Hass 2012) pese a la complejidad intrínseca del fenómeno migratorio per se. Tales distinciones reflejan las dinámicas de poder que connotan la regulación (jurídica) de las migraciones, sobre todo con referencia a la defensa de las prerrogativas soberanas de los Estados nacionales en el control de las fronteras y en la categorización y limitación de los flujos migratorios de entrada. Aunque los términos "migrante internacional", "migrante forzoso" y "trabajador migrante" o migrante "en situación irregular" no han sido definidos formalmente en el Derecho Internacional, sino que a veces son utilizados de forma diferente por las distintas partes interesadas. El trasfondo de la expresión "los refugiados no son migrantes" (Feller, 2005,2007), tal y como señala Backwell (2011, 17) o Meyer y Boll (2018), consolida una narrativa dominante sobre la clasificación binaria entre aquellos que merecen protección y asistencia particular, frente otros que no la merecen o incluso son una amenaza; cosa que justificaría, de un lado, las políticas migratorias de carácter defensivo, restrictivo o represivo y, de otro lado, las categorías de exclusión que los Estados ponen en acción frente a ellos. Sin embargo, más allá de estas narraciones hegemónicas, es muy difícil establecer que migraciones son realmente voluntarias en el siglo XXI: ¿es realmente posible, por ejemplo, considerar voluntarias (en sentido fuerte) migraciones que son dictadas por el hambre, por la extrema pobreza, por las emergencias sanitarias o por el cambio climático? Las clasificaciones jurídicas crean por tanto fracturas artificiales en fenómenos fluidos, globales y complejos. Ciertamente, distinciones y clasificaciones son elementos esenciales de la forma en que el derecho opera; aun así, si no son ponderadas con atención, pueden convertirse en fuente de discriminación, exclusión y marginalización, creando condiciones de vulnerabilidad. En esta perspectiva, la propuesta plantea una reflexión teórico-crítica sobre el uso y abuso de la dicotomía refugiado/migrante económico (por ejemplo, por el Derecho de la Unión Europea) y de la distinción entre migraciones voluntarias y migraciones forzadas explícita en los dos Global Compact. En particular, se discute la obsolescencia de estas categorías frente a la categoría emergente de las "migraciones mixtas", sobre todo a la luz de su capacidad de crear exclusión y de producir jerarquías entre los sujetos en razón de las diferencias de status que el derecho les atribuye.

Diaspora del Austro Ecuatoriano: Practicas Transnacionales y Ayudas

(1127) Pablo Israel Canar Tenenpaguay, Investigador autónomo, Spain

Asentados en tres ciudades diferentes (Madrid, Nueva Jersey y Londres), la diáspora proveniente de una comunidad pequeña (Gonzanamá) del austro del Ecuador han formado organizaciones migrantes que se han venido configurado y adaptando para dar respuesta a todo tipo de situación tanto "allá" lugar de asentamiento como "acá" comunidad origen. Mediante entrevistas, utilizando metodología de corte cualitativo y estudio de caso comparativo descriptivo. Este ensayo esboza brevemente de forma sincrónica la evolución de la diáspora gonzanameña, poniendo de manifiesto: 1) las organizaciones migrantes existentes y sus características, 2) las prácticas transicionales y 3) el trabajo en red que realizan a favor de Gonzanamá. Con una trayectoria de dos décadas los transmigrantes en sus inicios formaron organizaciones migrantes informales que con el paso del tiempo se han configurando según la realidad de los transmigrantes, de estas tres organizaciones que nacieron con un objetivo se derivan varios grupos de camarillas que persiguen un objetivo específico, en algunos casos buscan dar respuesta a las necesidades tanto "allá" como "acá", en otros se enfocan en realizar prácticas transnacionales (deportivas, cívicas, religiosas) dando paso a "coaliciones" cómo por ejemplo la práctica transnacional religiosa que reúne a cientos de migrantes de todo Ecuador, varios países de Latinoamérica y las personas del lugar de asentamiento, o la camarilla que con el actuar diario de los transmigrantes dan paso a la práctica transnacional deportiva de ecuavóley que es una variante del voleibol adaptada en

Ecuador donde recrean el terruño e interactúan con otras organizaciones de migrantes ecuatorianas, o las prácticas transnacionales cívicas donde enseñan a las nuevas generaciones sobre juegos, comida, baile, música y artesanías tradicionales de Gonzanamá. Finalmente se expone el trabajo en red que realizan las organizaciones migrantes para el envío de remesas tangibles e intangibles a la comunidad origen, ayudas que cada vez es mayor y cuenta con mayor número de participantes.

Palabra claves: Transnacionalismo, práctica transnacional, coaliciones, transnacionalismo desde abajo.

7C   Migration and Religion

Chair: Deniz Cosan Eke, University of Vienna, Austria

1029   "I had to reinvent my Jewishness": Personal and Professional Identity Perceptions of Jewish Culture Teachers from the Former Soviet Union

Iris Yaniv, Oranim College, Israel
Adi Binhas, Oranim College, Israel

1038   Religion and Migration, Diaspora Biography & Faith Case Study: 'Mary' A Christian Syrian Widow

Dua'a Al-Namas, Social Sciences University of Ankara, Turkey

1164   Transnationalism among Muslim Immigrants in Japan

Marie Sato, Kyoto University, Japan

539   Interfaith Initiatives and the Impact of Religious Leaders on Politics

Deniz Cosan Eke, University of Vienna, Austria

"I had to reinvent my Jewishness": Personal and Professional Identity Perceptions of Jewish Culture Teachers from the Former Soviet Union

(1029) Iris Yaniv, Oranim College, Israel

Adi Binhas, Oranim College, Israel

This study examines the identity and professional perceptions of teachers who teach subjects related to Jewish identity in non-religious schools in Israel. As immigrants, they face the consequences of the migration process on their personal, cultural, political and social identity (Berry, 1992). Since they came to Israel over twenty years ago - they are familiar with both Israeli and Russian social and cultural systems, accordance with transnational theory (Dinnerstein, Roger and Reimers, 1990; Gold, 2002).   In the last decade of the twentieth century, about a million immigrants from the former Soviet Union immigrated to Israel, most with atheistic or secular worldviews. While living under communism, they were distanced from their Jewish roots. Indeed, the Jewish population in Israel was disappointed with the lack of Jewish identity among the 1990s immigrants from the USSR (Remennick and Pershitsky, 2013). The immigrants, for their part, were disappointed by the cold reception they received and by lack of ethnic solidarity among Israelis Jews, making it difficult for them to experience Aliyah as a "return home" (ibid.). Upon arriving in Israel, the immigrants encountered Israeli Judaism and adopted the signs and symbols of a Jewish lifestyle (ibid). The research question was: What was the impact of immigration on shaping the participants' Jewish-Israeli identity, and how is this process reflected in their professional perception as teachers of Jewish subjects? The study used a qualitative research method that entailed conducting 12 semi-structured interviews. We sought to learn about the teachers' perceptions of being Jewish, the reasons they chose to teach Jewish subjects, and the impact of their personal worldview on their educational perspective. The study's findings indicated that the development of the teachers' own sense of Jewish identity had a significant impact on the formation of their educational perspectives regarding teaching Jewish subjects and on their definition of Jewish identity. The themes emerging from the interviews described the development of their Jewish identity since immigrating to Israel and revealed that their decision to become teachers of Jewish subjects is part of their personal journey in defining their identity.

Religion and Migration, Diaspora Biography & Faith Case Study: 'Mary' A Christian Syrian Widow

(1038) Dua'a Al-Namas, Social Sciences University of Ankara, Turkey

Diaspora and migration has long been existing, for many centuries in the world. What has changed in recent centuries is the reasons behind these migration journeys, some which could be related to economic reasons, educational reasons, conflicts and wars, or religious reasons. Examples are abundant, yet, religion counts for one main reason of migration, it could play both roles for individual, could play a push and pull factor. Could provide *"psychological, spiritual, and social support"*, (Hagan, J. M. 2015) and could be the reason for the exact opposite.

This paper will concentrate on one case to represent religious migration, and it happened to be a well determinate women, "Mary"[15] religious migrant from a Christian background, who moved from Syria to Canada with her kids after the death of her husband at an early stage of the conflict in Syria.

Qualitative in depth interview was conducted with the case study, which was introduced by a gatekeeper, (a common friend) This lady used all terms of religious and migration means in order to secure a safe journey from Syria to Lebanon and then to Canada for her and her sons. They went through many obstacles and difficult times, yet, nothing stopped her from fighting for her and her sons hopes of a better future. Eventually she managed and turned the harsh situation into a great advantage for herself and her most beloved two boys. With all the obstacles she faced and still facing from different culture, education system and language, to the small things like freezing cold weather and adapting to completely new style of life and food, She is safe and stable living in Canada, with her sons, within a Christian community, were she feels she is a productive, useful individual in a community that she feels welcomed in, and belongs most from a religious point of view.

In conclusion, the movement within the religious field can take on a variety of trajectories and has significant effects on the level of individual religiosity. Mary used her religion as a gate to gain refuge and shelter in different parts of the world. The study shows clear involvement and role of religion in Mary's case, as the church had a great psychological

---

[15] Mary is the name I chose for the case, not her real name.

and sociological impact on aiding the stabilizing of the small refugee family life, despite the origins of this family.

Bibliography:

Beckford. James A. (2019). *Religions and migrations – old and new Beyond the refugee crisis: migrations and religions in Europe. Sociology in public. Page:15-32.*

Pierret, Thomas, And Alrefaai, Laila. (2021). *Religious Governance in Syria Amid Territorial Fragmentation.*

Hagan, J. M. (2015). *Migration Miracle: Faith, Hope, and Meaning on the Undocumented Journey.*

Özisik, S. (2016). *Intergenerational changes in the religiosity of Turkish Islamic immigrants in contemporary Germany: a qualitative analysis using the faith development interview. Bielefeld: Universität Bielefeld.*

(2012) Migration and New International Actors: An Old Phenomenon Seen With New Eyes Edited by Maria Eugenia Cruset

Transnationalism among Muslim Immigrants in Japan

(1164) Marie Sato, Kyoto University, Japan

Japan's parliament has approved a new law allowing hundreds of thousands of foreigners into the country to ease labor shortages. Japan has traditionally been wary of immigration, though the number of foreign nationals is rapidly growing. Muslim population and their activities also grow. So how the Muslim immigrants in Japan develop their social networks, form activities and patterns of living that span home and host societies? The aim of the paper is to analyze transnational connections and networks through Muslim immigrants in Japan form.

The studies of transnationalism on Muslim immigrants are positioned in the discussion of religion and development. This is because Islamic principles and guidelines are closely related to charitable activities, and many Muslim immigrants establish organisations to commit in charitable activities. Their work such as Islam's obligatory practice of giving charity motivate Muslim immigrants not only to engage in development, but also to work in humanitarian aid, sustainable development, investment in education, and infrastructure development, both in their country of origin and beyond, which are secular and humanitarian in nature (Erdal and Borchgrevink 2017:143). While the homeland development that immigrant remittances play as its major example has been discussed in many cases, when this transcends ethnic relations and emerges as a humanitarian role is not adequately addressed from the perspective of migration studies (Rosenow-Williams and Sezgin 2018). The few cases are available, although they are regionally biased, concentrated in Europe and the United States. There is little follow-up on cross-border humanitarian assistance undertaken by Muslim immigrants.

This paper adopts a qualitative case study of Muslim immigrants' voluntary association named 'JIT: Japan Islamic Trust' in Tokyo Japan, registered as a religious cooperation. JIT's activities are supported by Muslims immigrants in Japan from more than 25 countries. They have built trust with Japanese society through their proactive humanitarian work, participation in local events and outreach activities. The representatives and Muslims living in Japan who participate in JIT activities are motivated by the Islamic teachings of reaching out and helping their "neighbours" and "neighbours" in need. Based on an analysis of their discourses, this paper will argue that their actions are considered by them as "everyday rituals" that are rooted in Islamic beliefs as well as Japanese social norms and practiced daily.

References:

Erdal, Marta Bivand., and Kaja Borchgrevink. 2017, "Transnational Islamic charity as everyday rituals", Global Networks, 17(1), pp.130-146.

Levitt, P., and N. Glick Schiller. 2004. "Conceptualizing Simultaneity: A Transnational Social Field Perspective on Society." International Migration Review 38 (3): 1002–1039.

Rosenow-Williams, Kerstin., and Zeynep Sezgin. 2018. "Islamic Migrant Organizations: Little-Studied Actors in Humanitarian Action", International Migration Review, 48(2), pp. 324-353.

Interfaith Initiatives and the Impact of Religious Leaders on Politics

(539) Deniz Cosan Eke, University of Vienna, Austria

Despite the secularization debate in Europe, the influence of religious leaders on people's political attitudes has continued to grow. Increasing international migration processes in recent years have affected both religious diversity and the effectiveness of clergy in religious communities. Rituals led by religious leaders have important implications for the dissemination of collective feelings of religious groups and the development of their collective memories. The main question in this article is whether religious groups influence political attitudes, within both their own religious communities and other faith groups, through the interfaith dialogue activities of religious leaders.

The influences of religious leaders and faith-based associations show that their positions in politics and society are reformulated throughout the migration process. Recently, interfaith initiatives have emphasized on expanding into European cities and maintaining peaceful coexistence based on dialogue rather than one religion. In this article, I will explore how interfaith initiatives can contribute to the migration process and the impact of religious leaders on the politics. The main purpose of this study is to contribute to the thinking of peaceful ways against the increasing polarization of society and politics and the need for cultural and religious understanding to build social cohesion.

7D   COVID-19 and Migration

Chair: Alina Botezat, Romanian Academy, "Gh. Zane" Institute for Economic and Social Research, Romania

987   Return Migration: Decision-making among Nigerian Physicians working in the NHS

Mohammed Abdullahi, University of Warwick, UK

1292   Challenges in Access to Healthcare of Syrian Refugees in Turkey: The Case of Mardin

Tuna Kılınç, Social Sciences University of Ankara, Turkey
1011   Migration and Covid-19 in Europe

Sibel Yanık Aslan, Pendik Municipality, Istanbul, Turkey
1059   How has COVID-19 pandemic affected the migration intentions of medical students? Survey evidence from Romania

Alina Botezat, Romanian Academy, "Gh. Zane" Institute for Economic and Social Research, Romania

Return Migration: Decision-making among Nigerian Physicians working in the NHS

(987) Mohammed Abdullahi, University of Warwick, UK

Many migrants depart their home countries with an aspiration to return. Flahaux and de Haas (2016) argue that sometimes when migrants leave home, their relationship with the home country may become distant, and sometimes strained, yet many still aspire to return home in the future. Although most migrants do not know when they intend to return, Borjas and Bratsberg (1996) and Dustmann and Weiss (2007) have documented that around 20 percent to 80 percent of migrants return home within five to 20 years of their migration. Despite this high percentage of returning migrants, interest in return migration research has lagged behind in migration scholarship. Over 20 years ago, King (2000:7) already stated that return migration is the "great unwritten chapter"□ in migration research. Despite some increase in research in this area, research on return migration is still limited. Debnath (2016:iii) puts this issue succinctly by stating that "limited research has been conducted to understand the decision-making dynamics behind migrants' returning to their home countries and the effectiveness of policies and programs in their reintegration process"□. Stefansson (2004) gives a plausible explanation of why return migration is not deeply researched, arguing that some researchers assume that return migration is a straightforward reinsertion of people back into a familiar community. Another credible explanation of why the return migration of highly skilled migrants remains under researched is provided by Ley (2010) who claims that people generally assume and expect that highly skilled migration is a one"□ way, permanent movement, as professionals stay on and settle in the destination country. However, just like departure, return migration is a complex decision-making process involving multiple factors (Abdullahi 2020). My current study uses a mixed-methods approach to provide insight into the return migration decision-making of Nigerian physicians working in the NHS, where the knowledge of the aetiology of this kind of migration is still lacking (Abdullahi and Uzomah 2021). As well as adding to this general understanding, a better awareness of the return propensities of Nigerian physicians in the UK could help in bringing about changes in the current healthcare sector and academic policies in Nigeria, and comparable nations. Moreover, there is still a dearth of information summarising the overall migration experiences of Nigerian physicians who have migrated. Hence, this research hopes to address this shortfall by analysing the labour market experiences of Nigerian physicians working in the UK, in order to establish the patterns of Nigerian physicians' migration trends.This research will also address the gap in the literature by extending academic understanding of return migration and adding to evidence. Such information will lend itself to relevant policy making and development at national and international levels regarding migration, labour market behaviour, and possible incentives to return to Nigeria.

Challenges in Access to Healthcare of Syrian Refugees in Turkey: The Case of Mardin

(1292) Tuna Kılınç, Social Sciences University of Ankara, Turkey

The right to health is a fundamental human right, regardless of migratory status. Access to healthcare is also crucial for refugees, since they are already traumatized by poor living conditions (Bilecen & Yurtseven, 2018). In the early years of the mass migration flows, Turkish government took an emergency response towards Syrian "guests" who were in dire need for protection. Later on, the whole access was redesigned from a short-term humanitarian emergency to a longer-term service provision that started to include Syrian national medical professionals into the frame (Yıldırım et al., 2019). There are empirical studies that focus on the problems encountered by medical personnel, patients, and translators (Demir et al., 2016; Köşer Akçapar & İdrisoğlu Dursun, 2019). However, access to routine and/or specialized healthcare services for refugees in Turkey still remains challenging. In the light of these recent studies, the aim of this paper is to understand what problems are being encountered by Syrians under temporary protection in access to healthcare services and the expectations of Syrian refugees from healthcare and what the current system provides. Fieldwork was carried out in Mardin in the two state hospitals, one in city center and one in Kızıltepe district of the city, and a refugee health center in the city. Mixed methodology was adopted for the research: 128 surveys were conducted among 35 male and 93 female respondents. 12 in-depth interviews with Syrian patients and 6 key informant interviews with medical personnel were also conducted. Reaching male participants is especially difficult, since they work on daytime and women mostly take their children to hospital if a child is sick. Although almost all the survey participants and interviewees noted that they are able to access to healthcare in Turkey, they have problems in healthcare services. They underlined the problems of language barrier, discrimination, difficulty in transportation and not enough number of appointments due to the pandemic conditions. Other than the problems faced by Syrian patients, interviews with medical personnel indicated unearthed challenges from the perspective of Turkish medical personnel. The preliminary findings of this fieldwork can be grouped under two categories. First, language barrier limits the patients' understanding of their medical condition as well as required steps for a treatment. The levels of satisfaction of Arabic and Kurdish speaking Syrians from the healthcare services are based on the language skills of the host community. Arabic speaking Syrians living in Mardin find relatively easy access to healthcare in Mardin due to the main ethnicity in Mardin being Arabs. The same can be said for Kızıltepe, in where host community is mainly Kurdish. This enables Syrians to overcome language barrier in healthcare access easily. It shows that without language barrier and much less difference in culture due to same ethnicity result in more easy adaptation and social cohesion. Second, already over-busy Turkish medical personnel are left alone to care for Syrian patients. Although SIHHAT project enabled refugee health centers for Syrians to access to healthcare, these centers operate either as small clinics or rather for referring patients to nearby state hospitals. Especially in surgical branches of hospitals, this results in new malpractice legal cases. This translates into medical personnel being reluctant to treat Syrian patients, which in turn understood as discrimination and shaming by patients.

Migration and Covid-19 in Europe

(1011) Sibel Yanık Aslan, Pendik Municipality, Istanbul, Turkey

To stop the COVID-19 outbreak, which first appeared in China's Hubei province in December 2019, countries around the world are taking various control measures, including strict quarantine measures, passenger screenings, mask-wearing and banning large social gatherings[16] As a result of the World Health Organization's declaration of the Coronavirus epidemic as a *Pandemic* at the beginning of 2020, people in many countries have become almost unable to even leave the provincial borders. Information from around the world shows that immigrants are one of the most vulnerable social groups, as in previous large-scale economic crises. In addition, with the Pandemic, the conditions of immigrants seem to have worsened.Unemployment, restrictions on movement, in some cases failure to comply with anti-epidemic rules and lack of access to adequate health services put migrants on the brink of death. Migrants are living in panic with the fear of being deported, not being able to return home due to closed borders, getting sick and being deprived of medical care during the COVID-19 epidemic. Tens of thousands of migrants struggle for survival in migrant camps around the Mediterranean. Measures to prevent the Pandemic, such as social distancing and cleaning rules, do not fit the reality of overcrowded refugee camps, where even access to soap or water is limited[17] These camps, where there is a lack of basic infrastructure and hygiene, are risky environments for spreading of Coronavirus. In some parts of the Moria camp in Greece, it is possible to say that there is one tap (and no soap) for every 1300 migrants. In addition, the number of showers and toilets is well below the minimum recommended standards for the emergency environment.Thousands of migrants, stopped on their way to Europe and forcibly detained on the North African coast, are living in dire conditions without food or water, and without health care. Meanwhile, resettlement practices and migrant transfers are coming to a standstill due to travel restrictions. As a result, more people are forced to live together in camps and temporary settlements on the European borders, where human health is at high risk. In addition, most of the migrant workers who work in heavy and low-income jobs in many sectors from tourism to factory have been unemployed due to the COVID-19 outbreak. Although unemployment rates have generally increased during the pandemic process, migrant workers have been more affected by unemployment due to their short-term contracts, their vulnerability and the sectors they work in. The aim of this study is to show that in European countries with a large number of migrants, the measures taken against the epidemic can only be successful with the inclusion of migrants. Considering the existence of millions of African and Asian migrants in Europe, it is an undeniable fact that segregation of migrants will neutralize all quarantine measures taken by European countries.

---

[16] World Health Organization (2020). Coronavirus Overview, Prevention, Syptoms. https://www.who.int/health-topics/coronavirus#tab=tab_1
[17] ECDPM (2020). https://ecdpm.org/talking-points/migration-mobility-covid-19-tale-of-many-tales/? Fbclid =IwAR1hPeEWDpv-M6FjCa2FTlnl17qkcVpLF7BPCleiCK8rzC-h9fISIeOW5gA

Abstract: Migration; COVIT-19; Pandemic; Europe

How has COVID-19 pandemic affected the migration intentions of medical students? Survey evidence from Romania

(1059) Alina Botezat, Romanian Academy, "Gh. Zane" Institute for Economic and Social Research, Romania

The COVID-19 global pandemic has caused major disruptions to economic and health systems, and changed the patterns of international migration flows. In the past decade, out of all the Eastern European countries, Romania experienced the highest number of young physician migrants. In this new and challenging situation, the question arises of how the pandemic will affect the decisions and trajectories of migration of medical students. This study aims to contribute to this literature by comparing migration intentions of Romanian medical students before and during the COVID-19 pandemic. We use a unique data set obtained from two in-school surveys carried out among medical students attending the "Gr. T. Popa"□ University of Medicine and Pharmacy in Iasi. We had previously studied the migration intentions of medical students enrolled in 2017 (N=1038, response rate 65%). During the pandemic, we started a new survey among the current medical students enrolled at the same University in order to examine how the pandemic has changed intentions to migrate among medical students. Our results show the pandemic has significantly reduced the average probability of migration intention among Romanian medical students by almost 10 percent. However, for males and those originating from small towns, COVID-19 has not affected their overall desire to migrate after graduation. Before the pandemic, students with a family background in medicine were more likely to express the intent to migrate after graduation. Recently collected data no longer shows the same trend. We also find that individuals who reported that the COVID-19 crisis has affected their plans to perform an internship abroad are more likely to want to migrate, despite the current global crisis. Interestingly, the older students and those who had planned to migrate before the ongoing pandemic canceled their future migration plans in response to the COVID-19 pandemic, compared to the younger students and those who initially had no plans to move abroad.

7E   Conflicts, Insecurities, Migration

Chair: Beja Protner, University of Cambridge, UK

1290   Displacement/emplacement and political movement: The production of internationalist spaces of radical politics with the Kurdish and left-wing political refugees from Turkey in Greece

Beja Protner, University of Cambridge, UK

1019   Using the Narratives to Explore the Life Experiences of Kurdish Refugees

Afrouz Zibaei, Manchester Metropolitan University, UK

1103   The Kurdish Question in the Shadow of Sheikh Said: Analyzing the Effects of Early Twentieth Century Migration on Twenty-First Century Regional Politics

Jackson House, SOAS University of London, UK

1172   Russia's war in Ukraine: Refugeeism and Way Ukrainians to Victory

Oksana Koshulko, The Technical University of Munich, Munich, Germany

Displacement/emplacement and political movement: The production of internationalist spaces of radical politics with the Kurdish and left-wing political refugees from Turkey in Greece

(1290) Beja Protner, University of Cambridge, UK

Large numbers of Kurdish and left-wing political refugees from Turkey and Kurdistan have been coming to Greece as asylum seekers since the 1980s. At least parts of the radical Left in Greece has always had comradely relations with the Kurdish and socialist movements of Turkey. Yet, there has been a new growth of interest and connections, particularly between the radical Left/anarchist movement of Greece and the Kurdish Freedom Movement, since the mid-2010s in the context of the internationalist support to the Rojava Revolution in Northeast Syria. Based on the ongoing ethnographic research among the Kurdish and left-wing political refugees from Turkey in Greece since 2018, this paper focuses on the participation of the exiles from Turkey/Kurdistan in the dynamic production of internationalist spaces of radical politics in Athens and Lavrio. This paper explores the materialized practices, intercultural encounters, co-habitation, and transnational political connections in particular places, and the ways in which these collective experiences shape places materially, socially, and politically. Building on Stavros Stavrides's (2006) concept of "urban porosity," it discusses these places of refugeehood and radical politics as thresholds, which allow for the emplacement of the exiles from Turkey/Kurdistan in Greece through spatiotemporal transgressions.

Political refugees from Turkey/Kurdistan have mostly considered Greece as a transitional zone and aimed to seek asylum in other European countries that host large Turkish and Kurdish diasporas. However, since 2016, the EU migration, border, and asylum regimes have made the journeys to safety increasingly difficult. Many refugees remain stuck in Greece for long periods of time in a situation of legal precarity, economic hardship, and "existential waiting" (Hage 2009). Most of the Kurdish and left-wing political refugees from Turkey live in the marginalized spaces of central Athens and the autonomous Kurdish refugee camp in Lavrio. Some of these spaces, particularly the squatted neighborhood of Prosfygika, the "anarchist neighborhood" of Exarcheia, and the Lavrio camp, are also spaces of intercultural encounter and radical left-wing politics. The Kurdish/Turkish exiles participate in the production of these spaces through the inscriptions of their political symbols into the materiality, communal co-habitation and political organizing, informative public events, discussions, and acts of solidarity with the struggles in Turkey and Kurdistan, and intercultural encounters and exchange during meetings, commemorations, celebrations, and spontaneous gatherings. Even if the exiles stay in Greece temporarily, they leave the marks of their histories in the material environment and affect the political character of the internationalist spaces of radical politics in Greece through their political engagement.

In the places conceptualized as porous urban thresholds, different histories of local movements, international visitors, and political exiles from Turkey/Kurdistan get connected through common practices that aim to produce an alternative future. This paper argues that in the conditions of spatiotemporal entrapment and instability, caused by the European migration regime and the dysfunctional asylum system in Greece, the (displaced) political movements of the exiles from Turkey/Kurdistan allow for a particular kind of emplacement through common spatialized political practices, which transgress spatiotemporal boundaries and reshape the landscape of radical politics in Greece.

References:

Hage, Ghassan. 2009. "Introduction." In *Waiting*, edited by Ghassan Hage, 1-14. Carlton South: Melbourne University Press.

Stavrides, Stavros. 2006. "Heterotopias and the Experience of Porous Urban Space." In *Loose Space*, edited by K. Franck and Q. Stevens, 174-192. London: Taylor and Francis.

Using the Narratives to Explore the Life Experiences of Kurdish Refugees

(1019) Afrouz Zibaei, Manchester Metropolitan University, UK

Using the Narratives to Explore the Life Experiences of Kurdish Refugees Afrouz Zibaei Faculty Health and Education, Department of Social Care and Social Worker Manchester Metropolitan University UK Afrouz.zibaei@stu.mmu.ac.uk In recent years, the subject of Refugee and Migration has become a high-profile political issue. I believe it is important to understand the reasons why people are forced to run away from their home countries. Placing the life stories of Kurdish refugees at the heart of this study, I conducted interviews with fifteen women and men who live as refugees in Finland. This research study attempted to develop a better understanding of the Kurdish refugees based on investigating the concept of safeguarding the refugee process's impact on their life in Finland. Awareness of the knowledge, the Kurdish refugee process reality in the research world. The reality of the Kurdish people's refugee process is very challenging to remove from the country that has been divided into four pieces and invaded by four stranger states. Most Kurdish people have a political problem, lack freedom and equality, and struggle for identity, which is critical for seeking asylum. Life story intends to explore the personal experiences of Kurdish refugees during the refugee process that would enable their voices to take centre stage of the research study. Therefore, illustrate Kurdish refugee voices of faith and trust by understanding their life story experiences. (Beazley and Ennew 2006; Holt, 2004)

The Kurdish Question in the Shadow of Sheikh Said: Analyzing the Effects of Early Twentieth Century Migration on Twenty-First Century Regional Politics

(1103) Jackson House, SOAS University of London, UK

In the 1920s and 1930s there were a series of Kurdish rebellions against the nascent Republic of Turkey.[1] In the context of this political upheaval and violent repression by the Turkish government, there was a significant migration of Kurds from Turkey into modern-day Syria which, at the time, was part of the French Mandate. An overlooked aspect of this migration is its effect on the regionality of the Kurdish question. The primary methodology of the paper is that of Historical Sociology which provides a framework "for doing macro level analysis on State formation, State failure and conflict."[2] Therefore, in order to assess the effects of these migrations, this paper begins with historical and sociological analysis of Kurdish migration to the Jazira region during the period following the Sheikh Said Rebellion (1925) until the de facto end of the French Mandate (1946).[3] Pierre Rondot's work "Les Tribus Montagnardes de l'Asie Antérieure" is an important reference point for early migration and later French studies by tienne De Vaumas as well as "La Djezireh syrienne et son réveil économique" by André Gibert and Maurice Févret provide sociological and ethnographic data. Mohannad Al-Kati summarizes this period in saying that "the French also encouraged the reception of refugees in Jazira, and the number of Kurds in the region increased from 6000 in 1927 to 56,340 in 1939." [4]The second section moves toward an analysis of the contemporary political dynamics between the Syrian Kurds and the Republic of Turkey. This analysis also has a historical component with the development of a Kurdish nationalism in exile[5] and the subsequent support of these nationalists for the Ararat Rebellion in 1930.[6] There is also a contemporary regional component with Kurdistan Communities Union which unites political parties in Kurdistan. Of particular importance to this paper is the connection between the PKK in Turkey and PYD in Syria, which is at the root of tension between the Turkey and the Autonomous Administration of North and East Syria. This paper concludes that this period of migration continues to influence Turkish foreign policy on Syria.[1] Hamit Bozarslan, Gunes, C., and Yadirgi, V., Editors. The Cambridge History of the Kurds. Cambridge: Cambridge University Press.[2] Raymond Hinnebusch, "State De-Construction in Iraq and Syria" Politische Vierteljahresschrift 57, No. 4 (2016): 561[3] Tejel, Jordi. Syria's Kurds: History, Politics and Society. New York: Routledge, 2009. 144. Ministre des Affaires trangres - Centre des Archives Diplomatiques (CADN), Fonds Beyrouth, Cabinet Politique, no. 1367. Distribution of population in Upper Jazira. Beirut, April 1939[4] Al-Kati, Mohannad. "The Kurdish Movement in the Arab World: The Syrian Kurds as a Case Study" AlMuntaqa 2, no. 1 (April/May 2019): 46.[5] Hakan Özogllu, "Exaggerating and Exploiting the Sheikh Said Rebellion of 1925 for Political Gains," New Perspectives on Turkey, no. 41 (2009): 181-210.[6] Naida Lahdili," Sheikh Said Rebellion (1925): The Controversy between Nationalist &Religious Motivations," International Journal of Humanities and Social Science Invention 7 no. 05 (May. 2018): 13-19.

Russia's war in Ukraine: Refugeeism and Way Ukrainians to Victory

(1172) Oksana Koshulko, The Technical University of Munich, Munich, Germany

The research presents some results of field research on Russia's war in Ukraine during the first month of the war. The hot phase of Russia's war in Ukraine has started on the 24th of February 2022, and Putin has started this war, like Hitler, at 4 a.m., but the war did not start during this moment. During the last eight years, since 2014, the Ukrainian state stayed in the situation of war, annexation and occupation of Crimea and Donbas (Koshulko & Dluhopolskyi, 2022). During these eight years, the state of Ukraine faced a lot of hybrid threats from the side of Russia, and Ukraine became a shield for the civilized world during these eight years of war, but the world did not listen to Ukraine, and only since the 24th of February, the world has understood the real threats from country-occupant Russia for all the civilized world (Koshulko, 2020). Because of the hot phase of Russia's war in Ukraine in 2022, ten million Ukrainians fully or partially lost their homes and became internally and externally displaced persons, around four million women with children fled Ukraine as Ukrainian refugees. The research methodology consisted of field research in Ukraine, Poland and Germany. In Ukraine, the research has been conducted among Ukrainian people who continue to stay in the rear and help the Army and the country in general in any way how they can. In Poland and Germany, field studies have been conducted among Ukrainian refugees, who came to these host countries during the first month of the war. According to the preceding results of the research, previously unknown cohesion emerged among Ukrainians in the rear. Every day, the Ukrainians in the rear do everything in their power to bring victory closer. A lot of the Ukrainian refugees, who came during the first month of the war in Poland or Germany, faced difficulties with the language barrier in Poland and Germany, and because of that some rules of staying in their host countries. In general, the way to victory and freedom is very difficult for Ukrainians, but the Ukrainian citizens (among them Crimean Tatars, and a lot of minorities of Ukraine) will be the winners in this war because it will be the victory of light over darkness, and after the victory, the majority of the Ukrainian refugees will come back to home.

7F   New Challenges in Migration Studies

Chair: Mala Arunasalam, Global Banking School, UK

1260   Problematizing Issues about Migration and Displacement: A Critical Study of Kiran Desai's, 'The Inheritance of Loss'

Nuzhat Fatima Rizvi, Symbiosis International University, India

1284   Permeable borders and technologies of control: A study of the Kafala migration regime

Shreya Katyayani, IIT(BHU), India

1003   Asymmetric Impact of Migrant' Remittances on Parity in Higher Education in Morocco: An Application of NARDL

Oussama Zennati, Université de Pau et des pays de l'Adour, E2S UPPA, CNRS, TREE, pau, France

Jamal Bouoiyour, Université de Pau et des pays de l'Adour, E2S UPPA, CNRS, TREE, pau, France

605   Evaluating Peer Assisted Study Skills Leaders Experiences: A Global Banking School Perspective

Vasilica Munteanu, Sonia-Elena Badulescu, Felicia Iroha and Mala Arunasalam, Global Banking School, UK

Problematizing Issues about Migration and Displacement: A Critical Study of Kiran Desai's, 'The Inheritance of Loss'

(1260) Nuzhat Fatima Rizvi, Symbiosis International University, India

The theory of diaspora and migration has deeply influenced writers across the globe. Literary work is influenced by the role played by the diaspora and its influence on the world politics. Diasporic literature encompasses various themes of migration, displacement, alienation and longing for homeland and cultural identity. In diasporic literature, 'exile' is often identified with misery and estrangement. With the advent of globalization, there has been a remarkable growth in the concept of Diaspora. Objective: The present paper, with a special reference to Kiran Desai's Booker award winning novel, "The Inheritance of Loss", aims to foreground the problems and complexities faced by the migrants of third world nations, specifically Indian migrants and bring forth their longing for homeland. It aims to highlight their struggles to cope up with the challenges of displacement and identity crisis. It aims to explore the positivist claim of 'economic globalization' can ever become a route to prosperity, the fast track for the downtrodden to navigate their way to prosperity. Literature Review: If we trace the origin of the term, 'Diaspora', it was originally used to describe the Jewish migration from their home land and lately has come to be applied for more or less as an inclusive term that is "metaphoric designations" (Safran, Williams) for all displaced people, immigrants, exiles, expatriates, emigrants, homeless individuals and refugees or the 'Cultural Diaspora' (Cohen). This physical and mental nomadism of diasporic life is what Homi. K. Bhabha described as the condition of being "unhomed", a desire to reclaim the past yet revolt against it the yearning to show solidarity to the homeland but unwillingness to threaten relations with the host country. Avtar Brah comments, "The concept of Diaspora places the discourse of 'home' and dispersions in creative tensions, inscribing a homing desire while simultaneously critiquing discourses of fixed origins" (Brah 192-193). According to Edward Said, desperate attempts are made to "overcome the crippling sorrow of estrangement". In diasporic discourses, these problems and tensions have been explored and debated through varied angles and sometimes prompting to a "displaced homeward journey" (Stuart Hall 399) CONCLUSION: The diaspora, in alien land are always in search of their roots. There is a painful longing for their homeland, left far behind. Though they adapt themselves and assimilate the new culture and practices of the foreign land, they are unable to negate the strains of umbilical collect with their motherland. There is always a hidden yet sincere effort to guard their cultural identity and tradition. Kiran Desai, through the portrayal of various characters, in her narrative highlights the concept of home, not as fixed one but, as an uncertain fluctuating and temporary location. In the narrative, "The Inheritance of Loss", the diasporic author Kiran Desai, illuminates the pain of exile and foregrounds the complexities of post colonialism experienced by the displaced people (of the globalized world), who are longing for their homeland. It is also suggested that the positive claim of the global economy can never become a route to prosperity for third world Nations.

Refrences:

Safran, Williams. "Diasporas in modern Societies": Myths of Homeland and Return", Diaspora: A Journal of Transnational Studies, 1.1.1991.

Cohen, Robert. Global Diasporas: An Introduction (U.C. Press, 1997)

Bhabha, Homi K. The Location of Culture. New York: Routledge, 1994

Brah, Avtar. Cartographies of Diaspora: Contesting Identities (Routledge, 1997).

Edward Said. Reflection of Exile and other Literary and Cultural Essays, New Delhi: Penguin Books, 2001. p.173 Hall Stuart "Cultural Identity and Diaspora" from Colonial Discourse Post-Colonial Theory: A Reader, eds

Permeable borders and technologies of control : A study of the Kafala migration regime

(1284) Shreya Katyayani, IIT(BHU), India

This paper entitled " Contract-based Modern Slavery: Technologies of Control in the Kafala Regime " tries to study the methods used by GCC nations to control the migrant population on their land with special reference to migrants from the Bhojpuri region of Bihar, its main argument being -the Kafala system as practised in the GCC nations, for organising the guest workers, is more than just an arrangement handling migration but rather is a migration technology in itself wherein the "sponsorship delegates to the citizens the responsibility for controlling and regulating the presence and activities of foreigners on the national territory, which is everywhere else a state prerogative and there is partial privatisation of control". For this, they have refurbished the age-old Kafala to craft it into a cutting-edge technology of migrant control and surveillance by linking every migrant to his citizen-sponsor, who, on behalf of the state, wields complete control on the mobility, social life and employment of the Makful (migrant). The paper, through the concepts of porous and indeterminate borders, tries to show how borders do not "exclude" but there is "differential inclusion" of the migrants, which is no less violent than exclusionary measures, wherein borders exist between the male migrant and the female, between the skilled migrant and the unskilled, between the migrant from South East Asia and the Expats from OECD countries- by the use of tactics like ethnic stereotyping, structural violence and the technologies of control inflicted on the guest workers, for example- different kinds of visas provided to them based on their skills, sponsors retaining workers' passport controlling their mobility, regulating their salary, their forced confinement and restrictions on their channels of communication thus, mapping them in a system of "structural dependence". From an outside onlooker's viewpoint- one cannot find any dearth of empirical material to support the claim of power imbalance in favour of the kafeel. Nevertheless, a complete understanding of a power relation needs that the analysis is built on a threefold approach- as seen by the onlooker, as told by the dominant actor and an account of the dominated, for this one has to understand the application of Kafala as a technology of control and surveillance of the migrants. (Longva 1999 p-20).

Asymmetric Impact of Migrant' Remittances on Parity in Higher Education in Morocco: An Application of NARDL

(1003) Oussama Zennati, Université de Pau et des pays de l'Adour, E2S UPPA, CNRS, TREE, pau, France

Jamal Bouoiyour, Université de Pau et des pays de l'Adour, E2S UPPA, CNRS, TREE, pau, France

This study examines the asymmetric effect of remittances on parity in higher education in Morocco, by controlling GDP per capita, the rate of feminization of educational staff in the three cycles, democracy and the rate of foreign direct investment for the period between 1975 and 2019 and using the Non-Linear Autoregressive-Distributed Lag

(NARDL) approach. Our results show the existence of a long and short-term asymmetric effect of remittances on higher education parity. In addition, our results show that GDP per capita and the feminization of educational staff in secondary and tertiary education are positively related to parity in higher education. While democratization and the increase of female teachers in primary education decrease parity in higher education. Our results also allow us to conclude that public expenditure in education consolidates in the long term the gains in terms of parity in higher education. Our results also allow us to conclude that public expenditure in education consolidates in the long term the gains in terms of parity in higher education.

Evaluating Peer Assisted Study Skills Leaders Experiences: A Global Banking School Perspective

(605) Vasilica Munteanu, Sonia-Elena Badulescu, Felicia Iroha and Mala Arunasalam, Global Banking School, UK

This abstract provides the Peer Assisted Study Skills (PASS) leaders views of their personal, academic and professional development during the pilot project (June-August 2022) in Global Banking School (GBS). Academics in higher education institutions are continuously developing a variety of methods to enhance student learning. However, globally, Peer Assisted Learning or Peer Assisted Study Session or Peer Assisted Study Skills is recognised as a by students for students support scheme. In this initiative, senior students facilitate interactive and engaging activities to support students in their lower years. In this GBS pilot project, (n=6), Level 4 students from the University of Suffolk partnership and (n=4), Level 5 students from Pearson Higher National Diploma were involved. These students were provided with a two-day PASS leader training. The leaders meet regularly with small groups of foundation/first year students on the same programme to facilitate interactive activities to enhance learning experiences. The What I know, Want to know and What I have Learnt (KWL) form used before training and evaluation forms from the two-day leader training; leading PASS sessions and at the end of the pilot project were used to identify the leaders personal, academic and professional development. It will identify the training and resources needed to further improve their soft/employability skills. This data will also provide information of the impact of being a leader on their engagement, retention, performance and grades.

7G   Youth Migration

Chair: Liat Yakhnich, Beit Berl College, Israel

933   Immigrant youth from the FSU and France in Israel: Adaptation and risk-taking

Liat Yakhnich, Beit Berl College, Israel
Keren Michael, The Max Stern Yezreel Valley College, Israel

1098   Little Migratory Birds: Re-framing Chinese' left-behind' Children, Beyond the Binary of the 'left-behind' and Migration

Kaidong Guo, SRI, IOE, UCL, UK

1219   Voices from transnationals from the US to Mexico and back: young adults' cosmologies, geographic itineraries and processes of integration.

Irasema Mora-Pablo, University of Guanajuato, Mexico
1296 Citizenship Education: intercultural dialogue and sustainable development. The case of young people from Western Mediterranean countries

Albino Cunha, Universidade de Lisboa, Portugal

Immigrant youth from the FSU and France in Israel: Adaptation and risk-taking

(933) Liat Yakhnich, Beit Berl College, Israel

Keren Michael, The Max Stern Yezreel Valley College, Israel

The immigration experience is especially complex for adolescents, since their mental equilibrium is more delicate than that of adults and they require a more stable environment to develop normally. Immigration, which involves coping with differences in language, values, norms, and rules of social interaction, can hamper immigrant youth's development and undermine their process of identity formation. One of the adverse consequences observed in this context is the high incidence of risk-taking behavior among immigrant youth. This phenomenological study aimed to explore the adaptation process of immigrant youth at risk who immigrated to Israel from the former Soviet Union and from France (two prominent groups of immigrants to Israel in the recent years). We sought to reveal the main challenges involved in their adjustment to the host country and the way they perceive them, and to understand how these challenges are related to the youth's involvement in risk behaviors. To attain etic, as well as emic, perspective and reach a holistic view of the studied phenomenon, we collected data from both the youth and the practitioners who work with this population. Three groups of participants were interviewed for this study: eleven immigrant youth from France, ten immigrant youth from the FSU, and six practitioners. The youth were recruited in educational and afterschool settings that work with youth at risk. Data analysis yielded the following themes, which represent the participants' experiences and perceptions of the adaptation process characteristic of French and FSU immigrant youth in Israel: the transition, factors involved in immigrant youth's adaptation (peer relations, cultural identity, school integration, parent-child relations), and risk behaviors among immigrant adolescents. Generally, the youth described immigration as a complicated experience that involves multiple confounding emotions. However, differences were found between the FSU and French participants' narratives and the way they perceived certain components of the adaptation process. Moreover, the practitioners' view of youth's adaptation was characterized by a wider ecological perspective which addressed such factors in the youth's lives as parent-child relations, developmental processes, etc. Moreover, although all the young participants that were interviewed for this study were recruited in settings that work with youth at risk, they addressed the issue of risk behaviors in a very limited manner. The practitioners, on the other hand, widely discussed youth's involvement in risk behaviors and believed it is related to the adaptational difficulties experienced by the youth. The findings stress cultural and developmental factors involved in immigrant youth's adaptation and have implication for research and practice.

Little Migratory Birds: Re-framing Chinese' left-behind' Children, Beyond the Binary of the 'left-behind' and Migration

(1098) Kaidong Guo, SRI, IOE, UCL, UK

In recent decades, China's sequence of economic reforms has rapidly encouraged the country to integrate into the global capitalist market, resulting in 137 million workers migrating to cities in order to earn a living (NBS, 2018). However, due to the restrictions of the hukou (household registration) system and the urban-rural system in education, in contrast with the migration of their parents, approximately 61 million children in rural areas are compelled to remain in their hometowns (ACWF, 2013). Public media and policies refer to this group as 'left-behind' children. Since these children represent a widespread social phenomenon in China, they have gradually become a matter of concern within public discourse and research. However, mainstream research on such children is conducted within a 'left-behind' paradigm, focusing exclusively on their 'left-behind' life while ignoring their mobility. The fact that these children also present certain aspects of mobility has been noted by only a small number of pioneering researchers (Zhang, 2015; Xiao, 2015), who indicated that it creates a more complex dynamic of family separation and reunion. Building on the above, this research aims to intensify our understanding of 'left-behind' children's mobility and its impacts on family life. Therefore, this research utilises the ethnographic method to participate in the lives of eight 'left-behind' families who live in the Sichuan Province of China, for a period of eight months, and uses a range of methodological tools including participant observation, interviews, and photo-voice to generate the data. This research identifies three different models of Chinese 'left-behind' children's mobility, including (i) short-term migration to cities; (ii) a contrary pattern of being born in an urban area, but migrating to a rural location where they become 'left-behind' children; and (iii) cyclical transformations between 'left-behind' and migrant children. Their different mobility models have caused their childhood to be characterised by instability, resulting in an experience of multiple separations in the dimensions of both time and space with different family members, thereby compelling them to adjust their roles and strategies periodically in order to navigate their ever-changing intimate lives. Nevertheless, in current mainstream research, 'left-behind' children are often regarded as a homogeneous and static group, encountering the same social and emotional challenges (Pissin, 2013). This research reminds us that the recent increasing mobility of 'left-behind' children has caused their experiences to be complex. This has led to such children facing various dilemmas, but such differences are often ignored by public media, policy, and current researchers. Furthermore, the complexity of their lives also challenges the existing conceptualisation of 'left-behind' children. Consequently, in contemporary China, 'left-behind' and migration cannot be treated as a simple binary opposition, but rather as a more intricate, interwoven process.

Voices from transnationals from the US to Mexico and back: young adults' cosmologies, geographic itineraries and processes of integration.

(1219) Irasema Mora-Pablo, University of Guanajuato, Mexico

This presentation reports on the findings of a longitudinal study which aimed at examining life stories of two young transnationals at different moments in their lives. This study is the result of almost 10 years of work with two young adults since the moment they started their university studies in Mexico (after living in the US for a number of years) until they are now back in the US due to educational or family reasons. I use the concept of 'cosmologies of destinations' (Belloni, 2020) as a theoretical lens to provide an understanding of the meaning of these migrants' journeys. Belloni (2020) asserts that the concept of 'cosmologies of destinations' "[â€¦] feed into the trend studies aiming to overcome simplistic mechanistic models of migration by employing a more culturally sensitive approach [â€¦] by recognizing the role of agency, aspirations and emotions in migrants' pathways" (p. 5). Methodologically the research approach was qualitative in nature, utilizing narrative inquiry. These participants studied a BA in English language teaching and later, an MA in applied linguistics to English language teaching in Mexico. As they wanted to pursue doctoral studies, they decided to come back to the US. Participants recall their experiences in the Mexican educational system where teachers called them by different derogatory names ("pocho", "cholo") and even asked them to leave the classroom because they speak English better than the teacher. Adaptation in the Mexican education system represented a convoluted, challenging, and oftentimes painful and violent process, as once they were in Mexico, they were caught between two worlds posing cultural, linguistic and identity conflicts (Despagne & Suárez, 2019). However, later they experienced a new adaptation process when returning to the US to start a new stage in their lives. The results show how these two young participants experience and build notions of transitions, identity formation and their processes of integration, in social and educational spheres. The participants speak both languages, but they do not completely meet the social expectations of both educational communities on either side of the border. When they are back in Mexico they are usually seen as a threat, since they speak another language (English) but are not highly proficient in what is supposed to be their mother language (Spanish). This, together with the difficulties they face when trying to adapt socially and culturally, put them in a fragile space where transnationals describe a complex navigation of belonging. This is challenged by different factors: the position of the family within the new society, their migration status in the US and the linguistic identity they carry with them wherever they go. I conclude by highlighting that if we listen to these young adults and what they have to say about their experiences, we can move away from superficial descriptions, capturing the emic, producing richer information that can allow us to be intermediaries to transnationals' multiple and varied cosmologies. This can be a catalyst to illustrate how their processes of integration can be understood if analyzed within their worldviews. Belloni, M. (2020). Cosmologies and migration: on worldviews and their influence on mobility and immobility. Identities, 1-19. Despagne, C., & Jacobo Suárez, M. (2019). The adaptation path of transnational students in Mexico: Linguistic and identity challenges in Mexican schools. Latino Studies, 17(4), 428-447.

Citizenship Education: intercultural dialogue and sustainable development. The case of young people from Western Mediterranean countries

(1296) Albino Cunha, Universidade de Lisboa, Portugal

In the UNESCO document entitled Education for Citizenship for the 21st Century, it is stated that "citizenship education addresses both the individual and the citizen and provides an avenue for each individual citizen to acquire an understanding of the issues of peace in the world and the challenges of globalization of economic, environmental and cultural problems."Since sustainable development of human beings and the world they live in is linked to the quality of education, the time has come to regard citizenship education as a vital part of any education system and any teaching programme.According to UNESCO, culture shapes our identity and the development cannot be sustainable without including culture. Culture is recognized through a majority of the Sustainable Development Goals (SDGs), including those focusing on quality education, sustainable cities, the environment, economic growth, sustainable consumption and production patterns, peaceful and inclusive societies, gender equality and food security.In relation to Sustainable Development in the Western Mediterranean area we believe that the valuation and knowledge of a common cultural heritage and the promotion of intercultural dialogue, it is necessary first of all to work particularly through the new generations, to change and evolve the perceptions and attitudes towards the Other and to the common environment by promoting a more effective form of cooperation, and highlighting the benefits, for all peoples and cultures of the diversity of culture and the need for an intercultural dialogue in order to promote peace in the world and promoting a sustainable development that will preserve the environment and will improve the quality of life of all mankind.In the particular context of the Western Mediterranean, the reciprocal presence of peoples and cultures on both sides: past, present, future implies a common, integrated, shared, inclusive and sustainable vision.This means focusing on the new generations and developing short, medium and long-term cooperation and integration mechanisms such as the 5 + 5 Dialogue, highlighting in particular the areas of education and culture and their effective contribution to sustainable development.

7H   International Refugee Protection System and Crises

Chair   Parvathi Vijay, Symbiosis School for Liberal Arts, India

1229   The Paradox of Human Rights: A Case study of the Rohingya Muslim Refugee Crisis

Parvathi Vijay, Symbiosis School for Liberal Arts, India

1097   Extreme Refugee Vetting in Response to the Migration 'Crises'

Ozgun Topak, York University, Canada

982   Rehabilitation and Resettlement through a Development Paradigm: A Study of Partition Refuges in India

Madhusmita Jena, CIPOD/JNU, India

1223   A Study on Syrians in Turkey: Soft Power and Migration Issue

Özcan Çetin, Dumlupınar University, Turkey

544   The EU's democracy and human rights promotion in its Southern neighbourhood: is the migration crisis a chance or a dilemma?

Smaro Boura, University of the Peloponnese, Greece

The Paradox of Human Rights: A Case study of the Rohingya Muslim Refugee Crisis

(1229) Parvathi Vijay, Symbiosis School for Liberal Arts, India

The Declaration of the Rights of Man in the 18th century paved the way for a novel epoch of emancipation. Henceforth, man, not merely a tradition or religion, was to be adjudged the source and fundament of law. The declaration of universal emancipation, from the very beginning, found its roots in the emancipation of concrete masses. While the French revolution remains a battle for the emancipation of the French people, it was fought under the pretence of universal emancipation of man. The very rights of man, therefore, are historically tied to the nature of citizenship.[1] The universal declaration of human rights, despite its establishment in 1948, has perhaps only reinstated the nature of the argument - that upon losing one's citizenship, one is only left with the rights they claim as human beings, and such has been mainly left unenforced by most governments and authorities. To prove this point and provide the reader with contradictions within the very nature of human rights, I take the case of the refugee crisis, particularly the deadly crackdown on the Rohingya Muslims and its deadly aftermaths. In tying this with Hannah Arendt's theorisation of the paradoxical tie between the nation-state (particular rights) and human rights (universal rights), we are met with a critical entanglement between human rights and citizenship. This highlights a fundamental foundation of western nationalism, which bases itself on principles of exclusion, wherein only-citizens remain equal before the law. The marginalised - Rohingya Muslims - are therefore left beyond the periphery of legal protection, and even if not entirely, the protection granted to the community remains largely unenforced. A key aspect in the subjugation of Rohingya Muslims may be attributed to the nature of rights possessed by the groups. Theoretically grounding it in relation to Foucauldian biopower, the sovereign, here, constitutes that which is armed with a "power to foster life, or disallow it to the point of death". The members of the Rohingya community are, as perhaps Foucault would put it, the alien 'monster' - or bodies which transgresses the law by simply existing remains essential to this understanding. From here, Giorgio Agamben's conceptualisation of the Homo Sacer, I believe, aptly highlights the plight of the community and its relationship with rights and sovereign power. This paper aims to analyse the inadequacies in the protection granted to refugees - Rohingya Muslims in particular - whilst grounding it theoretically with critiques of the nature of human rights and its relationship with citizenship. [1] We see this in the very title of the civil rights document, "Déclaration des droits de l'homme et du citoyen" (Declaration of the Rights of Man and of the Citizen)

Extreme Refugee Vetting in Response to the Migration 'Crises'

(1097) Ozgun Topak, York University, Canada

This presentation is about the refugee vetting process. The United States, under the Trump's Presidency, took the lead in establishing 'extreme vetting' procedures, as a key policy-security tool to govern migration. Other Western states and entities, including Canada and the European Union have followed. Extreme vetting includes detailed interviews, biometrics surveillance, social media surveillance, phone surveillance, and more recently algorithmic surveillance. It also includes data-sharing among security agencies, and international database checks. The vetting officers use these practices to assess the credibility of the applicants and the level of security risk they pose. This paper will demonstrate how extreme vetting has contributed to the normalization of invasive surveillance, even if such surveillance might be necessary for public security. The paper will problematize the use of extreme vetting as a key response mechanism to the migration 'crisis' by Western countries.

Rehabilitation and Resettlement through a Development Paradigm: A Study of Partition Refuges in India

(982) Madhusmita Jena, CIPOD/JNU, India

India's experience as a host state began with the partition of the subcontinent and movement of people across the borders of the two newly independent states. The new Government of India was initially unprepared for the vast humanitarian crisis which it faced in the immediate aftermath of Independence. Nearly eight million displaced persons in India constituted 2.2 per cent of the population; five million from West Pakistan and 3.5 million from East Pakistan (Brahmananda 1947). In 1947, there were few models for refugee protection and settlement that India could examine and adopt. Although India was aware of the post-war and post-conflict refugee management processes, the magnitude of the Indian case was first of its kind. The suddenness of huge population transfer, an absence of models of refugee protection and explosion in expectations of people for national reconstruction, with competing priorities in the face of severe resource constraints acted as formidable constraints for India to manage huge streams of refugees on its territory. Despite being unprepared for the vast humanitarian crisis, the Government of India was soon pressed into action against the backdrop of an unprecedented violence, an obvious outcome of religious diasporas (Zolberg et al 1979). India did not have the opportunity and challenge of bouts of refugee influxes prior to addressing the problem of Partition refugees. Neither did it have any prototype model to examine and adapt. India took the conventional humanitarian assistance design to a development paradigm, which was unheard at that point of time and much later too. GOI viewed refugees as human beings with capabilities, will and aspiration to better their lives. In no way they were considered different from other normal human beings. Rather they represent groups of "new-normal" people who can better their life opportunities with development inputs. With this realisation in view, GOI quickly shifted from simplistic humanitarian assistance to development-linked empowerment of refugees. Resettlement was linked with development and rehabilitation with reconstruction. Guided by the commonly held assumption that development-based approaches should only be introduced after the emergency phase of a refugee situation, GOI followed this pattern. The refugees were empowered, through several capability-building schemes, to be active agents of the nation-building programme of the state. Expansion of "freedoms"□ and "choices" for empowerment was the priority of priorities. It was a move to take refugees from a state of total dependency to a state of total autonomy to meaningfully reconstruct their distressed lives. This exceptionalism of GOI offers a form of 'Laboratory' and 'innovative entrepreneurship' which has an enormous vector worthy of replication in case of other groups of refugees not only in India but in different parts of the globe. Against this backdrop, the present paper explores India's responses to the Partition refugees premised on the idea of - empowering refugees will enable them in rebuilding and reconstructing their own lives. We, therefore, need to recognise that refugees are not just, or even predominantly, a humanitarian issue. We have to go beyond humanitarianism.

A Study on Syrians in Turkey: Soft Power and Migration Issue

(1223) Özcan Çetin, Dumlupınar University, Turkey

Decades-long military conflicts in different Middle East countries have been causing mass migration of vulnerable groups to more developed countries. However, the immigration that caused by Syrian Civil War has perhaps contributed the international community to discuss immigration issues more serious than ever. Alongside the unexpected course of the Civil War, involvement of super powers and regional actors to settle old scores in Syria, the question of "how many more immigrants should we receive?" that rose in societies of developed countries, have fuelled the discussions. Consequently, the factors mentioned above have encouraged the European governments to review their immigration policy and formulate new policies. The new immigration policies have amounted EU- Turkey immigration deal which can be considered as first of its kind, at least in terms of implementation. In this study, it has been examined in context of Syrian refugees in Turkey that which countries and why the immigrants are willing to live in? Prima facie, the answer is "immigrants would rather to live in European countries due economic reasons". However, as in the case of the Syrian family who decided to live in Turkey concerning the cause of religion while they are holding Germany visa, to illustrate the economics concerns as sole reason of migration is regarded as an inadequate analyze. Therefore, the study aims to address that which factors are affecting the migrant. From this point on, the study suggests that popularity, religion, culture and life-style, in other words, the soft-power of host-countries is attracting the migrants as well as economic reasons. The findings of the research study are based on observation and one-on-one interviews with Syrian community members in different regions of Turkey.

The EU's democracy and human rights promotion in its Southern neighbourhood: is the migration crisis a chance or a dilemma?

(544) Smaro Boura, University of the Peloponnese, Greece

EU's policies and instruments for democracy and human rights promotion in the Mediterranean region shaped by different parameters either depending on its internal decision-making mechanism or by the willingness and motives of each partner country to actively engage in the process. Bilateral initiatives have long been established by individual Member-States with the Southern partners. On the other side, multilateral partnering frameworks are based on the engagement of many partner countries, often with different interests, under a common agenda, while unilateral cooperation strategies are either based on incentives or coercive means. In both cases, the implementation of strategies is the result of a certain rationale that shapes EU's decisions influenced at a certain degree by European interests in geopolitical and/or economic terms. The nature of policy-making processes in democracy and human rights field determines the strategies that the EU adopts and the instruments that deploys to achieve its objectives. Its regional agenda is designed according to the interests of involved actors in this field and is influenced by internal and external factors and events. The migration crisis is one of these factors which determine regional dynamics. The examination of this factor and the nature of EU policies in the Southern Mediterranean in relation to specific events is crucial to understand whether it tries to pursue a normative pathway as a democracy and human rights promoter or its policies are shaped by securitisation.

Day Three 9 September 2022 Friday

Day Three 9 September 2022 - 13:15-14:45

Plenary Session III: Modernity, Aspirations, and the Culture of Migration in India [ONLINE]

Moderator: Dr S. Irudaya **Rajan**, IIMAD, Kerala, India
Keynote Speakers:

- Dr Samir Kumar **Das**, University of Calcutta, India
- Dr Parvati **Nair**, University of London, UK
- Sanjay **Awasthi**, IOM

Day Three 9 September 2022 - 15:00-16:30

8A   L'Immigration en Afrique [FR]   AMPHI 1

Chair: Zeynep Banu Dalaman, Istanbul Topkapi University, Turkey

945   The determinants of Sub-Saharan migration in Morocco

> *Chaabita Rachid, Université Hassan 2 Casablanca, Morocco*
> *Kamal Zehraoui, Université Hassan 2 Casablanca, Morocco*

956   La problématisation de l'immigration en Equateur: d'un pays des migrants vers un pays d'accueil

> *Martha Alexandra Vargas Aguirre, University of Ottawa, Canada*

501   Le processus de sécuritization de l'immigration au Maroc

> *Serrhini Hanane, l'Université Moulay Ismail de Meknès, Morocco*

1210   The Impact of the Recent European Migration Policies on the Aspirations of the Sub-Saharans African Migrants and Refugees in Presence in Morocco

> *Mohamed Tahar Es Siddiki, Mohammed V University of Rabat, Morocco*
> *Yamina El Kirat El Allame, Mohammed V University of Rabat, Morocco*

The determinants of Sub-Saharan migration in Morocco

(945) Chaabita Rachid, Université Hassan 2 Casablanca, Morocco

Kamal Zehraoui, Université Hassan 2 Casablanca, Morocco

The subject of migration has often been studied through Moroccan emigrations to the Europe. It is recently that studies have focused on Morocco as a host country, especially for Sub-Saharan. Indeed, Morocco has tried through its new migration policy to create a favorable and warm welcome context for the sub-Saharan migrants. Through our article we seek to define the factors that influence settlement decision of sub-Saharan migrants in Morocco. we try to understand what differentiates sub-Saharan migrants who intend to settle permanently in the Kingdom of Morocco from those who take Morocco as a country of transition. In this sense, our article attempts to describe and explain the differences and specificities that may exist between migrants from different sub-Saharan countries in terms of the choice of Morocco as a country of residence. This is to detect the homogeneity or heterogeneity that may exist between different groups of sub-Saharan migrants in terms of socio-cultural and economic integration. To define factors of permanent residence decision in Morocco, we conducted a survey with a sample containing 200 individuals. We concluded that several variables may explain the Sub-Saharan residence decision in Morocco (age, gender, educational level, membership in ethnic association).

La problématisation de l'immigration en Equateur: d'un pays des migrants vers un pays d'accueil

(956) Martha Alexandra Vargas Aguirre, University of Ottawa, Canada

La constitution actuelle de l'Équateur, adoptée en 2008, marque une rupture sans précédent dans la politique d'immigration de ce pays. Pour la première fois, le cadre constitutionnel établit que « personne n'est illégal » et reconnaît aussi une série de droits aux immigrants. Ainsi, les visas touristiques ont été éliminés pour tous les pays. Cette mesure a conduit à une augmentation évidente du nombre d'étrangers entrant dans ce pays (Ramirez, 2015). Pour plusieurs d'entre eux, l'Équateur est devenu un point de transit, et pour d'autres, une destination permanente (Herrera, 2019). Le gouvernement équatorien a fait face à ces « Conséquences inattendues » avec une série de modifications erratiques dans la politique migratoire, qui contredisent notoirement le cadre constitutionnel. Afin de mieux comprendre ces développements, mon étude cherche à répondre à la problématique suivante : comment l'immigration irrégulière a-t-elle été problématisée en tant qu'objet d'intervention gouvernementale prioritaire depuis l'adoption de la Constitution de 2008 en Équateur ?

Les travaux portant sur la politique d'immigration équatorienne adoptent généralement une perspective juridique (Arcentales, 2019). Ces études mettent en évidence certaines logiques sous-jacentes au gouvernement de l'immigration irrégulière. Cependant, elles ne permettent pas de comprendre la complexité des processus de production et de mise en œuvre des politiques migratoires. Afin de répondre à cet angle mort dans la littérature scientifique, ce projet cherche à analyser les multiples dynamiques du régime complexe et diffus qui prend en charge la régulation de l'immigration (Valverde, 1994).

Pour ce faire, mon projet s'inscrit dans la perspective foucaldienne des études critiques des politiques publiques (Foucauldian Critical Policy Studies), et étudie le gouvernement de l'immigration irrégulière à partir du concept foucaldien de « problématisation ». Ceci implique l'analyse des processus hétérogènes qui l'ont produite comme un objet de réflexion et d'action gouvernementale (Foucault, 1988). Ainsi, la formulation des politiques est analysée comme un processus complexe et désordonné (Gale, 2001), et son étude comporte l'analyse des logiques contenues dans les textes politiques et législatifs, mais aussi l'analyse des échanges stratégiques contenus dans les pratiques gouvernementales.

Dans cette perspective, j'articule ma recherche autour de trois objectifs : 1) identifier les rationalités qui sous-tendent la gestion de l'immigration irrégulière en Équateur pour dégager comment elle a été conceptualisée, questionnée et classée ; 2) tracer comment les rationalités ont été traduites en programmes gouvernementaux ; 3) étudier quelles technologies (des techniques, des instruments) sont mobilisées pour réguler ce champ et comment elles alimentent le processus de problématisation.

Pour atteindre ces objectifs, ma recherche suit la démarche méthodologique appelée « l'ethnographie de la gouvernementalité » (Brady, 2014). Je combine donc l'analyse des sources documentaires publiques avec la réalisation d'entretiens menés avec des acteurs des trois principales agences qui forment le système de régulation migratoire en Équateur : Police, Ministère de l'intérieur, et Ministère des affaires étrangères et mobilité humaine (N=45). L'analyse de ces données repose sur la méthodologie de l'analyse thématique de contenu (Paillé et Mucchielli, 2003).

Le processus de sécuritization de l'immigration au Maroc

(501) Serrhini Hanane, l'Université Moulay Ismail de Meknès, Morocco

Cet article s'inscrit dans le cadre de mon travail de thèse sur: «La politique migratoire

Marocaine entre les impératifs sécuritaires et les exigences humanitaires». Il s'agit de

démontrer que la problématique migratoire est d'enjeu multiple pour le Maroc. Ce dernier est contraint d'une part à assumer ses engagements régionaux avec ses partenaires européens pour lutter contre la migration irrégulière et d'autre part il est confronté aux respects des droits humains des migrants. Il propose d'étudier l'articulation et vérifier l'équilibre entre ces deux logiques sécuritaire et humanitaire. Dans le volet sécuritaire objet de cet article, la sécuritization comme processus pour créer de l'insécurité sous prétexte de défendre la sécurité. C'est la construction d' un événement en tant que «problème politique», pour faire appel à des moyens sécuritaires. Dans le domaine de la migration l'arrivée des flux des migrants et demandeurs d'asile ne peut seule imposer un sécuritization, mais il faut interpréter le contexte des migrations internationales comme u enjeu de sécurité pour le Maroc (la lutte contre le trafic: illicite des migrants, de la drogue, de la traite des personnes et du terrorisme...) pour justifier la sécuritization et le contrôle. La sécuritization justifie alors les politiques répressives contre les migrants Cet article aborde le processus de la sécuritisation de l'immigration avec une attention particulière aux différents mesures et pratiques de l' Union européenne en coopération avec le Maroc pour dissuader les migrations. Il vise aussi à relever le lien entre criminalité et migration au Maroc, et à répondre à la question si le migrant présente une menace à la sécurité nationale du Maroc? La réponse serait évidemment négative, et les contraintes seront lourdes sur les droits humains des migrants. L'étude du taux de la criminalité des étrangers au Maroc s'est basée à analyser les données de leur représentativité dans les structures de la délinquance au Maroc de la période allant de 2011 à 2018, selon leurs nationalités et selon les crimes commis. Il s'agit des données obtenues des établissements suivants: la Délégation Générale de l'Administration Pénitentiaires et de la réinsertion, le Ministère public au Maroc, le ministère de la justice au Maroc et l'Observatoire marocain des prisons. Bien que les études relatives à la sécuritisation des migrations ne soient traitées exhaustivement qu'en théorie, la base empirique demeure incomplète et limitée. Au Maroc, ces études sont quasiment absentes, c'est ainsi que cet article tente de combler ces lacunes. Au Maroc, la politique migratoire est multidimensionnelle, elle est justifiée d'un coté par la lutte contre les crimes et menaces contraire à l'ordre publique et à la souveraineté territorial du pays et d'un autre coté par les engagements du Maroc avec les partenaires européens pour le contrôle des frontières.

Bibliographie:

-Thèse, *La politique migratoire marocaine entre les impératifs sécuritaires et les exigences humanitaires,* soutenue le 21 avril à la FSJES Tanger, Maroc.

- B.ZYGMUNT, *Le cout humain de la mondialisation, traduit de l'anglais par Alexandre Abensour,* Hachette Littératures, 1999, 204p.

-C.INTRAND, *Les accords de réadmission et la politique du donnant-donnant,* Plein Droit, juin 2003, n° 57.

-C.JAFFRELOT et C.LEQUESNE, *L'enjeu Mondial: Les migrations,* presses de sciences Po-l'Express, 2009, 320p.

-D.BIGO, *Polices en réseaux, l'expérience européenne,* Paris, Presses de la Fondation Nationale des sciences politiques, 1996, 356p.

-D.LOCHAK, *Immigrés sous contrôle. Les Droits des étrangers: un état des lieux ,* Le Cavalier bleu, 2008, 171p.

-D. LOCHAK, *Étrangers: de quel droit ?,* Paris, Puf, 1985, 256p.

-D. LOCHAK, *Face aux migrants: Etat de droit ou état de siège?,* Paris, textuel, 2007, 112p.

-E.BALIBAR, *Europe constitution frontière,* édition du Passant, 2005, 164p.

-E.BALIBAR, I.WALLERSTAN, *Race, nation, classe : les identités ambigües,* édition la découverte, Paris 1988, 322p.

The Impact of the Recent European Migration Policies on the Aspirations of the Sub-Saharans African Migrants and Refugees in Presence in Morocco

(1210) Mohamed Tahar Es Siddiki, Mohammed V University of Rabat, Morocco

Yamina El Kirat El Allame, Mohammed V University of Rabat, Morocco

Over the last decades, sub-Saharan human mobility towards the European Union has largely characterized international migration. Flows of forced migrants and refugees from many African regions have fled their home countries for reasons of civil wars, religious and political persecution, and climate disasters. Whatever the drivers of this human mobility might be, it has shaped, developed and used various trans-Saharan and trans-Mediterranean routs crossing political borders of many countries to reach their final migratory destinations in the European continent. No one can deny that post-war Europe has relied heavily on African labour migration for decades to reconstruct its economy. However, surprisingly, since the 1980s, human movements from North and sub-Saharan African regions towards the UE countries have become critical issues at the crucial stage in the European political agendas. The European opposition to African migration and its political desire to curb African mobility has intensified following the 2013 and 2015 international refugee crises. Consequently, these migrants and refugees' dreams and 'aspirations' have been obstructed by a number of interrelated factors including the on-going restrictive migration policies, which have been criticized for being based on security requirements to protect the European Union rather than on global approaches to human rights' agendas (Jaulin,2010). The EU migratory security policy considers the externalization of border control of the "Fortress Europe" the most effective strategy to fight African migration to Europe. Relying on data from the International Migration Determinants (DEMIG) and the Migration between Africa and Europe (MAEF) projects, Beauchemin, Flahaux & Schoumaker (2020) found that European restrictive policies could not hinder largely mobility flows from African countries. However, these policies have encouraged more unauthorized migration from the continent. These migratory developments taking place in the North bank of the Mediterranean constitute new challenges that require from the Global South countries including Morocco, and many other North African nations, to generate new strategies of migration, asylum and integration to share the burden of African migration. As a result, Morocco, a major exporter of Moroccan migration and a transit country for international mobility, has been changing steadily to a host location where thousands of 'involuntary immoblities' aspire to settle. The aim of this paper is to determine the impacts of European migratory agendas on Sub-Saharan forced migration aspirations in the Moroccan context. The main objective is to shed light on these sub-Saharan migrants and refugees' migration projects. The study addresses two main questions, namely (i) in what ways are the recent European migration policies impacting the sub-Saharan migrants and refugees' migratory projects? (ii) To what extent have the European restrictive migration policies pushed sub-Saharan African migrants and refugees to consider Morocco as their final destination? The study adopts a combined mixed approach making use of both qualitative and quantitative research tools. Data analysis and interpretation reveals the impact of the recent European migration policies on the Sub-Saharans Africans migrants' aspirations and how this is progressively leading some of them to consider settling in Morocco as the ideal alternative.

8B   Migration and Integration

Chair: Deniz Yetkin Aker, Tekirdag Namik Kemal University, Turkey

1082   A Comparative Analysis of Turkey and Germany's Housing Policies for Syrian Immigrants

Pınar Savaş-Yavuzçehre, Pamukkale University, Turkey
Gökhan Yağmurlu, Independent

1239   Positioning of Women in Migration Studies and Marginalisation of Women's Knowledge: The Case of Syrian Women in Turkey

Hulya Sahin-Erbektas, Hacettepe University, Turkey

1004   The effects of international migration on the total fertility rate: evidence from Morocco by the Rolling window ARDL and the Granger causality test of Toda Yamamoto

Oussama Zennati, Université de Pau et des pays de l'Adour, France
Jamal Bouoiyour, Université de Pau et des pays de l'Adour, France

958   Constructing a sense of home: The case of lifestyle migration in the Arabian Gulf

Emina Osmandzikovic, Sorbonne University Abu Dhabi, UAE

A Comparative Analysis of Turkey and Germany's Housing Policies for Syrian Immigrants

(1082) Pınar Savaş-Yavuzçehre, Pamukkale University, Turkey

Gökhan Yağmurlu, Independent

Countries have changed, reasons have diversified, actors have increased, but the phenomenon of migration has always remained fresh. In this process, which is as difficult for the host countries as for the immigrants, the countries need to regulate new public policies in many aspects (housing, education, employment, social policies, etc.). Housing policies for immigrants will be discussed in this study.As a result of the Syrian Civil War in 2010, millions of Syrians first immigrated to neighbouring countries and eventually to European countries. Turkey and Germany, the countries most affected by this migration, are the subjects of this study. The study aims to compare the housing policies of the two countries for Syrian immigrants. Izmir from Turkey and Berlin from Germany were taken as samples. In the research, Konak, Buca, and Bayraklı districts of İzmir and Neukölln, Pankow, Mitte, and Tempelhof-Schöneberg districts of Berlin were selected in terms of workplaces and residences; as a method, interviews were held with immigrants in the field, and as a result of on-site examination and observation, it has been tried to determine which actors and factors have an effect on the change. There are temporary shelters consisting of containers, tents, or reinforced concrete partitions for the accommodation needs of displaced persons (Syrian and Iraqi) at a total of 26 points in 10 provinces in Turkey. On average, only 1.4% of Syrians under temporary protection are in temporary shelters; 98.6% of them are distributed to 81 cities of Turkey, excluding the camps. In Germany, the accommodation needs of the displaced are met with three different types of accommodation. These are; Initial Reception Centres, Collective Accommodation Centres, and Decentralized accommodations. In 2008, a total of 375 thousand 145 people "whether they have status or not" benefited from three different types of accommodation. 83% of displaced persons who have attained a status have been accommodated in private properties.The housing crisis was experienced in both cities as a result of immigrants preferring to live in individual houses instead of accommodation centres. While choosing a house in both cities, Syrians have taken into account their citizenship law and kinship status and concentrated in certain parts of the cities. In the neighbourhoods they live in, Syrians shop at grocery stores opened by Syrians. Although the places where they live and work in Berlin are generally located in two different regions far from each other, these areas in Izmir are mostly located close to each other. In both countries, i) housing prices and rents increased due to increased housing demand by immigrants; ii) local people reacted after price increases; iii) Syrian immigrants made their own cultures visible in the places they settled. In order for immigrants to have better quality living conditions and not to interfere these conditions with the rights of local people: receiving countries should improve their housing policies for Syrian immigrants and increase/diversify the housing supply.

Positioning of Women in Migration Studies and Marginalisation of Women's Knowledge: The Case of Syrian Women in Turkey

(1239) Hulya Sahin-Erbektas, Hacettepe University, Turkey

Migration is a complex phenomenon in which different disciplines such as political science, sociology, psychology, economy, anthropology, and geology are analyzed through their own assumptions. Nevertheless, in these disciplines, the common feature is that they have a gender-blind perspective nature. After gender studies became the center of migration research, although it is possible to see wider perspectives in the literature, it is seen that most of the studies are still far from the feminist point of view and continue to produce traditional knowledge. Based on these realities, in this paper, the knowledge production process of Syrian women was problematized in the context of Turkey. For this purpose, the published reports, academic papers, and thesis on Syrians were critically analyzed by covering the period between 2017 and 2022. While analyzing these reports and academic research, four main themes of Feminist Standpoint Theory, which are "Strong Objectivity", "Epistemic Advantage", "Situated Knowledge", and "Power Relationship", were used. In this way, achieving a response to how the knowledge of Syrian women is marginalized was aimed. While Syrian women's knowledge was being researched, the document analysis research method was used. In this paper, the meaning of marginalization, how Syrian women were positioned in the reports which are the subject of this study, the relation between power and production of information, and in which spheres are Syrian women presented as marginal were discussed. In the conclusion of the study, it has been recognized that the knowledge of Syrian women is marginalized within the findings that are limited to the reports and academic studies examined. In these studies, the Syrian women, who migrated to Turkey, were generalized as victims in a vulnerable group instead of making visible their voices of them by moving from their standpoint of views.

The effects of international migration on the total fertility rate: evidence from Morocco by the Rolling window ARDL and the Granger causality test of Toda Yamamoto

(1004) Oussama Zennati, Université de Pau et des pays de l'Adour, France

Jamal Bouoiyour, Université de Pau et des pays de l'Adour, France

This article aims to explore the link between international migration and the total fertility rate in Morocco, by controlling the GDP, the infant mortality rate, the rurality rate, the overall primary enrollment rate and the rate of consumer price inflation for the period between 1975 and 2017. The Autoregressive-Distributed Lag (ARDL) approach was used to estimate the short and long term coefficients and the Toda and Yamamoto test to explore causality between the variables. To take into account the variability of the coefficients of the ARDL model over time, the rolling regression window technique was used. Our results show that both remittances and fertility norms reduce significantly the fertility rate in Morocco. Both in the long and short term, the effect of fertility norms is greater than that of remittances. In addition, Toda and Yamamoto's test shows that the causality between remittances and the total fertility rate is bidirectional. In contrast, the causality between fertility norms and fertility rate is unidirectional. Our results show that

Moroccan migrants can play the role of agents of social change to achieve the demographic transition in Morocco. Particularly that in recent years we have witnessed the exhaustion of family planning methods in Morocco.

Constructing a sense of home: The case of lifestyle migration in the Arabian Gulf

(958) Emina Osmandzikovic, Sorbonne University Abu Dhabi, UAE

Lifestyle migration among the high-skilled professionals has been on the rise as a global phenomenon, exponentially rising in popularity amidst the Covid-19 pandemic and the resulting crisis. A range of countries, from Spain and Portugal to Singapore and South Korea, have been offering green and golden visas for high-skilled professionals, enabling greater permanence and integrating them better into the national socio-economic schemes. While traditionally governed by the 'kafala' system of sponsorship for non-nationals, the Gulf countries have diversified their visa portfolios in line with the rising global trends. The Golden Visas across the Gulf countries have been launched in the last three years, marking a historic shift and an unprecedented milestone in the way these countries approach their residents and non-national communities. Through my research, I examine the short-term impact of the changing residency policies in the Gulf with a special focus on the resident community of the United Arab Emirates, the socio-economic impacts of such policies and the perception of the domicile populations.

8C   Education and High Skilled Migration 3

Chair: Mala Arunasalam, Global Banking School, London, UK

1122   Educational Outcomes and Technology Access among Refugee Populations from Africa: A Needs-Assessment Study

Mythili Menon, Karissa Marble-Flint, Sophia Gami-Kadiri, Miriam Mangaza, Wichita State University

1042   Cultural capital and consumption practices for embodied acculturation: The case of educated and affluent Chinese immigrants in Hong Kong

Connie K. Y. Mak, University of Lincoln, UK
Bill Xu, The Hong Kong Polytechnic University, HK

1132   When Intercultural Experience Contributes to Creativity: International Students in Russia

Maria Bultseva, National Research University "Higher School of Economics", Moscow, Russia
Aytaj Mammadova, National Research University "Higher School of Economics", Moscow, Russia

1194   Exploring Social Capital Among the Non-Displaced Kashmiri Pandits in Kashmir, India

Avinash Koul, Symbiosis International University, India

Educational Outcomes and Technology Access among Refugee Populations from Africa: A Needs-Assessment Study

(1122) Mythili Menon, Karissa Marble-Flint, Sophia Gami-Kadiri, Miriam Mangaza, Wichita State University

Although the city of Wichita, the largest city in the U.S. state of Kansas, has resettled nearly 2,500 refugee families within the last decade, no studies exist on refugee integration. To bridge this gap and understand how refugees are integrating, we conducted a needs-assessment survey to assess refugees' perceived needs, barriers, technology access, and related it to educational outcomes. We report results of the study in Wichita among resettled refugee families (N = 48) from the African countries of The Democratic Republic of the Congo, Burundi, Kenya, Tanzania, and Uganda. Primarily, 42% of the participants spoke Kiswahili as well as other Bantu languages such as KiBembe and had limited English proficiency. Among participants who had children enrolled in local school districts, the study showed that mathematics was their favorite subject, while history and social studies was their least favorite. Less than half of the participants had access to a laptop/desktop or a smartphone at home, suggesting inequitable outcomes for educational attainment during online pivoting of classes throughout COVID-19. Most of the participants had internet access. In addition, the results found that the two main hardships for African refugees in Wichita are lack of quality employment opportunities and lack of English language classes, which in turn makes it difficult for them to find well-paying jobs and form new friendships in the community. The results of this survey can inform policymakers, educators, and humanitarian and resettlement agencies on the needs of this community, and aid in improving and prioritizing refugee needs.

Cultural capital and consumption practices for embodied acculturation: The case of educated and affluent Chinese immigrants in Hong Kong

(1042) Connie K. Y. Mak, University of Lincoln, UK

Bill Xu, The Hong Kong Polytechnic University, HK

While acculturation research on migration tends to adopt a psychological orientation and focuses on migrants' adaptation challenges in distinct host cultures, our study draws on the practice theories (e.g. works of P. Bourdieu, E. Shove and A. Warde) to explore the 'process' of how educated and affluent immigrants from the Mainland China and Taiwan adapt to their new life in the city of Hong Kong. We explore how this particular group of migrants mobilize cultural resources and embodied consumption practices to negotiate for existence and new identity in the new social setting. Do migrants with similar ethnic background and relatively good economic capital find the need of acculturation and integration at all? How do they mobilize their cultural competence and practices to achieve acculturation by embodying desirable habitus? From where do migrants acquire those cultural skills and knowing? Are they pre-exist before migration or acquired and accrued over time (Skeggs, 2004)? Unlike most existing research which take a cross-sectional view, we adopt a processual perspective to unveil the dynamics of how embodied practices and sources of acquiring them change over the trajectory of migration.

While acculturation studies for Asia regions are comparatively scarce, the three places of Hong Kong, Mainland China and Taiwan present a unique bordering case study to understand the malleable structure-agency relationship. Though sharing common historical roots and ethnic Chinese background, the three places have been undergoing dissimilar political regimes and value socialization, yet increasingly converging in terms of economic mutuality. The educated and affluent group is chosen in this study since the government has launched policies to attract such group of 'talents' and aims to see successful assimilation. Further, this group of migrants tends to have higher economic capital and lower financial concerns, and thus enable the study to focus on the role of cultural capital in acculturation.

The biographic narratives generated from 15 migrants suggest that nuanced cultural competence constitutes their proficiency in accommodating migration hysteresis. Their embodied practices and performative knowing determine their perceived well-being in the new destination. Cultural barriers or borders are found to be better traversed and acculturation efficacy are better attained through prior familiarity with the host culture, readiness for integration, language similarity, appreciation of host virtues and prudent fusion of consumption practices. While these cultural resources and practices are crucial, their relative salience evolve over time and induce a process of using, not using and adjusting. Migrants also shift between impalpable cultural borders to broaden their resource scope to optimize their consumption competence in daily life. Sources of socialization are also found changing over stages of migration. For instance, the influence of workplace counterparts and immediate family members or relatives gradually subsides with the emergence of other social acquaintances and quotidian observations, including social media, neighbourhood, market communications and even referent others on the streets. Our data show the mutability of habitus in cross-border cultural assimilation. The evolution of nuanced competence found in the study also provides practical implications to policy makers and migration authorities.

Hong Kong

References:

Berry, J.W. (1997), "Immigration, acculturation, and adaptation", *Applied Psychology*, vol. 46, no. 1, pp. 5-34.

Bourdieu, P. (1984), *Distinction: A social critique of the judgement of taste*, Harvard University Press, Cambridge, Mass.

Bourdieu, P. and Wacquant, L.J. (1992), *An Invitation to Reflexive Sociology*, University of Chicago Press, Chicago.

Shove, E., Pantzar, M. and Watson, M. (2012), *The dynamics of social practice: everyday life and how it changes*, Sage Publications, London.

Skeggs, B. (2004), *Class, self, culture*, Routledge, London.

Warde, A. (2005), "Consumption and theories of practice", *Journal of consumer culture*, vol. 5, no. 2, pp. 131-153.

When Intercultural Experience Contributes to Creativity: International Students in Russia

(1132) Maria Bultseva, National Research University "Higher School of Economics", Moscow, Russia

Aytaj Mammadova, National Research University "Higher School of Economics", Moscow, Russia

In this study we imply that intercultural experiences students get studying abroad may stimulate creativity under certain conditions. When a person comes across intercultural experiences, exposure to a new culturally specific information can stimulate creativity. However, in order to get positive otcomes, it is necessary for a person to have the ability to recognize and consider for cultural differences. As intercultural sensitivity, and mainly its relativistic stage, shows capacity of a person to cultivate positive emotions toward other cultures as truly appreciating these differences, it seems like intercultural sensitivity should contribute to creativity. However, preconditions of own culture of an individual matter. Specifically, cultural tightness can be a relevant antecedent for a way how intercultural experience influences an individual. So we investigated the relationship between intercultural experience, intercultural sensitivity and creativity of international students and considered the role of cultural tightness in these relationships. The cross-sectional study was conducted in a Russian university on a sample of 102 international students from more than 20 countries with the help of such instruments as Intercultural Sensitivity Scale Questionnaire (Holm, Nokelainen, & Tirri, 2009), Many Instances Game (Runco, 2011) and Tightness-Looseness Scale (Gelfand et al., 2011). The results have shown that, indeed, intercultural experience during exchange studies can be positive for students' intercultural sensitivity and creativity, while cultural tightness strenthens direct effect of intercultural experience on intercultural sensitivity and its indirect effect on creativity.

Exploring Social Capital Among the Non-Displaced Kashmiri Pandits in Kashmir, India

(1194) Avinash Koul, Symbiosis International University, India

Over the last thirty years, Kashmir, the northern frontier state of India, often referred to as the 'paradise on earth' for its scenic and beautiful landscapes has faced militant insurgencies, religious conflict, and separatist propaganda. This has led to the displacement of the local Kashmiri population including Sikhs, Muslims, Buddhists, and Hindus. Targeted attacks and selective killings of the Kashmiri Pandits (KP), one of the Hindu communities by militants between 1989-1990 has led to their mass exodus(Koul, 1991). The data available indicate displacement of 300,000 to 600,000 KPs(Evans, 2002). While most of the KP families left Kashmir, a small number chose to stay back in the conflict-ridden home state. A robust body of literature is available on the displaced Kashmiri Pandits, but little is known about the non-displaced Kashmiri Pandits or those who chose to stay back through the conflict and continue to do so till today.

Violent conflicts, displacement, and increasing lack of trust at both the inter and intra community levels have led to a loss of the 'sense of community, 'social networks' and 'civic engagement' among the people. The primary relation of individuals tends to become robust during conflict and while the secondary relations weaken (Colletta & Cullen, 2000), leading to a decline of the 'social and societal capital' for the individual and the community.Social capital is essential for the smooth functioning of a society as it maintains the balance and helps resolve conflict through collective action while conflict within a society weakens social capital and deviates people from ideal social norms resulting in an imbalance within the society.

The paper is drawn from an ongoing study that aims to explore how violent conflict and displacement affect social capital, both bonding and bridging capital, within the minority non-displaced population (here the Kashmiri Pandit population) and in their interaction with the other members of the society (here the Kashmiri Muslim and other Hindu and Sikh community) who traditionally and culturally have engaged and interacted with each other within the same space. The study uses qualitative data and an ethnographic method to illicit information from the participants. The preliminary results indicate that the traditional social network of the community is plagued due to mass exodus and a lack of trust, leading to the isolation of the non-displaced Kashmiri Pandits. The inter-and-intra bonds with and among the people have weakened due to a lack of interconnectedness arising from restrictions on travel and increasing physical distances among members of the community. The results have important implications for government and non-government agencies working in the region to bring normalcy to the life of the local people in this conflict-ridden zone for the past thirty-two years.

References:

Colletta, N. J., & Cullen, M. L. (2000). *The Nexus Between violent Conflict, Social capital and Social Cohesion:Case Studies From Cambodia and Rwanda.* International Bank for Reconstruction and Development/World Bank.

Evans, A. (2002). *A departure from history: Kashmiri Pandits, 1990-2001.* Contemporary South Asia, 11(1), 19–37. https://doi.org/10.1080/0958493022000000341

Koul, A. (1991). *The Kashmiri Pandit.* New Delhi: Utpal Publications.

8D   New Challenges in Migration Studies

Chair: Sebnem Koser Akcapar, Social Sciences University of Ankara, Turkey

1075   Syrian Refugeedom, Knowledge Production, and Subaltern Potential in Turkish Scholarship

Sandra Cvikić, Institute of Social Sciences Ivo Pilar

1131   Ethnography from a distance? The Pandemic and Aftermath in shaping qualitative method in migration studies

Sebnem Koser Akcapar, Social Sciences University of Ankara, Turkey
Aysima Calisan, Social Sciences University of Ankara, Turkey

1294   The Limitations of Extraterrestrial Migration: Theoretical Interstellar Space Travel toward Habitable Exoplanet Candidates and the Wait Calculation

Stefani Stojchevska, South East European University, N. Macedonia

1087 Narrating migration: media discourse and biographic accounts of recent Brazilian immigration in Portugal

Patricia Posch, University of Minho, Portugal
Rosa Cabecinhas, University of Minho, Portugal

Syrian Refugeedom, Knowledge Production, and Subaltern Potential in Turkish Scholarship

(1075) Sandra Cvikić, Institute of Social Sciences Ivo Pilar

In response to Adele E. Clarke's call 'to be creative in using' Sociology of Knowledge Approach to Discourse (SKAD) as an open and flexible way to conduct research in 'new and diverse' fields of social sciences (Clarke, 2020, p.xv); this paper provides an insight into experimental sociological attempt to form 'epistemic friendship' between constructivist grounded theory and Foucauldian discourse analysis inside SKAD framework (Keller, 2020, pp.16-47). Far from being confident in its generalized applicability, this paper presents a modest 'alternative form of research practice' based on a study case (Denzin et al., 2017, p.495). Namely, this paper is premised on a critical qualitative sociological inquiry into Turkish scholarly/expert knowledge production about Syrian refugeedom since the 2015/2016 European 'migration crisis/refugee crisis' (De Genova et al., 2016, p.1) which was financed in 2021/2022 by the Scientific and Technological Research Institution of Turkey (Tübitak). Building on this critical sociological inquiry, the aim of the paper is to outline a balanced study of knowledge production and the global process of refugeedom while bridging epistemological, methodological, and empirical divergences between critical sociology/sociology of knowledge and forced migration/refugee studies. Based on the research findings presented in the paper that is currently under review (International Migrations), further analysis of scholarly/expert knowledge production has unraveled 'elements of the unknown and unanticipated' leaving this critical sociological endeavor open-ended and deeply engaged 'with the moral' while taking full responsibility for its own contribution to the knowledge production about Syrian refugeedom (Denzin et al., 2017, pp.495-496). In its conclusion, this paper will not only provide answers as to how and what kind of scholarly/expert knowledge was produced by Turkish scholars/experts, and to what extent their research findings converge with data collected by their international counterparts. It will also propose a subaltern counteracting way of doing critical qualitative sociological research on forced/refugee migrations detached from the powerful structural dependency on the hegemony of the Global North knowledge discourse (Chimni, 1998, 2001, 2002, 2009; Connel, 2020; Hanafi, 2021, 2019; Said, 1978; Spivak, 1988, 1989; Malkki, 1995; Zetter, 1991, 2007; Harrell-Bond and Voutira, 1992).

Ethnography from a distance? The Pandemic and Aftermath in shaping qualitative method in migration studies

(1131) Sebnem Koser Akcapar, Social Sciences University of Ankara, Turkey

Aysima Calisan, Social Sciences University of Ankara, Turkey

The pandemic has forced social scientists to rethink the methodological and epistemological standpoints of their original research plans due to unavoidable limitations to their access to the participants, resources, and traditional techniques. This is particularly challenging for those whose research adapts qualitative method with the aim of obtaining in-depth information. Therefore, the need to design a method suitable for the pandemic conditions has become more crucial than ever to address the pressing challenges of conducting fieldwork and reaching participants due to the COVID-related restrictions and measures. While the opportunities already offered by modern information and communication technologies seem to be an important facilitating tool in overcoming these challenges, there are also some pitfalls that need careful consideration, such as the changing position of the researcher.[18] By comparing two studies conducted in 2021 with different categories and nationalities of migrant and refugee populations in Turkey, this paper aims to reflect on the advantages and disadvantages of online and face-to-face qualitative methods. The first study employs mostly online in-depth interviewing method to understand the impact of the pandemic on a sample group of 100 participants that consists of mixed migrants living in different cities of Turkey. The second one analyzing the relations between gender, forced migration, and deskilling, on the other hand, involves face-to-face interviews with 50 refugees residing in Ankara, Bursa, Gaziantep, İstanbul, and Mersin. The main difference between the two is not only about the use of traditional and online methods but also the combination of many issues, such as constant negotiation of the researcher's positionality,[19] subjectivity, self-reflexivity, exposure to second-hand trauma, the power dynamics[20] between the researcher and the participant, building rapport through the screen, and underrepresentation of disadvantaged people due to digital gap. Consequently, we assessed that even though the online method has increased its popularity during the pandemic, its challenges should not be overlooked. Therefore, in order to avoid these methodological and ethical pitfalls, hybrid methods that successfully combine in-person and online data collection techniques could be integrated to facilitate greater understanding of current migration trends and processes in the societ

---

[18] Akcapar, S.K. and Çalışan, A. (2022). Pandemi Döneminde Göçmenlerle Araştırma Yürütmek: Niteliksel Yöntemde Yeni Normal Üzerine. Sosyoloji Araştırmaları Dergisi, 25 (1): 8-22.

[19] Regarding difficulty of the ethnographer in drawing emotional, spatial, and temporal boundaries between work and everyday life, see Till, K. (2001). Returning home and to the field. Geographical Review,91(1-2): 46-86.

[20] Many authors pointed out existing hierarchies and asymetrical relationship in ethnography suggesting that intersubjective processes are often shaped by power relations. See for example, Faubion, J.D. & Marcus, G.E. (2009). Fieldwork Is Not What It Used To Be: Learning Anthropology's Method in A Time of Transition. Ithaca, NY: Cornell University Press. See also Bourdieu, P. (1999). Understanding P. Bourdieu. In The Weight of the World: Social Suffering in Contemporary Society. A. Accardo, G. Balazs, S. Beaud, F. Bonvin, & E. Bourdieu (Eds.) (pp. 607-626). Stanford, CA: Stanford University Press.

The Limitations of Extraterrestrial Migration: Theoretical Interstellar Space Travel toward Habitable Exoplanet Candidates and the Wait Calculation

(1294) Stefani Stojchevska, South East European University, N. Macedonia

Migrating the negative effects of overpopulation on Earth, as well as its established arguments, represent a multidisciplinary challenge for humankind as yet. With regard to the field of space sciences, particular emphasis is placed upon the concept of extraterrestrial migration, which is often envisioned through space development and habitation beyond low-Earth orbit (LEO) and even within the Earth-Moon system. However, when considering extraterrestrial migration through interstellar space travel toward habitable exoplanet candidates, its limitations reflect corresponding problems as derived from the wait calculation and low technological feasibilities. The primary objectives of this scientific research are to examine the limitations of extraterrestrial migration by considering theoretical interstellar space travel, all while addressing two of its most crucial hurdles: (1) vast distances between solar systems and (2) enormous fuel requirements. On such cosmic distance scales, the methods utilized in this scientific research include comparative approaches concerning Einstein's special relativity theory and non-relativistic Newton's physics. Both theories are essential in examining the wait calculation in terms of interstellar space travel toward habitable exoplanet candidates given that unlike Newton's theory in which gravity supposedly exerts its force instantaneously over any distance, in general relativity gravity travels at exactly the speed of light, fully in keeping with the central dictum of the special theory of relativity that nothing can exceed light speed. The results obtained from this scientific research include precise calculations which display contrasting requirements between Einstein's universe and Newton's universe, which further conclude the fact that interstellar space travel does not represent a highly established argument in response to migrating the negative effects of overpopulation on Earth. Despite interstellar space travel not violating any physical laws, its achievement is currently deemed impossible due to low technological and economic feasibilities. Moreover, underlying legal constructs of interstellar travel would not be appropriately manifested given that the high inefficiency of international space law regulating interstellar space. While the 1967 Outer Space Treaty contains no provisions in regard to extraterrestrial migration, this scientific research aims to guide space jurisprudents and policy-makers in setting forward its theoretical limitations.

Narrating migration: media discourse and biographic accounts of recent Brazilian immigration in Portugal

(1087) Patricia Posch, University of Minho, Portugal

Rosa Cabecinhas, University of Minho, Portugal

In contemporary times, international migrations are already part of the structure of industrialized societies (Massey, Arango, Hugo, Kouaouci, Pellegrino and Taylor, 1993), constituting an important vector of influence of social transformations (Castles and Miller, 1998). In the case of the migration route from Brazil to Portugal, after a period of deceleration, from 2015 onwards, the entry of Brazilian documented immigrants into Portugal began to grow significantly, reaching a peak of 143.74% in 2018 (SEF, 2019). Accompanying this growth, which has already been interpreted as a third (cf. França &

Padilla, 2018) or even fourth (cf. Fernandes, Peixoto & Oltramari, 2021) migratory wave, there is also a growing interest of the Brazilian media in producing content in which these migrations and their subjects are represented. These social representations are embedded in discourses that become part of social meaning networks (van Dijk, 2018) without losing their operative nature, which position them as mechanisms for the maintenance of social power and authority structures through knowledge management (Foucault, 1969/1972). In this regard, we see in Cogo (2007) how different media processes that deal with contemporary migrations contribute towards forging what the author called a communicative citizenship. In this sense, we developed a study with the objective of investigating how the social representations that involve the migratory experiences and experiences conveyed in the media discourse in the Brazilian context relate to those that are reported by Brazilian immigrants themselves who migrated to the North region of Portugal in the last years. Therefore, two empirical researches were conducted. The first one was an analysis of the discourse, through the approach of Critical Discourse Analysis, and also socio-semiotic, according to the theory of Kress and van Leeuwen (2006), of the episodes that make up the first season of the television series "Portugal by Brazilians", broadcasted in Brazil in early 2018. The second was the collection and analysis of stories of the migratory experience of Brazilian immigrants who migrated to the North of Portugal between 2015 and 2020, having adopted the Life Stories method for this purpose. By comparing the results of the previous analysis of the biographic narratives (cf. author, 2020a; 2020b; 2021) with the media discourse of the television series, it was possible to elucidate the similarities and differences in the discourse on Brazilian immigration in Portugal that is conveyed in the Brazilian media. The results of this analysis point to the fact that, although this is an important movement of television to reposition itself as an important player when it comes to the source of information about the phenomenon and its subjects, contributing to its social visibility through visuality, it is not possible to neglect how the framing that is made of a phenomenon as plural as Brazilian emigration to Portugal and the use of the biographical approach in the media context can be seen as strategic decisions that meet interests that often do not show themselves in the media content.

8E   Workshop: Identities, Ethnicities, Minorities, Religions

Chair: Eric M. Trinka, James Madison University, USA

1193   Patterns of Self-Identification among Turkish immigrants in North Cyprus

Aysenur Talat Zrilli, Eastern Mediterranean University, North Cyprus

549   'I Thought I Was Coming to Heaven': Expectation-Reality Discrepancy Among Nigerian Migrants in the United Kingdom

Tunde Alabi, University of Cape Town, South Africa

1282   "I am not who you think I am": Multiple, hybrid and racialized identities of Canadian Muslim Youth in the negotiation of belonging and citizenship

Wasif Ali, University of Calgary, Canada
Aamir Jamal, University of Calgary, Canada
Clive Baldwin, St. Thomas University, Canada
Swati Dhingra, University of Calgary, Canada

Abstracts Book

516   What does it mean for migrants to be religious? Revisiting

Eric M Trinka, James Madison University, USA

1163   Migrants, Religious Beliefs and Social Integration

Olivia M Joseph-Aluko, Reinvent African Diaspora Network (RADET), UK

1101   The influence of Islamic civilization in Europe

Răzvan Dacian Cârciumaru, University of Oradea, Romania

Patterns of Self-Identification among Turkish immigrants in North Cyprus

(1193) Aysenur Talat Zrilli, Eastern Mediterranean University, North Cyprus

Constructed as Turkish Cypriots' 'ethnic kin' by dominant Turkish-nationalist discourses of the state-building era in North Cyprus during 1970s, the populations that were transferred from Turkey to the island have remained largely invisible as immigrants both in politics as well as in the academia. Thus, literature on their acculturation experiences has remained rather scarce. Drawing on an ethnographic study conducted during 2011-2015 in a village settled by Turkish nationals after the partition of Cyprus, we aim to contribute to filling this gap. We will argue in this regard, that the newcomers have been going through experiences of self-identification which are necessarily marked and complicated by the experience of immigration and relocation. Conceptually, this study chooses to talk about 'identification' as opposed to 'identity' so as to underline the dynamic character of how these groups reflect about themselves and their relations to their host society (Hall, 1989; Brubaker and Cooper, 2000).

There exist three separate waves of migration from Turkey to North Cyprus (Kurtuluş and Purkis, 2014). Whereas the latter two waves of migration resemble international labour movements driven by economic and structural factors, the first of these stands apart. This wave was initiated as a bilateral project of Turkish mainland and Turkish Cypriot governments with not only economic but also political motivations, after Cyprus was partitioned into two ethnically homogenized sections and Turkish Cypriots declared sovereignty in the north. Continuing as a state-facilitated movement between years 1975-80, this migratory wave resulted in the settlement of a proportionally large population, which was depicted by the nationalist elite of the era as an element to be included so as to boost population, create a national economy by filling the labour gap, and to validate and make sustainable Turkish Cypriots' separation from their former Greek Cypriot partners (Talat Zrilli, 2019). The newcomers were settled mainly in rural areas in the northern part of Cyprus that were evacuated by a displaced Greek Cypriot population. In these locations they mostly remained within their own communities, spatially segregated from native Turkish Cypriots.

Under these circumstances and due to their group characteristics, such as low levels of formal education and non-transferable skills, many of the first-generation immigrants have had to rely on their own communities' cultural and social resources. This paper will argue that these are the main factors, along with perceived discrimination in the host society that affects these groups' self-identification. They strengthen not only the groups' emotional linkages to Turkey, but also reinforce its presence, via vigorous transnational ties, in their everyday-life practices. Identification with Cyprus among this group remains largely instrumental. The second-generation on the other hand, through increased social and cultural interaction with native Turkish Cypriots have increased emotional and habitual attachment to North Cyprus. Another finding of the study, which is similar to findings in pertinent migration literature, is that there also exists a state of 'in-betweenness' across generations.

References:

Brubaker, R., & Cooper, F. (2000). Beyond „Identity". *Theory and Society, 29, 1-47.*

Hall, S. (1989). Ethnicity: Identity and Difference. *Radical America, 23 (4), 9-20.*

Kurtuluş, H., & Purkis, S. (2014). *Kuzey Kıbrıs'ta Türkiyeli Göçmenler. Türkiye İş Bankası Kültür Yayınları.*

Talat Zrilli, A. 2019. Ethno-nationalism, state building and migration: the first wave of migration from Turkey to North Cyprus, *Southeast European and Black Sea Studies, 19:3, 493-510.*

'I Thought I Was Coming to Heaven': Expectation-Reality Discrepancy Among Nigerian Migrants in the United Kingdom

(549) Tunde Alabi, University of Cape Town, South Africa

Being abroad or having a family member in the West is an indicator of achievement in many African households. However, there is an exaggerated view of life in the West. African migrants do have pre-migratory expectations, which may (not) be congruent with their post-migration experiences. Disparities between expectation and reality may have implication for experience of disappointment, frustration and migrants' overall wellbeing. Migrants are beginning to form solidarity and educational groups on social media where they express their precarities in the host country and educate intending migrants. This study investigates (in)congruence between expectation and reality among Nigerian migrants in the United Kingdom (UK). The study asks: how do Nigerians in the UK express expectation-reality in(congruence)? In what areas of do Nigerians in the UK experience discrepancy between pre-migration expectations and post-migration reality? What are the factors in the UK encouraging Nigerians to stay back in the UK in the face of adversity? Data were drawn from (1) 666 online comments on a popular Instagram blog post asking migrants in the UK to narrate their expectation-reality discrepancy; (2) 12 interviews with Nigerian migrants across different cities in the UK. Data were organized and analyzed thematically using Nvivo (version 12). It was found that actual experiences fall short of pre-migratory expectations, and these discrepancies are often expressed in form of sarcasm, advice and argument in online space. The major areas of expectation-reality discrepancy are health, housing, bills/cost of living, aesthetics, and social life. As one migrant commented "the healthcare is not perfect at all as it is overstretched funding wise and this affects everything. COVID made it x20 worse". Nigerian migrants are disappointed by the lack of "ubuntu" in the UK as everyone is calculative. Despite these experiences, some prefer to remain in the UK because (1) the system is working as they get the value for their payment; (2) it's easier to get a job to pay bills even if such job results in occupational downgrading; (3) "it's better to cry in heaven than crying in hell".

"I am not who you think I am": Multiple, hybrid and racialized identities of Canadian Muslim Youth in the negotiation of belonging and citizenship

(1282) Wasif Ali, University of Calgary, Canada

Aamir Jamal, University of Calgary, Canada

Clive Baldwin, St. Thomas University, Canada

Swati Dhingra, University of Calgary, Canada

This study explores identity construction among Canadian Muslim youth (CMY). While there have been studies exploring the challenges faced by Muslim youth in the west, this study particularly focuses on the development of a meaningful a stable Canadian-Muslim identity in an era of global conflicts, collective surveillance, and suspicion. Identity-formation is a complex process involving the configuration of many influences - direct and indirect, local and global, personal and impersonal. Sometimes aspects of fluid, multiple identities conflict and an individual is faced with having to navigate competing and not necessarily commensurable influences. "Canadian Muslim Youth: Identity Construction in the Context of Global Conflicts" project is funded by the Social Sciences and Humanities Research Council of Canada. The project consists of three phases, at this point, study findings are being shared with broader audiences through conferences and forums and peer review research papers. The insights of this study derive from 30 in-depth interviews with Muslim youth from three Canadian metropolitan cities. Participants were identified through social networks, mosques, community organizations, schools and universities in Calgary, Toronto, and Vancouver, with 10 participants from each location. Convenient and snowball strategies of data collection were applied with attention to maximum variation strategy to gain a diverse religious and ethnic perspective. In all, we interviewed 18 males and 12 females between the ages 18 and 30, belonging to a variety of ethnic and cultural backgrounds and coming from various countries of origin including Afghanistan, Egypt, India, Indonesia, Pakistan, Palestine, and Turkey. Narrative inquiry, located within the constructionist framework, has developed as a means of exploring lived experience, making sense, communication, and the interplay of individual and social, cultural and discoursal factors. Thematic analysis of 30 interviews with CMY from Toronto, Calgary, and Vancouver, identified five major themes: a) The journey of navigating multiple, complex, and hybrid identities; b) Religious identity and spirituality; c) 'I am not what you think I am' - Media portrayals of Muslims; d) Claiming inclusion and belonging in the face of anti-Muslim racism; and e) Recommendations. This research contributes to the literature on Muslim youth in western countries and supports a better understanding of the concept of Islamophobia in those societies. Listening to the voices of CMY will help policy makers, practitioners, Muslim communities, and organizations to develop strategies for positive youth development. Understanding Muslim youth identity formation from the perspective of youth themselves has brought forward opinions on Islam as a religion and the perceptions about the Islamic teachings and Islamic way of life. Study findings will help the Muslim communities and organizations to develop strategies for positive youth development keeping in view these shared experiences and perceptions. Overall, this study will contribute to the public discourse and policymaking to address the pressing issue of Islamophobia by supporting CMY, reiterating the need for pluralism in Canadian society.

What does it mean for migrants to be religious? Revisiting

(516) Eric M Trinka, James Madison University, USA

There has been great debate within the fields of migration and religious studies regarding the salience of religion among migrants. Timothy L. Smith was the first to argue that migration was a "theologizing" experience. Some scholars have affirmed Smith's claims by providing qualitative evidence and concluding that the disruptive nature of migration spurs further reliance on the superhuman and a heightened religious consciousness among migrants that frequently results in increased religiosity. Others have challenged this perspective and argued that the nature of migration as a disruptive experience leads to decreased religiosity. Internal disagreement persists among researchers in this camp regarding the scope and duration of this decrease. The contention is whether deviations in religiosity are short-term responses to the immediate demands of building networks, finding a home and job, and learning a language or whether they signal long-term acculturative adaptation to a new context wherein previous religious identity is diminished. There is, however, consensus that disconnection from known religious contexts and social systems reduces the accountability for participants. Likewise, it is agreed that the demands of the migrational experience leave less time for religious participation or the building of religious social networks. Beyond these questions, researchers continue to debate the role of religion as a selection mechanism for migration.

This paper probes the roots of these topics by asking what it fundamentally means for migrants to be religious.

In doing so, it first presents an overview of current research on religion as a selection mechanism for migration. Subsequently, it explores the place of religion at various stages of the migrational undertaking. Finally, the paper reviews present scholarship on religious fluidity and conversion among migrants.

The overarching goal is to reflect further on our own methodological predilections for studying religion among migrants.

Short Bibliography

Phillip Connor, "International Migration and Religious Selection," Journal for the Scientific Study of Religion 51 (2012): 184-94.

Timothy. L. Smith, "Religion and Ethnicity in America," American Historical Review 83 (1978): 1115-85.

S.R. Warner, "Religion and Migration in the United States," Social Compass 50 (1998): 59-69;

Helen R. Ebaugh and J. Chafetz, eds., Religion and the New Immigrants: Continuities and Adaptations in Immigrant Congregations, (Walnut Creek, CA: AltaMira, 2000)

Holly Straut Eppsteiner and Jacqueline Hagan, "Religion as Psychological, Spiritual, and Social Support in the Migration Undertaking," in Intersections of Migration and Religion: Issues as the Global Crossroads (New York, NY: Palgrave Macmillan, 2016), 49-70.

Phillip Connor, "Increase or Decrease? The Impact of the International Migratory Event on Immigrant Religious Participation," Journal for the Scientific Study of Religion 47, no. 2 (2008): 243-57.

Claudia Diehl and Matthias Koenig, "God Can Wait—New Migrants in Germany Between Early Adaptation and Religious Reorganization," International Migration 51 (2013): 8-22.

Valerie A. Lewis and Ridhi Kashyap, "Piety in a Secular Society: Migration, Religiosity, and Islam in Britain," International Migration 51 (2013): 57-66.

F. Van Tubergen and J.I. Sindradottir, "The Religiosity of Immigrants in Europe: A Cross-National Study," Journal for the Scientific Study of Religion 50 (2011): 272-88.

Diana Wong and Peggy Levitt, "Traveling Faiths and Migrant Religions: The Case of Circulating Models of Da'wa among the Tablighi Jamaat and Foguangshan in Malaysia," Global Networks 14 (2014): 348-62.

Kim Knott, "Living Religious Practices," in Intersections of Religion and Migration: Issues at the Global Crossroads, Jennifer B. Saunders et al., eds. 71-90. (New York, NY: Palgrave Macmillan, 2016).

James A. Beckford, ed. Migration and Religion Vols. 1 & 2 (Cheltenham and Northampton: Elgar, 2016).

Karen I. Leonard, et al., eds. Immigrant Faiths: Transforming Religious Life in America (Lanham: Altamira, 2005).

Migrants, Religious Beliefs and Social Integration

(1163) Olivia M Joseph-Aluko, Reinvent African Diaspora Network (RADET), UK

For many migrants, religion is an integral part of social identity. However, tensions emerge when migrants are members of religious and ethnic minority groups. Recent studies have demonstrated that religion plays a significant role in the reception of migrants, refugees and asylum seekers in European societies, and many are forced to navigate between practising their religion and experiencing discrimination and harassment for adhering to their beliefs. This study examined the ways that religion is embedded in migrants' social identities and explored challenges associated with being an ethnic and religious minority.

This study consulted primary sources and reports to obtain data on migrants' religious affiliations. Ethnographic studies were explored to understand the role of religion in migrant communities. In addition, the study explored the legal and policy literature as well as government and NGO-authored human rights reports to uncover European government actions in relation to religious freedom.

The ethnographic literature widely attests to the centrality of religion in many migrant communities; religious practice provides a sense of community and maintains links to home. However, the literature also demonstrates that many migrants are concerned that they will have to give up their religion and culture to be fully accepted into their host society.

The legal and policy literature evinces that Europe has seen some of the world's largest increases in religious restrictions during the last decade. Europe had the world's second-highest share of countries where governments interfered in worship or harassed religious groups (91%).

Numerous European countries and cities have prohibited the wearing of religious symbols or clothing, in daily life or for public service jobs. Since 2011, France has outlawed full-face coverings such as burqa or niqab in public. Several cities in Catalonia instituted similar bans, which extend to face-covering veils, since 2010. Such bans have not been limited to Muslims; in 2021, a Cologne Regional Court classified male religious circumcision—a practice shared by Muslims and Jews—as constituting bodily harm, and in 2018, an Icelandic bill proposing to ban male circumcision for non-medical reasons was only put on hold following a groundswell of international pressure.

Societal hostility has also brought constraints on religious practice. Across Europe, religious minorities have been subject to intense pressure to convert to the dominant form of Christianity in their host countries. In 2015, Russian separatists in Ukraine held four Jehovah's Witnesses at gunpoint and took them to the local military headquarters, where they were tortured and forced to confess Orthodox Christianity as the only true religion. In 2019, a Jehovah's Witness in Moldova was physically assaulted for preaching in a village and subsequently fined by the authorities for 'insulting religious feelings'. Overall, 24 of 45 European countries failed to protect religious groups from discrimination or abuse in 2019.

It is critical to engage with public agencies and private organizations to better promote migrants' integration into European societies. In particular, legal advocates and social organizations can be leveraged to advance legal protections and policy change.

Referencesi

Ambrosini, M., Bonizzoni, P., & Molli, S. D. (2021). *How religion shapes immigrants' integration: The case of Christian migrant churches in Italy. Current Sociology, 69(6), 823–842.* https://doi.org/10.1177/0011392120979018

Boland, C. (2020). *Hybrid identity and practices to negotiate belonging: Madrid's Muslim youth of migrant origin. Comparative Migration Studies 8, 26.* https://doi.org/10.1186/s40878-020-00185-2

Meyer, B. & van der Veer, P. (2021). *Refugees and Religion: Ethnographic Studies of Global Trajectories. Bloomsbury Academic.* http://dx.doi.org/10.5040/9781350167162

Molteni, F. & Dimitriadis, I. (2021) *Immigrants' religious transmission in Southern Europe: Reaction or assimilation? Evidence from Italy. Journal of International Migration and Integration 22, 1485–1504.* https://doi.org/10.1007/s12134-021-00815-3

NoVaMigra. (2021). *Norms and Values in the European Migration and Refugee Crisis: Final Report.* https://novamigra.eu/index.php?s=file_download&id=104

Pew Research Center. (2019, 19 July). *A Closer Look at How Religious Restrictions Have Risen Around the World.* https://www.pewforum.org/wp-content/uploads/sites/7/2019/07/Restrictions_X_WEB_7-15_FULL-VERSION-1.pdf

Pew Research Center (2021, September 30). *Globally, Social Hostilities Related to Religion Decline in 2019, While Government Restrictions Remain at Highest Levels.* https://www.pewforum.org/wp-content/uploads/sites/7/2021/09/PF_09.30.21_religious_restrictions-Full_PDF.pdf

Shanneik, Y. & Tiilikainen, M. (2019). *Sudanese and Somali women in Ireland and in Finland: Material religion and culture in the formation of migrant women's identities in the diaspora. In Muslims at the Margins of Europe, eds. T. Martikainen, J. Mapril, & A.H. Khan (pp. 245–268). Brill.* https://doi.org/10.1163/9789004404564_013

Abstracts Book
United Kingdom Foreign & Commonwealth Office. (2022). *Human Rights and Democracy Reports.* https://www.gov.uk/government/collections/human-rights-and-democracy-reports

U.S. Department of State (2022). *International Religious Freedom Reports.* https://www.state.gov/international-religious-freedom-reports/

The influence of Islamic civilization in Europe

(1101) Răzvan Dacian Cârciumaru, University of Oradea, Romania

"Whoever seeks a way to pursue knowledge, Allah will make it easier for him to enter Paradise" [Prophet Muhammad]

The Golden Age of Islam has made massive contributions to various sciences. The numbers we use today in mathematics are called Arabic numerals and were brought to Europe in the 12th century by Muslim mathematicians. Medicine is another science in which Muslim scholars have made major contributions, so in addition to the establishment of the first hospital in history (706/707), **Al-Walid Hospital** in Damascus, shortly after, in 872, the Cairo **Al-Fustat Hospital** was founded, the first institution to share many features in common with modern hospitals. **Al-Rāzī's** medical work has become well-known among medieval European practitioners and has profoundly influenced medical education in the Latin West. Some of his volumes have become part of the medical curriculum in Western universities. Until modern times, **Al-Zahrāwī's** contributions to surgery had a huge impact in East and West, and some of his discoveries are still used in medicine today. Scholars such as **Ḥasan ibn al-Haytham** and **Abbas ibn Firnas** have also made significant progress in optical research.

In 859, **Fatima bint Muhammad Al-Fihriyya** founded the first graduate university in Fez, Morocco. An adjacent mosque was founded by Miriam, her sister. Later, the university and the mosque become the first educational complex and was named **Al-Qarawiyyin** Mosque and University.

The first map of the earth was commissioned by Caliph **Abu al-Abbas Abdallah ibn Harun al-Rashid** in 831. Muslim astronomers have established sophisticated observatories, discovered many new stars and conducted careful studies of planetary motion. An in-depth knowledge of astronomy helped Muslims develop the astrolabe, a precise navigational instrument that measures the height of stars. With the help of navigational instruments such as the astrolabe, Muslim scholars from all over the world are known, such as **Ibn Battuta**, who traveled more than any other explorer in pre-modern history, totaling about 117,000 km. The first authentic work on life at the North Pole was written by **Ahmad ibn Faḍlān**, a 10th-century Arab Muslim traveler. During the journey, Muslims not only brought precious treasures such as silk and spices, but also acquired scientific and technological knowledge that was later spread to Europe.

The history of coffee dates back to at least the 9th century, in East Africa, from where coffee later spread to Egypt and Yemen. From the Muslim world, coffee then spread to and from the rest of Europe.

Miswak is a toothbrush made from Salvadora persica tree, predominant in areas inhabited by Muslims and has been used for about 7,000 years, being the first toothbrush and found in Islamic hygienic jurisprudence.

Islamic civilization was the birthplace of innovation, technology, science and philosophy, greatly influencing the European Renaissance of the 15th and 16th centuries, as well as the birth of the modern scientific method in the 17th century.

8F   Historical Narratives of Migration in the Turkish Context

Chair: Caner Tekin, Ruhr University Bochum, Germany

527   Two sides of the same coin? Contrasting narratives of Bosnian-Muslims migration to Turkey in late 19th century

Nikola Lero, Carl von Ossietzky Universität Oldenburg, Germany
Omer Merzić, University of London, UK

528   German-Jewish Scholars in Turkish Exile 1933-1945: From the Winter of Despair under Nazism to the Spring of Hope in Turkish Academia

Filiz Künüroğlu, İzmir Katip Çelebi Üniversitesi, Turkey
Ali Onder, University of Portsmouth, UK

529   From Religious to Ethnic Minorities: The Cultural and Social Integration of Pomaks into post-Ottoman Turkey

Gözde Emen Gökatalay, Independent Scholar, Turkey

1236   Trade Union Attitudes towards Turkish Guest Worker/Immigrant Organisations in Federal Germany: Contradictions between Official Narratives and Local Cooperation in the 1970s

Caner Tekin, Ruhr-University Bochum, Institut for Social Movements, Germany

Two sides of the same coin? Contrasting narratives of Bosnian-Muslims migration to Turkey in late 19th century

(527) Nikola Lero, Carl von Ossietzky Universität Oldenburg, Germany

Omer Merzić, University of London, UK

The decline of the Ottoman Empire at the end of the 19th century caused numerous consequences for the region of South-eastern Europe, like that of mass Muslim migrations from Ottoman regions in Europe to Anatolia. In Bosnia, thousands of local Muslims feeling intra-state, but also external pressure by the non-Muslim population, left their homeland to find a refuge. Recognizing limited scholarly attention which was given to the sphere of the lived experiences of the migrant trajectories, this paper aims to give an in-depth and detailed portrayal of the reality regarding the arrival, work, and everyday life of Muslims from Bosnia at the turn of the century in the Ottoman Empire. It predominantly accomplishes it through a narrative analysis of two letters sent by Bosnian Muslims who migrated to the Anatolian town of Durgut. The oddity of these letters is in two heavily conflicting views on the lived experience of migration. The first one embarked on a highly nostalgic, sceptical, and pro-return perception reflecting on a specific "othering" of Bosnian Muslims in Turkey. In contrast, the other one, which was sent as a response to the first one, portrays a joyous assemblage of numerous benefits of migration to Durget, mainly through the prism of economic benefits of migration to Durget. However, to comprehend these pro and contra migration narratives, it is necessary to layout the socio-cultural background of both Bosnia and Anatolian Ottoman Empire in that period. Herein lies the supplementary contribution of this paper, as it, through examination of five letters from the 1860s by the Ottoman scholar and administrator Ahmed Cevdet Pasha sent from Bosnia to Istanbul, expands previous studies of migrations from Bosnia to Turkey in the late 19th century. By providing an additional layer of the socio-cultural mosaic that coloured the ambiguous Bosnia-Turkey relations in the period, this paper delivers a more resonant understanding of the broader context that encompassed migrations of Bosnian Muslims to Turkey at the same time answering can you put a value on nostalgia.

German-Jewish Scholars in Turkish Exile 1933-1945: From the Winter of Despair under Nazism to the Spring of Hope in Turkish Academia

(528) Ali Onder, University of Portsmouth, UK

"It was the best of times, it was the worst of times, it was the age of wisdom, it was the age of foolishness, it was the epoch of belief, it was the epoch of incredulity, it was the season of light, it was the season of darkness, it was the spring of hope, it was the winter of despair."

— from A Tale of Two Cities by Charles Dickens

This paper documents the migration experiences of German-Jewish scholars who fled from the Nazi regime and sought refuge in Turkey in 1930s. Reflecting on the historical narratives -e.g. oral documents, personal letters, memories or journals, we analyze the dynamics of forced migration processes of a highly qualified immigrant group, namely German-Jewish scholars and to scrutinize the factors affecting their psychosocial adaptation processes in Turkey. This unexpected brain gain came at a time when the young Republic of Turkey was reforming its higher education as part of an unprecedented attempt to widely modernize its political, social, and economic institutions. The large influx of German-Jewish scholars taking up lecturer positions, guest professor positions or even permanent professorships contributed extensively to the modernization and restructuring of the academic and scientific landscape in Turkey, leaving its mark in the Turkish academia until today. On 7th April 1933, only a few months after the National Socialist German Workers' Party (Nazi Party) secured its majority in the German parliament, they passed the "Law for the Restoration of the Professional Civil Service" – short version in German Berufsbeamtengesetz (BBG). According to the BBG, a civil servant was not allowed to have any Jewish grandparent, and any civil servant who failed to fulfil this criterion at that time was released from the civil service with immediate effect. One of the areas that were hit particularly severely by the BBG was higher education and research. Most of the permanent positions and chaired professorships in research institutes and universities in Weimar Republic were officially positions of civil service and hence were subject to laws and regulations thereof. This meant that many prominent professors such as Albert 2 Einstein and Erwin Schrödinger in physics, or Richard von

Mises in mathematics, or Fritz Neumark in economics needed to look either for alternative careers or new destinations. Kröner (1983) [1] documents 1522 German-Jewish professors and scientists whose jobs were directly or indirectly jeopardised by the BBG. The Turkish government at that time did invite several of these scholars to Turkey in an effort to restructure the Turkish university system. As a result of these efforts, many prominent German-Jewish scholars came to Turkish universities during 1930s. The paper is composed of two parts. In the first section, we provide a full account of all German-Jewish scholars whose emigration from the Nazi Germany took them to Turkey. We document rigorously background information on the migration conditions such as their field of study, their age at emigration to Turkey, duration of stay in Turkey, and when and where they left afterwards. In the second part, we focus on the narratives of individual scientists to gain to better insight into their individual circumstances and experiences during these times. Based on the personal narratives, we will reflect on the consequences of their migration as well as factors causing them to return or stay from their own perspective. To take a deeper perspective, we focus on the cases of mathematics stars Richard von Mises and Hilde Geiringer; world-renowned development economist Alexander Rüstow, and an iconic public economist Fritz Neumark. Our study is novel for several reasons. Although the experiences of German-Jewish scholars settling in Western contexts such as the US and the UK is extensively documented in the literature, much less is known about the scholars who settled in Eastern countries like Turkey. Besides, we adopt a comprehensive approach and focus on the whole migration cycle; pre-migration process; post migration process and return of Jewish refugees. There is a dearth of research focusing on the psychosocial processes of Jewish refugees and discussing their experiences from their own perspective within the socio political context of Turkey. We believe our study will provide valuable insight for academics on a neglected group in Turkish migration history.

Reference:

Kröner, Peter (1983) Vor fünfzig Jahren: Die Emigration deutschsprachiger Wissenschaftler 1933-1939. Gesellschaft für Wissenschaftsgeschichte, Münster.

From Religious to Ethnic Minorities: The Cultural and Social Integration of Pomaks into post-Ottoman Turkey

(529) Gözde Emen Gökatalay, Independent Scholar, Turkey

Hundreds of thousands of Muslims migrated to modern-day Turkey from the Balkans and the Caucasus in the late-nineteenth and early-twentieth centuries. While some of them saw themselves as Turks, others came from other ethnic backgrounds and spoke languages other than Turkish as their mother tongue. This difference between Turkish and non-Turkish immigrants played a key role in their integration into Turkish society. While some natives accepted the non-Turkish immigrants as Muslim fellows and considered them within the broader category of Turks, other indigenous groups discriminated non-Turkish immigrants because of their ethnicity. This tension illustrated a larger confrontation between secular and Islamic nationalists in early Republican Turkey. Secularist groups within the ruling elites wanted to define the Turkish nation in ethnic and linguistic terms whereas Islamic ones advocated areligious definition of the nation. With a focus on Pomaks, Bulgarian-speaking Muslims, this presentation explores the social and cultural experience of non-Turkish immigrants in post Ottoman Turkey. It argues that the debates between different segments of elites about the formation of a new identity at the national level did not only affect official policies but also had far-reaching cultural and social effects on such immigrants. Although there is rich literature on the migration of Muslim groups and official policies against them, to which extent political decisions and discussions shaped the construction of immigrant identities at the local level have received little attention in scholarly studies. This study sheds light on the negotiation of a novel identity of immigrants in the context of their daily life. To demonstrate the importance of local factors and variations, it consults a wide range of primary and secondary sources that both state and non-state actors produced.

Trade Union Attitudes towards Turkish Guest Worker/Immigrant Organisations in Federal Germany: Contradictions between Official Narratives and Local Cooperation in the 1970s

(1236) Caner Tekin, Ruhr-University Bochum, Institut for Social Movements, Germany

The relationships between Turkish guest worker associations (after 1973 migrant associations) and German trade unions have not found much attention in the literature. According to few studies, in the aftermath of the respective guest worker agreements trade unions marginalised the emerging migrant mobilisations outside DGB (German Trade Union Confederation) on the ground that migrant associations followed extremist (communist, ultra-nationalist and ultra-religious) views.(1) Based on archive research referring to the documents published by the DGB-affiliated trade unions (primarily DGB, IG Metall and IG BE) as well as the leading Turkish associations in the 1970s, the present article challenges this argument and highlights the interplays between trade unions and migrant associations, and it lays a specific emphasis on the historical developments in the city of Frankfurt.

In their official narratives (conference documents, communications etc.) trade unions remained distant to many migrant umbrella organisations which they deemed 'marginal' and often warned German authorities about their activities. Turkish migrant associations, according to the DGB's Foreigners Department, "were pursuing to carry ideological conflicts from their country to Federal Germany".(2) A closer look into the period yet reveals that contacts and even limited cooperation became possible between trade unions and local migrant associations at least in certain cities. In view of the highlighted documents three arguments thus emerge. First, in respective cases, some leading members of these (so-called marginal) organisations also assumed executive positions in trade unions as well as in Workers' Welfare Association. Second, DGB-affiliated trade unions had differentiating opinions and even disagreements about the migrant associations. Third, against the growing problems and injustice the immigrants faced in social and work life, the trade unions, migrant associations and other civil organisations joined their forces for protest events in certain cities, such as in Frankfurt, where Turkish workers and local actors held common demonstrations in the early 1970s.

Simon Goeke, The Multinational Working Class? Political Activism and Labour Migration in West Germany During the 1960s and 1970s. Journal of Contemporary History. 2014; 49(1), 176-177; Karin Hunn, "Nächstes Jahr kehren wir zurück...": Die Geschichte der türkischen "Gastarbeiter" in der Bundesrepublik (Wallstein Verlag, 2005): 395-396

Karl Schwab/Heinz Richter: „Türkischer Arbeiterkongress. Polit-Ausländer wirbeln durch die Bundesrepublik. DGB stellt richtig, wie es zu dem Düsseldorfer Kongreß kam", in: Welt der Arbeit, 18.03.1977.

8G   PANEL: Indian Diaspora: Shaping Cultures, Perceptions, and Patterns of Mobility [ONLINE]

Moderator: Dr. Shweta Sinha Deshpande, SSLA, India

Speakers

Dr. Shinder Thandi, University of California Santa Barbara, USA

Dr. Syed Ali, Long Island University, Brooklyn, USA

Dr. Chinmay Tumbe, Indian Institute of Management Ahmedabad (IIM-A), India

Dr. Ram Bhagat, International Institute for Population Sciences, India

Day Three 9 September 2022 Friday

Day Three 9 September 2022 - 16:45-18:15

9A   International Migration and Vulnerability

Chair: Mala Arunasalam, Global Banking School, London, UK

1308   A migrant's own culpable conduct: Critical perspectives towards an interpretative design in the European Court of Human Rights

Elina Nieminen, Tampere University, Finland

1020   Country of Origin Information Reports on Refugee Status Determination Procedures: open access or classified documents?

Melissa Martins Casagrande, Lawyer / Independent Consultant
Derek Assenco Creuz, Legal Researcher / Independent Consultant
Carolini Machado Bandeira, Researcher / Independent Consultant

1012   Vulnerable and Voiceless: 'Losing the pride of African sovereignty through Migration'

Richard Osei Bonsu, Organization for Migrants and Non Immigrants for African Education (OMANIAE Ghana); PICUM, IVCA, VZW, EASO, Belgium; Ministerial of Foreign Affairs, Office of the Diaspora, Ghana

1064   Pandemic, Precarity, and Vulnerability: Lessons Learned from Diverse Migrant Experiences in Canada

Amrita Hari, Associate Professor, Carleton University, Canada

A migrant's own culpable conduct: Critical perspectives towards an interpretative design in the European Court of Human Rights

(1308) Elina Nieminen, Tampere University, Finland

This paper looks into what is regarded as culpable conduct of a migrant in the European Court of Human Rights (the Court). Furthermore, this paper observes what kind of legal interpretation the Court is adapting in such situations. The Court attaches the test of a migrant's own culpable conduct to cases dealing with collective expulsions, especially under the recent case of N.D. and N.T. By looking into the criteria that apply for a migrant's culpable conduct this paper aims to make sense of and look critically what is understood as culpable conduct. Furthermore, the paper seeks to demonstrate how a migrant's culpable conduct lies in the core of migration control. From this perspective, a migrant's conduct is in attachment of circumventing the immigration restrictions or to a failed attempt of a regular stay. Therefore, a migrant's (culpable) conduct is not necessarily limited to collective expulsions cases. Rather, the more broad scope of the Court's case law focusing on the inability to follow the immigration restrictions supports the development of the construct of a migrant's culpable conduct and migrant responsibility. Therefore, a selected piece of the Court's case law focusing on the unauthorized entry or residence is looked in parallel. In this regard, it is also assessed how the Court is balancing between the interpretative design of a culpable migrant and vulnerable migrants more generally. I am reaching the conclusion that an interpretative focus on the culpable migrant is a step towards a decline in the protection of migrants more generally. By consolidating migrants' own (culpable) conduct as a legal construct may act as a dangerous passing lane for the states for disclosing their obligations towards migrants.

Country of Origin Information Reports on Refugee Status Determination Procedures: open access or classified documents?

(1020) Melissa Martins Casagrande, Lawyer / Independent Consultant

Derek Assenco Creuz, Legal Researcher / Independent Consultant

Carolini Machado Bandeira, Researcher / Independent Consultant

This paper aims to contribute to the ongoing debate as to whether Country of Origin Information (COI) reports should be publicly accessible through official channels of the Refugee Status Determination (RSD) application country or be kept confidential as internal documents by the governments that issue them. There does not seem to be an international consensus on whether COI reports should be widely available to the public. Arguments in favour of wide public access to COI reports are transparency and accountability in RSD procedures, as well as the provision of reliable information to RSD applicants, legal practitioners, and civil society. Arguments against relate to COI issuing country's position not to publicly divulge information that could be perceived as a political assessment of the country of origin's internal affairs, which might trigger diplomatic friction and affect trade. This paper aims to explore and critically assess the publicization of COI reports in RSD procedures, outlining and analysing arguments for and against the public availability of State-drafted COI reports. Arguments for and against the public accessibility of COI reports are gathered through literature review and public statements and contrasted with International Refugee Law norms and protection guidelines. This paper's conclusions include insights on how the use of certain arguments related to publicizing COI reports in detriment of others may hinder, or promote, an effective assessment of RSD applications by the countries issuing the COI report. Moreover, the paper seeks to access risks connected to COI reports being made public by certain countries and being used by other countries without considering nuances of displacement towards different countries of destination.

Vulnerable and Voiceless: 'Losing the pride of African sovereignty through Migration'

(1012) Richard Osei Bonsu, Organization for Migrants and Non Immigrants for African Education (OMANIAE Ghana); PICUM, IVCA, VZW, EASO, Belgium; Ministerial of Foreign Affairs, Office of the Diaspora, Ghana

Every day, tens and hundreds of unaccountable African youth are confidently tricked into modern day slavery through irregular migration. Majority are been sent to Kuwait, Qatar, Saudi Arabia,and Lebanon whiles others taken through the desert and Mediterranean sea by the human smugglers and traffickers finds themselves in Niger, Algeria, Libya, Spain and Italy.The trend of these irregular migration represents one of the biggest humanitarian tragedies,rendering most African youths who were intellects and vision holders to be hopeless and vulnerable within the scope living as undocumented migrants and slaves for which they constitutethe greater work force of their nation.Twenty-first (21st) century promises to be a new age of migration. African migrants will risk all to reach Europe, their dreamland of greener pastures 'the land of Paradise', eighty percent (80%) will be confronted with almost certain death whiles the twenty percent (20%) do make it but aresoon confronted with shattered dreams and unattainable expectations. These brain-drain have been a major challenge to both African and European governments on the growing negative effect of the over 80% African migrants been displaced whiles the gap between documented and undocumented migrants keep growing by 90% yearly, in exception of those who survived the deadly voyage, African migrants faces various decree of inhumane treatment when caught up by the law as Illegal immigrants. Over Thousands youth are been kept in various detentions centre (a prison name branded for illegal immigrants) across Europe between 3 months to one (1) year. Majority of these youth between 19-42 years passes through mentally, physiological and emotional trauma before been forced to return to their country of origin. While 35% of the returnee re-migrates.

Pandemic, Precarity, and Vulnerability: Lessons Learned from Diverse Migrant Experiences in Canada

(1064) Amrita Hari, Associate Professor, Carleton University, Canada

The COVID-19 pandemic, like previous epidemics (e.g., HIV/AIDS in the 1980s), is predicted to have a disproportionate impact on vulnerable segments of Canadian society (Bowleg, 2020). Existing structural inequalities that leave migrants vulnerable socioeconomically are the very same conditions that increase their risk of contagion. Using precarity as a conceptual tool, we conducted a systematic qualitative review of publicly available data on the impact of the current pandemic on the lives of different categories of migrants in Canada, including temporary migrant workers, highly skilled immigrants, international students, asylum claimants and refugee newcomers, as well as undocumented detainees.

The Government of Canada implemented emergency legislations, such as social distancing, lockdown, travel restrictions and border closures to mitigate the spread of COVID-19 (Firang, 2020; Macklin, 2020). These responses resulted in a decline of 64% in all immigration categories (Jedwab, 2020; El-Assal, 2020). The government reconfigured its immigration regime to designate 'non-essential travellers' (e.g., refugees and family members awaiting resettlement or reunification) and 'essential travellers' (e.g., migrant farmworkers) further disrupting pre-pandemic patterns of migration (Macklin, 2020).

Temporariness is a common lens to understand migrant vulnerability in Canada. It implies limited rights based on temporality (often limiting period of stay) and conditionality (rights conditional upon behaviour such as requirements to satisfy a specific employer to remain in the country) (Hari, 2014). There is extensive documentation of the multitude forms of temporariness (Rajkumar et al., 2012; Lenard & Strahele, 2012; Goldring & Landolt, 2013). A key feature is its emphasis on the relative advantage of highly skilled migrants as compared to their lower-skilled counterparts. Precarity as a conceptual tool has gained prominence recently and is especially relevant to understand migrant populations. Paret & Gleeson (2016) argue that the central significance of the concept lies in its capacity to connect the micro and the macro, situating experiences of insecurity and vulnerability within historically and geographically specific contexts. Migrant lives are precarious in multiple and reinforcing ways and not all migrants experience all conditions.

Like Paret & Gleeson (2016), we find precarity to be a useful point of analytical departure to understand the conditions of migrants impacted by a global pandemic. It gets beyond a skill-differentiated comparison - central to temporariness - which we argue is a common yet adequate lens to understand migrant vulnerability during the ongoing pandemic. Instead, we analyze pandemic-specific public health and immigration policy shifts to understand how the lives and livelihoods of migrants with varying characteristics and migratory pathways were reshaped and highlight their particular vulnerabilities. Examining these differences is critical to Canada's post-pandemic recovery.

Canada is in the process of increasing the annual immigration targets between 2021 and 2024 with plans to admit more highly skilled immigrants in the healthcare and technology sectors. Meanwhile, plans to support low-skilled immigrants in service industries (e.g., hospitality, retail, and tourism) are undetermined. During this critical window of reform, we provide policy recommendations and directions for future research. Additionally, we share lessons learned from Canada to encourage pandemic oriented and internationally comparative migration policy research.

References:

Bowleg, L. (2020). *We're Not All in this Together: On COVID-19, Intersectionality, and*

Structural Inequality. American Journal of Public Health, 110, *917.* https://doi.org/10.2105/AJPH.2020.305766

El-Assal, K. (2020, April 30). *How Canada is helping international students.* CIC News. *https://www.cicnews.com/2020/04/how-canada-is-helping-international-students-0414222.html#gs.4ggmr2*

Firang, D. (2020). *The impact of COVID-19 pandemic on international students in Canada. International Social Work, 1-5.* https://doi.org/10.1177/0020872820940030

Goldring, L. and P. Landolt, eds. (2013). *Producing and Negotiating Non-Citizenship: Precarious Legal Status in Canada. Toronto: University of Toronto Press.*

Hari, A. (2013). *Temporariness, rights, and citizenship: The latest chapter in Canada's exclusionary migration and refugee history. Refuge, 30(2), 35-44.*

Jedwab, J., (2020). *Canadian views on immigration levels and immigration categories in the*

COVID era [PowerPoint presentation]. *https://acs-aec.ca/wp-content/uploads/2020/08/ACS-Immigration-levels-August-2020.pdf*

Lenard, P.T., and C. Straehle. (2012). *Legislating Inequality: Temporary Labour Migration in Canada. Montreal: McGill-Queen's University Press.*

Macklin, A. (2020). *(In)Essential Bordering: Canada, COVID, and Mobility. Frontiers.* *https://doi.org/10.3389/fhumd.2020.609694*

Paret, M., & S. Gleeson. (2016). Precarity and agency through a migration lens. *Citizenship Studies, 20(3-4)*, 277-294.

Rajkumar, D., Berkowitz, L., Vosko, L.F., Preston, V., and R. Latham. (2012). *At the*

Temporary-Permanent Divide: How Canada Produces Temporariness and Makes Citizens through Its Security, Work, and Settlement Policies. *Citizenship Studies, 16(3-4), 483–510.*

9B   Migration Theory and Methods

Chair: Atinder Pal Kaur, Punjab Agricultural University, India

1202   Culture of Migration: Depicting Punjabi migration trends from Historical to Present times

Atinder Pal Kaur, Punjab Agricultural University, India

1162   (Im)Mobility in and out of Afghanistan: Analysis of Factors Shaping Migration Aspirations

Sebnem Koser Akcapar, Social Sciences University of Ankara, Turkey
Hidayat Siddikoglu, BILIM Organization for Research and Social Science Studies, Kabul, Afghanistan

1169   Experimentation with Data Imputation Methods to Improve Refugee Regression and Classification Prediction Models

Esther Mead, COSMOS Research Center, University of Arkansas Little Rock, US
Kazi Tanvir Islam, COSMOS Research Center, University of Arkansas Little Rock, US

1300   On 'crisis': The construction of vulnerability

Cristina Schaver, Universidad CEU San Pablo, Spain

Culture of Migration: Depicting Punjabi migration trends from Historical to Present times

(1202) Atinder Pal Kaur, Punjab Agricultural University, India

Most of the studies on migration include how people migrate in economic terms and the network connection they use. The present study explores the culture of migration among Punjabi people and the desire for migration which has become a norm. Review of Literature: Kindel and Massy (2002) examined the "culture of migration" in the Mexican community, with a high rate of internal youth migration from Mexico to the USA. Mexican youth, especially males, come to see migration as a normal part of life and become a norm in their life. Timmerman (2008) defined marriage migration in Turkish people from Turkey to Belgium as a migration culture. While Ali (2007) ethnographically defined the culture of migration in Hyderabadi Muslims, in which migration became a way of life and norm in Muslims, marrying daughters with Gulf people also became prevalent for economic return. Horva´th(2008) depicts migration in Romina youth due to economic reasons and uplift of family status, which cause a culture of migration in the Romina community. Connell (2008) mentioned that the culture of migration created a favorable milieu where people become habitual towards migration. In Punjabi migration, more focus was given to their migration experience, place of migration, and the Diasporic activity in the place of migration. Methodology: For the present study, data was obtained from the Doaba region of Punjab, a hub of migration. The data was collected through semi-structured interviews and participant observation in different settings using ethnography and sociological interpretation. 48 case studies were conducted with left-behind families in Punjab. In addition, 10 KII were conducted with return migrants, and 10 open-ended interviews with young males and females were also taken to know the culture of migration in the Doaba region of Punjab. Lastly, interviews were also conducted with 6 Gulf migrants during their holiday visit to their homeland Punjab. Finding: Migration from Panjab is not new; it is as old as Indian migration. Punjabi migrated to various parts of the world as indentured labor and army men during the British empire. The first migration started after 1849, when the Britishers captured Punjab. Till 1947 migration from Punjab was mainly found among army men. Later on, Punjabi started migrating to developed countries for their livelihood. Recently, Gulf migration became a norm in the villages and is also seen as a positive, acceptable, and inevitable practice of mobility among Punjabis to seek better employment opportunities. Conclusion: the study finds that migration culture embedded in Punjabi families that migration becomes generational. After seeing successful years of migration, their elder, now the younger generation, is on the move. The migration becomes a family ritual after the father, a son, is on the move, and after the elder brothers, the younger brother is thinking of migrating. In the case of young female marriage, migration or educational migration become more prevalent. In the nearby city, IELTS and visa agents' businesses are mushrooming to provide aid in youth migration.

(Im)Mobility in and out of Afghanistan: Analysis of Factors Shaping Migration Aspirations

(1162) Sebnem Koser Akcapar, Social Sciences University of Ankara, Turkey

Hidayat Siddikoglu, BILIM Organization for Research and Social Science Studies, Kabul, Afghanistan

After the takeover of government by Taliban in August 2021, hundreds of thousands of Afghans flocked to the Kabul International Airport. After 20 years of occupation, the exit strategy of the US and NATO allies included an injudicious call only for some Afghan partners, including politicians, high-level bureaucrats and those whose lives are in grave danger to be airlifted and provided safe havens. At this critical time when Afghanistan is going through political turmoil, countries already hosting large refugee populations but also the EU are increasingly alarmed by the unprecedented mass displacements in Afghanistan. Concerned with the political shift of power and precarious situation, Turkey raised concerns that she cannot handle an additional refugee burden while Pakistan and Iran also followed suit. Despite erection of high fences and high securitization of migration, many Afghans continued to risk their lives to get out of the country. This paper, however, is not about those who migrated but rather those who stayed with some migration aspirations. Yet, migration aspirations do not necessarily mean that potential migrants can actualize their migration motives. Most of the migration literature takes up mobility as the norm. Nevertheless, it is important to theorize immobility since 96% of the world's population does not fall under any category of international migrants. Contrary to the dominating 'mobility bias' in migration studies, this paper, therefore, sets off with the premise to understand the reasons why people stayed and levels of constraints on mobility. In an attempt to analyze different forms of (im)mobility, we adopt the aspiration-capability model (involuntary immobility - mobility - voluntary immobility - acquiescent immobility).[1] To this end, mixed methodology was adopted for this research that consists of in-depth semi-structured interviews with 42 men and women still living in Kabul, Afghanistan and life-history interviews with 3 selected participants. We also carried out follow-up interviews to see to what extend these migration aspirations are realized since these are often fluid and subject to change. A series of research questions guide our research: How do structural factors at the macro level (political, social, economic reasons and migration policies of host countries) impact migration aspirations and contribute to the agency (i.e., power of the individual to freely make choices and perform actions) in forced migration? At the meso level, how does information flow among Afghan migrants and diaspora members contribute to shaping knowledge and changing the attitudes and actions of potential migrants back home? How does prior migration experience impact the decision to return or to stay put? At the micro level, what kind of role does the intersection of different variables, such as ethnicity, socio-economic status, age, marital status, and gender, have on migration aspirations? Starting from these research questions stated above, the objective of the paper is two-fold. 1) To find out and analyze how migration decision mechanisms and country preferences are formed regardless of migration outcomes, 2) To examine what factors contribute to (im)mobility. [1]Schewel, K. (2020). Understanding Immobility: Moving Beyond the Mobility Bias in Migration Studies. International Migration Review, 54 (2): 328-355.

Experimentation with Data Imputation Methods to Improve Refugee Regression and Classification Prediction Models

(1169) Esther Mead, COSMOS Research Center, University of Arkansas Little Rock, US

Kazi Tanvir Islam, COSMOS Research Center, University of Arkansas Little Rock, US

The UNHCR reported that 82.4 million people were "forcibly displaced globally by the end of 2020" [1]. About 26.4 million were classified as "refugees", meaning they "fled war, violence, conflict, or persecution" seeking protection in another country.[1] This work builds on our previous work [2], wherein we demonstrated the potential refugee count predictive power of a variety of features. One of the limitations of our previous work was small datasets due to missing data. The objective of this work is to experiment with data imputation techniques to determine if a better predictive performance can be achieved with imputed datasets as opposed to datasets wherein rows containing missing values are simply removed.Data shortage is a prevalent problem in data-driven research, and data imputation is one of the most efficient techniques to deal with missing values [3]. There are several data imputation methods, but incorrectly imputed data can turn out to be worse than having missing values, so vigilance must be used when selecting methods. In general, the use of sophisticated machine learning data imputation techniques improves predictive quality more than statistical imputation techniques [4]. For this work, we chose regression imputation because it maintains the mutual relationship among the variables and reduces the chance of bias in prediction. We experimented with two regression methods: deterministic (DRImp) and stochastic (StRImp). In DRImp, missing values are restored without considering random variation error, which reduces a variable's intrinsic variability. In contrast, StRImp infuses normally distributed noise into predicted imputed values, thus preserving a variable's inherent variability.Our experiments (Table 1) involved both a refugee count regressor and a refugee count category classifier based on 12 predictive features. In general, the regressor and classifier performed best when a manual implementation of an ensemble with scikit-learn[2] was used and when the datasets were normalized using a min/max scaler as opposed to no scaler or a standard scaler. Despite containing less data, overall, the learners performed best when the datasets were compiled based on the removal of missing values as opposed to imputing using DRImp and StRImp. Nonetheless, among the two imputation methods when the datasets were full (included outliers), the regressor performed best when DRImp was used, while the classifier performed best when StRimp was used. When outliers were removed (trimmed), the regressor performed equally well using DRImp and StRImp, while the classifier performed best when DRImp was used.In our case, the use of data imputation methods did not result in an increase in performance over a simple removal method. This is most likely due to the complexity of our model, and further investigation will be conducted. However, the use of data imputation techniques for refugee prediction will still be required in many cases; for example, when making predictions for countries that do not have any recorded ground-truth metrics. This research shows that the use of DRImp and StRImp can produce both regression and classification predictions that are competitive with, and in most cases supersede, that reported in previous works (Table 2).

On 'crisis': The construction of vulnerability

(1300) Cristina Schaver, Universidad CEU San Pablo, Spain

The migration of nonwhite people toward Europe, especially by land or sea, is denominated a 'crisis'. It is not a crisis for the people who are attempting to migrate amidst dangerous conditions exacerbated by bureaucratic intransigence; instead, we are told that this is a crisis for the wealthy, stable, and institutionally capable European states who would receive them. By coding migrants as destabilizing and dangerous forces, the European security state becomes justified as protection for a vulnerable Europe. This paper argues that such vulnerability is entirely self-imposed and constructed to excuse practices of exclusion. It is also at odds with how the EU often chooses to present itself—Fortress Europe, capable of being autonomous and strong—yet this contradiction is useful to the EU, providing versatility of justification to the security state.

The EU constructs its own vulnerability, thus enabling a discursive positioning of victimhood. When thousands of Middle Eastern refugees sought to enter the European Union (EU) from Belarus in 2021, European Commission President Ursula von der Leyen spoke of a "hybrid attack" against the EU. If the EU did not implicitly regard migrants as a threat, if it did not pay billions of euros to externalize its borders, then neighboring countries would not have leverage over the EU nor be in a position to make threats of migrants. A 'hybrid attack' is only real because the EU makes it real, but it is not, in fact, true. If Poland had fulfilled its obligations under international law to receive asylum applications, then what would the threat have been? The EU could have foiled President Lukashenko's intentions to destabilize the bloc by simply refusing to see migrants as a destabilizing force. This begs the question, why is victimhood useful to the Europeans? This paper argues that constructed vulnerability and the imagined identity of victimhood serve as justification for border militarization, as cover for the absence of solidarity and humanity, and as apology for xenophobic discourse. Anti-migrant policies become acceptable as matters of national security and the securitization of European life and policy is further reinforced.

The projection of threat upon the personhood of migrants is directly linked to Islamophobic paranoia and the conflation of migrants with terrorists. The language of crisis presupposes a threat to Europe and Europeans that aligns with white supremacist and nationalist rhetoric. The open welcome of millions of Ukrainian refugees to the EU in February and March 2022 demonstrates the discrimination that permeates European approaches to migration. White, Christian Europeans are acceptable refugees, and suddenly their number is of no matter. It is correctly discussed as a humanitarian crisis that people fleeing war face. This paper draws upon critical migration studies and studies of race, while seeking to contribute to the literature of border theory.

9C   New Challenges in Migration Studies

Chair: Olgu Karan, Başkent University, Turkey

978   Artificial Intelligence in Migration Interventions: The Panacea for Integration Program in Finland

Frank Ojwang, University of Lapland, Finland

Artificial Intelligence in Migration Interventions: The Panacea for Integration Program in Finland

(978) Frank Ojwang, University of Lapland, Finland

Artificial Intelligence (AI) is revolutionizing aided decision-making processes across various sectors all over the world for improved holistic service provision. This research forecasts AI-aided integration program potential to offer accelerated, concrete and specifically tailored integration support for new immigrant and for 'old' resident immigrants that did not receive sufficient integration support during their arrival and throughout their stay in Finland. The algorithms help in profiling the immigrants into the various taxonomies and topologies for accelerated integration into the Finnish society. This is an action research article that analytically reviews high-quality peer-reviewed publications on AI across disciplines through systematic reviews and meta-analyses combining results from multiple impact evaluation studies to draw conclusions for the use of AI in accelerating and enhancing new migrants' settlement into the Finnish society. This article uses grounded theory to come up with and test theories, and analyzes the pareto principle as a concept that underscores the role and impact of AI in accelerating integration into the Finnish society. The application of AI in healthcare system for diagnosis and treatment will inform the approach of the article and theoretically guide experts to develop a holistic integration package. This study is the first of a three-phase analysis that culminates in the rollout of an AI pilot model that accelerates integration in Finland.

Climate-induced Migration: A District-level Empirical Analysis in Bihar, India

(1307) Richa Choudhary, Indian Institute of Technology Roorkee, India

The increased frequency and severity of natural hazards threaten the rural livelihood and accentuate rural to urban migration in developing countries (WMR, 2022). It is believed that climate change may play a role in causing these extreme events (IPCC, 2019). In this backdrop, the term climate-induced migrant is used to identify those leaving their place of origin because of being displaced/affected by an extreme event (Muttarak, 2021). India significantly faces the problems of both disasters and the management of internal migrants (Dallmann and Millock, 2017). Further, the internal migrants are mostly permanent residents of two states, namely Bihar and Uttar Pradesh (Census of India, 2011). North Bihar witness perennial flooding that affects lives and livelihoods and damages public infrastructure (BSDMA, 2020). These recurring floods increase the vulnerability of the economically weaker section of the population and others in Bihar, contributing to the exodus of people from the state annually (Jha et al., 2017). Given this background, this study aims to measure the extent to which the impact of climate change related disasters affect migration in Bihar. For this, the study uses data collected from statistical handbooks of Bihar over the period 2000-2016 for all 37 districts except Arwal. The primary dependent variable of the study is migration. The climatic variables (rainfall and floods-damages) capture the environmental change impact on mobility. The study also developed a flood intensity index (dummy variable) that measures the flood impact on the affected population. To develop the empirical specification, the study derives stylised construct of New Economics of Labour Migration (NELM, 1985). The study thus, uses a short panel model with cluster standard robust errors to assess the relationship. Several regression models estimate the impact of climate change related extreme events on migration. The results suggest that high flood disaster intensity causes approximately one (0.975) percent increase in migration outflow from the affected districts than non-affected. Also, the results indicate that one percent increase in crop damage as a proportion of total agricultural output also increase outmigration by 0.0469 percent. Finally, the rainfall variability affects the migration significantly in the model. All the coefficients are significant at one percent level of significance. The study concludes that the climate change and related disasters (floods in case of Bihar) triggers mobility. The use of disaster matrix enhances the econometric significance of the economic relationship between climate change and migration. Also, NELM is partially validated by these findings that household migration may happen on account of extraneous factors like climate change or relative deprivation. The implications of climate change induced migration-process and outcomes could be explored by using survey based studies in future.

A Sociological Appraisal of Conflict Model of Climate Migration

(1253) Olgu Karan, Başkent University, Turkey

Rising sea levels and drought due to global warming have affected millions of people. It threatens livelihoods and creates a global humanitarian security problem. By 2050, it is estimated that 200 million people will migrate due to climate change and access to resources, reduced food supply, and water scarcity expected to create instability and conflict. This study asks which social groups and regions are more likely to experience climate migration. What are the reasons behind the vulnerability of these regions and social groups? The paper employs the conflict model of climate migration which enables us to focus on the human security and insecurity continuum. While the reasons for unequal vulnerability in different geographical regions are questioned, it also focuses on the differences in experience based on social categories such as race, gender, and class in a particular place. In line with these questions, two distinct climate change-induced natural disasters such as hurricanes Sandy, Katharina and Haiyan and droughts in California, the Philippines and Turkey are analysed regarding the question of which regions and social groups are more likely to experience climate-induced migration. This comparison shows that similar natural disasters occurring in different geographies cause inequalities in vulnerability. The Global South is more prone to be affected by the consequences of climate change.

Best Practices in Sicily: Civil Society Responses to Sicily's Changing Demographics

(531) Lisa Di Carlo, Brown University, USA

The current demographic profile of Sicily is, in fact, a portrait of two regions in crisis. The island itself is heavily agricultural, with aging landowner farmers and city-bound offspring. Young incoming migrants from various African countries are fleeing environmental, political, and economic hardship. While the landowner farmers need labor migrants to keep farms operating, the larger Sicilian community tends to see the incoming migrants as a threat to the island's racial, social, and cultural fabric. The result is a system of hosting without accommodating, employing without supporting, and accepting the need for labor migrants without allowing for their integration or autonomy. Indeed, labor migrants work and live in conditions of precarity with no access to legal recourse. This paper looks at the work of key Sicilian civil society organizations that are trying to improve legal conditions for migrants, economic conditions for farmers in distress, and social relations for child refugees hosted by Italian families within communities across the island. An analysis of the missions and projects of Borderline Sicilia, Sicilia Integra, and AccoglieRete will reveal how residents of the island are working in specific ways to foster integration and acceptance of labor migrants and refugees throughout Sicily.

9D   Migraciones, Globalización and Transnacionalismo [ES]

Chair: Pascual Gerardo García Zamora, Universidad Autónoma de Zacatecas, México

1276   Estudio de Caso de la Coordinacion Interinstitucional de la Movilidad Humana en Loja – Ecuador

Jessica Andrea Ordóñez, Universidad Técnica Particular de Loja, Ecuador

1293   Reflexiones desde la epidemiología social a la migración en tránsito en América Latina post confinamiento por Covid-19

Pascual Gerardo García Zamora, Universidad Autónoma de Zacatecas, Mexico
Juan Lamberto Herrera Martínez, Universidad Autónoma de Zacatecas, Mexico
Cristina Almeida Perales, Universidad Autónoma de Zacatecas, Mexico

1067   Recepción del Derecho Internacional Humanitario en la tutela de los derechos de las personas migrantes

Diana Pamela Zambrano, Universidad de Colima, Mexico

Estudio de Caso de la Coordinacion Interinstitucional de la Movilidad Humana en Loja – Ecuador

(1276) Jessica Andrea Ordóñez, Universidad Técnica Particular de Loja, Ecuador

El estudio de caso da cuenta de los efectos locales que produce la inmigración en una ciudad pequeña que no había recibido una ola de personas migrantes como la actual procedente de Venezuela. El que se analiza es la necesidad de coordinación interinstitucional para gestionar y realizar acciones a favor de las personas inmigrantes y sus familias.

Reflexiones desde la epidemiología social a la migración en tránsito en América Latina post confinamiento por Covid-19

(1293) Pascual Gerardo García Zamora, Universidad Autónoma de Zacatecas, Mexico

Juan Lamberto Herrera Martínez, Universidad Autónoma de Zacatecas, Mexico

Cristina Almeida Perales, Universidad Autónoma de Zacatecas, Mexico

El presente trabajo es un acercamiento a la construcción del estado de la cuestión de la migración en tránsito post confinamiento, para la implementación de un estudio multicéntrico México-Ecuador con el objetivo de identificar los itinerarios de experiencias, rutas y necesidades de atención sociosanitarias percibidas por los y las protagonistas de estos procesos demográficos, así como protección a los derechos fundamentales de las personas. A partir de la declaración del Covid-19 como pandemia en marzo del 2020, todos los países del mundo realizaron acciones con el objetivo de contener su impacto en sus respectivas poblaciones, además del reforzamiento en equipo y medicamentos en áreas hospitalarias se promovió el autocuidado, el distanciamiento entre personas y restricción de movimientos migratorios, dejando varado y sin ninguna protección a grandes cantidades de migrantes en trayecto por todo el mundo. En México se calcula varias millas de personas afectadas, en su mayoría provenientes de centro y sur América, buena parte de ellos en la frontera norte, saturación de espacios en los albergues y extenuación de sus materiales y económicos, lo que dio por resultado que varios de ellos cerraran sus puertasMéxico tiene una tradición de más de cien años de ser expulsor de fuerza de trabajo hacia Estados Unidos y durante el siglo veinte se fue convirtiendo también como un país de destino para algunas poblaciones de los países de Centro y sur de América, pero en los últimos años, también como país de tránsito para esos países, el Caribe, algunos países de Ã frica e India. Un dato interesante es que durante la pandemia quedaron atrapados en México cerca de 21 mil; 12.500 personas en la frontera norte y 9.000 en albergues de la frontera sur. Actualmente con la reciente invasión de Ucrania por Rusia se han agregado ciudadanos ucranianos en este proceso, para el día de hoy 31 de marzo del año 2022 se habla de aproximadamente 1000 ucranianos acampados en la frontera entre Baja California México y el estado de California solicitando asilo en Estados Unidos. La pandemia del Covid-19 ha venido a complicar más las condiciones de riesgo para las personas migrantes en tránsito, por qué a los peligros ya conocidos de mucha vulnerabilidad física, psicológica y del ejercicio de los derechos fundamentales para los seres humanos, se agregó la al riesgo de infeccion por el coronavirus-19. Brindando la oportunidad a los Estados de América central, México y Estados Unidos a soportar sus políticas migratorias con el pretexto de control sanitario, al mismo tiempo, hiso sinergia con actitudes ya enquistadas en estos países de discriminación y xenofobia hacia las personas con nacionalidad diferente. El nuevo contexto de post confinamiento marca un parte aguas en las condiciones en que las personas realizan la odisea de ir en lograr mejores condiciones de vida para ellos y sus familias.

Recepción del Derecho Internacional Humanitario en la tutela de los derechos de las personas migrantes

(1067) Diana Pamela Zambrano, Universidad de Colima, Mexico

El pasado mes de octubre del año 2021, se publicó en la Gaceta Oficial del Estado de Veracruz, México, un Protocolo Interinstitucional para la atención a personas migrantes. Lo relevante de dicho documento es que fue realizado en coordinación de autoridades mexicanas así como por personal del Comité Internacional de la Cruz Roja, uno de los referentes del Derecho Internacional Humanitario, los cuales delinearon ejes de acción y señalaron a las autoridades que deberán conocerlo a fin de que lo implementen y con ello mitigar las vulneraciones que padecen las personas migrantes en cualquier punto de la ruta migratoria. El documento en cita representa un importante avance para el Estado mexicano en materia de protección a los derechos de las personas migrantes, debido a que en reiteradas ocasiones la Corte Interamericana de Derechos Humanos, ha señalado a través de su línea jurisprudencial que muchas de las violaciones cometidas en perjuicio de las personas migrantes es en virtud de un desconocimiento de la norma, de tal suerte que exhorta a que los Estados capaciten a sus autoridades en materia de Derecho Internacional de los Derechos Humanos y de Derecho Internacional Humanitario. Derivado de lo anterior, el proceso de recepción de los principios humanitarios que se manifiestan en el protocolo en comento se traduce como un reto que el Estado mexicano deberá atender a fin de velar por la tutela efectiva a los migrantes. En este orden de ideas, el Estado de Veracruz es la entidad que lo ha adoptado pero, es imprescindible señalar que otras entidades federativas que conforman al Estado mexicano y por las cuales se aprecia con mayor ahínco el flujo migratorio, también puedan replicar el modelo con el propósito de coadyuvar en la protección de la persona migrante.

9E   Türkiye'nin Göç Deneyimi [TR]

Chair: Yakup Çoştu, Hitit University, Turkey

1114   Kimlik-Mekân İlişkileri ve Göç-Benlik-Ötekilik Tasavvurlarının Dönüşümü Üzerine Bir Değerlendirme-

Mehmet Evkuran, Hitit University, Turkey

1176   Göçmen Çocukların Örgün Eğitim ve Din Eğitiminde Karşılaştığı Sorunlar

Kamil Coştu, Turkey

570   Göçmen Çocukların Eğitimde Entegrasyonu ve Okullaşma Süreci

Sibel Terzioğlu, Istanbul Rumeli University, Turkey

1113   Göçmen Dini Örgütlenmesi Olarak Türk Diyanet Vakıfları; Avrupa Örneği

Yakup Çoştu, Hitit University, Turkey

Kimlik-Mekân İlişkileri ve Göç-Benlik-Ötekilik Tasavvurlarının Dönüşümü Üzerine Bir Değerlendirme

(1114) Mehmet Evkuran, Hitit University, Turkey

Mekân-kimlik ilişkileri, evsizleşme-yurtsuzlaşmanın yoğunlaştığı XX. Yüzyıl başlarından itibaren önce edebiyatta ardından sosyal bilimlerde ele alınmaya başlayan temel araştırma-soruşturma alanlarından biri haline geldi. Evsizleşme-yurtsuzlaşma ister bir metafor ve zihin durumu ister bilfiil yaşanan istenmeyen sürpriz bir deneyim olsun, kimliğin yeniden tanımlanmasını zorunlu kılan farkındalıklara yol açmaktadır. Yerinden-mekânından edilen kimlik, mekân sadece bulunulan yer değildir. Kelimenin etimolojisi bize mekânın 'olunan yer' olduğunu, olan şeyin öyle olması için varoluş imkânı sunduğu ve o şeye tanıklık ettiğini söyler. Kimlik söz konusu olduğunda mekân fiziksel değil ontolojik bir kategori olup çıkar. Göçün, mekâna sıkı bağlı kimlikler üzerindeki etkisinin daha derin ve kapsamlı olduğu söylenebilir. Bu benlik ile olduğu kadar ötekilik ile de ilgilidir. Zamana ve mekâna yoğun göndermelerle örülü kimlikler, yakın düşmanlıklar ve ötekilikler üretmek konusunda daha yaratıcı ve kararlıdır. Oysa göç, öteki ile planlı ya da ani karşılaşmalarla ile empati/sempati yollarının sıkça aşındırıldığı bir süreci zorunlu kılar. Bu, kimliğin koordinatlarını yıpratır. Aslında postmodern teori ötekiliği sevimli ve meşru bir kategori olarak resmetmişti. Merkezîliklere, hiyerarşilere ve mutlaklaştırmalara itiraz eden ve hakikatin çoğulculuğunu, ötekini anlamayı, farklılıkları yüceltmeyi savunan postmodern teori, ben-öteki sınırını yumuşatmaya başlamıştı. Ancak bilinçli ve sistemli bir entelektüel çabaya dayanan yersizleşme-yurtsuzlaşma deneyimi ile korku, dehşet içinde maruz kalınan yersizleşme-yurtsuzlaşma ayrıştırılması gereken bir karmaşık durum yarattı. Ötekiliklerin arttığı ve yaygınlaştığı postmodern dünyada eşit ve saygıya dayalı ben-öteki karşılaşmaları yerine, ötekine sığınan ben'in çaresizliğinden kaynaklanan dezavantajlarla dolu bir mecburiyet/mahrumiyet olgusu yaygınlaşmaya başladı. Bu çalışmada mekâna bağlı/bağımlı kimliklerin göç karşısında ya da sürecinde yaşadığı değişim, ötekinin dönüşümü ve yeni karşılaşmaların etik dayatmaları tartışılacak ve önerilen çözümler analiz edilecektir.

Göçmen Çocukların Örgün Eğitim ve Din Eğitiminde Karşılaştığı Sorunlar

(1176) Kamil Coştu, Turkey

Savaş, ekonomik etkenler vb. sebeplerle dünyada milyonlarca insan hem ülke içerisine hem de dışına göç etmektedir. Yetişkinlerle birlikte göç yolculuğuna çıkan çocukları çok farklı problemler beklemektedir. Belki de en zoru ikamet ettiği bölgenin gelenek ve gelecek algısına yabancı kalması, entegrasyonu sağlayamamasıdır. Türkiye özellikle 2011'den sonra kütlesel dış göç dalgasına maruz kalmıştır. Suriye'deki iç karışıklıklar sebebiyle yaklaşık 5 milyon insan Türkiye'nin çeşitli şehirlerine yerleşmiştir. Bu durum hükümetin pek çok alanda olduğu gibi eğitim alanındaki ihtiyaçları da göz önüne almasına etki etmiştir. Aynı zamanda bu problem akademianın da ilgisini çekmiştir. Bu araştırmada konu hakkında yapılan bilimsel araştırmalardan yola çıkılarak örgün eğitim ve din eğitimi alanında yaşanılan sorunlar konu edilecek ve çeşitli öneriler de bulunulacaktır.

Göçmen Çocukların Eğitimde Entegrasyonu ve Okullaşma Süreci

(570) Sibel Terzioğlu, Istanbul Rumeli University, Turkey

Ekonomik, toplumsal, siyasal, sosyal sebeplerde bireylerin ya da toplulukların yaşam alanlarını değiştirmelerini göç olarak tanımlanır (TDK,2018). Türkiye coğrafi yapısı itibariyle , sosyal ,ekonomik ve kültürel yapısıyla sürekli göç hareketliliğine maruz kalmış dolayısıyla fazlasıyla göç alıp vermektedir. Sınır bölgelerinde yaşanan gelişmeler sonucunda son zamanlarda göç deneyimini daha sık yaşanmakta ve bu bağlamda göçe ve göç eden bireylere karşı farklı stratejiler geliştirme konusundaki ihtiyacın önemini deneyimleyerek görmüştür (Ünal, 2014, s. 68). Bu bağlamda göçler hem göç eden hem göç alan yer ve toplum açısından değişimin kapılarını aralamaktadır (Akıncı m, 2015, s.60).

Çocukların sosyal hayata katılımı kendilerine verilen hakların aktifleşmesi açısından hem refahları hem toplumsal iyi olma halinin arttırılması açısından faydalıdır. Fakat gözardı edilmemesi gereken önemli bir ayrıntı da hala yetişkin olamamış, kişisel gelişimlerini tamamlayamamış çocukların farklı kulvarlarda alınan kararlara nasıl katılabileceği bilinmediği gibi bununla alakalı var olan emsal kararların yeterli görülmediği kanaatidir. Çalışmamızın amacı, mülteci çocukların göç ettikleri toplumda maruz kaldıkları dışlanma etkisi, akran zorbalığı ve katılım hakkını kavramsal olarak tartışmak, bu konuyu entegrasyon sürecinin hassas kesimi olan göçmen çocuklar açısından ele almaktır.

Göçmen çocuklar açısından ele aldığımız eğitimde entegrasyon ve okullaşma sürecinde herkesin üzerine düşüp onların uyum ve entegrasyonlarının sağlanması için ortak bir paydada buluşması gerekliliği kanaatine varılmıştır. Okula giden göçmen çocuklarda adaptasyonlarının kolaylaşması, dışlanma ve yabancılaşma sorununa maruz kalmamaları için kolaylaştırıcı tedbirler ve önlemler alınmalıdır. Yapılan çalışmalar sadece okul içerisinde kalmamalı yukarıda da değindiğimiz gibi ortak paydada buluşulan donanımlı meslek elemanları ile beraber, göçmen çocuklar ve aileleri de dahil edilerek, sosyal, psikolojik, kültürel cinsiyetleri ve çevresel faktörleri çerçevesinde ortaklaşa bir çalışma yürütülmesi önerilmektedir.

Kaynakça:

Akıncı, B., Nergiz, A., Gedik, E. (2015). Uyum Süreci Üzerine Bir Değerlendirme: Göç ve Toplumsal Kabul. Göç Araştırmaları Dergisi, Cilt:1, Sayı 2, s.58-83.

Ünal, S. (2014). Türkiye'nin Beklenmedik Konukları Öteki Bağlamında Yabancı TDK. (2018) http://www.tdk.gov.tr/index.php?option=com_gts&arama=gts&guid=Erişim Tarihi:21.06.2022

Göçmen Dini Örgütlenmesi Olarak Türk Diyanet Vakıfları; Avrupa Örneği

(1113) Yakup Çoştu, Hitit University, Turkey

Türkiye'de din hizmetleri ve dini irşat görevini kamusal düzeyde Diyanet İşleri Başkanlığı (DİB) yürütmektedir. Anayasal bir kurum olarak DİB, merkez teşkilatı, taşra teşkilatı, yurtdışı teşkilatı ve medya kanalları vasıtasıyla toplumun dini ihtiyaç ve gereksinimlerini karşılamaya çalışmaktadır. DİB 1980'lerin başlarından itibaren, yurtdışında yaşayan vatandaş ve soydaşların dini ve kültürel konularda bilgilendirilmesi, milli ve dini değerlerinin güçlendirilmesine yönelik olarak yurtdışında teşkilatlanmaya başlamıştır.

Diyanet İşleri Başkanlığı, Avrupa ülkelerindeki Büyükelçilikler nezdinde 'Din Hizmetleri Müşavirlikleri', Başkonsolosluklar nezdinde de 'Din Hizmetleri Ataşelikleri' ve 'Ataşe Yardımcılıkları' adı altında yurt dışı teşkilatı olarak örgütlenmiştir. Diyanet İşleri Başkanlığının yurt dışındaki Türkiye Cumhuriyeti Büyükelçilikleri ve Konsoloslukları nezdindeki teşkilatlarıyla organik bağı bulunan "Türk Diyanet Vakıfları" adı altında bir sivil örgütlenmesi de bulunmaktadır. Diyanet İşleri Başkanlığı, 1985 yılından itibaren maaşları Türkiye Cumhuriyeti Devleti tarafından karşılanmak suretiyle, yurt dışındaki teşkilatları bünyesinde faaliyet yürüten cami ve mescitlere din görevlisi gönderme uygulamasını başlatmıştır. 1982'de Belçika'da "Belçika Diyanet Vakfı", 1982'de Hollanda'da "Hollanda Diyanet Vakfı (HDV)",1984'te Almanya'da "Diyanet İşleri Türk İslam Birliği (DITIB)", 1984'de İsveç'te "İsveç Diyanet Vakfı", 1985'te Danimarka'da "Danimarka Türk Diyanet Vakfı", 1986'da Fransa'da "Fransa Diyanet İşleri Türk İslâm Birliği (DİTİB)", 1990'da Avusturya'da "Avusturya Türk İslam Birliği (ATİB)", 2001'de İngiltere'de "İngiltere Türk Diyanet Vakfı (İTDV)" ve 2011'de Norveç'te "Norveç Türk Diyanet Vakfı (ITDV)" kurulmuştur Yabancı bir ülkede kalıcı hale gelen ve anavatana geri dönme ümitleri de git gide azalan topluluklar olarak Avrupalı Türk göçmenlerin bulundukları yerleşim bölgelerinde kendilerine özgü kimlik ve aidiyet dünyaları inşa etme girişimlerinden biri de dini sivil örgütlenmelerdir. Tesis edilen bu sivil örgütlenmeler, topluluğu oluşturan her bir alt grubun etnik, kültürel, ideolojik ve politik söylemlerine göre farklılaşmaktadır. Topluluğa ait bu kuruluşların sayısı hakkında kesin bir bilgi olmamakla birlikte bunların, göçmen grupların nüfus oranlarının yoğunlaştığı bölgelerde toplandığı görülmektedir. Avrupalı Türklerin gündelik dini yaşamlarında etkin bir rol üstelenen söz konusu bu sivil dini örgütlenmeler etrafında gelişen sosyal, kültürel ve dini hayata yakından bakmak önem taşımaktadır. Türkiye Cumhuriyeti Diyanet İşleri Başkanlığı'nın topluma deklare ettiği çatışmadan uzak, karşılıklı hoşgörü ve uzlaşıya dayalı din hizmet politikasının yansımasını Avrupa ülkelerindeki Türk Diyanet Vakıflarının faaliyetlerinde de gözlemlenmektedir. Kaynaklara uygunluk, süreklilik, denetlenebilirlik ve kamu yararına uygunluk ilkelerine dayalı bir misyon çerçevesinde hizmet sunmaya çalışan bu dini sivil örgütlenmeler, Türk göçmenlerin gündelik dini hayatında önemli katkı sağlamaktadır. Bu bildiride, Almanya, Fransa, İngiltere, Avusturya, Belçika, Hollanda, Danimarka, İsveç ve Norveç'te çatı kuruluş olarak tesis edilen Türk Diyanet Vakıflarınca yürütülen faaliyetlerin göçmenlerin dini kimlik, sosyal uyum ve birlikte yaşama kültürü bağlamında gündelik dini hayatlarına katkıları makro sosyolojik bir yaklaşımla incelenecektir.

9F Economics of Migration

Chair: Afsal K., International Institute for Population Sciences, India

1183   Diaspora philanthropy; A study on the motives and causes of philanthropic activities of migrants from Kerala

Afsal K, International Institute for Population Sciences, Mumbai, India

926   Remittances Effects of Islamic Financial Development

Farid Makhlouf, ESC Pau Business School, France
Abdelhamid Addi, University of Pau, France
Oussama Ben Atta, University of Pau, France

1212   Migrants Remittances and Fertility in the Post-Soviet States States

Rashid Javed, Westminster International University in Tashkent, Uzbekistan
Boburmirzo Ibrokhimov, Westminster International University in Tashkent, Uzbekistan
Mazhar Mughal, ESC Pau Business School, France

1099   COVID-19 and Remittances to Mexican States

Jaime Lara, Universidad de Monterrey, México
Ana Paula Goerne Luna, Universidad de Monterrey, México
Luz Daniela Montañez Martínez, Universidad de Monterrey, México
Regina Saracho Cueto, Universidad de Monterrey, México
Alonso Torre de Silva, Universidad de Monterrey, México
Iliana Michelle Zaldivar Galindo, Universidad de Monterrey, México

Diaspora philanthropy; A study on the motives and causes of philanthropic activities of migrants from Kerala

(1183) Afsal K, International Institute for Population Sciences, Mumbai, India

Diaspora and philanthropy are two different words, 'Diaspora', simply refers to migrants' communities overseas who still keep relationship with the homeland, not necessarily as 'dispersed political subjects' (Werbner, 2002). On another hand, philanthropy word means 'love of humanity', a term singularly associated with giving altruistically or acts of charity to others outside of one's family (Espinosa, 2016). Furthermore, it is an effort to promote human welfare, usually manifested by giving money, support and help needy person, society and other social institutions as well as the generosity towards the socially useful purpose (Newland, 2010). In this migration era, diaspora philanthropy has a significant role in social and economic development as remittances. In the context of Kerala, migration is an important factor in its socio-economic and demographic aspects, especially the Gulf migration after the 'oil boom' of the 1970s (Shekhar, 1997; Prakash, 1998; Prakash, 1998; Zachariah, 1999; Babu, 2005). The study of migration and remittances has been well studied and documented, but few studies have been conducted on diaspora philanthropy and charity (Osella, 2009; Rahman, 2019; Sahasranamam, 2019). It has been proven that the expatriates are helping the Keralites on many occasions, just as a UAE-based migrant organization sent R.s 100 million in emergency aid to Kerala during the catastrophic floods of 2018 and 2019. And as part of the relief, they have planned a rehabilitation plan that includes a financial package to repair, rebuild homes and restore business (Gulf News 2018). Expatriate charities are believed to have helped backward areas and communities such as the UAE-based Keralites organization, which launched the Beit Al Rahima Charity project to build 1000 houses for the homeless in Kerala (Emirates 24, 2013). When the Nipha virus hit Kerala in 2018, a UAE-based Malayalee healthcare provider sent a chartered plane with medical equipment to fight the Nipha. (Gulf News, 2018). In addition, there are numerous educational and health institutions, and multidisciplinary charities that provide full or partial funding from migrants. Therefore, the study seeks to explore the motives of diaspora philanthropy using a primary sample survey conducted among 300 returning migrants and 'migrants on vocation' who supported the diaspora philanthropic organizations working in various fields, including education, health, social welfare and the community level. The study found that the main motivating factors and causes of philanthropy are religion and community relations, the moral and ethical response, and the serious issue to be considered and supported. And they were also inspired by colleagues, friends, religious scholars, family and locals. In addition, they mainly contributed to the health sector, education and social welfare programs such as housing and poverty alleviation.

Remittances Effects of Islamic Financial Development

(926) Farid Makhlouf, ESC Pau Business School, France

Abdelhamid Addi, University of Pau, France

Oussama Ben Atta, University of Pau, France

Diaspora and philanthropy are two different words, 'Diaspora', simply refers to migrants' communities overseas who still keep relationship with the homeland, not necessarily as 'dispersed political subjects' (Werbner, 2002). On another hand, philanthropy word means 'love of humanity', a term singula

Migrants Remittances and Fertility in the Post-Soviet States States

(1212) Rashid Javed, Westminster International University in Tashkent, Uzbekistan

Boburmirzo Ibrokhimov, Westminster International University in Tashkent, Uzbekistan

Mazhar Mughal, ESC Pau Business School, France

The possible demographic consequences of remittance flows has so far received scant attention. In two studies on the question, Anwar & Mughal (2016) and Ben Atta et al (2021) examined the role of migrant remittances on fertility in South Asia and North Africa. In this study, we examine the impact of migrants' remittances on fertility by employing panel data for Post-Soviet states from 1990 to 2020. Post-Soviet states are an interesting case study. First, there is large-scale out-migration and receipt of migrants' remittances is also substantial. Second, like other parts of the world, this region also passed through a demographic transition moving from a high mortality and high birth rate to low mortality and low birth rate. Third, in these states, there is the existence of a traditional family structure with rapid social change. By employing standard panel estimation methods, we find a significant negative association between remittances and fertility rate. The findings of the study highlight the contribution of Post-Soviet state's migrant community to the demographic transition.

COVID-19 and Remittances to Mexican States

(1099) Jaime Lara, Universidad de Monterrey, México

Ana Paula Goerne Luna, Universidad de Monterrey, México

Luz Daniela Montañez Martínez, Universidad de Monterrey, México

Regina Saracho Cueto, Universidad de Monterrey, México

Alonso Torre de Silva, Universidad de Monterrey, México

Iliana Michelle Zaldivar Galindo, Universidad de Monterrey, México

With the onset of the COVID-19 pandemic and its negative effect on economic activity, a decrease in remittances was expected. However, on the contrary, remittances have increased in countries like Mexico. Objectives: This study aims to deepen the relationship between the COVID-19 crisis and the sending of remittances to Mexico at the subnational level Methods: In a fixed-effects model we incorporate the registered cases of the pandemic at the state level as an explanatory variable of remittances Results: Our results indicate that a new case of COVID-19 has been associated with a $490 increase in remittances. However, consistent with the results in previous literature, remittances did not increase in the face of the employment decline at the local level in Mexico during the pandemic crisis. Moreover, the robustness of the effect depends on the inclusion of quarter effects, showing a significant increase in remittances to all Mexican states during the pandemic. Conclusion: Remittances could serve as an insurance mechanism for some recipient households and can be considered countercyclical in more aggregate terms. However, results show that remittances as an insurance mechanism could face difficulties identifying the most affected regions. Therefore, remittances cannot be considered a close substitute for public policies for COVID-19 shocks at the local level.

9G   Workshop: Migración y arquitectura [ES]

Chair: Dr. Emanuele Giorgi, Tecnológico de Monterrey in Chihuahua, Mexico

506   Sistemas constructivos más adecuados para viviendas de migrantes a larga estancia. El caso de Ciudad Juárez, Mexico

Ana Laura Díaz Rojas, Escuela de Arquitectura, Arte y Diseño, Tecnológico de Monterrey, Mexico

507   Albergues para niños migrantes, lo que se busca de un entorno arquitectónico seguro

Victoria Ernestina Reyes Ríos, Escuela de Arquitectura, Arte y Diseño, Tecnológico de Monterrey, Mexico

508   Soluciones urbano-arquitectónicas para facilitar la recepción de migrantes en ciudades saludables

Dariana Alitzel Lerma Bringas, Escuela de Arquitectura, Arte y Diseño, Tecnológico de Monterrey, Mexico

509   Estudio sobre modelos eficaces para una vivienda digna para refugiados climáticos

Frida Patricia Holguín Bustillos, Escuela de Arquitectura, Arte y Diseño, Tecnológico de Monterrey, Mexico

510   Intervención de la arquitectura en la protección de la mujer en su proceso de migración

Ana Sofía Romero Coello, Escuela de Arquitectura, Arte y Diseño, Tecnológico de Monterrey, Mexico

Sistemas constructivos más adecuados para viviendas de migrantes a larga estancia. El caso de Ciudad Juárez, Mexico

(506) Ana Laura Díaz Rojas, Escuela de Arquitectura, Arte y Diseño, Tecnológico de Monterrey, Mexico

Ciudad Juárez se encuentra en la frontera septentrional de México y tiene un alto flujo de migrantes que en busca de una mejor calidad de vida viajan a los Estados Unidos; sin embargo, no todos logran cruzar la frontera, por lo que terminan quedándose en esta ciudad. Según la COESPO, en el año 2019 existían más de 5,600 migrantes en Juárez que solicitaron asilo político a los Estados Unidos y que actualmente están viviendo en la ciudad (2019). Aunado a esto, el INAMI señala que en el mismo año fueron retornadas más de 12,500 personas de habla hispana por los Estados Unidos, mismas que permanecieron en México mientras se definía su situación migratoria. Después de haber sido deportadas, muchas de estas personas se quedan en Juárez por un largo periodo de tiempo, ya sea porque no cuentan con la documentación necesaria o los recursos suficientes para regresar a su país de origen. Esto origina que en la ciudad exista una necesidad apremiante por la existencia de opciones de hospedaje de larga estancia o programas de vivienda social pero que posiblemente tendrán que tener características diferentes a la vivienda social tradicional dirigida a la población nacional. La investigación busca concluir cuáles son los sistemas constructivos más adecuados para edificar viviendas de largo plazo para migrantes en la frontera norte de México (principalmente Ciudad Juárez, Chihuahua), caracterizada por un clima desértico con muchos extremos en altas y bajas temperaturas. En México existen sistemas constructivos vernáculos, como el adobe, que permiten una edificación eficiente y de bajo costo, con la capacidad de proveer un hogar digno y seguro. Estos sistemas tienen la posibilidad de utilizarse para edificar viviendas económica y rápidamente para proveer alojamiento a los migrantes. Por medio de casos de estudio en ciudades fronterizas mexicanas y de otras partes del mundo, se compararon características clave para determinar sistemas y elementos constructivos adecuados para la construcción de vivienda para migrantes en ciudades fronterizas.

Albergues para niños migrantes, lo que se busca de un entorno arquitectónico seguro

(507) Victoria Ernestina Reyes Ríos, Escuela de Arquitectura, Arte y Diseño, Tecnológico de Monterrey, Mexico

En los últimos dos años el fenómeno migratorio ha crecido de una forma excepcional, convirtiéndose en un cambio histórico. Las causas principales de los movimientos migratorios globales tienen origen en varios factores; situaciones económicas, políticas y educativas; así como emergencias relacionadas a violencia extrema, pobreza, hambruna y cambio climático. Se estima que de los 272 millones de migrantes internacionales, dos tercios son migrantes laborales (OIM, 2020). México se encuentra en un área geográfica muy importante, pues se localiza al sur de Estados Unidos y Canadá, países líderes en economía mundial, y al norte de países como El Salvador, Guatemala y Honduras, que presentan extremos casos de violencia e inseguridad. Por ello, México es el enlace hacia el llamado sueño americano. Esta investigación se enfoca en la situación vivida al norte de México, en donde 3 de cada 10 migrantes, son niños, niñas y adolescentes no acompañados en busca de asilo en Estados Unidos, con el objetivo de reencontrarse con familiares que anteriormente han migrado y ahora trabajan en EE.UU. (DAES, 2020). De estos, entre el 70% y el 90% son deportados sin hacerse los procedimientos legales necesarios que son estandarizados tanto por leyes internacionales como nacionales (Ley sobre Refugio, Protección Complementaria y Asilo Político en México; the Trafficking Victims Protection Reauthorization Act of 2008, the 1996 Flores v. Meese en Estados Unidos; el Pacto Mundial sobre los Refugiados de UNICEF y ACNUR) (Amnistía Internacional, 2021). Teniendo en cuenta la situación tan complicada que precede a estos infantes y adolescentes, el entorno arquitectónico de los refugios debe representar para ellos un espacio seguro, por lo que su arquitectura juega un papel fundamental para su readaptación a una nueva realidad. Por lo tanto, para los arquitectos es un reto responder a estas nuevas necesidades y dar instrumentos que puedan ofrecer soluciones constructivas y de diseño ideales para niños, niñas y adolescentes migrantes. La metodología empleada para realizar esta investigación ha sido nutrida con otros documentos de investigación, de diferentes perspectivas, (legal, psicológica, etc.) que han sido comparados con la opinión de experimentados arquitectos, psicólogos y pedagogos de la región. Además, se ha buscado entrevistar a niños migrantes para conocer su vivencia dentro de estos centros de refugio. Los resultados han sido especialmente interesantes, pues no ha surgido una guía como tal que especifique el tamaño de los espacios, sino más bien, se invita a un espacio de reflexión y de diseño participativo, en donde no solo se diseñe basado en la opinión de los profesionales, sino también con ayuda de los usuarios.

Soluciones urbano-arquitectónicas para facilitar la recepción de migrantes en ciudades saludables

(508) Dariana Alitzel Lerma Bringas, Escuela de Arquitectura, Arte y Diseño, Tecnológico de Monterrey, Mexico

La inquietud de no encontrar lugares adecuados y seguros a lo largo del camino hacia el destino final es uno de los temores principales para los migrantes. Estos casos generan la inquietud de ¿cuáles características básicas tienen que tener las ciudades fronterizas para ser consideradas preparadas para recibir a los migrantes? UN-Hábitat es un programa con la finalidad de, a través de proyectos, lograr una mejor ciudad a futuro. Uno de sus proyectos es "Urban Health", el cual ha impactado a alrededor de 10,000 personas a nivel mundial, y se han estudiado aproximadamente 100 casos de estudio. El proyecto "Urban Health" consiste en buscar la manera adecuada de la planificación y del diseño urbano, debido a que estos juegan un papel importante en la promoción de entornos más saludables. El factor de la salud urbana es un factor que, sin duda alguna, es una pieza clave en cualquier ciudad. Sin embargo, esto vale aún más por las ciudades fronterizas, por sus grandes flujos de personas que además son ajenas al país. En México ciudades como Tijuana, Ciudad Juárez y Nuevo Laredo son las 3 ciudades fronterizas más importantes del país. Sin embargo, las 3 ciudades presentan estándares altos de violencia, que sin duda afectan directamente a la salud mental y física de las personas. Tijuana presenta un gran desarrollo económico, generación de riquezas, pero a su vez, mucha pobreza. Ciudad Juárez, un problema grave es la violencia pues es conocida como "la ciudad asesina de mujeres", "la ciudad más violenta del mundo". Finalmente, Nuevo Laredo por su parte, se caracteriza por ser una frontera con mucho crecimiento económico, turístuco, y es el cruce más grande de mercancía en la zona norte del país. La investigación buscó definir las características que hacen "saludable" una ciudad que recibe migrantes y, por medio de casos de estudio, se buscaron estas características en las principales ciudades fronterizas del norte de Mexico: Tijuana, Ciudad Juárez y Nuevo Laredo.

Estudio sobre modelos eficaces para una vivienda digna para refugiados climáticos

(509) Frida Patricia Holguín Bustillos, Escuela de Arquitectura, Arte y Diseño, Tecnológico de Monterrey, Mexico

Según expertos, se estima que, para 2050, alrededor de 200 mil personas se verán obligadas a desplazarse anualmente a causa del cambio climático (Brown, 2008). Por un lado, el aumento repentino del nivel del mar, la desertificación, la erosión del suelo y la escasez del agua serán causas de migración cada vez más constantes. Por otro lado, los cada vez más frecuentes desastres naturales y fenómenos meteorológicos extremos como tormentas, inundaciones o, ciclones, causarán amplias migraciones de emergencia (Brown, 2008). Frente a este fenómeno global, se tiene que abrir una importante reflexión interdisciplinaria sobre el acceso a soluciones de hospitalidad dignas. De hecho, lo que al principio se piensa como una solución temporal, la mayoría de las veces resulta en una estadía permanente o de largo plazo (Aburamadan, 2022). No obstante, los campos de refugiados climáticos no cumplen con los requisitos de confort y características socioespaciales para que las personas vivan dignamente. Por este motivo, esta investigación busca entender cuál es la forma más factible de ofrecer una vivienda digna a los refugiados climáticos. La investigación tomó en cuenta diversas condiciones de vida en campos de refugiados climáticos que migraron en diferentes contextos -desastres naturales, desertificación y erosión del suelo, escasez de agua, aumento repentino del nivel del mar-, esto para establecer las necesidades espaciales y determinar líneas bases para un modelo eficaz de vivienda digna para migrantes en ambientes de desplazamientos extremos, capaz de adaptarse a las condiciones relacionadas a un caso específico y cumplir con el confort de los desplazados.

Intervención de la arquitectura en la protección de la mujer en su proceso de migración

(510) Ana Sofia Romero Coello, Escuela de Arquitectura, Arte y Diseño, Tecnológico de Monterrey, Mexico

En el presente artículo, se integra una investigación realizada en torno a cifras migratorias y experiencias de violencia hacia las mujeres que han atravesado por un proceso de migración irregular, haciendo énfasis en la importancia de la creación de espacios sostenibles que auxilien a aquellas que buscan cumplir el "sueño americano", tomando como prioridad el daño que presentan gran cantidad de mujeres al no contar con otra alternativa de supervivencia al migrar y tomar rutas clandestinas. Todo en búsqueda de una mejor calidad de vida, bienestar personal y de familia. En cifras generales se observa que las mujeres se acercan a la mitad de los 19.6 millones de migrantes refugiados registrados por la OIM, de las cuales cerca del 80% presentan alguna experiencia de violencia sexual, e incluso siendo el género un motivo por el cual la mujer se ve obligada a cambiar de lugar de residencia. La feminización de la pobreza restringe a la mujer de su independencia debido a la carencia de igualdad económica y discriminación que se presenta en todos los países, abarcando el 70% de las personas en situación de pobreza, indican datos de la ONU. Se trabajará un sector de migración a Estados Unidos en frontera Juárez, en donde se investiga y diagnostica con el fin de proponer espacios que apoyen a tratar inquietudes sociales del proceso migratorio de la mujer, como lo son casos de estrés post traumático, dificultad con trámites legales, conocimiento del inglés, entre otros factores. Se pretende tomar como pieza clave el educar a la mujer para su destino, facilitar y sanar un fragmento de la trayectoria ocurrida.

Day Four 10 September 2022 Saturday

Day Four 10 September 2022 - 09:30-11:00

10A   Integration, Acculturation and Diasporas

Chair   *Gül Ince-Beqo, University of Bari, Italy*

1145   International Migration and Integration: Turkish Immigrants in Poland

Gizem Karaköse, Anadolu University, Turkey
Filiz Göktuna Yaylacı, Anadolu University, Turkey

1299   The feeling of integration of Cypriot-Turkish, Turkish and Kurdish Migrant Women in London

Tuba Tayfun Kayalarli, University of Roehampton, UK

1062   A historical and multilevel approach to migration trajectories: The case of changing migration patterns from Turkey to Italy

Gül Ince-Beqo, University of Bari, Italy
Sahizer Samuk Carignani, IMT School for Advanced Studies Lucca, Italy
Matilde Rosina, Kings College London, UK

502   Rural poverty in African contexts and the changing nature of community resilience: insights for migration studies

Sónia Frias, University of Lisbon, ISCSP, CEsA, ISEG, Portugal

International Migration and Integration: Turkish Immigrants in Poland

(1145) Gizem Karaköse, Anadolu University, Turkey

Filiz Göktuna Yaylacı, Anadolu University, Turkey

This paper focuses on the social and system integration (Esser, 2000, s.56-58) processes of Turkish immigrants in Poland based on identity, host society policies, communication with the host society and ethnicity. The research was planned according to the qualitative methodology based on interviews and participatory observation in Warsaw, Gdansk, Bydgoszcz, Torun, Poznan and Wroclaw between October 2020 and August 2021. According to the obtained data during the research process, it can be said that Turkish immigrants in Poland provide social and system integration. On the one hand, the identity perceptions of Turkish immigrants in Poland have affected communication, which has an important role as well as in the social and system integration process. But on the other hand, while the Turkish immigrants are loyal to their ethnic identity, they have moved away from the perception of ethnicity. Turkish immigrants spend more of their free time together with the members of the host society, use the language of the host society in daily life and find a place for themselves in social spaces. In other words the system integration of Turkish immigrants in Poland consists of an easy process, while social integration has different stages for different groups. Therefore, immigrants who are intertwined with the host society shape their social integration processes and identity perceptions in the direction of their relationships.

The feeling of integration of Cypriot-Turkish, Turkish and Kurdish Migrant Women in London

(1299) Tuba Tayfun Kayalarli, University of Roehampton, UK

This paper aims to examine the feeling of integration of Cypriot-Turkish, Turkish, and Kurdish (hereafter 'CTK') migrant women that live in London. Globally women play a significant role in migration. Although they comprise 48.1% of the 135 million global international migrants, they often face more discrimination and are more vulnerable to mistreatment (UN Desa, 2020). The UK Census data (2011) and the existing information about the CTK community reveals a high degree of socio-economic disadvantage of this community compared to other minority communities in London. Furthermore, the percentage of economically inactive population of the CTK women who also have the lowest education level gives a clear indication of disadvantage of women in the CTK communities. Nevertheless, the recent migrations change the socio-economic characteristics of the CTK women as the new comers have higher levels of education, economic status, and language capability. This paper highlights the diversity of the CTK migrant women in terms of ethnicity, education, socio-economic status, language capability and migration background which make some of them disadvantaged and some more advantaged. It adopts cross-sectional survey design with qualitative interviews and takes the CTK women who live in London (N=241) as the population to draw the sample from. With a two-group study, this paper intends to explore the experiences and perceptions of feeling of integration of two groups of the CTK women. Group one comprises CTK migrant women who have work permit (Ankara Agreement or Business sponsorship) (N=87,36%) and Group two includes the CTK women who have naturalised legal status (N=90,37%). With the help of the Immigration Policy Lab Integration Index (which captures psychological, economic, political, social, linguistic and navigational dimensions of integration) and the semi structured interviews (with the CTK women who have different characteristics) the multiple forms of disadvantages and advantages that the CTK women experience are examined. Preliminary results of the quantitative data analysis indicates that the level of linguistic integration (t=.040, p<.05) and social integration (t=.001, p<.05) is significantly higher for the CTK women who have naturalised legal status compared to the ones with work permit where as for the psychological integration there is not a statistically significant difference between the two groups. Nonetheless, it should be noted that there could well be other factors (i.e., duration of living, age of participants) that affect the preliminary results. For this reason, at this stage the results give only an indication of a likelihood of a difference between groups. The semi-structured interviews are on-going with two groups of women. After the results of both survey and qualitative interviews are combined, it will be possible to better evaluate the feelings of integration of two groups of the CTK women. This will help us to utilise this knowledge to explore the experiences of other similar groups and communities of London and therefore contribute to the study of migrant integration widely.

Selected Bibliography

Anthias F. (1998) Rethinking Social Divisions: Some Notes towards a Theoretical Framework. The Sociological Review. 46(3), pp.505-535. doi:10.1111/1467-954X.00129.

Bryman, A. (2016) Social Research Methods. 5h ed. Oxford: Oxford University Press.

Creswell, J.W. and Plano Clark, V.L. (2011) Designing and Conducting Mixed Methods Research. Thousand Oaks, CA: Sage.

D'Angelo, A., Galip, O. and Kaye, N. (2013) Welfare Needs of Turkish and Kurdish Communities in London, Social Policy Research Centre, Middlesex University, London.

Enneli, P., Modood, T. and Bradley, H. (2005) Young Turks and Kurds: A Set of Invisible Disadvantaged Groups, Joseph Rowntree Foundation, York.

Great London Authority, (2009) Turkish, Kurdish and Turkish Cypriot Communities in London. Greater London Authority, London.

Harder,N. et al. (2018) Multidimensional Measure of immigrant integration, PNAS, 115 (45).

King, R.,Thompson, M., Mai, N. and Keles, Y. (2008) Turks in London: Shades of Invisibility and the Shifting Relevance of Policy in the Migration Process. Working Paper 51. Sussex Centre for Migration Research, University of Sussex.

Oliver,C. (2016) Review of the Research Literature on Integration and Resettlement in Europe and the Impact of Policy Interventions, Centre for Migration and Policy Research and Refugee Studies Centre, University of Oxford.

Phillimore, J. (2012) Implementing integration in the UK: lessons for integration theory, policy and practice, Policy & Politics, 40 (4), pp:525–45.

Simsek, D. (2012) Identity Formation of Cypriot Turkish, Kurdish and Turkish Young People in London in a Transnational Context. Phd Thesis. City University. Available at: https://openaccess.city.ac.uk/id/eprint/1234/ (Accessed: 25 March 2020).

Sirkeci,I. (2016) Little Turkey in Britain. London: Transnational Press.

UN DESA (2020) Available at: https://www.un.org/development/desa/dspd/wp-content/uploads/sites/22/2020/02/World-Social-Report2020-FullReport.pdf (Accessed:21March2021).

Yanasmayan, Z. (2019). The migration of highly educated Turkish citizens to Europe: from guestworkers to global talent. London; New York: Routledge.

A historical and multilevel approach to migration trajectories: The case of changing migration patterns from Turkey to Italy

(1062) Gül Ince-Beqo, University of Bari, Italy

Sahizer Samuk Carignani, IMT School for Advanced Studies Lucca, Italy

Matilde Rosina, Kings College London, UK

This article explores the evolution of Turkish migration to Italy, and the reasons behind its changes. Turkish migration to Italy presents key peculiarities, in the European context: While several EU member states used labour recruitment schemes since the 1960s to promote migration from Turkey, no such scheme was in place in Italy (which only became a destination country in the late 1980s similar to Turkey). On the contrary, initial Turkish migration to Italy was predominantly characterised by flows of asylum seekers and refugees since 1990s. Gradually however, the profile and motivations of Turkish migrants varied over the years, especially in the last decade Today, Italian universities and companies receive increasing numbers of students and high-skilled professionals from Turkey. From a theoretical viewpoint, neo-classical theories would expect migration to be a function of spatial disequilibria (for instance, pull and push factors with macro explanations). Yet, such representation cannot adequately capture the complexities and changes observed with migration from Turkey to Italy over time if a historical approach to the characteristics of migration is analysed. Investigating migration drivers at the macro, meso, and micro level, this article, thus aims to shed light on the under-explored phenomenon of Turkish migration to Italy. To do so, it relies on official datasets on migration dynamics (ISTAT, Eurostat, TUIK), as well as on interviews with both refugees/migrants who arrived with the first flows and students/professionals who arrived more recently, to understand migration trajectories and aspirations. The thematic analysis and comparison of these diverse patterns will further have implications on how the phenomenon of migration is linked with domestic policies, historical circumstances, bilateral and international relations.

Rural poverty in African contexts and the changing nature of community resilience: insights for migration studies

(502) Sónia Frias, University of Lisbon, ISCSP, CEsA, ISEG, Portugal

The flows of populations from the countryside to the cities, whatever they may have been the reasons for their consolidation in the different african countries, have also contributed to a strong transformation of the rural world. In addition to the spatial dimension of the movement, there are socio-economic and cultural dimensions that, much more than inducing changes, have been transforming rural realities very firmly and quickly, not only in terms of space, but also at the level of communities. There are changes that are more evident because they relate to production and its impact on the agricultural system, the impoverishment of families, environmental changes and migration. But alongside these, more discreet issues must be addressed, namely the need for populations to adapt to changes, which require an almost permanent adjustment and development of new skills, logics of thought and behavior, and mosto f all resilience. In this presentation I intend to try to read some of the challenges communities have to deal with. This text is based on a very simple methodology, supported by bibliographic research and data collected during fieldwork in Mozambique and Angola in the years 2016 and 2018 respectively.

10B   Türkiye'nin Göç Deneyimi [TR]

Chair: H. Yaprak Civelek, Anadolu University, Turkey

1058   Göç Çalışmalarının Türkiye'deki Serencamı: Uluslararası İlişkiler Alanındaki
        Doktora Tezleri Üzerine Bir Değerlendirme (2000-2021)

                        Pınar Çağlayan, Uşak University, Turkey
                        Özge Özkoç, Ankara University, Turkey
603   Uyum ve Entegrasyona Karşılaştırmalı Bir Bakış

                        Deniz Yetkin Aker, Namik Kemal University, Turkey
604   Çukurova Bölgesinde Göç Karşısında Kentsel Direncin Arttırılması ve Rezilyans
        Deneyimi

        Özge Çopuroğlu, Adana Alparslan Türkeş Bilim ve Teknoloji Üniversitesi, Turkey
535   Bir Metafor Olarak Deniz: Avcılar Sahilleri ve Suriyeliler

                        H. Yaprak Civelek, Anadolu University, Turkey
                        Gülden Büyükdağ, Ministry of Education, Turkey

Göç Çalışmalarının Türkiye'deki Serencamı: Uluslararası İlişkiler Alanındaki Doktora Tezleri Üzerine Bir Değerlendirme (2000-2021)

(1058) Pınar Çağlayan, Uşak University, Turkey

Özge Özkoç, Ankara University, Turkey

Uluslararası kitlesel göç hareketleri, I. Dünya Savaşı ile birlikte devletlerarası bir soruna dönüşmüş olsa da aynı dönemde doğan ve gelişen uluslararası ilişkiler disiplininde ayrı bir çalışma alanı olarak kendisine yer bulamamıştır. II. Dünya Savaşı'nın ardından başlayan Soğuk Savaş döneminde ise güvenlik, savunma, güç dengesi ve dış politika gibi konular öncelikli çalışma alanları olarak uluslararası ilişkiler disiplinini domine ederken, göç olgusu ikincil öneme sahip ve sosyal alana ilişkin ulusal bir sorun olarak görülerek araştırmacıların ilgisine mazhar olmamıştır. Göç çalışmalarının uluslararası ilişkiler alanında önemli bir yer edinmesi, Soğuk Savaş döneminin sona erdiği 1990'lı yıllara tekabül etmektedir. SSCB ve Doğu Bloku'nun dağılmasıyla ortaya çıkan istikrarsızlığın yanı sıra, Afrika ve Asya ülkelerinde yaşanan iç çatışmalar çevre ülkelerden Batı'ya doğru büyük bir göç dalgasını tetiklemiştir. Böylece, göç sorunu uluslararası ilişkiler alanında birincil derece öneme sahip bir politika meselesi haline gelmeye başlamıştır. Bu durum, 2000'lerde de devam edecektir. Nitekim, 11 Eylül 2001 saldırılarının ardından göçün güvenlik başta olmak üzere diğer temel küresel konularla ilişkisini merkeze alan akademik çalışmalarda artış olduğunu söylemek mümkündür. Yukarıda değinilen dönüşüm, şüphesiz Türkiye'yi de etkilemiştir. 1990'lı yıllardan itibaren yoğun bir transit mülteci/sığınmacı nüfusa ev sahipliği yapan ve özellikle 2012'den sonra Suriye iç savaşından kaçan 4 milyona yakın Suriyeli göçmeni sınırları içerisinde barındıran Türkiye'de de göçe yönelik akademik ilginin son yıllarda arttığı gözlemlenmektedir. Fakat, Türkiye'deki göç çalışmalarının 2000 sonrasındaki gelişimini ve uluslararası ilişkiler disiplini içerisindeki yerini derinlikli bir şekilde analiz eden çalışmaların varlığından bahsetmek mümkün görünmemektedir. Bu çalışmanın temel amacı, uluslararası ilişkiler alanında yazılmış doktora tezlerini baz alarak göç çalışmalarının Türkiye akademisindeki yerinin genel bir fotoğrafını çekebilmektedir. Bunu yaparken, ilk olarak, göç çalışmalarına ilişkin akademik ilgi artışının Türkiye'de kaleme alınmış uluslararası ilişkiler doktora tezlerinde kendisine ne denli yer bulduğu ortaya konmaya çalışılacaktır. İkincisi, söz konusu ilginin hangi temalar etrafında kümelendiği yine uluslararası ilişkiler alanında göçü temel alan tezler bağlamında değerlendirilecektir. Buradan hareketle, Türkiye'deki Ulusal Tez Merkezi'nde yer alan ve 2000-2021 yılları içerisinde uluslararası ilişkiler alanında yazılmış doktora tezleri ele alınacak ve göç, diaspora, sığınmacı, mülteci, yabancı işçi, göçmen vb. konularda kaleme alınmış doktora tezleri araştırmanın örneklemini oluşturacaktır. Söz konusu tezler öncelikle yıllara göre ve konu bazında istatistiki olarak değerlendirilecek, sonrasında ise içerik analizi yöntemi ile tematik olarak çözümlenecektir.

Uyum ve Entegrasyona Karşılaştırmalı Bir Bakış

(603) Deniz Yetkin Aker, Namik Kemal University, Turkey

Bu çalışma, uluslararası göç tanımından yola çıkıp göçün olası etkilerini tartıştıktan sonra, uyum/entegrasyon kavramını inceleyecektir. Uyum kavramını entegrasyonla eş anlamda alacak, yapısalcı yaklaşımla, kavramın söylem içinde inşa edildiğini iddia edecektir. Yakın dönemde nasıl değiştiği, ne gibi pratik ve olgularla ilişkili olduğu tartışıldıktan sonra BM tanımı ve bazı ülke örnekleri kullanılarak, uyum kavramının söylem içinde inşa edildiği ve ülkelerin söylemlerine göre kavramın içeriğinin değiştiği iddiası desteklenecektir.

Çukurova Bölgesinde Göç Karşısında Kentsel Direncin Arttırılması ve Rezilyans Deneyimi

(604) Özge Çopuroğlu, Adana Alparslan Türkeş Bilim ve Teknoloji Üniversitesi, Turkey

Rezilyans kelimesi Latince geri sıçrama veya geri gelme anlamına gelen "resilire" fiilinden türemiş olup dayanıklılık, sarsıcı etkiyi karşılama yeteneği ve hayatı normale çevirme yeteneği gibi bağlama göre değişkenlik arz eden anlamlara sahiptir. Söz konusu çalışma Çukurova bölgesindeki belediyelerin göç karşısındaki rezilyanslarını ele almayı amaçlamaktadır. 2011 yılında ortaya çıkan Suriye kriziyle birlikte başlayan ani ve yoğun göç, en çok yerel yönetimleri etkilemiştir. Özellikle kendi yerleşik nüfusuna kıyasla önemli bir oranda göçmen nüfusu alan bu belediyeler, merkezi bütçeden ayrılan paylar aynı kaldığı için hizmet sunumu konusunda kısa vadede olumsuz etkilenmiş olup, aynı bütçeyle daha fazla nüfusa hizmet götürmek gibi zorluklarla karşı karşıya kalmışlardır. Çalışmada Çukurova bölgesindeki belediyelerin göç ve göçün etkileri karşısında daha dayanıklı, hazırlıklı ve tedbirli hale gelmeleri için geliştirilmeye çalışılan sistematik yaklaşımlar ve rezilyans değerlendirmeleri ele alınacak, göçten kaynaklanan olumsuz etkileri karşılamada, hizmet sunumlarını normale çevirmede ve kentlerin eskisinden daha iyi bir hale gelmelerinde ne gibi inisiyatifler alındığı değerlendirilecektir.

Bir Metafor Olarak Deniz: Avcılar Sahilleri ve Suriyeliler

(535) H. Yaprak Civelek, Anadolu University, Turkey

Gülden Büyükdağ, Ministry of Education, Turkey

Bir metafor olarak deniz mevzusu aslında bir tür ayrımcılığın sık sık gözlenmesi üzerine ortaya çıkan sorularla gündeme geldi. İstanbul'un Kadıköy, Caddebostan, Avcılar, Büyükçekmece ilçelerinde kış aylarında da gözlenmesi muhtemel fakat yaz aylarında bir "sorun" olarak yerel halkın şikayetlerine karşılık belediyelerin yaptırımlar getirmesine de vesile olan deniz kenarlarına akın etme eylemidir. Sahillerde özellikle Suriyeli ve Afgan göçmenler olduklarını anladığımız çocuklu ailelerin ve genç bireylerin geniş kalabalıklar üretecek şekilde deniz kenarlarına akın etmeleri, piknik yaparak, denize girerek ya da sadece sohbet edip seyrederek vakit geçirmeleri toplumsallaşma biçimleri, öğrenme, kültürleme, kültürlenme, kültür şoku, sosyal ilişki ve uyum koşulları gibi pek çok temel sosyolojik, antropolojik ve psikolojik kavramı düşündürdü elbette. Dahası, emlakçılardan öğrendiğimiz kadarıyla sosyo-ekonomik olarak iyi durumda olanların çoğu sahile yakın evleri kiralamış ya da satın almışlardı. Ancak biz iki araştırmacı, meselenin bu kavramsal boyutlarını çoktan kabullenmiş insanlar olarak asıl şu soruya odaklandık: Savaştan insan püskürtür gibi sahillerden dışarı atılmak istenen göçmenlerin zihinlerinde deniz nasıl bir anlama sahiptir? Onların gözlerinde, alabildiğine uzanan denizlerin varlığı, bir ülke ve vatandaşları için nasıl bir avantaj sağlamaktadır? Denize yakın olmaktan duyulan coşku neyi ya da neleri temsil ediyordu? Teorik-politik platformda elbette akla ilk gelen Montesquieu'dur. Biz de onun denize yüklediği anlamlardan yola çıkarak sahada saptadığımız sosyal psikolojik yansımaları, sosyo-politik anlamlandırmalarla birleştirdik. Teorik bir açılımı, niteliksel araştırma çerçevesinde pratiğe bağladık. Suriyeli göçmenler nezdinde deniz bir metafor olarak en çok özgürlük, bir anlamda baskısız ve rahat bir yaşam demek. Deniz aynı zamanda iyi ve iyileştirici duygulara işaret eden bir simge. Deniz, bolluk bereket, genel olarak ülke ekonomisi için kazanç, ticaret ve turizmde çok işe yarayan, karayı, ülke sınırını korumada çok fazla katkısı olan, saflığın, sonsuzluğun, huzurun kaynağıdır. Kendi ülkeleri bazında daha çok politik bir sınıfsallık hatta baskıcı bir gücün iktidar alanına dahil edilmiş bir bölgenin korku yaratan özelliği.

10C   Migration Politics

Chair: Sinan Zeyneloglu, Istanbul Kent University, Turkey

994   Trafficking in human beings for the purpose of labour exploitation in Gulf States on light of international reports.

Benzidane Cherifa, University of Oran 02, Algeria

1142   The socialisation of precarity and precarious solidarities: Conclusions from a covert period of observation of migrant labour in Glasgow

Panos Theodoropoulos, University of Glasgow, UK

543   Successes and Failures in the Implementation of Migration Policies in Africa

David Oluwsegun Yusuf, University of Pretoria, South Africa
Maryam Mangai, University of Pretoria, South Africa
Oscar Otele Meywa, University of Nairobi, Kenya

Michel Tshiyoyo, University of Pretoria, South Africa

526   Multilateral Development Banks and Migration: from a country-specific approach to shared responsibility

Dimitra Manou, Aristotle University of Thessaloniki, Greece
Anastasia Blouchoutzi, University of Macedonia, Thessaloniki, Greece
Jason Papathanasiou, University of Macedonia, Thessaloniki, Greece

Trafficking in human beings for the purpose of labour exploitation in Gulf States on light of international reports.

(994) Benzidane Cherifa, University of Oran 02, Algeria

Each year, the Gulf States attract many foreign workers, especially Asian workers, in search of improving their socio-economic conditions. According to World Bank Statistics 11,7 % of total world migrants were living in the Gulf States, which were well known for their oil wealth and high revenues. However, these states are under the pressures of several international organizations that issued reports referring to victims of trafficking in human beings for the purpose of labour exploitation, they are requesting the GCC to end the abusive practices of foreign workers and reforming labor laws (International organization of Migration report, the other migrant crisis protecting migrant workers against exploitation in the Middle East and North Africa 2015, p.05). In this context, we ask questions: What are the challenges of labour migration? What are the indicators of international reports of violations of migrant labour rights in the Gulf countries? For Global Slavery Index in 2018, the forced Labour percentage is 51 % in Arab States (Global Slavery Index,2018,walk free foundation,p.83) the indicators of exploitation of migrant workers in the construction sectors they are subject to practices that may amount to forced labour including extortionate recruitment fees, withholding and non- payment of salaries,unhygien living conditions, unlawfully excessive work hours performed under the threat of deportation, physical and sexual abuse (The Global slavery index, Arab States Report, 2018,Walk Free foundation,p.04) The domestic workers remain the most exploited and the GCC region has an estimated 2,1 million migrant domestic workers, but they often work under xenophobic physical and sexual abuse (International Trade Union Confederation, facilitating exploitation: a review of labour laws for migrant domestic workers in Gulf Cooperation Council Countries,2017,p.13) In Qatar, in report of Amnesty International in 2016 entitled « the ugly side of beautifulgame » exploitation of migrant workers in Qatar 2022 World Cup Site the country embarked on massive construction projects to build stadiums and other infrastructure to host the tournament .However, there are violations threaten migrant labor including accumulation of debt due to high recruitment fees, terrible and insecure living conditions, denial of the right to strike, Lack of grievance mechanisms to improve their conditions, Forced labor (Amnesty International report, the ugly side of beautiful game, exploitation of migrant workers on a Qatar 2022 World Cup Site,2016,p.7.8) Where international organizations described Qatar as a modern slavery state due to violating the rights of workers who building the facilities of the 2022 World Cup championship, after that the Geneva Summit for Human Rights summoned Qatar to attend the twelfth annual summit of human rights in February 2020 to discuss slavery of workers, which caused death 676 Nepalese workers and 1,345 Indian workers. For UAE , Despite its creation Ministry of Happiness but in report of The Euro-Mediterranean Observatory for Human Rights in 2017 affirmed that domestic workers are suffering forced labor, With hours of work that may reach 21 hours per day, and the absence of rest periods or vacations, and they are subjected to psychological, physical and sexual abuse. In other hand, Human Right watch and International Labour Organisation requested GCC to abolishment of Kafala (sponsorship) system that violates workers' rights, and allow to migrant worker is dependant the sponsor ,so the workers are unable to enter or leave the country or seek alternative employment without their sponsor's written consent (reform of the Kafala System "sponsorship" system,policy brief N°02,migrant forum Asia,p.01)

The socialisation of precarity and precarious solidarities: Conclusions from a covert period of observation of migrant labour in Glasgow

(1142) Panos Theodoropoulos, University of Glasgow, UK

In an economy intentionally designed to attract and exploit migrant labour, migrant workers are frequently pushed to the forefront of the precarious condition. Despite the multiple, intense, and intersecting inequalities they experience, examples of autonomous migrant mobilisations in pursuit of labour rights in the UK are rare. The study that this paper is drawn from sought to understand how structure and subjectivity intersect to form barriers to the autonomous organisation of migrant workers. This consisted of a sustained period of covert participant observation in six workplaces that heavily relied on migrant labour under precarious and intensely exploitative conditions in the hospitality, food processing, manufacturing, and logistics industries. These observations were further supplemented by in-depth semi-structured interviews with 20 migrant workers. A series of useful and original concepts emerged from the research that concern the relationship of the structure (e.g., national economic and migration frameworks and employment practices) and migrant subjectivities (e.g., the dual frame of reference, cultural and linguistic barriers, disorientation in the new society). These include the 'agency arena', which describes the cumulative debilitating effects of workers competing amongst each other for limited but insecure and exploitative jobs in the context of labour agencies and zero hours contracts, and the 'socialisation of precarity', which describes the gradual effects of sustained experiences of precarity on worker subjectivities. Further noteworthy insights emerged regarding the complex interactions between co-ethnic migrants in precarious workplaces; shared ethnicity and experiences do not necessarily trigger solidarity, and it would be more accurate to position these relations on a continuum ranging from exploitation and dependency to various forms of contingent support. The first part of this paper will discuss the use of using covert participant observation to analyse the lived realities of migrant workers in precarious occupations. This is a useful but sensitive methodological approach which is rarely employed in migration research but is connected with embedded anthropological approaches such as Holmes' (2013) work on Mexican fruit pickers in the United States, and merits further consideration. The second part of the paper will present some of the findings as they pertain to the socialisation of precarity and the complex nature of solidarity amongst migrant workers in precarious workplaces.

Successes and Failures in the Implementation of Migration Policies in Africa

(543) David Oluwsegun Yusuf, University of Pretoria, South Africa

Maryam Mangai, University of Pretoria, South Africa

Oscar Otele Meywa, University of Nairobi, Kenya

Michel Tshiyoyo, University of Pretoria, South Africa

There have been various attempts to manage and govern migration both globally and in Africa. However, these attempts with innovative and excellently developed migration policies have not been beneficial during implementation. This paper analyzed and reviewed various continental and country level migration polices and eventually developed an innovative, beneficial, and inclusive model of co producing and co-implementing migration in Africa.

Using a case study design of data (in Benin City, a Nigerian migration hotspot) obtained from multiple focus group sessions and in-depth structured interviews with the members of the Benin Case Management Committee of the IOM along with returnee migrants and NGOs involved in migration management. Data were gathered based on the experiences and perspectives of the participants regarding migration. The qualitative data was analysed using a content analysis in ATLAS Ti 9 to develop a conceptual model in respect to the commissioning and implementation of migration policies to make migration more fair, orderly, predictable, and sustainable.

The study's findings revealed that migration management is successful during the process of agenda setting, policy formulation, development, and analysis. Whereas much failure have been recorded during policy implementation and policy evaluation. The participants acknowledged and recommended that coordinated follow-up efforts involving the global, country-level, and local-level migration agencies especially at the implementation phase will ensure successful and beneficial migration governance. These findings were reflected in the conceptual model for migration.

This paper contributes to the practical understanding of beneficial migration management in Africa and the potentials of coordinated (post) implementation in improving migration governance. To the best of the authors' knowledge, no previous scientific research has studied how migration is affected by post-implementation adequacies and this paper aims to fill this gap. The paper concludes that implementation using coordinated, innovative, and inclusive partnerships have far reaching effects at improving migration.

Multilateral Development Banks and Migration: from a country-specific approach to shared responsibility

(526) Dimitra Manou, Aristotle University of Thessaloniki, Greece

Anastasia Blouchoutzi, University of Macedonia, Thessaloniki, Greece

Jason Papathanasiou, University of Macedonia, Thessaloniki, Greece

The discussion on migration and development in the agendas of Multilateral Development Banks (MDBs) has been evolving already since their implementation agreements and throughout the decolonization period and has grown dramatically in the last decade including other aspects, such as environmental factors causing migration and the relation of migration to trade. As the policy discussion on migration within MDBs moves forward to new directions, we should not lose sight of their way so far: from dealing with migration on a country-specific basis to new policies establishing an enhanced cooperation between MDBs and adopting concepts of "shared responsibility".

This paper explores the policies and strategies related to migration of the World Bank, the Asian Development Bank, the African Development Bank, the European Bank for Reconstruction and Development, the Inter-American Development Bank and the Islamic Development Bank. It analyses the different approaches followed by these organizations through time, while matching each time their policies with the dominant development concepts of that period (i.e. economic growth, human development, sustainable development, etc.) and examines every time their most prominent tools and initiatives. It concludes that MDBs have been moving towards to adopting new concepts of "shared responsibility", as global challenges nowadays demand enhanced cooperation between MDBs and between MDBs and other actors (International Organizations, states, donors and others).

10D   Wellbeing and Migration

Chair: Margarida Martins Barroso, Universidad Autonoma de Madrid, Spain

1247   (Re)Shaping identities through literacy classes. Migrant women learning to read and write.

Margarida Martins Barroso, Universidad Autonoma de Madrid, Spain

960   Subjective well-being of internal migrants in China: The role of absolute and relative income

Peihua Deng, Freie Universitate Berlin, Germany

1091   Post traumatic withdrawal state in children seeking asylum - a case report and review of literature

Sisan Sillo, Black Country Healthcare NHS Foundation Trust
Reka Ajay Sundhar, Black Country Healthcare NHS Foundation Trust
Kiruthika Sivasubramanian, Black Country Healthcare NHS Foundation Trust

1008   The impact of Covid-19 and its consequences on labor migrants living in Georgia

Tatiana Sitchinava, Tbilisi State University, Georgia

(Re)Shaping identities through literacy classes. Migrant women learning to read and write.

(1247) Margarida Martins Barroso, Universidad Autonoma de Madrid, Spain

Background:

More than a process of cognitive acquisition of skills and competencies, learning to read and write is an important point in the definition of individual and social identities. In contemporary societies, largely referred to as knowledge societies, the generally higher levels of literacy tend to neglect this relevant marker in one's life, and to treat adults' inability to read and write as an invisible social phenomenon.

Although migrants tend to possess above the average education when compared to the population of their home countries, recent estimates show an increase in the proportions of migrants, in Europe, without or with low levels of formal education and basic literacy (Eurostat, 2019). Women represent most of the world's illiterate population (UNESCO, 2015), and around half of Europe's international migration (ILO, 2022). Even though statistics are limited, estimates also reveal that the percentage of illiterate migrant women has been rising in some European countries, tending to equal that of men.

Together with language classes, several organizations and institutions are offering literacy courses to those migrants who were not schooled. This raises the interest in understanding how migration, gender and the acquisition of literacy are shaping and reshaping the identities of migrant women who are learning to read and write in the host country.

Following the New Literacy Studies approach (Street, 2012), that conceives literacy as a social practice shaped by relations of power and sociocultural determinants, the main objectives of this paper are: 1) to discuss literacy courses and classes as practices that define and redefine individual and social identities of migrant women; and 2) to discuss migration, gender and education, and its interplay, as social markers of domination in contemporary knowledge societies.

A case study was undertaken in a local association offering literacy classes to migrant women in Spain. The research was supported by 1) three-month classroom observation, with descriptive registers of the classes' structure, dynamics, and general functioning, and fieldnotes and diaries; and 2) semi-structured interviews with teachers and students.

Absolute illiteracy, or the inability of reading and writing a simple sentence in any language, conditions the everyday lives of a segment of the female migrant population. Literacy has an empowering dimension, that promotes change and transformation, not only in the ways society sees these women, as also in the ways they see themselves. As such, learning advances such as being able to write one's name, or reading a simple instruction, reshape their individual and social identities.

The results allow to question how gender, migration and education interplay in the identity redefinition that illiterate migrant women often face in the learning process, and how the condition of being a woman, a migrant, and (un)able to read and write shape their lives.

References:

Eurostat (2019), Migration and migrant population statistics, retrieved from: https://ec.europa.eu/eurostat/statistics-explained/index.php?title=Migration_and_migrant_population_statistics, consulted 14th February 2022.

IOM (2022), World Migration Report, retrieved from: https://publications.iom.int/books/world-migration-report-2022, consulted 14th February 2022.

Street, B.V. (2012), "Contexts for literacy work: New literacy studies, multimodality and the 'local and the global'", in Tett, L., M. Hamilton and J. Crowther (eds), *More powerful literacies*, Leicester, National Institute for Adult Continuing Education.

UNESCO (2015), *Narrowing the gender gap. Empowering women through literacy programmes*, Paris, UNESCO.

Subjective well-being of internal migrants in China: The role of absolute and relative income

(960) Peihua Deng, Freie Universitate Berlin, Germany

Employing a novel dataset, the China Migrants Dynamic Survey (CMDS), this paper examines the association between income and subjective well-being among Chinese internal migrants. By revisiting the dispute over the link between individual's absolute income and their well-being, rural-urban migrants are found to be more significantly affected by their absolute income compared to urban-urban migrants. There is no "saturation point" for rural-urban migrants, those with the highest income are still found to be positively and significantly influenced, most likely because money could help rural-urban migrants to get rid of their stigmatized rural Hukou status. Additionally, linking administrative data and survey data of CMDS, striking differences between migrant's objective and subjective measures of relative income status are found. More importantly, objective relative income status is proved to be a relatively weak predictor of SWB. This helps explain why Chinese internal migrants generally stay in urban areas for a relatively long time, most of those misestimated people are overestimating their relative income positions when compared to the mainstream population in host city, making them to ignore their disadvantaged situation in the host city, the reality cannot hurt them if they do not realize it.

Post traumatic withdrawal state in children seeking asylum - a case report and review of literature

(1091) Sisan Sillo, Black Country Healthcare NHS Foundation Trust

Reka Ajay Sundhar, Black Country Healthcare NHS Foundation Trust

Kiruthika Sivasubramanian, Black Country Healthcare NHS Foundation Trust

Objective: To present a case of a post traumatic withdrawal state in an asylum-seeking adolescent and compare with current literature. Background: Several non-organic conditions comprising of potentially life-threatening symptoms like refusal in eating, drinking, speech, mobilisation, and personal care accompanied with social withdrawal and apathy have been reported in children since the early 1990s. Trauma, cultural factors and hostile asylum processes are specific risk factors for refugee and asylum-seeking children. Diagnostic nomenclature for the presentation in this demographic includes Pervasive Refusal Syndrome (PRS), Depressive Devitalisation (DD), and Resignation Syndrome (RS). We present our case accompanied with a literature review. Case Presentation: A then 15 year old Middle Eastern boy seeking asylum in the UK, was referred to our outpatient CAMHS by GP in January 2020. His family had fled their home country in

2017 due to persecution and their marginalised stateless status. He spoke minimally and selectively and required heavy prompting and encouragement for activities of daily living, some of which his parents were simply doing for him. Physical examination and investigations (including bloods, ECG and EEG) were unremarkable. The MDT has taken a holistic approach to management, with a particular focus on the social and psychological aspects of his care. We are noticing very slow and gradual improvements in his ability to participate in psychological therapy. Literature Review: We analysed reviews of case series and case reports of asylum-seeking children who develop social withdrawal symptoms (including PRS, DD and RS). Various articles highlight a complex interplay of moderating and mediating factors within the formulation. Vulnerable premorbid personality types and previous history of mental illness were reported as predisposing factors. Precipitating factors were traumatic events and infections. Difficult and dysfunctional parent-child relationships, and ongoing delays with asylum applications were perpetuating factors. Psychological and social support were protective factors. Cases initially presented with a psychiatric disorder (such as Depression or Post traumatic stress disorder) with a gradual progression into refusal to eat, mobilise, speak and self-care. Neurological symptoms were described only in a few cases, and physical health investigations ruled out organic explanations for the presentations. Children were of ethnic or political minority status in their home countries. Management usually took a multidisciplinary approach with CAMHS, paediatric, nursing and physiotherapy teams being involved. Many cases required lengthy inpatient admission and nasogastric feeding. A recent retrospective cohort study showed that environmental therapy, with patients separated from their parents and distanced from the asylum process, resulted in remission. Conclusion: We propose that our patient presents with a moderate version of a post traumatic withdrawal syndrome. Previous reviews of the topic suggest that treatment amounts to promoting and maintaining a secure and hopeful environment. Further research is required into the management of this presentation as an unprecedented number of children are displaced from their homes, and it is likely that we will encounter further cases in the UK and worldwide.

The impact of Covid-19 and its consequences on labor migrants living in Georgia

(1008) Tatiana Sitchinava, Tbilisi State University, Georgia

The Covid-19 pandemic became the major challenge for the entire world, and of course, Georgia is no exception. After the collapse of the Soviet Union, Georgia became a country of intensive emigration. Due to the inflow of immigrants, the last decade has marked a fundamental transformation in the country's migration profile. Covid-19 revealed complications that exist in Georgian immigration policy. The pandemic posed legal, socio-economic, health and other problems for the migrants. The purpose of the following paper is to identify the impact of the Covid-19 pandemic and the resulting tightened immigration policy on the situation of labour migrants in Georgia. The results of the research are based on a qualitative sociological survey. The 54 in-depth interviews were conducted with migrant workers in the two biggest cities of Georgia (Tbilisi, Batumi) and 13 experts in the field were interviewed. A similar complex scientific study on labour immigrants has not been conducted in Georgia yet. The research (PHDF-21-137) has been supported by the Shota Rustaveli National Science Foundation of Georgia. The results of the study identified the most affected migrant groups of pandemics. These include people employed in the local labour market in the tourism and service sectors and less-skilled jobs. The research indicated that the less effective government policies during the pandemic period significantly hampered the integration process of migrants. A particular challenge during the Covid-19 was the maintenance of legal status for migrant workers, which was compounded by socio-economic challenges, the problem of awareness, and restrictions on access to health care services.

10F   New Challenges in Migration Studies

Chair: Pinar Yazgan, Mobility Research Centre, International Business School, UK

1045   Stable and migrant peoples: the sketch of a paradigm

Orazio Maria Gnerre, University of Perugia, Italy

513   How Media and Technology Help Refugees Cope with COVID-19

Amira Halperin, University of Nottingham Ningbo, China

1205   Social vulnerability of international migrants in the context of the COVID-19 epidemic

Mariia Ivanova, St Petersburg University, Russia

545   Is there a home to go back to? Return and mobility aspirations among Turkish and Albanian migrants in Italy

Gül Ince-Beqo, University of Bari, Italy
Eralba Cela, University of Milan, Italy

1168   Impact of Covid-19 Pandemic on Gulf Migration: A Study of Telangana, India

Sudhaveni Naresh, Centre for Economic and Social Studies (CESS), Hyderabad, India

Stable and migrant peoples: the sketch of a paradigm

(1045) Orazio Maria Gnerre, University of Perugia, Italy

Often, during the modern age, the idea of the people was linked to the stability of life on a territory, and there is no doubt that the essence of an environment, that is its morphology, its endowments in terms of resources, and last but not least flora, fauna and anthropogenic patterns, constitute a strong influence on the culture of a human community. Nonetheless, in the nineteenth and twentieth centuries it was often forgotten that many peoples developed within large human movements, just as for some cultures the transience of the environment of birth is a central element of their tradition. This intervention aims to give a partial and non-exhaustive vision of how stability and transience can both form the vision of the world of a people or of a cultural tradition, and to propose a draft of integration of these two perspectives within a governmental policy proposal of human migrations.

How Media and Technology Help Refugees Cope with COVID-19

(513) Amira Halperin, University of Nottingham Ningbo, China

Although 2020 was a year in which the COVID-19 pandemic severely disrupted the lives of people across the world, thanks to the lockdowns and other strict anti-pandemic measures, it was also the year, which saw a significant increase in the number of people fleeing their countries to escape the horrors of war and violence. COVID-19 only exacerbated the refugees' problems and risks (World Economic Forum, 2020).

By the end of 2020, about 82.4 million people were displaced, 35 million of whom were children, according to 2022 Global Humanitarian Overview; more than 2 million people have fled Ukraine, according to UN High Commissioner for Refugees' Operational Data Portal.

The role of information and communications technology (ICT) during these turbulent times became critically important, even more so during the pandemic. Soon after the refugee crisis in Ukraine erupted, tech companies started playing an active role in helping the fleeing people.

Millions of refugees rely on smartphones and apps; they use them as survival tools to escape conflicts, to navigate border crossings, to receive and send warnings about attacks in real time, and to disseminate photographic evidence from conflict zones. The use of ICT is vital for refugees in all stages of their migration. After arriving in a new country, they use technology and apps for multiple reasons; most importantly, to receive settlement services.

My research focuses on the use of media Technology by Middle Eastern refugees who seek safe haven in Canada. While migration and media studies have focused on media representation of migrants (Leurs and Smets, 2018; Smets and Bozdag, 2018), little is known about how refugees make use of media or how this might have been impacted by COVID-19. Facebook information on the pandemic in local languages might be the difference between life and death for refugees who do not watch the news and cannot understand English.

Social vulnerability of international migrants in the context of the COVID-19 epidemic

(1205) Mariia Ivanova, St Petersburg University, Russia

The COVID-19 epidemic has exacerbated the existing discrimination and social vulnerability of international migrants. Migrants now constitute a significant proportion of the labor force in many countries. Migrant workers and their families made a considerable contribution to economic development in their countries of origin, as well as to their countries of destination. The crisis made quite clear systemic inequalities between the native population and migrants . The Covid-19 pandemic has increased the vulnerability of international migrants. The research task related to the analysis of the main determinants of migrant vulnerability in current conditions is identified.As a theoretical framework for the study were the theory of social vulnerability" the pressure and release (PAR) model and the determinants of migrant vulnerability (DoMV) model. Research methods: the first stage of the study analysed background information based on data collected from available governmental and non-governmental sources (legislative acts, official statistics on international migration).The second stage of the study included the qualitative methods . In order to assess the general conditions of the COVID-19 pandemic crisis and the extent of its impact on the migration community, semi-structured expert interviews were conducted with heads of non-profit NGOs dealing with migration issues and in-depth interviews with international migrants in St. Petersburg, Russia. The findings of the study: The legal status of international migrants. The lack of official legal status of a migrant is a key determinant of vulnerability to the consequences of the COVID-19 pandemic; Access of international migrants to health services. Many migrants do not receive medical care during the pandemic, which negatively affects not only the health of migrants, but also the epidemiological situation in general; Professional risks of international migrants. Significant difficulties in the labor market are associated with informal relations with employers. In addition, the pandemic mainly affected employment in the service sectors, where migrants are mostly represented; The housing conditions of migrants. The housing conditions of migrants is characterized by a higher population density, which makes it difficult to provide of social distancing, thereby migrants are more vulnerable to COVID-19 infection and at the same time pose an epidemic threat to others; The public attitudes towards international migrants. Respondents among migrants claim that during the pandemic they have faced an increase in xenophobia; The education of migrant' children. Many children often do not have technical opportunities for online education, in addition, the low level of education and poor Russian language skills of their parents make difficult the home education since online classes require the support of adult family members; Social support for international migrants. Social support for migrants is fragmented, there is no systematic approach to reducing the social vulnerability of the migration community during the pandemic. The social vulnerability of migrants affects not only the social situation of migrants themselves but also the host society; that is especially important to take into account in the situation of the COVID-19 epidemic. Acknowledgment. The research was carried out in St. Petersburg University with the financial support of the RSF, the project– 19-18-00246

Is there a home to go back to? Return and mobility aspirations among Turkish and Albanian migrants in Italy

(545) Gül Ince-Beqo, University of Bari, Italy

Eralba Cela, University of Milan, Italy

Migration and return are two interconnected phenomena. Leaving aside those who move as asylum seekers, for many migrants return is often part of the migratory project at the time of departure. As time goes by, however, migrants face many opportunities and constrains in the destination countries which might shape their life plans. Moreover, different life events and trajectories may change the intention to return home and force migrants to continuously postpone it until it never really happens, transforming the dream to return into the myth of return. Return migration is one of the most debated dimensions of international mobility. Its definition is complex and may cover different types and circumstances like occasional, seasonal, temporary and permanent return, "after a significant period abroad or in another region." (King, 1986b, p.4). In this paper we focus on two groups of migrants, Albanians and Turks living in Italy. Relying on qualitative data collected through semi-structured interviews, we investigate their future return plans or intentions for onward and/or circular migration movement. Previous research has shown that despite being one of the most stigmatized migrant nationalities in the Italian public discourse at their arrival, Albanian migrants are one of the most integrated groups among non-EU migrants due to their increasing employment advancements and desire to remain in Italy. Differently, migrants from Turkey, consider Italy as a country of transit rather than a country of settlement; it becomes an alternative place to live for good for those who have not succeeded to settle elsewhere in Europe. Considering the significant socio-cultural and religious differences between the countries of origin and host countries and the different requirements for exercising the right to family reunification in each context, we argue that migrants' attachment and evaluations of the country of arrival, as a desired or undesired destination, strongly influences their mobility aspirations.

Impact of Covid-19 Pandemic on Gulf Migration: A Study of Telangana, India

(1168) Sudhaveni Naresh, Centre for Economic and Social Studies (CESS), Hyderabad, India

The millions of the migrant workers in Gulf countries were directly affected by the Covid-19 pandemic who are mostly employed as semi-skilled and low skilled contract or temporary worker in construction and allied sectors. The Gulf countries well known and historically has been the most favoured destination for such employment. However, the Covid-19 pandemic has stopped construction projects in this region due to the drastic fall in oil prices which has affected Gulf oil and non-oil economies harshly. It had an unfavourable effect on migrant labour from India particularly from Telangana as they threat of unemployment, leading to their voluntary or forced return to origin place. For instance, at the end of 2021, half a million Telangana emigrants, most of them in the Gulf, has lost their employment abroad because of the Covid-19 pandemic, making their return unavoidable given their temporary status in this region. This paper examines how India in general and Telangana in particular is prepared to handle the changing trends in Indo-Gulf migration and the subsequent return emigration from the Gulf. The paper explores the major sending-state perspectives, such as that of Telangana, Andhra Pradesh, Kerala and others, and their responses towards Gulf returnees. Moreover, it provides insights by revisiting the existing economic and social security measures for returning migrants and their families within the framework of state welfare schemes, thereby examining rehabilitation and re-integration mechanisms for return migrants at the central and state levels in India.

11A   Managing Migration and Asylum

Chair: Türkan Özkan, Bolu Abant Izzet Baysal University, Turkey

1197   Russo-Ukrainian War: Positions of the political groups in the European Parliament on Ukrainian refugees

Kamber Guler, Konya Food and Agriculture University, Turkey

1310   The Immigration Admission Policies of Japan: Change or Continuity?

Türkan Özkan, Bolu Abant Izzet Baysal University, Turkey

1069   Travel bans by Governments amid the COVID-19 pandemic: Exploring the impact in the contemporary transnational world

Thebeth Rufaro Masunda, University of Zimbabwe
Pranitha Maharaj, University of KwaZulu-Natal, South Africa

Russo-Ukrainian War: Positions of the political groups in the European Parliament on Ukrainian refugees

(1197) Kamber Guler, Konya Food and Agriculture University, Turkey

Russia's annexation of the Crimean Peninsula from Ukraine in March 2014 was followed by this country's invasion of Ukraine in February 2022, resulting in more than four million Ukrainian refugees as well as about six and half million internally displaced people as of March 2022. The European Union (EU) has decided to grant these people temporary protection in the Member States for at least one year, which includes a residence permit, access to the labour market and housing, medical assistance, and access to education for children. Among all EU Member States, Poland is the leading receiving country with more than 2 million refugees from Ukraine, and it is followed by Romania, Hungary and Slovakia, respectively. Given these realities, this study aims at understanding and exposing the positions of political groups in the European Parliament (EP) on Ukrainian refugees. By doing so, it also aims to contribute to the literature on migration in terms of political views on refugees from different countries of origin. With these aims in mind, the relevant discourses delivered by the members of these political groups during the EP debates from March 2014 until today are analysed on the basis of the literature on critical discourse analysis (CDA) with some references to Norman Fairclough, Ruth Wodak and Teun A. van Dijk. Finally, the study concludes that the members of the political groups in question mostly deliver inclusive and tolerant discourses regarding Ukrainian refugees.

The Immigration Admission Policies of Japan: Change or Continuity?

(1310) Türkan Özkan, Bolu Abant Izzet Baysal University, Turkey

On the eve of global border closures introduced due to Covid-19 pandemic, the Japanese Prime Minister, Shinzō Abe, approved an act to release the strict immigration admission policy, despite the averseness of the opposition and most of the public in general. Enacted in 2018, the Immigration Control and Refugee Recognition Act (hereinafter ICRRA) (出入国管理及び難民認定法- Shutsunyūkokukanrioyobinanmin'ninteihō) regulates the conditions for the revocation of refugee status, the detention of refugees, obtaining of residence and working permit. ICRRA not only readjusts the widely criticized provisions for the refugees and asylum seekers, but also opens the tightly closed doors for unskilled or semi-skilled foreign labor force. Nevertheless, due to pandemic period measures and the end of Abe's term, the full fruition of this policy change has not been reached.

One may have doubts about whether Japan ever would realize such an immigration admission policy, since it is notorious for being one of the most 'closed to migration' countries. Yet, the high rate of the aging population and the need of low-cost employment for the declining economy have urged the decision-makers to change the longitudinal policy of discountenance to foreigners.

The aim of this study is to discern the characteristics and determine the importance of the recent policy choice of immigration admission to Japan. For this aim, in the first place the past policies either for refugees and asylum seekers or economic migrants will be touched upon and compared with the recent one. Also, the economic and political incentives behind the process leading to policy change and the much intriguing point, whether the new arrangement would align the Japanese migration regulations with the international law will be addressed. Finally, the situation after the pandemic restrictions and the new hotspot of Ukraine will be evaluated.

Travel bans by Governments amid the COVID-19 pandemic: Exploring the impact in the contemporary transnational world

(1069) Thebeth Rufaro Masunda, University of Zimbabwe

Pranitha Maharaj, University of KwaZulu-Natal, South Africa

This paper seeks to unpack the impact of Covid-19 on the social and economic functioning of today's society. Migration has gained momentum over the past decades and has been adopted as a livelihood strategy by many in developing countries. People leave their families and dependants in their countries of origin to seek better livelihoods in other countries. Due to the increased interconnectedness as a result of globalisation, both social and economic aspects of life have become transnational. By so doing, human capital and resource mobility has increased with global citizens dispersed across the globe. Human life is no longer confined in a particular country's borders. Under such circumstances, the levels of mobility and the need to travel across borders have increased. Transnationalism has become a major feature of the contemporary society. However, with the Covid-19 pandemic, the world has been compelled to impose travel bans, with governments introducing laws for closure of borders and restriction of both internal and external mobility. Governments across the globe have undertaken various measures that halt human mobility to curb the spread of coronavirus. With the restrictions on both internal and external movements, the flow of incomes from remittances and informal trading has been compromised. The impact of these restrictions can be more appalling on the livelihoods of populations dependent on cross-border mobility, especially informal traders as well as households that depend on remittances from the migrant family members. Such disruptions can have dire consequences on household poverty levels as some families are pushed below the poverty datum line. It is, therefore, crucial to explore the effects these travel bans imposed due to Covid-19 pandemic have on the lives of global citizens in this transnational society.

www.ingramcontent.com/pod-product-compliance
Lightning Source LLC
Chambersburg PA
CBHW071735270326
41928CB00013B/2684